KU -121-794

# Managing without Growth, Second Edition

I dedicate this book to my grandchildren Rio, Sacha, Gryffin, Acacia, Viggo and Dante . . . and to theirs.

# Managing without Growth

Slower by Design, not Disaster

Second Edition

Peter A. Victor

*Professor Emeritus, York University, Canada*

Edward Elgar
PUBLISHING

Cheltenham, UK • Northampton, MA, USA

© Peter A. Victor 2019

All rights reserved. No part of this publication may be reproduced, stored
in a retrieval system or transmitted in any form or by any means, electronic,
mechanical or photocopying, recording, or otherwise without the prior
permission of the publisher.

Published by
Edward Elgar Publishing Limited
The Lypiatts
15 Lansdown Road
Cheltenham
Glos GL50 2JA
UK

Edward Elgar Publishing, Inc.
William Pratt House
9 Dewey Court
Northampton
Massachusetts 01060
USA

A catalogue record for this book
is available from the British Library

Library of Congress Control Number: 2018946016

This book is available electronically in the **Elgar**online
Economics subject collection
DOI 10.4337/9781785367380

MIX
Paper from
responsible sources
FSC
www.fsc.org    FSC® C013604

ISBN 978 1 78536 737 3 (cased)
ISBN 978 1 78536 739 7 (paperback)
ISBN 978 1 78536 738 0 (eBook)

Typeset by Servis Filmsetting Ltd, Stockport, Cheshire
Printed and bound by CPI Group (UK) Ltd, Croydon, CR0 4YY

# Contents

# Preface and acknowledgments to the first edition

In 2001 I received an invitation from Gideon Rosenbluth to collaborate on a book. Gideon had supervised my Ph.D. dissertation in the later 1960s and over the years we had kept in touch. The chance to work with Gideon again came just at the right time. I had just completed my term as the Dean of the Faculty of Environmental Studies at York University, having worked for many years as a consultant and public servant, and I was eager to get my teeth into something truly academic. We agreed on the general outline of what we wanted to do and produced three papers on managing without growth, out of which this book developed. Gideon let me write the book on my own but he read significant parts of it in draft and provided his customary insightful and critical comments. I am greatly indebted to him for his lasting guidance so generously given all those years ago at the University of British Columbia and for his continuing interest, advice and support that was so valuable in writing this book.

Another economist whose influence on me has been considerable is Herman Daly, the leading contributor to and exponent of ecological economics. I have known Herman since the mid-1970s when he republished a paper of mine in his edited book *Economics, Ecology, Ethics. Essays Toward a Steady-State Economy*. Herman has helped shape my view of economies as subsystems of the biosphere and his influence on my thinking about these matters is substantial.

The main argument I make in this book is that we in the rich countries can and should manage without economic growth so that people living in poorer countries can enjoy the benefits of economic growth where it really makes a difference to their well-being. At the very least, we should demote economic growth from its position atop the hierarchy of policy objectives in rich countries and concentrate our efforts on more specific welfare-enhancing policy objectives. I think it is implausible that the biosphere can support the nine billion people, more or less, who are expected to be on Earth by mid-century at a standard of living remotely like that of current day North Americans. In any case, there is plenty of evidence to show that economic growth is doing very little to increase the happiness of most of us in rich countries. So as Clive Spash writes, our economies should be 'smaller by design rather than smaller by disaster' (Spash 2007), which inspired the subtitle of this book.

In the book I employ some simulation models to help illustrate specific parts of this argument and in particular to explore the possibility for Canada to meet important economic, social and environmental objectives without relying on economic growth. I am very grateful to Matthias Ruth for introducing me to the Stella programming language which is designed for building models based on systems dynamics. I use Stella in all of the models described in the book. I began to learn Stella while on sabbatical leave at Keele University (UK) in 2001 where I discussed some of my early thinking on the issues dealt with in the book with John Proops.

I owe much to colleagues in the Toronto area who have helped me in various ways: Peter Timmerman who read several chapters in draft and helped me improve the exposition of my ideas, economists George Fallis and John Grant who encouraged me to pursue a topic which is anathema to most members of our shared profession, and my long-time friend, environmental scientist Ed Hanna with whom I have had many discussions about the relationship between the economy and the environment.

It is doubtful whether I could have written this book without the help of my students. Over a period of three months in early 2007 I met with a group of six MES students at York University to review and discuss early drafts of most parts of the book: Howie Chong, Ed Crummey, Katie Fotheringham, Roberto Garcia, Andreas Link and Nathan Okonta. The tables were turned and they critiqued my work, often with gusto. It was a terrific stimulus to produce something in writing on a weekly basis and by the start of the summer of 2007 I had drafted substantial portions of the book.

I owe a special thanks to Ed Crummey who worked as my research assistant for six months and helped me in so many ways. He tracked down information, reviewed literature, estimated equations and checked the model in which they are incorporated, helped with the bibliography, read drafts and wrote notes on issues such as technology assessment, the capital tax and the reports of the IPCC on which parts of the book are based. Ed has a very bright future in ecological economics.

Another student to whom I am indebted is Tatiana Koveshnikova who worked with me on a systems dynamics model of Hubbert's peak that is used in the book. While there is considerable debate about whether and when the production of conventional oil will peak at the global level there is no doubt that it did so long ago in the United States. Our interest is in how the USA will reduce its dependence on imported oil, which is a matter of great concern if world peak oil materializes within the next decade as more and more commentators are predicting. Tatiana has been a very conscientious co-researcher on this question and contributed much to the design and construction of our Hubbert's peak model.

I have drawn extensively on publicly available information from Statistics Canada, Canada's first class statistical agency. By providing easy electronic access to vast quantities of well-organized and well-documented data, Statistics Canada makes possible an incredible range of research in the social sciences in Canada. What impressed me even more than the data was the excellent technical support that Statistics Canada provides. On many occasions Ed or I would call a member of staff at Statistics Canada if we could not find what we were looking for or if we required further explanation. The response from staff at Statistics Canada was always professional in the very best sense of the term, and was matched only by the extraordinarily fine service we received from Walter Giesbrecht, the data librarian at York University.

In developing my ideas I had the opportunity to present papers at many seminars and conferences where I received helpful comments: the Faculty of Environmental Studies at York University (2004), the University of Newcastle in Australia (2004) at the invitation of Philip Lawn which was the first time that I aired the main argument and analysis publicly, the biennial meeting of CANSEE (2005), as a guest in a course run by Doug Worts at George Brown College (2005), the Progressive Economics Forum at the annual meeting of the Canadian Economics Association (2005), and at a conference at the University of Ontario Institute of Technology (2006).

Above all I thank my wife Maria for her confidence in me and in her belief that what I was writing about really does matter. She has encouraged me continually and provided a home thoroughly congenial for work of this kind, even while writing a book of her own. It is to her, our daughters Carmen and Marisa, their husbands Mischa and Marc, our grandchildren Rio, Sacha and Gryffin, and their great grandmother Ruth that I dedicate this book.

# Preface to the second edition

In the decade that has passed since I wrote the first edition of this book, there have been significant changes in the world. Consider the following. Demographically, from 2007 to 2017 the global population increased from 6.7 billion to 7.6 billion with most of the increase concentrated in the global south. The percentage of people living in urban areas worldwide surpassed 50 percent in 2007 and the number of displaced persons has risen dramatically. Income and wealth inequality are at their highest levels in the past half century.

Environmentally, the concentration of carbon dioxide in the atmosphere exceeded 400 parts per million (ppm) in 2015 for the first time since measurements began in 1958, greater than at any time in the last 10–15 million years. This was aided and abetted by the decline in the price of crude oil from an all time high of $145 in 2008 to less than $30 in 2016. The global ecological footprint continued to increase such that as of 2012, the equivalent of 1.6 planets are needed to support the current living standards of the world's populations. China became the world's second largest national economy, overtaking Japan in 2010, and the world's largest emitter of greenhouse gases, overtaking the USA in June 2007. Twenty-five years ago, 1700 environmental scientists warned that 'a great change in our stewardship of the Earth and the life on it is required, if vast human misery is to be avoided'. In 2017 over 15 000 scientists from around the world issued a second 'Warning to Humanity'. After reviewing the trends of the previous quarter century, they concluded that 'with the exception of stabilizing the stratospheric ozone layer, humanity has failed to make sufficient progress in generally solving these foreseen environmental challenges, and alarmingly, most of them are getting far worse. . .'.

Not all that has happened in the past 10 years has been bad, far from it. For example, the number of people living on less than $1.25 a day continued its downward trend from 1926 million in 1990 to 825 million in 2015. Similar progress was made towards the other Millennium Development Goals (MDG) relating to education, gender equality, child mortality, maternal health, disease, sanitation and access to clean water (United Nations 2015b). In January 2016, the MDGs were replaced by a broader set of more ambitious Sustainable Development Goals. Much rests on whether these goals can be achieved and later surpassed as the 21st century unfolds or whether resource and environmental conditions, coupled with inadequate governance, rising inequality and social strife in the global north and south will prevent it.

In 2007/2008 the world experienced a major and largely unforeseen financial crisis which brought a serious economic recession in its wake. Vast sums of money were created by and for the banking system to avert financial and economic catastrophe, making many wonder where it all came from if governments were as short of funds as they claimed. The concentration of wealth and incomes continued to climb, with eight men now owning as much wealth as the poorest 3.8 billion people, and the richest 1 percent owning more than everyone else (Hardoon 2017). And most pertinent of all to the thesis of this book is that rates of economic growth virtually everywhere declined. The possibility of 'secular stagnation' (Summers 2016) – an era of sustained low growth and high unemployment – has begun to surface even in an era where 'technology' has become ubiquitous (think smart phones, robotics, artificial intelligence, and social media) and venerated, despite misgivings by some that people, especially children, are spending far too long in front of screens (Dunckley 2014) and are soon to immerse themselves in virtual reality.

The implications of these trends provide the backdrop for the second edition of a book which argues that advanced economies such as Canada and other OECD countries could and should work out how to manage without economic growth, if not now then soon. Such an argument, which seemed somewhat novel, even perverse, only a decade ago, is more pertinent than ever, reinforced by an explosion of literature, some directly on topic by such luminaries as Tim Jackson, Richard Heinberg, Juliet Schor, Brian Czech, and degrowth proponents led by Serge Latouche and Giorgos Kallis. Other literature, such as Piketty's treatise on capitalism and inequality and Gordon's prognosis for the USA of a long-term decline in its growth rate, help buttress the argument for an alternative to the continual pursuit of economic growth as a major priority for advanced economies. So does the work of many of the 800-plus participants in the Institute for New Economic Thinking (INET), founded in response to the global financial crisis. Their research reflects deep concern with the inadequacies of mainstream economics, as does the continued rise of a number of heterodox schools of thought. It is also evident in the growing number of economics students protesting the narrowness of the standard curriculum. Much of this disillusionment provides grist for the mill of alternatives to economic growth.

International agencies have also got into the act through important work on issues such as alternatives to GDP, sustainable finance, the changing nature of work, and the impact of new technologies and artificial intelligence on employment. Most closely allied to the theme of this book is their misguided enthusiasm for 'green' growth in which economic growth is 'decoupled' from material and energy inputs allowing economic growth to continue without limit. In addition to these efforts by international organizations to re-think economic growth, in 2012 we saw the end of the Kyoto Accord commitment period and the failure to secure even the modest reductions in greenhouse gas emissions to which the signatory countries committed themselves in 1997. We witnessed a further setback in Copenhagen in 2009 when no meaningful international agreement was reached to replace the expiring Kyoto Accord. Then in Paris in 2015 a more promising agreement to reduce greenhouse gas emissions was reached with commitments for monitoring and reporting but no specific binding targets for reduced emissions. The situation barely improved in the follow-up meeting in 2017, especially in light of President Trump's announcement earlier in the year that the USA would withdraw from the Paris Agreement, putting achievement of its modest objectives in jeopardy.

Finally, the emergence of organizations and movements calling for systemic change should not go unnoticed. Among them are the UK's New Economics Foundation, the Next System Project in the USA, the degrowth movement which began in France and has now spread to several other countries, Via Campesina in Latin America, the international divestment movement, and Transition Towns which now exist in more than 43 countries around the world. All of these initiatives call for changes that go far beyond the boundaries of mainstream thinking. They reflect the same angst that was expressed loudly but briefly in the Occupy movement of 2011–13 and other grassroots protests calling for substantive change.

So where does a book like this fit in? It is my hope and intention that it can help provide the intellectual foundations for the changes that are increasingly being sought. When it comes to an economic system that is compatible with the conditions confronting humanity on planet Earth and that provides for all in a just and sustained manner, are there alternatives to the continual pursuit of economic growth which exacerbates problems rather than solves them? Ideas without actions are bound to frustrate. Actions without ideas are bound to fail. It will take both to bring about the political, social and economic transformation we need to achieve change by design rather than by disaster.

In the first edition of this book I drew heavily on examples from Canada that applied in some degree to all rich developed countries. For this second edition, I refer to a wider range of national and international experiences to broaden its relevance. LowGrow, the macroeconomic model I used for simulating alternative economic futures and subsequently replicated in other countries, has been significantly expanded, updated and improved. It includes an explicit electricity sector and financial sector, and is 'stock-flow consistent'. This last feature in particular is an outcome of my ongoing collaboration with Professor Tim Jackson to develop ecological macroeconomics. Over the past few years we have published several academic papers in peer reviewed journals as well as more popularly written reports and articles on topics that are relevant to many parts of this book and which are duly referenced. I am delighted that Tim accepted my invitation to co-author Chapter 11.

This brings me to the subject matter of this book: the rationale for and inquiry into alternative economic futures not dependent on economic growth. Will we in the rich countries have to manage without growth? Should we? Can we? What might such a future look like? What can grow when the economy as a whole does not? Can some parts grow while others decline? How could we make the transition to a more sustainable economic system with as little disruption as possible? What institutions and policies will help? These are some of the questions that I tried to answer in the first edition and to which I received many useful responses from readers and encouraging reactions from a wide range of audiences. Indeed, speaking in a Buddhist temple in Japan a young student was so impressed by my argument that he pleaded with me not to die. So far, so good. In this second edition, as well as reflecting on all the feedback I have received, I have updated the data, provided a broader range of examples, and I present new modeling results in support of the argument that yes indeed, the time has come for rich countries to take the lead to manage without growth or face dire consequences.

# Acknowledgments

The first edition of this book was inspired by an invitation in 2001 from Gideon Rosenbluth to revisit questions about economic growth that we had discussed in the 1960s when he was my supervisor at the University of British Columbia. Gideon passed away in 2011, time enough to see the renewed interest in alternatives to the growth paradigm challenge the overarching priority of economic growth in academia and governments around the world.

In writing this second edition I am indebted to many people. First and foremost, I have benefited greatly from my ongoing research with Tim Jackson. Tim's multiple talents for modeling, analysis, writing, oratory, and his command of stock-flow consistent macroeconomics are impressive and have helped raise my own standards. Tim co-authored Chapter 11, much of which reflects the fruits of our collaboration since we met in 2008. We gratefully acknowledge the financial support we have received at various times to support our work from the Economic and Social Research Council, the Institute for New Economic Thinking, the Metcalf Foundation, the Ivey Foundation, and the Santa-Barbara Family Foundation.

For the past few years I have enjoyed the company of several of my former and current students at meetings of what has come to be known as the Gothic Group: Ed Crummey, Andreas Link, David Mallery, Eric Miller, Alvi Palazuelos and Martin Sers. The group gave me very useful feedback on several of the early chapters and our various discussions have informed my thinking on many key issues. I owe a special thanks to Martin Sers with whom I worked on the energy–emissions trap which is described in Chapter 5.

Sophie Sanniti is another of my former students who played a significant role in the production of this book. Working as my research assistant for several months, Sophie tracked down numerous references, checked others, and helped format the text, wrestling Word, which has a mind of its own, to the ground.

Environmental scientist and engineer Ed Hanna is one of my oldest friends. Many of the issues covered in the book reflect our discussions and consulting projects that began in the late 1970s. Ed was especially helpful in distinguishing between 'productive' and 'unproductive' green investments, a distinction that has implications for simulating the impact of green investment on economic growth as reported in Chapter 11.

Brett Dolter's excellent dissertation on Greening the Saskatchewan Grid inspired me to build a sub-model of the electricity sector which Brett kindly reviewed. The sub-model is used to simulate the environmental and economic impacts of transitioning away from fossil fuels.

Mark Onyr Kailer assisted with the econometric estimations that are incorporated in the macroeconomic simulation model that is described in Chapter 11 and I am grateful to him.

I made considerable use of Cansim, the easily accessible database of Statistics Canada. Whenever I needed further explanation I always received timely and helpful responses from the very professional staff employed by Canada's national statistical agency. I also made good use of the data bases maintained by the OECD and the World Bank and want to acknowledge all those who work in these organizations behind the scenes for bringing consistency to the data obtained from so many different countries.

I am grateful to Fridolin Kraussman for providing me with the most recent estimates of global materials use which are included in Chapter 5 and to Tom Weidmann for pointing me to the OECD data on the materials footprint. Several sources, identified in the text, granted me permission to reproduce figures for which they own the copyright and I thank them for that.

As professors, if we are lucky, our students learn as much from us as we do from them. In my case, in the winter term of 2017 I was fortunate to teach a course on ecological economics to 27 graduate students from York University, McGill University and the University of Vermont. The course was part of a collaborative program, Economics for the Anthropocene, offered by these three universities. One component of the course was student-led discussions of drafts of the first ten chapters of *Managing Without Growth*. The students wrote detailed reports on the drafts. Although I cannot claim to have fixed all the shortcomings noted by the students, I considered them all and the book is all the better for it.

After the publication of the first edition of *Managing without Growth* I exchanged ideas and material with numerous travellers along the same path, some old friends but mostly new ones, many of whom are quoted and cited in this second edition. I want to acknowledge and thank: Gar Alperovitz, Robert Ayres, Dennis Bardeen, Ross Beaty, Yannick Beaudoin, Mathias Binswanger, Alex Bowen, Francois Briens, Halina Brown, Peter Brown, Ingrid Bryan, Terry Burrell, Louison Cahen-Fourot, Emanuele Campiglio, Isabelle Cassiers, Ian Christie, Maurie Cohen, Mick Common, Mateo Cordier, Bob Costanza, Brian Czech, Simone D'Alessandro, Simon

Dalby, Herman Daly, Uchita de Zoyza, Federico Demaria, Bo Diczfalusy, Arnaud Diemer, Rob Dietz, Kristoffer Ditmer, Peter Doran, Angela Druckman, Ben Dyson, Paul Ekins, Ernie Epp, Jon Ericson, George Fallis, Josh Farley, Lorenzo Fioramonti, Marina Fischer-Kowalski, Tony Friend, John Fullerton, Jim Fyles, Christopher Gan, Dave Gardner, Geoff Garver, Neva Goodwin, Maja Gopel, John Gowdy, John Grant, Tom Green, Velma Grovers, Helmut Haberl, Nate Hagens, Alan Hallsworth, Colin Harbury, Jonathan Harris, Anders Hayden, Rob Hoffman, Thomas Homer-Dixon, Paul Jenkins, Bruce Jennings, Gareth Wyn Jones, Giorgios Kallis, Miriam Kennet, John King, Naomi Klein, Marcus Koch, Karen Kraft Sloan, Lisi Krall, Fridolin Kraussman, Ida Kubiszewski, Tom Kruse, Atif Kubursi, Aurore Lalucq, Serge Latouche, Phillip Lawn, Tim Lloyd, Brude Lourie, Donnie Maclurcan, Mikael Malmeus, Joan Martinez-Alier, Graeme Maxton, Elizabeth May, Angus McAllister, James Meadowcroft, Euan Mearns, Graciela Metternicht, David Miller, Frank Muller, Robert Nadeau, Sonja Novkovic, Doug Nutall, Dan O'Neill, Raj Patel, Derek Paul, Richard Pereira, Ellie Perkins, Elke Pirmaier, Jonathan Porritt, Louis Pradanos, Steve Pressman, Paul Pubelis, Stephen Purdey, Stephen Quilley, Jorgen Randers, Paul Raskin, Kate Raworth, Rupert Read, William Rees, Armon Rezia, Oliver Richters, Justin Ritchie, Johan Rockström, Dan Rosen, Frank Rotering, Jeff Rubin, Steve Running, Matthias Ruth, Toby Sanger, Jack Santa-Barbara, Juliet Schor, Charles Sing, Vaclav Smil, Dick Smith, Robert Smith, Steve Sorrell, Jules Speck, Gus Speth, Sigrid Stagl, Noël Sturgeon, David Suzuki, Asa Svenfelt, Vanessa Timmer, Peter Timmerman, Ralph Torrie, Graham Turner, Marco Ulvila, Jeroen Van den Burgh, Philip Vergraft, Mathis Wackernagel, Tom Walker, Stewart Wallis, Hayden Washington, Tom Webb, Ernst von Weizsäcker, David Welch, David Wheeler, Tommy Wiedmann, Anders Wijkman, Bob Willard, Susan Witt and Doug Worts. Apologies to anyone I failed to mention.

I owe a debt of gratitude to the staff of Edward Elgar Publishing. In particular to Alan Sturmer, Executive Editor, who encouraged me to write this second edition and then proved extremely patient when it took a lot longer than either of us expected. I also thank Erin McVicar and Rebecca Stowell for their hard work in checking the manuscript and preparing it for production.

I completed the manuscript a short time after retiring from the Faculty of Environmental Studies at York University. My association with FES goes back to 1975 when I began teaching a course on economics and the environment as a part-time faculty member. In 1996, I joined this truly interdisciplinary faculty full-time. I thank everyone there, past and present, who has contributed to the generous intellectual space without which an inquiry into managing without growth would not have been possible.

Finally, there is the enormous debt that I owe my wife Maria Paez Victor for supporting my endeavors, leaving me in peace for long hours in my study, checking references while in hospital recovering from a broken ankle, encouraging me to speak out, and reading the entire text.

To all I give a big vote of thanks. Your help and inspiration has kept me going and has made for a better book. You are welcome to share in any compliments that it may receive, but the responsibility for any errors that may remain is entirely mine.

# Prologue

> The great majority of men and women, in ordinary times, pass through life
> without ever contemplating or criticising, as a whole, either their own condi-
> tions or those of the world at large. (Bertrand Russell, 1918)

The end of World War II in September 1945 was celebrated in many ways.
I was the result of one such celebration, born some nine months later into
a middle class Jewish family in a north London suburb in the UK. I was
on the leading edge of the baby boom, the generation whose demographic
weight has given it a disproportionate impact on society for over half a
century. The adventure playgrounds of my childhood were an unsuper-
vised, overgrown field known as the barn, though there was no longer
a barn, and a local bomb site which became the site for a Woolworth's
store. I was educated at a private nursery school, a local primary school
and a highly regarded all boys grammar school from where I went to
Birmingham University and then to the University of British Columbia to
study economics.

I recount these few details of my early life not because they are especially
interesting but because they tell you something about the values that I
acquired growing up in post-war Britain. These were typical middle class
values which stressed the importance of family, education and hard work
and which generally equated success with a secure income earned in a
profession and the acquisition of material goods.

It is difficult, if not impossible, to step outside your own value system
and to reflect upon it, but that is what I try to do in this book. I also invite
you to do the same. The main value that I want to call into question is the
primacy that we in rich countries give to economic growth as the overriding economic policy objective for government. Sometimes growth comes
dressed in other clothes such as 'competitiveness' or 'free trade' or 'productivity', but underneath is a commitment to economic growth, defined and
measured as an increase in real, inflation-adjusted gross domestic product.
It is the policy objective against which all other proposals must be judged.
Environmental policy must not be allowed to impede growth, and where
possible should be advocated because it will boost growth. Apparently
a green economy will be even bigger than a brown one. Education
policy must see that students are trained for work in the 'new economy'.

Transportation policy should result in a more rapid movement of goods. Immigration policy should attract the most highly educated and wealthiest to meet the needs of a growing economy. Support for the arts, for sports, for child care, for less inequality, for better access to public goods, or for greater environmental protection all too often must be justified by their contribution to economic growth.

Growth of the economy supports and is supported by a variety of not necessarily compatible objectives such as maximizing profits, raising shareholder value, increasing sales and market share, higher wages, more consumption etc., etc. I do not include happiness in this list though it is often assumed that economic growth provides the means to fulfillment and therefore, I suppose, to happiness. We shall see later whether the evidence supports this assumption. Nor do I include freedom, justice or equity, or quality of life, or Maslow's 'self-actualization', or Sen and Nussbaum's 'capabilities', which some argue are fostered by growth if not guaranteed by it. And I certainly do not include peace and quiet and a contemplative life.

What I am most interested in, and what this book is about, is the rationale for a continued commitment to economic growth as the primary economic policy objective, and whether countries such as Britain, where I grew up, and Canada, where I have spent most of my adult life, or the USA, which still claims to be a world leader, can and should manage without growth. This is not to say that we should adopt zero growth as an alternative, overarching policy objective. Rather that we should not bother with economic growth as a policy objective at all or only as subsidiary to more specific objectives that have a clearer and more substantiated relation to well-being. Clearly, there are many areas where growth is to be welcomed, such as in well-being, literacy, life expectancy, social justice, security, conviviality, environmental quality, vibrant ecosystems and thriving populations of other species, and resource efficient sectors and activities, but we should not assume that these are only to be had in the context of economic growth – quite the opposite in many cases. And there is another list where stability or decline is to be welcomed, such as in material and energy use and related emissions causing degradation of air, land and water, habitat destruction from land conversion, the human population, stocks of physical capital and artifacts, and resource inefficient sectors and activities. As we shall see, more often than not, economic growth in rich countries exacerbates these problems.

In the first chapter I describe how economic growth emerged as the pre-eminent economic policy objective of government and how that commitment lives on, obscured perhaps by the language of 'sustainable development', 'sustainability' or 'smart prosperity'. In Chapter 2 I consider several reasons for managing without growth: from the implications of living in the Anthropocene, to the tempting but false hope of green growth and the permanent decoupling of economic output from its material and energy requirements, to the evidence that economic growth is slowing anyway and, like it or not, adjustments and accommodations to these new circumstances will have to be made. The third chapter presents an ecological economics perspective on the economy as a system with particular emphasis on the essential but imperfect role that prices play as the conveyors of information in the economic system. In Chapter 4, which is entirely new, I take a critical look at the fashionable interest in conceiving of nature as a form of capital and pricing it. Chapters 5, 6 and 7 provide an empirical assessment of some of the main connections between the economies and biosphere in which they are embedded: the sources of raw materials, the disposal of wastes into environmental sinks, and the impacts of these flows on the capacity of the environment to support life. In Chapter 8 I return to the issue of decoupling and its potential to prolong economic growth indefinitely by considering the interactions between the scale or size of an economy, what it produces, and the technologies employed. Next comes Chapter 9 on economic growth and happiness, and Chapter 10 on the disappointments of economic growth. Having laid all this groundwork for considering managing without growth, in Chapter 11, co-authored with Tim Jackson, we use a revised and updated version of the LowGrow macroeconomic simulation model to explore what might be achieved in terms of employment, poverty elimination, environmental protection, and fiscal prudence in a no or low growth economy. Notably, in this revised edition we go beyond the discussion of policies arising from the computer simulations of Chapter 11 and take up the question of whether substantive changes to the economic system itself will also be required to manage without growth. I touch on policy issues throughout the book but it is in Chapter 12 where I pull together policy implications of managing without growth.

If, like me, you have been inculcated with the virtues of economic growth, you may have to suspend your belief in this fundamental value of contemporary society as you read on. It is the best way to make the most of the journey. Of course, I expect that it will take more than this book to change your mind about something you may feel deeply, but humor me. I'm only asking you to think about managing without growth. The really exciting part comes later when enough of us in the rich countries are convinced that it's the best, if not the only way to go. Then we shall have some real work to do.

# 1. The idea of economic growth

Before the Enlightenment era there was little or no concept of progress. Over the short historical period since then Western culture has come to be built on the taken for granted conviction that technical and social progress is not only possible and normal, but potentially limitless. Economists have probably done most to reinforce the faith through making economic growth the supreme and unquestionable goal of national and global economic policy. (Trainer 2014, p. 168)

It is hard to imagine a time when economic growth was not paramount in the minds of politicians, the media, business, trade unions, and the public at large. For years Statistics Canada, Canada's world-class statistical agency, published annual estimates of Canada's gross domestic product (GDP). Then it started producing quarterly estimates and now it releases estimates each month; such is the appetite for information about Canada's economy. As in so many countries, the statistical news is spread in print and electronically by newspapers, TV, radio, the Internet and by banks and investment houses. The latest estimates of GDP are compared with previous ones. The greater the increase, the better. Or is it?

Comparisons with other countries of GDP, GDP per capita, and growth rates are also popular and made easier through the widely accessible data-bases of international organizations such as the World Bank and the OECD. A ready audience can always be found for anyone who expresses concern about threats to their country's position in the international GDP league tables. We are told to spend more on education to prepare employees for the 'new economy' (a term that quickly became old after the dotcom crash of the late 1990s), or 'knowledge-based' economy (as if the 'old' economy ran without knowledge). We need to reduce taxes, increase subsidies for research and development, raise productivity, promote innovation, expand trade and attract foreign investment, all in pursuit of economic growth. And when it comes to immigration, let's encourage those with marketable skills and capital. Even our universities are expected to promote commercialization through teaching and research (Fallis 2007). And if governments lose the confidence of the electorate in their ability to promote economic growth they risk being replaced by another party which claims it can do better.[1]

In fact, however, economic growth has only been an explicit objective of government policy since the middle of the 20th century. The history of the idea of economic growth has been succinctly told by H.W. Arndt in *The Rise and Fall of Economic Growth* (Arndt 1978) and more recently by Schmelzer (2016) and Timmerman (2017). To understand the ascent of economic growth to the summit of government policy objectives we must first examine the birth of an idea that is even more fundamental in our culture than economic growth. This is the idea of progress. A belief in progress is one of the most important defining values of Western civilization, along with private property, respect for human rights, individual liberty, separation of church and state, representative democracy and the rule of law. These were the beliefs and principles established during the European Enlightenment of the 17th and 18th centuries by people such as Locke in England, Voltaire in France, Hume in Scotland, Lessing in Germany and Paine in what became the United States. The list of influential Enlightenment philosophers and writers is much longer than this but these five show the international character of the movement that bequeathed so many of the main beliefs and principles adopted by liberal democracies around the world. Central among these beliefs is a commitment to progress, to economic progress in particular, and more specifically to economic growth. Thus, the belief in economic growth as a necessary and desirable feature of modern societies reflects an even deeper commitment to the idea of progress. But where did this idea come from, on what is it based, and how well are its several dimensions captured in the pursuit of economic growth? We must answer these questions before we look at managing without growth.

## 1.1 THE IDEA OF PROGRESS

The first thing to understand about progress is that it is an idea. It assumes a past and presumes a future. The idea of progress as applied to human affairs is that events are sequential in the sense that one event succeeds another in a causal, not random manner. The idea of progress also entails the belief that the sequence of events has led and will continue to lead to improvement. Events that repeat themselves in a cyclical pattern would not be considered progress. Sequential events leading to a worsening situation would not be considered progress. It is a combination of sequential events leading, in some sense, to improvement that defines progress (Pollard 1971).

As far as we know from oral, written and pictorial records, belief in the idea of progress that we take for granted is at odds with what people believed throughout all but the last moments of human history. Until the Enlightenment, if people thought about it at all, most believed either that life was lived pretty much as it always had been, as in traditional societies, or that humanity was on a downward path, descending from a previous Golden Age or Garden of Eden. Redemption, if it was ever to come, would have to wait until the afterlife.

These views did not necessarily mean belief in a static, unchanging world. The seasons in which birth, growth, decline and death repeated themselves provided obvious signs of change, but change without direction. A belief in larger cycles involving rebirth and reincarnation as propounded in Buddhism and Hinduism entailed a belief in change but change described as much by repetition and decline as by novelty and improvement. (See Timmerman 2017 for an account of the deep historical and religious roots of the idea of growth.)

The belief that events are not necessarily a repeat of what has come before and that change for the better is not only possible but observable and achievable by human action, is a very modern idea. Indeed it is the quintessential modern idea. It is modernity. It is the idea that history has a direction and that the direction is towards improvement of the human condition. It is the idea of progress.

Sydney Pollard (1971, p. 20) tells us that the idea of progress is only about 350 years old. He explains that the idea emerged in Western Europe in the 16th and 17th centuries from two sources. The first was the rise of science as a deliberate effort by some individuals to learn from experience and to build on the previous work of others. The practice of science was and is all about the accumulation of knowledge based on a mix of hypothesis, experiment, and observation. It also involves sharing results with others through publication for corroboration, refutation and further development. Scientists as great as Newton were aware of how much they were indebted to others who had gone before. 'If I have seen further, it is by standing on the shoulders of giants' (Moncur 2007: Newton in a letter to Robert Hooke, 5 February 1675).

Science has direction. It is a systematic process of knowledge accumulation and it yields results considered to represent an improvement in understanding. In the 16th and 17th centuries and even later, science was practiced by a very small number of people who were not necessarily even identified as scientists. Most people knew nothing of what these early scientists were up to. Literacy rates were low, schooling was only available to the wealthy and paid far more attention to Greek and Roman writers of antiquity than to contemporary developments in science.

Initially it was only within the intelligentsia that science began to influence the way people thought about change in society. In Britain for example, the Royal Society was officially founded in 1660 at Gresham College, following a lecture by Christopher Wren. It grew out of meetings that began in the mid-1640s of a group of natural philosophers who gathered to discuss the ideas of Francis Bacon, famous for his influential essays on the philosophy of science. To this day, the Royal Society remains the pre-eminent 'independent scientific academy of the UK dedicated to promoting excellence in science' (Royal Society 2007). Similar organizations developed in other Western European countries around the same time or shortly thereafter, many of which are still flourishing. And the Royal Society spawned similar organizations in ex-British colonies, so there are Royal Societies in Australia, Canada and South Africa. All of these organizations continue to play an important role in promoting the practice of science and in supporting technological change and public policy across an ever-widening range of fields.

The rise of science and the propagation of a scientific way of thinking was a slow process, one which would have taken much longer to influence how people think about the world were it not for other changes that were under way at the same time. Equally if not more important in the early development of the idea of progress was the fact that people in several European countries began to experience positive changes in their own lives. They began to realize that their lives might be a little better than those of their parents, and that their children's lives might be even better than theirs. Gradually, the idea began to grow that this kind of improvement from one generation to the next might be part of a larger process of change that came to be referred to as progress.

These two forces, the emergence of science and the experience of improvements in living standards over a lifetime were not sufficient, according to Pollard, to account for the widespread acceptance of the idea of progress. He argues that science did not emerge on its own but in concert with the gradual development of entrepreneurship, early capitalism and new technologies, all of which prepared people's minds to accept the idea of progress. 'Such men as Bacon, Rabelais, Le Roy or Bodin caught their first glimpses of the idea of progress when they observed the tangible proofs of compasses, printing, gunpowder, and the other by-products of the capitalist expansion of their day' (Pollard 1971, p. 29).

In his account of the idea of progress, Pollard notes that in the 18th century, the century of the Enlightenment, there was a marked distinction in the scope of discussions about progress in post-civil war Britain and pre-revolutionary continental Europe. Following the victory of the parliamentarians over the monarchy in England in the late 17th century, British philosophers accepted the basic structure of society. As a result, they concentrated much of their attention on progress as economic growth. They accepted the system, now they wanted to know what made it run and how to make it run faster. This was embodied in the rise of British political economy led in particular by Adam Smith.

> With Adam Smith we reach the parting of the ways. Henceforth, the unity of social philosophy is broken. British political economy (in due course to become 'economics') has taken off on a course of its own, manipulating with growing skill increasingly mobile variables within an increasingly rigid social framework . . . the link with history has disappeared. (Pollard 1971, p. 77)

Pollard contrasts the British approach to political economy and progress with that of Voltaire, 'the most influential single individual of the Enlightenment' (Pollard 1971, p. 53). Like so many other philosophers writing about progress in pre-revolutionary France, Voltaire stressed the structural changes in society required for continued social and economic progress. This difference between British and continental European writers in the 18th century anticipated the 20th-century distinction between growth and development. Nowadays growth is defined as increases in economic output within given institutional structures whereas development refers to a broader set of institutional changes as a precondition for ongoing increases in economic output. 'Because the realization of economic opportunities also depends on political liberties, the term "development" has increasingly encompassed political development as well as economic development' (Meier 2005, p. 6).

Another feature of the idea of progress that became generally accepted by 18th-century writers was that progress was not just about progress in science and technology. It also included 'progress in wealth, in civilization, in social organization, in art and literature, even in human nature and biological make-up' (Pollard 1971, p. 31). In their eyes, progress meant much more than economic growth. It meant improvement in all facets of individual and social experiences. As we shall see, such a broad conception of progress encompassing improvement in all aspects of the lives of individuals and communities has been severely curtailed as the idea of progress evolved from its historically broad origins to the narrower conception of progress as economic growth.

By the 19th century the idea of progress had become established not only in the minds of scientists, philosophers, politicians and educated people in general, but also in the minds of ordinary people, educated or not. It started in Britain, Western Europe, the United States, Canada and Australia and began spreading around the world. Much of 19th-century literature that dealt with the idea of progress was written by historians and others who sought to describe the transition of societies from one stage to the next in a fixed sequence. This idea was especially popular among the German historical school. 'According to them, history proceeded in stages, each of which had a recognisable character of its own, determining all facets of society, including its economic relationships, and each, by its own immanent constitution, inevitably prepared the way for and ushered in the next' (Pollard 1971, p. 136). Similar ideas, though with a more restricted focus, were popularized in the 1960s by W.W. Rostow in his influential book *The Stages of Economic Growth* (Rostow 1960).

In the 20th century, the idea of progress was fully accepted by mainstream society. There were still commentators who were pessimistic about the long-term prospects for progress but even Karl Marx, who had argued that capitalism contained the seeds of its own destruction, believed that a better world would emerge from its ashes. A growing majority of others were far more optimistic. Despite the failures of Western civilization – two World Wars, the Great Depression of the 1930s, the Holocaust, the Cold War – and the intellectual challenge from post-modernism, this optimism about the inevitability of progress continues into the 21st century though perhaps with less enthusiasm. Now few people, especially in rich countries, question the idea of progress.

## 1.2   ECONOMIC GROWTH AS PROGRESS

To say that we manage what we measure has become a cliché, but it is a useful one nonetheless. For societies that believe in progress based on science and technology, it is to be expected that they would develop ways of measuring it. In a world that seems overflowing with statistics, the one that is most highly favored over all others as a measure of progress is Gross Domestic Product (GDP). GDP can be measured in three equivalent ways. It is:

> (1) an aggregate measure of production equal to the sum of the gross values added of all resident institutional units engaged in production (plus any taxes, and minus any subsidies, on products not included in the value of their outputs); (2) the sum of the final uses of goods and services (all uses except intermediate consumption) measured in purchasers' prices, less the value of imports of goods and services; and (3) the sum of primary incomes distributed by resident producer units. (OECD 2001)

As economic growth became virtually synonymous with progress, increases in GDP became our main measure of progress.

> While the level of GDP per head of population is the most commonly used shorthand measurement of the economic well-being of a given country (most of all in international comparisons), its variation over time in real terms (in

other words at constant prices) measures economic growth, the maximisation of which is usually considered to be the main goal of economic policy. (Giovanni 2008, p. 13)

If we understand progress to mean an improvement in well-being then GDP is a poor measure. American economist Simon Kuznets was one of the main architects of the system of national income accounts from which GDP is obtained. When he appeared before the US Congress in 1934 he said the 'welfare of a nation can scarcely be inferred from a measurement of national income' (Kuznets 1934). However, as history has shown, his warning went unheeded. GDP includes many items that grow when things are or might be getting worse: for example, household expenditures on health care, repairs, commuting, pollution control devices, home security measures. It includes government expenditures on police and defense. Equally problematic as a measure of progress in terms of well-being is what is left out of GDP: voluntary work, unpaid housework, leisure time, illegal trades, capital depreciation, damage to the environment and the depletion of natural resources. Obviously GDP is not a reliable indicator of progress (Eisner 1994, Chapter 2; *The Economist* 2016).

GDP also tells us nothing about how the output of goods and services is distributed among the members of society. A growing GDP that is increasingly unequally distributed is a poor indicator of progress. Complementary statistics such as the Gini coefficient, which is a measure of distribution, can help but they are seldom produced and publicized with the same frequency. Rising GDP per capita improves upon GDP in one respect. It recognizes that the size of the population among whom an increase in GDP is shared affects the average amount of goods and services available to each person. Japan is an example of a country in which the rate of economic growth has declined from world-leading levels of 6 or more percent after World War II to around 2 percent or less since 1990. Yet the effects have been tempered by a declining rate of growth in the population, becoming negative in 2011, such that GDP per capita has continued to rise at a modest rate (World Bank 2016c). But since GDP per capita is a measure of the average GDP per person and not of its distribution, this fundamental deficiency of GDP as a measure of well-being remains.

Despite these well-known deficiencies of GDP as a measure of well-being it continues to reign supreme as a measure of progress. Consider this claim by the Commission on Growth and Development:

A growing GDP is evidence of a society getting its collective act together. As its economy grows, a society becomes more tightly organized, more densely interwoven. A growing economy is one in which energies are better directed; resources better deployed; techniques mastered, then advanced . . .. Growth is not an end in itself . . . but growth is a necessary, if not sufficient, condition for broader development, enlarging the scope for individuals to be productive and creative. (Commission on Growth and Development 2008, pp. 17, 1)

Significantly, the Commission acknowledges that 'accelerated growth has created new challenges . . . a clear divergence in incomes within and between countries . . . and new pressure on the planet's ecology and climate' (Commission on Growth and Development 2008, p. 19), but does not see them, especially the pressure on the planet, as being a problem that cannot be addressed by further growth in GDP. And the Commission, whose main purpose was to share its understanding of the experience of growth and development with political leaders and policy makers in developing countries, fails to connect ongoing economic growth in advanced economies with diminished prospects for growth in poorer ones.

One prominent politician who had an excellent grasp of the limitations of GDP as a measure of progress is Robert Kennedy, who in a speech in 1968 at the University of Kansas (Kennedy 1968) said about gross national product:[2]

> Too much and too long, we seem to have surrendered community excellence and community values in the mere accumulation of material things. Our gross national product . . . if we should judge America by that – counts air pollution and cigarette advertising, and ambulances to clear our highways of carnage. It counts special locks for our doors and the jails for those who break them. It counts the destruction of our redwoods and the loss of our natural wonder in chaotic sprawl. It counts napalm and the cost of a nuclear warhead, and armored cars for police who fight riots in our streets. It counts Whitman's rifle and Speck's knife, and the television programs which glorify violence in order to sell toys to our children.
>
> Yet the gross national product does not allow for the health of our children, the quality of their education, or the joy of their play. It does not include the beauty of our poetry or the strength of our marriages; the intelligence of our public debate or the integrity of our public officials. It measures neither our wit nor our courage; neither our wisdom nor our learning; neither our compassion nor our devotion to our country; it measures everything, in short, except that which makes life worthwhile.

We are so accustomed to hearing about economic growth and about what governments are doing to promote it, that we might think that governments have always taken responsibility for economic growth. This would be a mistake. National income accounting began in earnest in the USA and other countries during the economic depression of the 1930s. It received impetus from World War II. Knowledge of how much could be produced in economies working flat out was regarded as critical information for the conduct of the war especially by the Allies. This is when the expenditure estimates of GDP began to be produced systematically and regularly (Carson 1975).

Those charged with responsibility for measuring economic output did not have to start from scratch. William Petty (1623–87) estimated the national income of England through what he termed 'political arithmetick' (Petty 1691). Subsequently many scholars have considered the definition and measurement of the output of an economy and some made their own estimates. However, it was only when the measurement of national economic output, both actual and potential, became important for government policy that adequately standardized conventions, methods and data were developed. This started in the 1930s with contributions from many economists and statisticians (Bowley 1942) and continues to this day, led by the United Nations which has established the System of National Accounts for all countries to follow (United Nations et al. 2009).

As World War II drew to a close, governments in North America, Western Europe, Australia and New Zealand became concerned about the possibility of recession and high unemployment, even a return of the Great Depression of the 1930s. When literally millions of de-mobbed soldiers started looking for work, where would they find it? Fortunately there was now an answer based on the work of John Maynard Keynes, the most influential economist of the 20th century.

## 1.3 KEYNESIANISM, GDP AND FULL EMPLOYMENT

In his *General Theory of Employment, Interest and Money* (Keynes 1935) Keynes argued that the private sector, if left to itself, could settle on a level of economic activity far below the productive potential of an economy, resulting in very substantial unemployment. He found no automatic mechanism that guaranteed a level of total expenditure sufficient to employ all those who wished to work. He rejected the argument of what was then mainstream economics that unemployment resulted from wage levels that were too high and that a reduction of wages, resisted by unions, would entice employers to hire more people. On the contrary, Keynes argued that lower wages would mean less spending and even more unemployment as employers cut back production still further. Unemployment, Keynes argued, was a macroeconomic problem rather than a microeconomic one, a problem of the economy as a whole, a problem of a lack of aggregate demand, a problem then of inadequate GDP.

Keynes further distanced himself from the mainstream by arguing that if governments used their powers of expenditure and taxation appropriately, they could regulate the level of aggregate demand (the total level of spending in the economy), so that unemployment could be reduced to very low levels if not eradicated entirely. Keynes was aware of the risks of price inflation if aggregate demand was raised to a level in excess of the productive capacity of the economy. It would be the task of government to steer a course between total expenditures that were too little and too much.

The basic Keynesian message was that in the face of too much unemployment governments should spend more than they receive in taxes to stimulate the economy, and in the face of inflationary pressures, they should do the opposite. Over time, the ensuing budget surpluses (when expenditures minus tax revenues are positive) and deficits (when expenditures minus taxes are negative) would even out so that the national debt would remain relatively stable. Well, that was the theory. Its endorsement by many economists and politicians in the 1940s and 1950s allowed governments in most Western countries to take responsibility for full employment. That these countries had experienced full employment during the war when government expenditures had been running at record levels was all the proof they needed that Keynes was right.

The report by William Beveridge, *Full Employment in a Free Society* (Beveridge 1945) was very effective in transmitting Keynes's explanation of the causes of unemployment and its remedy. Paul Samuelson's highly successful textbook *Economics*, first published in 1948, and now in its 19th edition translated into 41 languages, also played a key role in spreading Keynesian ideas among generations of students. Britain's wartime coalition government committed itself to full employment using Keynesian methods. At about the same time the Australian government made a similar commitment, followed closely by the Canadian government in a White Paper in 1945 and the government of the USA, with some reservations, through the Employment Act of 1946. Full employment was also incorporated in the United Nations Charter (Arndt 1978, pp. 27, 28; Gross 1987).

It is important to note that before the advent of Keynesianism, it was widely believed that governments could help create the conditions for a well-functioning economy, but they could do very little directly to reduce unemployment. Typically, this meant limiting monopoly power, including that of trade unions, reducing tariffs, guaranteeing the right of private property, and keeping taxes and interest rates low. It might also include public education to secure a trained and capable work force. These policies had failed to ensure full employment or anything close to it for years, even decades, at a time, but they were the best available until Keynes came along. What was new after World War II was that governments believed they now had the tools with which to manage the economy and to ensure that it operated at or near full employment year after year, and for some 25 years they were not wrong. From 1960 to 1972 unemployment rates in OECD countries stayed well below 6 percent (Nickell et al. 2005, Table 1), in large measure due to the deliberate intervention of governments acting on Keynesian principles.

It was not until the early to mid-1970s that the Keynesian formula was found wanting. The new problem was 'stagflation', the simultaneous occurrence of economic stagnation (unemployment) and inflation following the rapid rise in oil prices in the 1970s. This was the time when monetarism began to flourish, first in academic circles led most notably by Milton Friedman in the USA and then adopted by governments who believed that control of the money supply, defined in various ways, and fiscal prudence were the order of the day. Keynesian policies did not provide an answer to stagflation but neither did monetarism (Allen and Rosenbluth 1992). The application of monetarist policies coupled with fiscal restraint and a call for balanced budgets reached its zenith in the 1990s. Canada was among the leaders of this movement, which achieved 10 consecutive budgetary surpluses between 1997 and 2007 (Statistics Canada 2016d). But even though there is still considerable enthusiasm for balanced budgets in some quarters (for example Speer and Emes 2014; Mitchell 2011; 2014) the gilt is off the monetarist lily. Macroeconomic policy has become more pragmatic and less obviously ideological. Central banks use the interest rate on overnight loans to the commercial banks to influence interest rates throughout the economy, lending by the commercial banks and hence the money supply. The primary objective of central banks is to keep inflation low while departments of finance implement fiscal policies governing taxation and expenditure broadly speaking along Keynesian lines, though with the 'non accelerating inflation rate of unemployment' (NAIRU) as their target rather than full employment. (See Chapter 10 for more discussion of NAIRU, inflation targeting and full employment.)

## 1.4   FROM FULL EMPLOYMENT TO ECONOMIC GROWTH

Keynes is famous for saying that his was a short run theory because 'in the long run we are all dead.' (This phrase comes from his earlier book *A Tract on Monetary Reform* (Keynes 1923, p. 80) but it also characterized his more famous *General Theory*.) One feature that made his a short-run theory was that he included investment (that is, expenditures on new infrastructure, buildings and equipment) as a component of aggregate demand without much concern with the fact that these expenditures also increase the productive capacity of the economy. When Keynes was writing and until quite recently, more investment meant more factories with more machines requiring more workers from an expanding labor force. Nowadays it might also mean more software, more computing power, more artificial intelligence and a requirement for fewer employees. The potential for capital investment to displace human workers did not go unnoticed by Keynes. Indeed he thought it offered the promise of a much better future with a much shorter work week (Keynes 1930[1963]), but it is one that has yet to materialize, a topic to which we return in Chapters 11 and 12.

In the *General Theory*, Keynes was primarily concerned with how governments could use their taxation and spending powers to achieve full employment. He saw that the key to this was for government to directly influence the level of aggregate expenditures in the economy such that it was sufficient for full employment. But this level of expenditure and the output to which it corresponds has to increase year over year in step with the increase in productive capacity to maintain full employment. Failing this, it would take fewer and fewer employees to produce an unchanging output unless working hours are reduced. This 'productivity trap' represents a significant threat to full employment in the absence of economic growth (Jackson and Victor 2011). The ongoing impact of rising labor productivity on employment as capital displaces labor explains why communities and the politicians that represent them celebrate the construction of a new factory not so much for the increase in supply of some needed product, but because of the jobs it creates. In advanced economies, the shortage of employment has become more important than the shortage of products. This is clear from media accounts of new production lines at car assembly plants that announce the number of new jobs, not new cars. It's as if the cars produce jobs rather than the other way around. In the past we needed more people at work because we needed the goods and services they produce. Now we have to keep increasing production simply to keep people employed so that they can earn an income and buy the goods and services they need and want. What was a problem of production has become a problem of distribution. If we are to manage without growth then we must find a way of overcoming this problem, and in Chapters 11 and 12 we will see how this can be done.

Keynes left it to others to work out the relationship between full employment and economic growth. This was the issue taken up in 1939 by R. Harrod in Britain and in 1946 by E. Domar in the USA, leading to the Harrod–Domar model of economic growth, as well as by other notable economists heavily influenced by Keynes. The Harrod–Domar model examined the conditions necessary for balanced growth in aggregate demand and productive capacity. It influenced much of the subsequent work by economists on the theory of economic growth.

A few years after governments committed themselves to the maintenance of full employment, they adopted economic growth as a policy objective. Domar stated that his and Harrod's work was 'concerned with unemployment and treated growth as a remedy for it rather than an end in itself' (quoted in Arndt 1978, p. 33). Arndt observed that 'there is in fact hardly a trace of interest in economic growth as a policy objective in the official or professional literature of western countries before 1950' (1978, p. 30). In 1936, Colin Clark published the first ever estimates of the annual rate of growth of real income per person (Arndt 1978, p. 32). 'The first annual *Economic Survey* for the United Kingdom in which the term "rate of growth" occurs was that for 1950' (Arndt 1978, p. 32). Referring to a statement by the US Council of Economic Advisors in October 1949, Arndt says 'it was perhaps the first explicit official pronouncement in favour of economic growth as a policy objective in any western country' (1978, p. 37).

How quickly things changed. By the end of the 1950s economic growth had been 'thrust to the top as *apparently* the supreme, overriding objective of policy' (Arndt 1978, p. 41). In analyzing the rapid ascent of economic growth atop the list of government policy objectives Arndt notes that 'more rapid economic growth came to be regarded as a prophylactic or remedy for all the major current ailments of western economies – balance of payments difficulties and especially dollar shortage, underemployment, and inflation whether due to excess demand or competing income claims' (1978, p. 43). In the USA, Arndt adds the Soviet challenge and the Cold War as another important reason why economic growth attained top priority. 'In the 1950s momentous political importance came increasingly to be attached to international comparisons of growth rates . . . The first UN *Economic Survey of Europe* to present growth rates of real GDP, based on the OECD estimates, was that of 1957' (1978, pp. 50, 51).

Why growth rates differ became a topic of intensive academic research in the early 1960s and 'from that year [1960], for a decade, economic growth occupied an exalted position in the hierarchy of goals of government policy both in the United States and abroad' (Arndt 1978, p. 55). Economic growth was a major campaign issue in the celebrated contest between Kennedy and Nixon. When Kennedy became President, faster economic growth became a central objective (Arndt 1978, pp. 55, 56).

The *UN World Economic Survey 1959* stated 'The reinterpretation of the objective of full employment under the United Nations Charter to embrace the goal of economic growth marks a second fundamental change in public policy thinking' (quoted in Arndt 1978, p. 62). 'Not only France and Britain, Sweden and the Netherlands, but also Germany, Belgium and Switzerland which had remained the citadels of non-interventionist policies . . . took in the sixties [steps] towards a more purposeful control of economic growth' (Arndt 1978, pp. 63, 64).

By the end of the 1960s the case for economic growth as an overarching policy objective of governments in developed countries had matured. The fully fledged case for economic growth had many facets but as Arndt notes,

> the belief that steadily, rapidly and (at least for the foreseeable future) indefinitely increasing productive capacity is an important policy objective even in the rich countries because higher living standards in the widest sense are desirable and demanded, undoubtedly constituted the core of the case for economic growth. (1978, p. 73)

Arndt based the case for economic growth in developed countries on five principles: the desire for continued material progress; the greater ease of dealing with competing claims when economic output is growing, making other problems such as achieving full employment more manageable; maintaining a 'cheerful state' in society; harking back to Adam Smith; and keeping up with others. In regard to this last principle Arndt quotes Domar, one of the fathers of modern growth theory who said that, in relation to international rivalry 'such motives have given rapid growth a status among the objectives of economic policy of the major (and even many minor) powers almost independent of rational assessment of benefits in terms of standard of living' (Arndt 1978, p. 76).

Recent research by Matthias Schmelzer (2016) has increased our understanding of the rise of the 'growth paradigm'. Schmelzer, an economic historian, defines the growth paradigm as 'a specific ensemble of societal, political, and academic discourses, theories, and statistical standards that jointly assert and justify the view that economic growth as conventionally defined is desirable, imperative, and essentially limitless' (2016, p. 264). In other words, the emergence of economic growth as the principal economic policy objective of so many governments was a reflection of a set of more deeply held beliefs. Based on an examination of early documents from the OECD and its forerunner, the Organization for European Economic Development, Schmelzer identifies four of these beliefs:

> (1) that GDP . . . adequately measures economic activity; (2) that growth was a panacea for a multitude of . . . socio-economic challenges; (3) that growth was . . . a necessary means to achieve some of the most essential societal goals such as progress, well-being, or national power; and (4) that growth was essentially unlimited, provided the correct . . . policies were pursued. (Schmelzer 2016, p. 264)

These beliefs were challenged at the time, with little or no effect (Schmelzer 2016, p. 265), but they became the focus of a wide-ranging critique of economic growth that has fluctuated over the past half century and is gaining momentum today.

## 1.5   ECONOMISTS QUESTION GROWTH

When economic growth was reaching the pinnacle of policy objectives some dissenting voices were beginning to be heard. One of the most widely read was John Kenneth Galbraith. In *The Affluent Society* published in 1958 and revised through multiple editions, Galbraith compared private affluence in the USA with public squalor. He also questioned the efficacy of dealing with poverty through a general rise in incomes (Galbraith 1958). Many academic economists regarded Galbraith as more of a political commentator than a serious economist because of his disdain for theoretical economics, and on these tenuous grounds they resisted his arguments. The same could not be said of British economist Ezra Mishan who published *The Costs of Economic Growth* in 1967 (Mishan 1967). Mishan was a highly regarded and well-published expert in 'welfare economics', the field within mainstream economics that is concerned with the relationship between economic activity and well-being. So although Mishan's analysis of the costs of economic growth was aimed at a broad audience, no one could dismiss the author as not really understanding modern economic theory.

Perhaps this is one reason why Mishan's critique of economic growth, unlike Galbraith's, ignited a heated debate that went on for several years between him and Wilfred Beckerman, another well-established British economist. Beckerman wrote 'Why we need economic growth' (1971) and *In Defence of Economic Growth* (1974). Later Beckerman wrote *Small is Stupid* (1995) in response to *Small is Beautiful*, Schumacher's critique of modern industrialized economies (Schumacher 1973). Many of Schumacher's arguments about the optimal scale of an economy were anticipated, echoed and augmented by other economists notably Kenneth Boulding in his seminal essay 'The economics of the coming spaceship earth' (1966), Georgescu-Roegen in his path-breaking work on entropy and economics (1971; 1975), and Herman Daly in *Steady-State Economics* (1977) and many other writings. Meanwhile Beckerman continued to resist criticisms of economic growth (Beckerman 2003).

So, within a couple of decades of economic growth becoming the supreme policy objective of most if not all Western governments, serious concerns were being raised even from within the economics profession.

The contemporaneous rise of modern environmentalism, largely a move-ment led by non-economists, buttressed the arguments of the economists challenging the growth paradigm, as did the widely read *Limits to Growth* (Meadows et al. 1972), which examined the implications of physical constraints on global economic growth. Fred Hirsch in *The Social Limits to Growth* (1976) used the concept of 'positional' goods to account for the disconnect between higher incomes and increases in well-being. We will examine arguments from this literature in later chapters.

Arndt titled his book *The Rise and Fall of Economic Growth*, which suggests that by the late 1970s he believed the critics of economic growth had managed to undermine its pre-eminence as a policy objective. This assessment was premature. The commitment to economic growth remains firmly entrenched as the number one priority of most governments today even though it may be promoted in the guise of free trade, competitiveness, productivity and the like or even as 'sustainable development'. Clearly Arndt himself was unconvinced by the critics of growth. His reasons are very similar to those still given for continuing the commitment to eco-nomic growth. That rich economies are already more than double their size when Arndt was writing in the 1970s seems not to matter when progress is at stake. Arndt expressed great faith in the price mechanism to handle scarcity. The standard argument is that if a resource becomes scarce its price will rise, providing incentives for further exploration, for extraction from sources not previously profitable, for the development of substitutes, for better technologies, and for more efficient resource utilization through better design, reuse and recycling. This is a well-established argument in the economics of environmental and natural resources (Tietenberg and Lewis 2014, Chapter 6). One limitation is that it only applies when property rights to resources are clearly established and enforceable in the courts, otherwise those who would respond to increasing scarcity by investing in more exploration and new technologies are discouraged from doing so because they cannot appropriate all the benefits. This is a very large problem especially with respect to many potentially renewable resources such as easily accessed forests, ocean fisheries, the atmosphere, and the gene pool.

Even with non-renewable resources prices may not give the right signals. The argument that prices will handle scarcity of these resources over time assumes that their owners and managers will behave in certain ways conducive to conservation rather than exploitation and this may not be the case. For example, if resource owners anticipate the development of a sub-stitute for their increasingly scarce resource they may expect the price to go down when the substitute becomes available rather than up in response to increasing scarcity of the resource they own. With this expectation, to maximize their profits they will *increase* the rate of extraction, not reduce it, which, in the short term, will depress prices fulfilling their expectations of a price fall. Such behavior runs counter to price induced conservation. It is not far-fetched either. For example, maintaining the supply of oil so that increases in oil prices are moderated, reducing the incentive for the development of alternatives, can be in OPEC's interests. Indeed, this became the strategy adopted by some of its members, notably Saudi Arabia, in response to the increase in 'unconventional' oil coming from the USA made possible by new extraction technologies such as hydraulic fracturing (fracking) and horizontal drilling (Critchlow 2015; Bader 2015).

While prices can and do play a useful role in dealing with resource scarcity it would be foolhardy to rely on them too much, especially for resources where the conditions for a well-functioning market do not exist (see Chapter 3). And even where they do exist, market prices cannot signal anything participants in the market are not concerned about, such as declining supplies decades or centuries ahead.

Sometimes we get the impression that human-induced impacts on the global environment, such as climate change, have only recently been identi- fied as serious. As we shall see in Chapter 5, this is far from true. Arndt was aware of large-scale environmental problems, noting that 'our ignorance about these matters is still great' (Arndt 1978, p. 144), but he was not particularly concerned about them, believing that 'on most of these dire predictions, of over-heating of the earth's atmosphere, destruction of the ionosphere and irremediable damage to ecological balance in other forms, the weight of reputable scientific opinion appears to have come down against the prophets of doom' (Arndt 1978). With all the evidence that has accumulated in the past four decades of climate change caused by human activities, depletion of the ozone layer from human-made CFCs, and the disturbing loss of habitat, species and biodiversity from the expanding presence of humanity on the globe, I doubt if he would hold the same opinion today. This evidence which informs the discussion in later chapters has been effectively summarized in the literature on 'planetary boundaries' (Rockström et al. 2009a, 2009b; Steffen et al. 2015b).

Arndt concludes with four prescient statements about the possibility and desirability of continued economic growth that resonate today and which, to a greater or lesser extent, are themes that will occupy us throughout the rest of this book:

[1.] there is little if any convincing scientific evidence that exhaustion of non- renewable natural resources or irreversible damage to the biosphere will set early limits to growth, though it is possible, but by no means certain, that economic growth will be slowed down over the next century by rising long-run cost curves for some key resources, such as fossil fuels.

[2.]   as per capita income rises, the costs of economic growth tend to increase relative to its benefits.

[3.]   there does not seem the least chance that people will voluntarily forgo opportunities for higher standards of living ... merely because enough is enough.

[4.]   therefore the realistic question to ask is ... what *kind* of growth we should aim at. To have focused public attention on this question is the major achievement of the critique of economic growth of the past decade. (Arndt 1978, p. 150)

We shall return to these contentious conclusions quite often as we consider the prospects and promise of managing without growth.

## 1.6  ECONOMIC GROWTH REMAINS PARAMOUNT

Arndt's cogent account of the rise of economic growth as a policy objective was published three-quarters of the way through the 20th century. Throughout the remainder of the century and into this one, economic growth has maintained its position at or near the top of policy priorities in most countries. Economic growth in developing countries and countries in transition (the old eastern bloc) is important though it is doubtful whether the adoption of a development path that tries to mimic the experience of the rich countries by stressing growth over distribution is feasible and desirable. However, this book is not about developing countries or countries in transition except indirectly. The continued aggressive pursuit of growth by the rich countries has many negative implications for much poorer countries because of global limits on resources and the capacity of the biosphere to absorb and recycle wastes. Managing without growth in advanced economies has a lot to do with leaving room for those whose need is greatest.

With the benefit of hindsight, Arndt's conclusion that by the mid-1970s the commitment to economic growth as the number one policy objective of government had crested was premature. The Organisation for Economic Co-operation and Development (OECD) was founded in 1960 by 20 developed countries and now has 35 members. Article 1 (a) of the OECD charter states,

The aims of the Organisation for Economic Co-operation and Development ... shall be to promote policies designed to achieve the highest sustainable economic growth and employment and a rising standard of living in Member countries, while maintaining financial stability, and thus to contribute to the development of the world economy. (OECD 1960)

The OECD continues to pursue growth with full vigor. In 2005, the OECD published *Economic Policy Reforms: Going for Growth* (OECD 2005). Donald Johnston, the OECD Secretary General, writes in the Foreword that: 'As policy makers and others grapple with the challenges posed by the increasing interdependence of our economies, growth has to be at the top of our agenda' (OECD 2005, p. 4). Since this first edition the OECD has published annual reports with the same title, giving advice to member governments on ways to promote economic growth. In the OECD, economic growth as a dominant objective of government policy is alive and well, albeit sometimes qualified as 'inclusive, sustainable growth' and 'green growth' (OECD 2014; 2015d). The insertion of these adjectives in front of growth is a welcome, if belated, recognition that the pursuit of economic growth per se is not necessarily inclusive, sustainable or green. Whether economic growth can be all of these things is what this book is about and if not, what the alternatives might look like.

This is not to deny that other policy objectives have taken center stage for a while. Objectives such as free trade, increased competitiveness, lower taxes, reducing governments' deficit, innovation, and higher productivity have all had their moments as the focus of government economic policy, but hardly as ends in themselves. They are all promoted as ways of securing increases in economic output; whether they do or not is another matter. The point is that they are best regarded as instrumental policies in the general pursuit of faster, more robust economic growth.

## 1.7   SUSTAINABLE DEVELOPMENT – NEW WINE IN OLD BOTTLES

In 1987, the UN World Environment Commission published the widely read report *Our Common Future* (World Commission on Environment and Development 1987), known as the Brundtland report, popularizing and promoting the concept of sustainable development. The subsequent commitment by many governments to sustainable development is best understood as more of the same rather than a radical departure from economic growth as the top economic policy objective. The absence of a completely unambiguous definition of sustainable development in the Brundtland report helped make it possible for governments, businesses and others to adopt the goal of sustainable development without compromising their adherence to economic growth. Now there are definitions and interpretations of sustainable development to suit everyone. Some of these place very heavy emphasis on economic growth. Only two years after publication of the Brundtland report, Pezzey listed over 60 definitions of sustainability from the literature. His catalogue of definitions includes six from the Brundtland report alone (Pezzey 1992).

Reflecting on the impact of the Brundtland report nearly 20 years after its publication, Jim MacNeill, one of its lead authors, commented that:

> I also never thought that the concept of sustainable development could and would be interpreted in so many different ways . . . Many of them, of course, are totally self-serving. I no longer shock easily but to this day I remain stunned at what some governments in their legislation and some industries in their policies claim to be 'sustainable development.' Only in a Humpty Dumpty world of Orwellian doublespeak could the concept be read in the way some would suggest . . .. In 1987, we thought the concept was plain enough. We defined it in several ways – ethical, social, ecological . . . Only one definition grabbed the headlines, however, and stuck, unfortunately to the exclusion of all the others. It's the one that features the need for intergenerational equity . . . 'development which meets the needs and aspirations of the present generation without compromising the ability of future generations to meet their own needs'. (MacNeill 2006 pp. 3, 4)

Where does economic growth fit within the Brundtland report's definition of sustainable development? Clearly, it is not a repudiation of growth. 'We see . . . the possibility for a new era of economic growth, one that must be based on policies that sustain and expand the environmental resource base' (World Commission on Environment and Development 1987, p. 1). To be fair the main concern of the Commission was with the prospects and possibilities facing developing countries and the threats to their future presented by a wide range of environmental factors that are thoroughly discussed in the report. However, the Commission did not consider whether these countries might find it easier to develop if they were not facing such vigorous competition from rich countries in pursuit of their own economic growth.

In a comparison of conventional and alternative interpretations of sustainable development, David Korten writes that sustainable development as conventionally understood 'is about achieving the sustained economic growth needed to meet human needs, improve living standards, and provide the financial resources that make environmental protection possible' (Korten 1996). In other words, Korten observes that sustained economic growth is a fundamental component of sustainable development as conventionally understood without any differentiation between rich and poor countries.

A good example of this conventional understanding of sustainable development is provided by the Canadian Department of Finance which defined sustainable development as 'long-term sustainable economic growth based on environmentally sound policies and practices. Environmental degradation at the local, national and international level undermines prospects for continued economic development' (Department of Finance Canada 2007). Apparently in 2007 the Department of Finance believed that sustainable development is all about sustaining long-term economic growth and that environmental degradation matters because it undermines the growth process. In terms of whether sustainable development has supplanted in any meaningful way the commitment to economic growth, Canada's Department of Finance could not have been clearer: it had not.[3]

Subsequently, the Federal Government's Sustainable Development Office, established by an Act of Parliament in 2008, stated that 'the Government's Plan for Responsible Resource Development ... was designed to *promote sustainable economic growth* while introducing significant new measures to ensure environmental protection, and supporting social development ...' (Environment and Climate Change Canada 2013, p. 4, emphasis added). The emphasis on economic growth within the context of sustainable development was reaffirmed in the Federal Government's sustainable development strategy for Canada 2016–19 where the promotion of economic growth is prominent throughout the document, for example '... sustainable development means achieving low-carbon, environmentally responsible economic growth ...' (Environment and Climate Change Canada 2016).

Further insight into how the Canadian Government understands sustainable development is provided by the following statement: 'Interconnections between the environment and the economy are evident in the federal government's efforts to support sustainable economic growth and responsible resource development – for example, by expanding Canada's international trade' (Environment and Climate Change Canada 2016, p. 8). Perhaps the most telling indication that sustainable development has done little to change government thinking about economic growth is provided by the Federal Government's budget for 2016 (Morneau 2016). In this fundamentally important statement of government priorities, 'economic growth' is mentioned 37 times and only twice does the word 'sustainable' appear before it. In stark contrast, sustainable development is only mentioned three times.

Similar statements about how sustainable development has been interpreted as another version of the growth agenda can easily be found from governments in other countries. Here are examples from the US and the UK. Explaining sustainable development, the United States Bureau of Oceans and International Environmental and Scientific Affairs (OES) states 'OES spearheads many partnerships and initiatives that advance our broad development goals of *promoting economic growth*, social development and environmental stewardship in such areas as forests, water, energy, climate, fisheries, and oceans management' (US Department of State n.d., emphasis added). The UK Government 'bases its vision of sustainable development on four broad objectives', one of which is 'Maintenance of *high and stable levels of economic growth* and employment' (UK Government 2005, emphasis added).

Economic growth remains the policy objective against which all others must be judged, despite statements made by highly placed people in the public and private sectors about balancing economic, social and environmental considerations in decision-making which are seldom acted on in any practical way. Within government, finance trumps environment almost every time. That is why ministers of the environment are considered junior to ministers of finance. That is why the Ministry of Finance in Ontario was able to extricate itself from inclusion under Ontario's path-breaking Environmental Bill of Rights legislation in 1996 (Ligeti 1996). That is why environment departments are the most vulnerable to cuts whenever governments decide they have to trim their budgets as Canadian governments did in the mid-1990s at the federal and provincial levels (Miller 2007), an experience that was replicated in many other countries (Howard 2015; Hook et al. 2011).

Yet not all of the enthusiasm for sustainable development, or sustainability as some prefer to say, is merely economic growth in disguise. There are many who see it as redefining the goals of society at least to include environmental and social considerations on a par with economic. The 'triple bottom line' of economic, environmental and social success and 'stakeholder value' rather than 'shareholder value' favored by some business scholars and writers suggests a broader approach (Elkington 1998). When all three components of the triple bottom line point in the same direction or when serving stakeholders and shareholders are consistent, the way ahead is obvious. But what happens when the economic conflicts with the environmental or the social, or when stakeholder interests conflict with shareholder interests? The financial imperative is very hard to resist and it usually decides the issue.

### 1.7.1 The Sustainable Development Goals

On 25 September 2015, the United Nations General Assembly adopted 'a plan of action for people, planet and prosperity' entitled *Transforming our World: the 2030 Agenda for Sustainable Development* (United Nations 2015a). The Agenda includes a wide-ranging and candid account of the economic, social and environmental problems confronting different parts of the world. To address these problems the Agenda specifies 17 sustainable development goals supported by 169 targets. The targets are defined as 'aspirational and global; with each Government setting its own national targets . . . taking into account national circumstances' (United Nations 2015a, p. 13). They build on the previous eight Millennium Development Goals established in 2000, which were partially achieved by the target year of 2015 (United Nations 2015b). It is intended that the sustainable development goals (SDGs) and targets 'will stimulate action over the next 15 years in areas of critical importance for humanity and the planet' (United Nations 2015b, p. 1). The SDGs cannot be faulted for a lack of ambition. Who could fail to be inspired by the resolution:

> between now and 2030, to end poverty and hunger everywhere; to combat inequalities within and among countries; to build peaceful, just and inclusive societies; to protect human rights and promote gender equality and the empowerment of women and girls; and to ensure the lasting protection of the planet and its natural resources. (United Nations 2015b, p. 3)

Being 'aspirational', the goals and targets are not legally binding, but nonetheless they are a bold statement of the shared values and objectives of the world's political leaders and have generally been well-received in the media and by the population at large. The issue here is whether and in what ways do they signify a change in the more traditional growth agenda of the UN and its member countries. Here the news is not so good. Economic growth, not just in developing countries, is still regarded as an essential component of sustainable development in the SDGs. Goal number 8 is quite explicit about the importance of economic growth though with the qualification that it be inclusive and sustainable: 'Goal 8: Promote inclusive and sustainable economic growth, employment and decent work for all' (United Nations 2015b, p. 14). Target 8.1 is more precise about the rates of economic growth that are to be achieved between 2015 and 2030 to meet this goal: 'Sustain per capita economic growth in accordance with national circumstances and, in particular, at least 7 per cent gross domestic product growth per annum in the least developed countries' (United Nations 2015b, p. 19).

Target 8.4 recognizes that if economic growth is to be sustainable, it will be necessary for it to be achieved at the same time as pressure on the biosphere is reduced. The target states: 'Improve progressively, through 2030, global resource efficiency in consumption and production and endeavour to decouple economic growth from environmental degradation, in accordance with the 10-Year Framework of Programmes on Sustainable Consumption and Production, with developed countries taking the lead' (United Nations 2015b, p. 19). According to the Framework, 'The most promising strategy for ensuring future prosperity lies in decoupling economic growth from the rising rates of natural resource use and the environmental impacts that occur in both consumption and production stages of product life cycles' (United Nations 2015c). Unfortunately, the Framework of Programmes on Sustainable Consumption and Development does not include quantitative targets for the rates of decoupling required to make economic growth truly green. We take up this issue in some detail in the next chapter and in later chapters as well. For now, suffice it to say that to achieve absolute reductions in natural resource use and in the waste flows causing environmental impacts, the rate of reduction in these flows must exceed the rate of economic growth by a considerable margin if ambitious targets for absolute reductions are required. It is a leap of faith to believe they can be achieved, not only between 2015 and 2030 but beyond, if economic growth continues at anything like the rates that are hoped for to 2030.

## 1.8 ECOLOGICAL MODERNIZATION AND GREEN GROWTH

The promotion of sustainable development is not the only effort that has been made to find ways of reconciling economic growth with the resource and environmental conditions and limitations of the planet and its various regions. Other well-intentioned efforts along similar lines are 'ecological modernization' and 'green growth'. Ecological modernization refers to the proposition that 'continued industrial development [offers] the best option for escaping from the ecological crises of the developed world' (Fisher and Freudenberg 2001). In other words, economic growth based on the further advancement of technology and industrialization is key to resolving the environmental problems resulting from past technology and industrialization: 'ecological modernization sees environmental protection not as a burden on the economy, but as a "precondition for future sustainable growth"' (Fisher and Freudenberg 2001, p. 703). Ecological modernization is also an agenda for political innovation such that 'the potential for improved ecological outcomes . . . is also seen as dependent on changes in the institutional structure of society' (Mol 2000, cited in Fisher and Freudenberg 2001, p. 702).

Green growth, which is closely related to ecological modernization, refers to the belief that the reduction in environmental impact per unit of GDP can outpace growth in GDP so that GDP can grow at the same time as environmental impact declines (OECD 2011a). This is the principle of decoupling, which is integral to all proposals for continuing economic growth and diminishing environmental impact. Green growth is usually promoted as a response to concerns about climate change but can be applied to any environmental problem. Indeed, if green growth is not generalizable to all environmental problems, that is a problem in itself since it would mean that economic growth could not continue indefinitely at anything like historical rates without further environmental deterioration. Strong claims have been made for green growth by international organizations such as UNEP (2016b) and the OECD (2011a; 2014; 2015d) and by individual researchers (for example Ekins 2017). We will consider the efficacy of these claims in the next chapter and provide a more comprehensive critique of an influential study on green growth by UNEP in Chapter 7.

## 1.9   CONCLUSION

In the past two hundred years or so we have seen the idea of economic growth find its way from the minds of some of the most influential writers of the Enlightenment to the top of the list of government policy objectives, in poorer countries where the case for growth is strong, and in rich countries where there is a case to answer. It is this case that we look at in the next few chapters.

## 1.10   WHAT COMES NEXT?

In Chapter 2 we ask the question, why manage without growth? It is there that we introduce the concept of economies as open systems. All systems rely on information. In Chapter 3, we consider the adequacy of prices for conveying accurate and useful information in large and growing economies, particularly with respect to economy–environment interactions, followed in Chapter 4 with a commentary and critique of pricing nature. In Chapters 5, 6 and 7 we consider whether economic growth can be sustained for much longer or whether the world's economies are or will be confronting severe constraints as we realize that nature's bounty is being run down, even to the point of exhaustion. The answer to this question provides part of the rationale for entertaining the idea that rich countries, having benefited most from economic growth, should manage without growth to make room for the poorer countries where the case for growth is much stronger.

In Chapter 8 we examine the relationships among the scale (the size of an economy), composition (the goods and services produced and consumed in an economy) and technology, and how they affect the impact of the economy on the environment. This will provide a framework for assessing the potential for decoupling environmental and resource impacts from economic growth on which the promise of green growth depends. We will analyze the contribution that slower growth in the rich countries could make to reduce global emissions of greenhouse gases and still leave room for poorer countries to benefit from growth.

What, if any, is the relationship between higher incomes and happiness? We address this question in Chapter 9. It seems that after an income level surpassed by most people in rich countries, relative income influences people's sense of well-being far more than their absolute level of income. Having more counts far less than having 'more than'. Since economic growth cannot make everyone better off in relation to others, it contributes little to increasing happiness. In Chapter 10 we look at how effective economic growth has been in helping countries meet other important objectives. Has it brought full employment? Has it reduced poverty (we know it has not eliminated it)? Has it protected the environment? Can we do just as well without relying on growth? Can we do better? Chapter 11 provides some answers to these questions and in some respects is the most important chapter of the book. It shows that a rich country like Canada can indeed achieve a variety of important objectives, often believed to be attainable only through economic growth, without relying on growth. Rich countries can manage without economic growth and if the arguments of the earlier chapters are sound, the sooner we move in that direction the better. The chapter ends with a consideration of whether the scope of changes required for a viable and desirable future are compatible with the kind of capitalist economy that has evolved over the past few centuries or whether the changes are so significant that they signal the dawn of something new.

In Chapter 12 we look at some policies for managing without growth in rich countries, recognizing that such policies should flow from broad public discussion. The objective in this chapter is simply to seed the discussion, not to complete it.

## NOTES

1. In the election platform of the Liberal party of Canada, which replaced the Conservative government in the general election of 2015, economic growth is mentioned many times and its pursuit is a primary objective of the new government (Liberal Party of Canada 2015). And who can doubt that President Trump's campaign slogan to 'make America great again' was all about faster economic growth?
2. Gross national product (GNP) equals GDP plus net income from abroad.
3. In 2017, the Department of Finance continues to use the definition of sustainable development it introduced in 2007 (Finance Canada 2017).

# 2. Why manage without growth?

> Providing for the well being of a still growing world population within the limits of a finite planet is *the* key challenge for our future. (Eleven National Organizations 2006, Consensus Statement 2006)

> We fail to see the deepest roots of our present failures, which have to do with the direction, goals, meaning and social implications of technological and economic growth. (Pope Francis, 2015, Laudato Si')

Most people understand the need to manage growth. Cities become unpleasant when they get too big. Urban sprawl, gridlock and road rage are well known to many of us and continue to challenge the best minds among planners and politicians. Greenbelts, car-free zones, intensification, transit – these are just some of the solutions that help but are not up to the job of containing urbanization as it spreads across the landscape. Still, we keep trying. Growth of entire economies also requires management. This is the job of departments of finance and central bankers who strive for but seldom achieve a steady year over year increase in economic output with high employment and stable prices, with additional objectives for government finances, savings rates, trade balances, capital flows, exchange rates and the like. Economic growth also brings related problems that must be managed. High on this list is what is commonly termed the environment, a catchall for a whole host of air, water, land and resource issues and concern for other species. That is why we have government departments and agencies charged with safeguarding the environment, protecting wildlife, and conserving natural resources. In most countries, their record in doing all this is mixed at best.

But this book is not about managing growth. It is about managing *without* growth, that is, without economic growth as conventionally measured: an increase in real, inflation-adjusted, GDP. More specifically, it is about growth as the prime policy objective in rich countries such as Canada and the USA and more than seventy other 'high income countries' as defined by the World Bank (2017b). Is the priority given to economic growth in countries with highly developed economies in the best interests of their own citizens or is growth in these countries already uneconomic in the sense that the costs of growth are exceeding the benefits, as Daly (2014) contends? Is the pursuit of growth impeding the achievement of other objectives that are more directly related to well-being such as health care, affordable housing, and environmental protection because they are not seen as contributing to the growth agenda? In that case would it be better to be indifferent or agnostic about growth in GDP, as Van den Bergh (2011) has argued? How might an advanced economy function in the absence of growth? Would it collapse or is there a configuration of production, consumption, employment and other aspects of importance that is both feasible and attractive without relying on economic growth? Could the financial system accommodate and support such a transformation? Is growth in these countries in the best interests of the rest of the world's much poorer population for whom economic growth remains a crucial objective? We attempt to answer these questions in the remainder of this book.

It is sometimes helpful to distinguish between growth in GDP and growth in GDP per capita. With a growing population, an increase in GDP is required simply to prevent GDP per capita from declining. This is not a problem if the population is stable and the rates of growth of population in all rich countries have been trending down for some time. According to the UN and World Bank, the population of many of these countries would already be declining were it not for immigration, since the number of births is less than the number of deaths (UN 2017a). Growth in GDP and GDP per capita come to the same thing if population is constant. While the difference between the two concepts can be important, it is less so as populations stabilize or decline so we shall make the distinction explicit only when it really matters.

## 2.1  GROWTH IS SLOWING DOWN

Historically, population growth has resulted from economic growth, which has made it possible to support more people by increasing the production of food, clothing, shelter and other necessities of human life. At the same time, population growth and the accompanying increase in the labor force has been one of the key drivers of economic growth. The other key driver of economic growth has been an increase in labor productivity, defined as the average output per employed worker or worker hour. An increasing labor force that is employed combined with rising labor productivity results in a growing economy since GDP = labor hours × output per worker hour.

Gordon (2016) has estimated that in the United States, the average annual rate of growth in labor productivity between 1890 and 1920 was 1.5 percent. It rose to 2.82 percent between 1920 and 1970 and then declined to 1.62 percent between 1970 and 2014 (Gordon 2016, p. 14). He attributes this decline in US labor productivity to growing inequality, poor education, changing demography, deepening debt, globalization, climate change and a

slower rate of innovation. Gordon notes that the increase in the participation of women in the paid labor force in the latter part of the 20th century
mitigated the impact on the rate of economic growth of the decline in the
rate of increase in labor productivity. Since this increase in participation
cannot be repeated, if US labor productivity growth continues to remain
low or declines further and population growth continues to decline, then the
USA will have to manage without growth for a long time to come. Gordon's
forecast for the average annual rate of growth in real US GDP per person
from 2015 to 2040 is 0.8 percent, compared with 2.41 percent from 1920 to
1970 and 1.77 percent from 1970 to 2014 (Gordon 2016, p. 637).

Figure 2.1 shows the annual average rate of economic growth for high-
income countries as a group, with a trend line added revealing the decline.[1]
Figure 2.2 groups the same data into 10-year averages for four high-income
countries: Canada, Sweden, the UK and the USA. It is clear that the
changes over time in the economic growth rates of advanced economies
have been very similar. Gordon attributes the increase in growth rates in
the mid-1990s that lasted into the early years of the next decade in the USA
to the impact of computers, which he believes has largely run its course in
its impact on economic growth (Gordon 2016, pp. 17, 441–60). A similar
pattern shows up in the average annual growth rates for other advanced

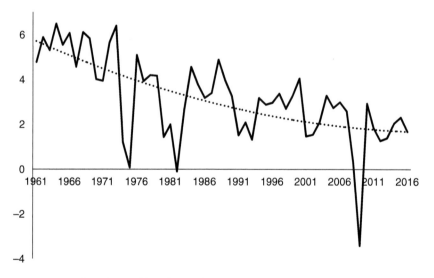

*Source:*    Data from the World Bank World Development Indicators July 2017 (World Bank
2017b).

*Figure 2.1    Average rate of economic growth (%) in high-income
             countries: 1961–2016*

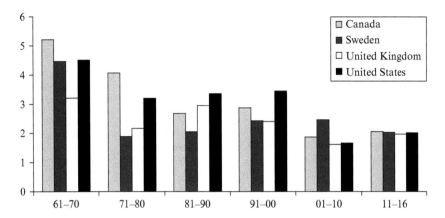

*Source:* Data from the World Bank World Development Indicators July 2017 (World Bank 2017b).

*Figure 2.2*   *Annual average rate of economic growth (%) in Canada, UK and USA by decade: 1961–2016*

economies. Of course, past trends cannot simply be extrapolated to predict the future but it would be foolhardy simply to assume that they will reverse themselves and carry on regardless. There are some very good reasons for expecting slower, even much slower, rates of growth in the future. Some, to which we now turn, stem from the profligate use of the biosphere to serve human purposes such that, according to some scientists, we are living in a brand new geological era, the Anthropocene.

## 2.2 THE ANTHROPOCENE

For most of human history economic activity has been small in relation to the biosphere. Impacts on the environment were local and sometimes regional, but most were limited in their geographic extent and duration. As the scale of economic activity has increased, some impacts have become global, such as climate change and biodiversity loss. Other more local impacts, the scarcity of fresh water for example, have been experienced in different parts of the world simultaneously, giving them a global dimension of a different sort. Awareness of the escalating impacts of human economies on the environment has led some scientists to argue that we have entered a new era, the Anthropocene, to denote a period during which human activity has become the dominant influence on climate and the environment (Crutzen and Steffen 2003).

Various dates have been proposed for the start of the Anthropocene from 10000 years ago, when agriculture and animal husbandry began, to the late 18th century and the advent of the steam engine. In their assessment of the literature on the Anthropocene, Crutzen and Steffen emphasize the period since 1950 as the one in which human activities rapidly change from merely *influencing* the global environment in some ways to *dominating it in many ways*:

- Human impacts on Earth System structure (e.g. land cover, coastal zone structure) and functioning (e.g. biochemical cycling) now equal or exceed in magnitude many forces of nature at the global scale.
- The rates of human-driven change are almost always much greater than those of natural variability . . .
- All of the changes in the Earth System . . . are occurring simultaneously, and many are accelerating simultaneously. (Crutzen and Steffen 2003, p. 253)

Another term closely related to the Anthropocene that is used to describe the rapid increase in a wide range of human impacts on the biosphere is 'the Great Acceleration'. The Great Acceleration refers to the simultaneous upturn in many socio-economic trends in the mid-20th century and the corresponding responses of multiple interconnected Earth systems. This is illustrated in Figures 2.3a and 2.3b for the period 1750 to 2010, which show in dramatic fashion how times have changed since the middle of the 20th century. In Figure 2.3a we see the rapid increase in growth in GDP, primary energy use, urbanization and population. In Figure 2.3b we see rising concentrations of carbon dioxide and methane in the atmosphere,

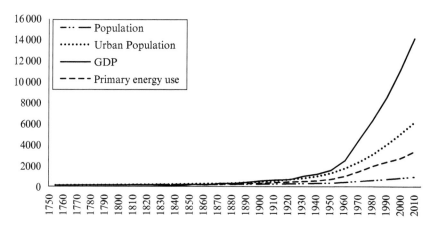

*Source:*  Based on data from Steffen et al. (2015a).

*Figure 2.3a   Global socio-economic trends 1750–2010*

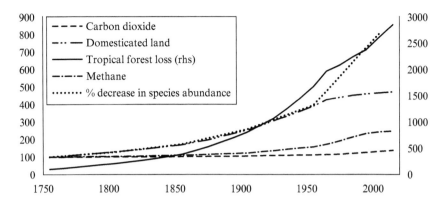

*Source:* Based on data from Steffen et al. (2015a).

*Figure 2.3b    Global earth-system trends 1750–2010*

*Table 2.1    Rates of change in the Great Acceleration*

| Global Socio-Economic Trends | 1750–1850 | 1850–1950 | 1950–2010 |
| --- | --- | --- | --- |
| Population | 0.6% | 0.7% | 1.7% |
| GDP | 0.6% | 2.2% | 3.7% |
| Urban Population | 0.8% | 1.8% | 2.6% |
| Primary energy use | 0.6% | 1.4% | 2.6% |
| Large dams | N/A | N/A | 2.9% |
| Fertillizer | N/A | N/A | 4.2% |
| Water use | N/A | N/A | 1.9% |
| Telecommunications | N/A | N/A | 16.4% |
| Global Earth-System Trends | 1750–1850 | 1850–1950 | 1950–2010 |
| Carbon dioxide | 0.0% | 0.1% | 0.4% |
| Nitrous oxide | 0.0% | 0.1% | 0.2% |
| Methane | 0.1% | 0.3% | 0.8% |
| Domesticated land | 0.5% | 0.8% | 0.3% |
| Tropical forest loss (rhs) | 1.4% | 1.5% | 0.9% |
| % decrease in species abundance | 0.6% | 0.8% | 1.3% |

*Source:* Based on data from Steffen et al. (2015a) available from IGBP (2015).

increasing domestication of land, the loss of tropical forests and decline in
species abundance.

Table 2.1 summarizes the average annual rate of increase in each of
these variables. The trends displayed in this table and the previous two

figures are a major cause for concern about the capacity of the biosphere to support the continuing expansion of the human population and our economies.[2]

## 2.3    DECOUPLE AND THE ECONOMY CAN GROW FOREVER?

One aspect of managing without growth that we need to address before going further is whether it is an unnecessarily blunt instrument for addressing problems that warrant a more detailed and precise approach. If, for example, there is concern with the impacts of accessing, extracting and using energy resources to fuel economic growth, then can't we find ways to reduce energy requirements and to reduce or eliminate the associated environmental impacts of the energy requirements that remain, without stifling growth? This is the essence of green growth, which is based on the premise that economic growth can be 'decoupled' from the full range of environmental impacts that we want to reduce while growth continues apace (OECD 2011a). We will consider specific examples of decoupling and its limits in later chapters. Here I want to make a simple but crucially important point about the intimate relationship between the rate of economic growth and the rate of reduction in energy use, land conversion, habitat destruction, greenhouse gas emissions, toxic waste release and any other environmental impact of concern that is required to meet any chosen reduction target.

Suppose that a target has been set for the reduction in a flow of wastes to be achieved at some specified future time. It follows that the higher the rate of economic growth, the higher must be the rate of reduction in the waste flow to achieve the target. Take the example of greenhouse gas (GHG) emissions. The top row of Table 2.2 shows the annual rate of growth of an economy. The first column shows the annual rate of reduction in GHG emissions per dollar of GDP, often called the GHG emissions intensity or GHG intensity, of the economy. The entries in the table show the reduction in GHG emissions that will be achieved in 35 years for each specific combination of a rate of economic growth and a rate of reduction in GHG intensity.

Assume a target of reducing GHG emissions by at least 80 percent in 35 years through a steady reduction in GHG intensity. Table 2.2 shows that an annual rate of economic growth of 2 percent/year and a rate of reduction of 7 percent/year in GHG intensity results in an eventual 84 percent reduction in GHG emissions within the time specified. A 3 percent rate of economic growth requires a 14 percent faster rate of reduction in GHG

*Table 2.2    Reduction in GHG emissions in 35 years*

| | | | Rate of Economic Growth | | | |
|---|---|---|---|---|---|---|
| | | 0% | 1% | 2% | 3% | 4% |
| Rate of Reduction in GHG Emissions Intensity | 0% | 0% | 42% | 100% | 181% | 295% |
| | −1% | −30% | 0% | 41% | 98% | 178% |
| | −2% | −51% | −30% | −1% | 39% | 95% |
| | −3% | −66% | −51% | −31% | −3% | 36% |
| | −4% | −76% | −66% | −52% | −33% | −5% |
| | −5% | −83% | −76% | −67% | −53% | −34% |
| | −6% | −89% | −84% | −77% | −68% | −55% |
| | −7% | −92% | −89% | −84% | −78% | −69% |
| | −8% | −95% | −92% | −89% | −85% | −79% |
| | −9% | −96% | −95% | −93% | −90% | −85% |
| | −10% | −97% | −96% | −95% | −93% | −90% |

*Source:*    Adapted from Victor (2010).

intensity to achieve the same result. When the economy does not grow, then the rate of reduction in GHG intensity for an equivalent reduction in emissions is a much more modest, though still ambitious, 4.5 percent/year.

A rule of thumb is that to achieve a reduction in GHG emissions of at least 80 percent in 35 years requires a reduction in the intensity about 5 percent per year greater than the rate of economic growth. This is useful for thinking about different combinations of rates of economic growth and rates of decline in GHG emissions intensity around the world allowing for very different national and regional circumstances. In poorer countries, where economic growth can still bring significant benefits, a faster rate of decline in GHG intensity will be required to reach any reduction target than if their economies were to grow more slowly. Richer countries contemplating slower growth will find that a different combination of the rate of economic growth and a decline in GHG intensity makes more sense.

In 2016 the International Energy Agency made much of the apparent stabilization of global carbon dioxide emissions from 2014 to 2015 (based on preliminary data) with the headline 'Decoupling of global emissions and economic growth confirmed' (IEA 2016c). Global GDP grew 3.1 percent in the same year (IMF 2016), which means that the rate of GHG intensity declined at the same rate.[3] If these rates of change are maintained into the future, with global GDP rising at the same rate that GHG intensity declines, then total GHG emissions will remain virtually unchanged. Decoupling at this rate, in combination with a rate of economic growth close to 3 percent, does no more than hold the line on emissions. As Table 2.2 shows, a sustained rate of decline in GHG intensity in excess of 7 percent per year is required to reduce GHG emissions by at least 80 percent by mid-century if the global economy grows at 3 percent per year. And if the rate of reduction in GHG intensity is less than 7 percent in any year, in subsequent years it must exceed 7 percent simply to meet the target 80+ percent reduction in GHG emissions in the same timeframe. What's more, each year the reduction on intensity falls short of 7 percent, as it clearly did in 2014 and 2015, there is an increase in the cumulative emissions to mid-century even if the target for reduced emissions is ultimately achieved.[4]

Decoupling GHG emissions from economic growth is just one example of how the two rates, intensity reduction and economic growth, should always be discussed together to understand the implications of what decoupling can achieve. A fundamental principle of decoupling is that the combination of the rate of growth in economic activity and the rate of reduction in the intensity of the unwanted flow stemming from that activity determines what happens to the level of the flow. The same considerations apply to any economic activity from local to global, from sector to sector, and to a reduction in environmental impacts, whether from resource use, land conversion or waste disposal. The key is to match the rate of economic growth with the rate of reduction in intensity required to achieve any particular total reduction target. Acting only on the rate of decoupling and not on the rate of economic growth puts too many eggs into a single basket.

Table 2.2 also illustrates the important distinction between *relative* decoupling and *absolute* decoupling. Relative decoupling requires that the rate of intensity declines but at a rate that is less than the rate of economic growth, with the result that GHG emissions (or any other environmental flow of concern) increases. Relative decoupling is shown in the cells in the upper right-hand side of Table 2.2. Absolute decoupling requires that the rate of intensity decline faster than the rate of economic growth because only then will the undesirable environmental flow also decline. Relative decoupling is easier to achieve than absolute decoupling so it is not surprising that there is much more evidence for it than for absolute decoupling (Mazzanti and Zoboli 2008; Jorgenson and Clark 2012; Fischer-Kowalski and Amann 2001; Sjostrom and Ostblom 2010).

There is a further complication that should give us pause when thinking about decoupling as the key to endless economic growth. So far, we have been talking about decoupling flows. GDP is defined as the output of final goods and services produced in an economy in a specified period of time, usually a year. It is a flow, measured in dollars per year. Annual GHG emissions are also a flow, measured in tonnes per year, as is energy consumption measured in tonnes of oil equivalent or some other measure of energy per year. The problem with this is that many environmental problems result from the accumulation or decumulation of a *stock* of some kind and not from immediate exposure to an excessive *flow*. For example, it is the stock of GHGs accumulated in the atmosphere that causes climate change, not the flow in any year, and it is the decumulation of the stock of habitat that matters for biodiversity rather than the result of a single annual change. Flows remain important because to mitigate stock-related environmental problems it is necessary to act on the flows that determine the stocks. A reduction in GHG emissions will slow the accumulation of greenhouse gases in the atmosphere. If the flow reduction is large enough the accumulated stock will eventually stabilize and decline as natural processes that reduce greenhouse gases in the atmosphere take over. The same is true for the loss of habitat from land conversion which requires elimination of (net) land conversion simply to prevent the stock of habitat from declining further.

The connection between flows and stocks also applies to natural resources, though in slightly different ways. Over-harvesting renewable resources such as fish or forests results in a reduction in the stocks. By reducing the rate of harvesting the stocks can recover. Again, we change the flows to achieve an objective that is about stocks. Properly managed stocks can yield sustainable flows available for human use, the usual management objective. With non-renewable resources such as fossil fuels and metals, there is concern that stocks are being depleted at such a rate that the flow of materials obtained from them cannot be sustained (see Chapter 5). This gives rise to questions about the feasibility of finding substitutes such as renewable sources of energy for oil, gas and coal that are not too costly and the possibility of making a smooth transition, again made more challenging if an ever-expanding economy is to have the energy it needs.

We can only properly assess the contribution of decoupling material and energy flows from GDP growth to meet a reduction target that is really about stocks when we take into consideration the links between the flows we think we can control and the likely rate of adjustment of the associated stocks. This is one reason why discussions about GHG emissions reduction goals have come to be expressed in terms of a carbon budget rather than a specific reduction in annual emissions sometime in the future (Levin and Tompkins 2014). If a GHG emissions reduction target expressed as a flow in 35 years' time is met with little or no reduction in flows, the stock of GHGs in the atmosphere will be much greater than if the target reduction in the flow of GHG emissions is steadily approached, as assumed in Table 2.2.

To conclude this discussion of decoupling, it is true that slowing the rate of economic growth to zero (or less) may be a relatively crude way of reducing environmental impacts. But Table 2.1 shows why it can be easier to reduce environmental impacts at lower rather than higher rates of economic growth. We will see later (Chapter 10) that the counter-argument that higher rates of economic growth are necessary to provide the resources to reduce environmental impacts is not well supported historically and we will also come to understand why.

Finally, it is worth reiterating that managing without economic growth does not mean that all growth should cease. If economies are successful in transitioning away from fossil fuels to renewable sources of energy, the coal, oil and gas industries will decline and the solar, wind, geothermal and tidal industries will expand. There will be similar patterns of growth and decline elsewhere in economies that manage without growth. It will be possible to secure ongoing improvements, growth if you like, in many things that make life worth living both for individuals and communities. Some writers such as Tim Jackson (2009; 2017) show how prosperity, understood as people everywhere having the capability to flourish as human beings, can be sustained within the ecological and resource constraints of a finite planet. Indeed, this has become the principal goal of the Centre for the Understanding of Sustainable Prosperity in the UK, which Jackson leads (http://www.cusp.ac.uk/about/). If prosperity without growth is the aim, managing without growth is the way to make it happen.[5]

## 2.4   MANAGING WITHOUT GROWTH IS NOT NEW

Managing without growth seems like a very radical, even crazy, idea, yet for all but the tiniest sliver of time since humans evolved, humanity has managed without growth. This is not to say that we have managed without change. But throughout history, excluding the very recent past, the pace of change has been so slow that people expected the lives of their children to be much the same as those of their parents. Change happened, but it was not apparent within most people's own lives – and yet most people managed.

It is only in the last few hundred years or less that the pace of change accelerated, in rich countries especially, to the point where people changed their expectations about the future, itself a modern idea. Parents began to expect that their children would have better lives than them and children began to expect it too. Just how this happened was the subject of Chapter 1. Suffice it to say that humans evolved without reliance on or anticipation of economic growth and that these circumstances have been typical of all but the last blink of human existence. Our mental faculties and emotional states are those of a species that spent almost its entire history without having to cope with growth and all that growth entails (Dubos 1965). With all this experience, we ought to be good at managing without growth. Well, at least we should not be afraid to contemplate it.

But why bother? Growth is good, isn't it? It has raised the standard of living of billions of people and provides the wherewithal to solve problems, whatever they may be. Not only is growth good, these days we think of it as essential. It is not hard to come up with all the standard arguments for promoting economic growth in countries whether they are rich, middling or poor. The value of economic growth in poor countries is easy to see. It is the arguments for growth in rich countries we need to question. Indeed it is because medium and low-income countries require economic growth that rich countries should make room for them, particularly in a world constrained by biological and physical limits which are becoming more and more apparent each day. They can do this by redirecting their policy objectives away from the pursuit of their own economic growth to far more specific economic, social and environmental objectives for themselves and for the other countries with which they share the globe. In doing so, they can set aside the increasingly outdated preoccupation with economic growth.

## 2.5   THE MEANING OF MANAGING WITHOUT GROWTH

What though does it mean to manage without growth? Answering this question will be a recurring theme throughout this book. Let us start with some dictionary definitions. Here are a few of the many definitions of 'to manage' from the *Oxford English Reference Dictionary* (Pearsall and Timble 1996):

1.   'To train a horse'.

This definition is included only because it is the original meaning of the word manage, coming to English from the Italian *maneggiare*, derived from the Latin *manus* meaning hand. To manage meant to guide a horse by the hand. Its meaning has come a long way since then. According to the dictionary, manage now means:

2.   'To meet one's needs with limited resources',
3.   'To organize; regulate; be in charge of',
4.   'To gain influence with or maintain control',
5.   'To cope with'.

Each of these definitions says something useful about managing as the term is used in this book. The second definition, meeting needs with limited resources, is what economics is all about according to the standard textbook definition of the subject. The same textbooks tell us that needs are insatiable so resources can never be sufficient to satisfy them all (Baumol 1977). Growth can ease the strain but not solve the economic problem entirely. The question now is whether and for how long the planet can support the historically unprecedented and massively unbalanced expansion of the world economy while limiting and ultimately reducing the serious adverse effects. Managing under these circumstances is a challenge that promises only to become more difficult with 7.6 billion people on the planet in 2017, approaching 11 billion, plus or minus, by the end of the century (Gerland et al. 2014). Organization, regulation, and maintaining control (the third and fourth definitions of to manage) are unavoidable, raising questions about the kinds of organization and regulation that are desirable, and about control over what, by whom and towards what ends. Who decides? Managing in this sense quickly becomes political and problematic.

Finally, there is managing as coping (the fifth definition). This sounds a lot drearier because coping suggests getting by rather than achieving great things. With the challenges of the 21st century before us, getting by might be ambition enough. The same dictionary tells us that coping also means 'to manage successfully; deal with a situation or problem', and under the circumstances this may be just the kind of managing we need.

Growth in general is simple to define: 'an increase in size or value' (Pearsall and Timble 1996) is one of several similar dictionary definitions that works very well. Growth can be an increase in the size or value of anything. Anything that is non-material, such as love and social justice, can grow without limit but growth of anything material or which has material and energy requirements will necessarily be constrained if dependent solely on resources available on planet Earth. Our interest here is in the increasing size or value of the economy as normally measured, that is, as an increase in real GDP. You would have thought that a definition of economic growth would be found in textbook treatments of the subject, but that is not necessarily so. For example, *Introduction to Economic Growth* by Professor Charles Jones and Dietrich Vollrath is a lucid and widely used textbook that provides an excellent overview of modern growth economics, yet the authors do not provide a definition of economic growth. They start out right away with data on GDP per capita and GDP per worker and take no time to reflect on the meaning of an economy or its growth (Jones and Vollrath 2013). It is also difficult to find official definitions of economic growth even from organizations such as the OECD, the IMF and the World Bank that are dedicated to promoting it. We are simply told that economic growth is measured by changes in real GDP or real

GDP per capita. What is being measured has become synonymous with its measurement.

Other writers, such as Herman Daly who believes that economic growth in rich countries is already doing more harm than good, have looked deeper into its meaning (Daly 1996). Daly makes a distinction between growth as quantitative and development as qualitative. Economic growth in this sense occurs when an economy is increasing its use of materials, and economic development occurs when the same quantity of materials is used to achieve more desirable goals (Daly 1996, p. 167). Economies can grow and develop at the same time. They can also grow without developing and, as Daly argues, develop without growing. He points out that GDP (he uses GNP) conflates growth and development so we cannot tell from increases in GDP to what extent an economy is growing in the sense of increasing its use of materials, or developing by using the same materials more effectively, or both (Daly 1996, p. 28). Daly's view has begun to resonate at the highest political level.

> There are a lot of people out there, environmental thinkers like Herman Daly and others, who talk about the fact that maybe endless growth within a finite system is not either possible or even desirable. Maybe we have to talk about shifting our focus so that instead of just growing, we're actually developing and improving. (Trudeau 2012)

A different and perhaps more widely used distinction between growth and development comes from the literature on development economics, as noted in Chapter 1. Development in poorer countries is expected to involve substantial institutional change, usually taken to mean towards the kinds of political, economic and legal institutions found in Western democracies. To underline this meaning of development, the rich countries are called developed and the rest, undeveloped, less developed, developing, in transition, or some other term implying that further institutional changes are required before such countries can be considered 'developed'. Having developed, all they need is growth and require no further fundamental changes in institutions.

When it comes to quantitative analysis of managing without growth, we have to rely on statistics collected and published by government agencies. These statistics do not generally reflect the distinction between growth and development that Daly emphasizes. Statistics on annual flows of materials, energy and wastes are available for some countries but there is a distinct lack of comprehensive accounts collected systematically over many years. Hence for empirical work we have to use changes in GDP as the measure of economic growth whether we like it or not. As it turns out, most people like it or at any rate do not question it, though we should note the extensive literature on ways to improve GDP (e.g. Costanza et al. 2009; Stiglitz et al. 2009). There is work under way at the United Nations and in various countries to develop 'satellite accounts' to accompany the standard set of national accounts from which GDP is derived. Clearly, the intent is to complement GDP rather than abandon it (Boyd 2006; Boyd and Banzhaf 2007; Muller et al. 2011; Ewing et al. 2012; UN et al. 2014).

Managing without growth entails measurement, whether of the value of market activity as with GDP or the measurement of flows of materials and energy, as favored by Daly and ecological economists generally. If our objective is to reduce these physical flows in order to reduce the burden that economies impose on the biosphere, and if GDP is becoming less material and energy intensive, then managing without growth of GDP will bring the reductions in physical flows that we are seeking. Alternatively, if decoupling is insufficient, desired reductions in physical flows will entail slower, zero or even negative growth in GDP. But managing without growth can also be understood as managing without growth as a policy objective. This is the position promoted by Jeroen Van den Bergh (2011) and Kate Raworth (2017). The rate of economic growth they say should emerge from the pursuit of other objectives but should not be an objective in its own right. While this view is not inconsistent with the position taken in this book, it seems likely that agrowth, as Van den Bergh names it, stands a better chance of adoption if it can be shown that managing without growth in GDP can, under the right circumstances, be better than pursuing growth for its own sake. We shall look further into this question in Chapter 11.

To summarize, managing without growth has two different but related meanings. The first is to drop economic growth as a distinct policy objective and give other more meaningful objectives priority. The second meaning of managing without growth is to explore the circumstances under which an economy that is not growing can outperform one that is. If it can be shown that, in the absence of economic growth, an economy can deliver on a range of economic, social and environmental objectives where a growing economy falls short, then it buttresses the displacement of economic growth as a policy objective. Succeeding with the second will facilitate the first. In this book, we use managing without growth in both senses.

## 2.6   ECONOMIES AS OPEN SYSTEMS

'Economic growth is usually measured by the pace of change of gross domestic product (GDP) after adjustment for inflation also known as real GDP' (Government of Canada 2007a). This conventional definition of economic growth is not accompanied by a separate explicit definition of the economy, that is, that which grows. This lack of differentiation between an economy, which is a complex arrangement of artifacts, people and institutions embedded in and dependent on the biosphere, and the goods and services it produces is not very helpful for considering alternative economic futures. Managing without growth is likely to require changes in the economy as well as in the level and mix of goods and services it produces, that is, in GDP. So, what is an economy? One definition is that an economy is 'the system of production and distribution and consumption' (Miller 2006). Economies can be distinguished in terms of their social arrangements and institutions, particularly those involving the ownership and deployment of the 'factors of production' (land, labor and capital) in the production and distribution of goods and services. Different social and institutional arrangements yield different types of economies. These may be classified as feudal, capitalist, socialist, communist, or as traditional, market, mixed, planned, or as local, regional and global, or as some other grouping depending on the features one wishes to emphasize.

A different conception of an economy that provides a better starting point for a book on growth is as an 'open system' with biophysical dimensions. An open system is any complex arrangement that maintains itself through an inflow and outflow of energy and material from and to its environment. You and I are open systems. We rely on food to build and maintain our bodies and for energy, and we produce wastes that must be discharged. A failure at either end can be fatal. While we are alive this 'throughput' sustains us. In the early years, material inflows exceed outflows and so our bodies grow until we reach a steady state in terms of mass, or something close to that. In later years, we enter a period of decline. When we die our bodies degrade. All animals, plants and microbes are open systems and they all go through this process of growth, stability and decline, though at very different rates. Ashes to ashes, dust to dust. The process does not end there because the dust becomes food for other organisms living within ecosystems powered by the sun, and life continues.

Ecosystems are open systems. Cities, towns and neighborhoods are open systems. In fact, virtually all of the systems that we can think of are open systems. Everything that lives is an open system. Many human-made artifacts are open systems. Consumer durables such as cars, computers and air conditioners are open systems; they need a supply of energy and material to function and for repair.

Planet Earth is a closed system, or virtually so. A closed system exchanges energy with its environment but not material. The Earth receives solar energy and re-radiates an equal amount of energy to outer space, maintaining the planet's temperature. The accumulation of greenhouse gases in the atmosphere from the operation of human-controlled open systems on the surface of the planet is disturbing this exchange of energy, causing the climate to change. Only insignificant amounts of material enter or leave the Earth and that is why it is a closed system.

Economies are open systems. All economies require energy and materials and all but energy from the sun comes from the planet. Even this solar energy is limited by the surface area of the planet. These material and energy inputs are used in many ways to produce goods and services. Some reuse and recycling takes place within economies but eventually all the materials and energy that enter an economy are degraded. They become less and less useful and are returned to the environment as waste. And here is the rub. Economies are open systems but they exist within and depend upon planet Earth, which is a closed system. All of the materials used by economies come from the planet and end up as wastes disposed of back in the environment. This includes all fossil fuels (coal, oil, natural gas) that enter the economy as materials and from which chemical energy is released during combustion. Solar energy, wind energy, hydro and geothermal energy are sources of energy used by the economy that are not first obtained as supplies of materials, though the equipment that makes their capture and use possible is. Fossil fuel combustion inevitably produces waste materials that re-enter the environment as ash, pollutants and carbon dioxide. The quantity of these wastes is equal in amount to the quantity of fuels themselves, though the chemical composition is quite different. This 'materials balance' principle applies to all materials used by economies (Ayres and Kneese 1969; Boulding 1966; Victor 1972).

An equivalent 'energy balance' principle applies to all uses of energy. The quantity of energy is maintained in any process, only its form changes. This is the first law of thermodynamics (Miller 2004). An example is the conversion of the chemical energy in gasoline to mechanical energy and heat when used to power an automobile. (The first law of thermodynamics is more properly expressed as the conservation of mass/energy allowing for the conversion of mass into energy, which happens when very small amounts of matter are converted into energy through atomic fission in the generation of electricity.)

It is the second law of thermodynamics that accounts for the inevitable decline in the capacity of energy to do work each time it is used (Georgescu-Roegen 1971). For example, in a conventional electric power station, energy from coal combustion is used to boil water. The steam drives a turbine that produces electricity. Some energy is released to the environment as waste heat, which is unavailable for further work. Only about 35 percent of the chemical energy in the coal leaves the power station as electricity and then there are further losses during transmission and use

(Hussy et al. 2014). In a 'cogeneration' system, some of the lower quality energy is used for industrial, commercial or domestic heating before release to the environment as waste. Cogeneration allows more useful work to be obtained from the same amount of fuel than conventional electricity generation. Nevertheless, there is no escape from the decline in the capacity of the energy to do work and from the impossibility of recycling energy in some form of perpetual motion machine. Reuse and recycling can reduce materials flows between an economy and the environment but some reduction in quality is inevitable as when recycled fine paper is used to produce cardboard. The concept of a 'circular economy' (Andersen 2006) raises as an ideal 100 percent reuse and recycling of materials (energy cannot be recycled though it can be used more efficiently) but the first and second laws of thermodynamics prohibit complete circularity.

As a result of these fundamental physical laws, open systems that depend upon their environment for material and energy must keep going back for more and must keep finding places to deposit their wastes. This applies to whole economies just as much as it applies to animals, plants and microbes and to people like us. The extent of the demands placed by any open system on its environment is largely a question of scale, composition and technology. A large and growing economy will impose a greater burden on the environment than a small and stable one if they produce and consume similar mixes of goods and services and employ comparable technologies. (In Chapter 8 we consider the difference that changes in the structure of an economy, such as more services, fewer goods, and changes in technology can make to mitigate the effects of growth.)

Open systems that keep demanding more and more from their environment will be limited in how they function if their environment is unable to sustain them. Is the limited supply of some natural resources a critical problem for growing economies? Those concerned with limits to non-renewable physical resources such as 'peak' oil – the supposed imminent decline in the production of crude oil from cheap conventional sources – certainly think it is (Tverberg 2016). Those more concerned with biological resources are sure it is (Rees 2006). Forestry and fishing are in decline as are wetlands, aquifers and some major lakes and rivers. We will consider these problems and their implications for growth in Chapters 5 and 6.

Figure 2.4 illustrates this conceptualization of economies as open systems. It shows the economies of two countries that are linked by trade in goods and services and flows of capital and labor. The different sizes of the rectangles for the two countries reflect the different sizes of their economies. The dashed oval is the boundary of this two-country, open-system, global economy. Both economies rely on inputs of matter and energy from the environment and dispose of matter and energy back to the

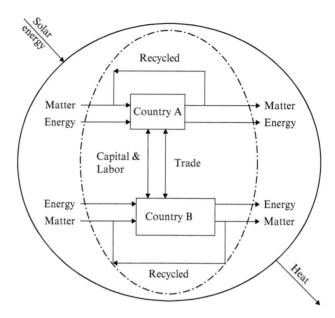

*Figure 2.4    The global economy as an open system*

environment. Some matter is recycled but not energy. The global economy is located in the planet, which is a closed system admitting solar energy and discharging heat.

Because of trade, goods, services, capital and labor flow between the two countries. The material that is extracted from the environment by one country may be discharged back to the environment by the other country though the effects on the environment do not necessarily respect national boundaries. This happens, for example, when oil from the Middle East is burned in automobiles in the United States or when minerals mined in Canada are used in products made in China. It can be difficult to track such flows and the lack of data complicates the assessment of the environmental impact of any one national, regional or local economy. The 'ecological footprint' is one method that relates human activities to the land-based resources required to support them on a sustainable basis (Wackernagel and Rees 1996). Another method is to track the materials that move in, through and out of an economy (Adriaanse et al. 1997), sometimes referred to as an economy's metabolism. A third approach is the uses of 'environmentally-extended' input–output models to estimate the materials and energy embodied in the consumption in one country regardless of the sources of these materials and energy (Miller and Blair

2009; Victor 1972). Work is under way on each of these approaches for measuring the physical dependence of economies on their environment (OECD 2008a).

Not only does the environment supply useful energy and materials to the global economy and receive wastes, it also provides a variety of 'ecosystem services' that are directly beneficial to humans. These ecosystem services are not shown in Figure 2.1 but they can be described; Lubchenco summarizes them well as:

> the purification of air and water; mitigation of floods and droughts; detoxification and decomposition of wastes; generation of renewal of soil and soil fertility; pollination of crops and natural vegetation; control of the vast majority of potential agricultural pests; dispersal of seeds and translocation of nutrients; maintenance of biodiversity from which humanity has derived key elements of its agricultural, medicinal, and industrial enterprise; protection from the sun's harmful UV rays; partial stabilization of climate; moderation of temperature extremes and the force of winds and waves; support of diverse human cultures; and provision of aesthetic beauty and intellectual stimulation that lift the human spirit. (Lubchenco 1998)

As we shall see in Chapter 6, these valuable and essential services are being compromised by the increasing burden that the world's economies are placing on the environment primarily through economic activities that transform land and sea, alter major biogeochemical cycles, and add or remove species and genetically distinct populations (Lubchenco 1998, p. 492). All of these activities require inputs of energy and material and all of them produce wastes. At low levels these material and energy flows have only local, short-term impacts on the environment but with the increases in scale their flows have impacts that are regional and global and of much longer duration.

Natural systems can be very effective in breaking down many of the wastes produced by people and machines, but local environments arc often overloaded causing polluted land, water and air. Historically these were the environmental problems typical of early industrialization. More recently, the scale and complexity of environmental problems have increased. Now we are confronted by broad regional problems such as acid rain and desertification, and global problems such as depletion of the ozone layer, climate change and extensive losses of biodiversity. We also have to deal with problems created by synthetic chemicals, nanotechnology and, through genetic engineering, novel biological forms with which nature has little experience and which it may not be able to accommodate without stress. Whether or not these kinds of environmental impacts present a greater constraint on growth than a shortage of energy and material supplies is unclear. In part, it depends on location since different regions are subject to different pressures. What matters more than determining whether limited resources or rising impacts are the greater threat to growth is that rapidly growing economies have to confront them both.

So far, we have focused on the materials and energy that enter and leave the economy but this is not the whole story. In activities such as mining and construction, very large quantities of material are moved around and sometimes processed without entering the economy as sources of value at all. The removal of overburden in mining or the separation of a mineral from crude ore can require the manipulation of enormous quantities of materials that in themselves have no economic value. In fact, they have negative economic value because they are unwanted. These movements of material, which are substantial, can have considerable environmental impacts and should be included in any complete reckoning of the material and energy requirements of an economy (OECD 2008a).

## 2.7   OPEN SYSTEMS AND RUSSIAN DOLLS

You may have seen those intricately painted Russian dolls that fit snugly inside one another. In a somewhat similar way, we can say that open systems are 'nested'. Smaller systems are contained within larger ones that are contained within even larger ones. Nested systems differ from Russian dolls in that they are different in many respects, not just size, and are connected through material and energy flows, whereas the dolls are just static. For example, leaves, branches, trees and forests are all open systems that are nested. The behavior of each system influences and is influenced by the systems nested inside it and by the systems in which it is nested. The faster changing, smaller systems stimulate change in the slower moving, larger systems. The larger systems regulate and limit the behavior of the smaller systems.

In *Panarchy*, Gunderson and Holling use these ideas to analyze how natural and human systems are transformed over time in repeated but not identical patterns (Gunderson and Holling 2002). They offer a general scenario for systems which start from the exploitation of an initially abundant environment, followed by a temporary period of conservation and consolidation. This situation, a climax forest for example, is not sustained because the system is vulnerable to disturbances from outside such as fire or a pest infestation. The next phases are release and regeneration, leading back to exploitation. This sequence describes some ecosystems very well. Gunderson and Holling believe that much the same analysis can be applied to social and economic systems (2002, p. 5). They note the similarity between their view and that of Schumpeter, who coined the phrase 'creative destruction' to describe processes of capitalism in which new technologies replace older ones and new companies obtain market dominance at the expense of older ones (Schumpeter 1950).

We can take the notion of an economy embedded in and dependent upon the environment one step further. Although we are accustomed to talking about the economy as a separate, identifiable component of our society, it has not always been like this and in some parts of the world is still not. For most of humanity's history, the economic and the social were intertwined. There was no such thing as the economy as a stand-alone entity worthy of study. The emergence of the 'economy' distinguishable from the rest of society can be traced back to the first industrial revolution, which started in Britain in the 18th century, and spread to other parts of Europe, North America and then to parts of the rest of the world.

It was not a coincidence that economics, or political economy as it was originally known, emerged in Britain out of philosophy at the same time and in the same place as the first industrial revolution. The founders of modern economics such as Smith, Malthus and Ricardo and later J.S. Mill and Marx were writing about changes they were observing in Britain as much as changes they were advocating. These writers were well aware of the links between the economy and its larger social setting. Some of them also paid attention to the links of the economy with nature. Unfortunately, most economists who followed concentrated on the internal workings of the economy, giving the false impression that the economy is disconnected from society and the natural world. This view was founded in the late 19th and 20th centuries by the development and diffusion of new technologies that made it seem that 'man had conquered nature'. Britain's imperial dominance, which provided access to global resources, and the United States' unmatched supply of resources from within its borders, influenced the development of economics in these countries based on circumstances that could not be repeated elsewhere.

The ways in which modern economies and societies are intertwined are many and varied. We are not born consumers and employees but that is what most of us become. We are socialized, through our families and educational, religious, political and media institutions, to adopt norms and values essential for the economy. Some people resist the pressures to consume and some, often through the fortunes of birth, have sources of income other than regular employment. But most of us accept the economic system as we find it.

Another aspect of society essential for the economy to function is the system of property rights enforceable through the courts. Exchanges of raw materials, and the products they are used to make, are exchanges of property rights. The owner of these rights can determine how and when the resources and products will be used and by whom. Conversely, with ownership comes the right of exclusion. Without the capacity to exclude others from using something, no one would pay to own anything. There would be no market transactions. Why would you pay for something if you could not assure yourself that you would be able to use it? For anything that is rival in consumption, you must be able to exclude others. (See section 3.3 in Chapter 3 for the meaning of rival.) This right of exclusion is the essence of property rights and it requires an effective legal system and supportive social norms to work. It is also the essence of trade, which is why economies that depend on trade treat crimes against property with such severity. A certain level of theft and robbery can be tolerated but when the legal system and supportive norms break down, vandalism and looting can become rampant and destroy an economy.

We are interested not just in how economies depend on nature for material, energy and space, but also in how economies are integrated with and supported by a whole range of social systems. Just as economic growth can undermine the natural systems on which economies depend, it can also damage and destroy important social structures. We see this in the demise of town centers when 'big box' stores are built on the outskirts, or when a one-industry town loses its main employer who has departed for higher profits elsewhere, or where entire industries migrate in search of cheap labor and lax environmental regulation.

One way of picturing economy, society and nature is as three concentric circles with the economy in the center, surrounded by the social system, which is surrounded by the natural system (Berkes 1993, p.66; Porritt 2005, p.46). This conception is better than the more common one in the sustainability literature of displaying the economy, society and environment as three legs or pillars supporting and defining a sustainable society (Dawe and Ryan 2003). Nature can get on very well without humans. It did once and will likely do again, but as humans we have an interest in staying around, which means attending to our dependence on the rest of nature and doing so through the kinds of society and economy that we create.

One problem with depicting the relationship between the economy, society and nature as concentric circles is that the edges are too hard and the interconnections among the three components are obscured. It is less neat but more informative to represent these three systems as in Figure 2.5. At the center is the economy shown with arms that reach into the social and some that reach all the way across to the natural.

There are several messages in Figure 2.5. First, the economy is connected to nature directly because some of the arms of the economy reach right into nature, unmediated by society. A good example is the air we

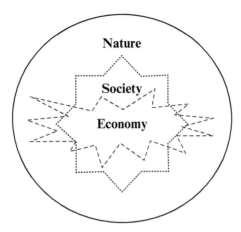

*Figure 2.5    Nature, society, economy*

breathe and the unregulated pollutants we generate. More commonly, the connections between the economy and nature are mediated by society. What we extract from nature as raw materials, how we use them and what we use them for, are all strongly influenced by the kind of society we have, the laws we enact and the prices we pay. Likewise, the economy influences and changes society as it also influences and changes nature. It is this dependence and the propensity of rich, growing economies to undermine the society and environment on which they depend, that has prompted this investigation into managing without growth.

## 2.8    COMMODIFICATION

Commodification is one of the processes by which the economy influences society and nature. It refers to the conversion of something outside the economy into a commodity for purchase and sale. In *The Great Transformation* (1944) Polanyi gives an insightful account of how traditional arrangements involving land and labor were converted into marketable commodities and became subject to economic transactions, valuations and calculations. The success of capitalism owes much to this process through which the market takes over aspects of society that were previously outside the economy. The conversion of human actions normally done by people for themselves into services that are purchased, such as being paid to do someone else's housework, is an example of commodification. Commodification raises GDP by converting activities into goods and services for sale even when there is no increase in overall output. Any extension of the market into realms not previously within the economy usually involves commodification.

These days we are more aware of the commodification of nature than we are of the continuing commodification of society in general. Perhaps this is because we are so used to the latter and are more willing to accept it, though there are occasional pockets of resistance. One such pocket is the loyalty of citizens in countries that have publicly funded health care systems based on the delivery of service according to need rather than ability to pay, in contrast to the system in the USA, which is heavily privatized. In Canada, for example, the legislated limits on private medicine reflect the belief that access to health care is a citizen's right, not a commodity to be rationed by the market (Health Canada 2005). Nevertheless, even this highly valued arrangement is under continual pressure from self-interested parties for privatization.

The commodification of nature shows up in such novelties as eco-tourism, the use of emissions trading for regulating air pollution, and payments for ecosystem services. And there are good reasons for thinking that the increasingly popular practice of regarding nature as 'natural capital' that delivers 'environmental goods and services' that can be valued in monetary units represents the commodification of nature (Costanza et al. 2014). Money is valuable because of the commodities (that is, goods and services for sale) that it can buy. To assign a monetary value to anything that lies outside the market necessarily implies that it has the same value as a commodity of the same monetary value. Equating the value of nature with the monetary value of a commodity is commodification. Resistance to the further commodification of nature can be seen in the deeply felt opposition of Canadians to bulk water exports from the Great Lakes. This resistance is notable in a country whose economic history has been characterized by the exploitation of its natural resources and on which much of its economy still depends (Hessing et al. 2005). As Liverman observed, 'this move to commodify nature and market its services is a massive transformation of the human–environment relationship and of the political economy of regions and landscapes' (Liverman 2004, p. 734).

In 2005 Pope Francis pressed home this point in his famous encyclical 'Laudato Si'':

> Even as the quality of available water is constantly diminishing, in some places there is a growing tendency, despite its scarcity, to privatize this resource, turning it into a commodity subject to the laws of the market. Yet *access to safe drinkable water is a basic and universal human right, since it is essential to human survival and, as such, is a condition for the exercise of other human rights.* (Pope Francis 2015, p. 23, emphasis in the original)

## 2.9   CONCLUSION

Understanding economies as open systems that are dependent on their environment raises questions about the longevity of economic growth. Is the environment capable of providing material and energy inputs and accommodating material and energy wastes of growing economies without doing more harm than good? Economic growth is usually measured by changes in GDP, which conflates quantitative and qualitative change. Conceivably, we can continue qualitative change (development) without quantitative change (growth). Questions about longevity would remain but they would be less urgent as we reduce the burden of the economy on the environment.

Generally speaking we lack the data to distinguish between quantitative growth and qualitative development. For the time being at least we have to conduct empirical work on economic growth using data for GDP and GDP per capita. If energy and material intensities (measured as physical amounts per dollar of GDP) and land conversion stabilize or decline when GDP is constant, then an economy in which GDP is not growing, or is shrinking, will coincide with constant or declining material and energy use, land conversion and waste emissions. And since GDP and GDP per capita are the measures most commonly used to judge the success of an economy, we have the advantage of using a language familiar to many even if, for reasons we consider in the next chapter, it is a language whose meaning is less than transparent.

## NOTES

1. High-income countries is a category defined by the World Bank (2015).
2. The data on which Figures 2.3a and 2.3b are based is displayed in panels showing multiple graphs using different scales resulting in very similar looking upward trends emphasizing the Great Acceleration (Steffen et al. 2015b). As Table 2.1 shows, the rates of change in the variables differ considerably.
3. This is a close approximation to the true value.
4. The IEA claims that global carbon dioxide emissions stabilized for two years but this is not fully supported by their own data, which shows global carbon dioxide emissions were 32.07 Gts in 2013, 32.13 in 2014 and 32.14 in 2015 (IEA 2016c). Furthermore, they only considered emissions of carbon dioxide from energy sources which account for about 50 percent of global GHG emissions – too early for a celebration, one would think. Then in 2017 global emissions of carbon dioxide from fossil fuel use and industry were projected to increase again by 2 percent (Futurearth 2017 and Tollerson 2017). 'We expect energy-related $CO_2$ emissions will increase again in 2018 after growing in 2017' (Fatih Briol, Executive Director of the International Energy Agency, https://twitter.com/IEABirol/status/1049172957858344960, last accessed 7 October 2018).
5. Unfortunately, Jackson's deep consideration of the meaning of prosperity and its requirements is not necessarily shared by others. For example, a report by Smart Prosperity 'a

new initiative launched by respected leaders to harness new thinking for Canada's environment and the economy' (Sustainable Prosperity 2016, p.i) defines smart prosperity as 'a thriving economy, healthy environment, and high quality of life, achieved through decoupling environmental harm from economic success' (Sustainable Prosperity 2016). This is a statement of what they think is required for prosperity without saying what prosperity means. It is clear in the report that they regard economic growth as integral to prosperity and that it can continue indefinitely while human impacts on the environment decline. 'The old idea that we must choose between strong economy and a healthy environment has been proven false' (Sustainable Prosperity 2016, p.1). Remarkably, very little evidence is presented to support this proof in the Smart Prosperity report.

# 3. Systems, information and prices

> the mainstream discipline [of economics] has not ... asked what types of information the price system systematically marginalizes or excludes, nor the consequences of these exclusions. (Babe 2002, p. 255)

Conceptualizing the economy, society and environment as nested systems as illustrated in Figure 2.5 reveals much that is important for understanding the economy and its dependence on a wider world. Modern, dynamic economies continually put pressure on the social and natural systems on which they rely. What is less clear from Figure 2.5 is how these other systems respond and adapt to this pressure and the effect of these responses on the economy. There are positive and negative feedbacks in play in all these systems and at all levels. These feedback loops determine how systems function and how they respond to external pressures. Fundamental to any feedback loop is the information that drives it. For example, a thermostat used to maintain room temperature at a particular level works by comparing information about the current room temperature with the desired level. If the temperature is too high the thermostat switches the heating off. If it is too low, the thermostat switches the heating on. It should be obvious that if the information fed to the thermostat is not accurate then the desired room temperature will not be maintained. Accurate information is extremely important for any system to function well.

Although they are not shown in Figure 2.5, there are feedback loops in all three of the systems: economy, society and nature, and among them. A comprehensive understanding of how the systems function and how they influence each other requires consideration of these connections and the information that drives them. In economies where markets play a key role in determining what gets produced, consumed and by whom, prices are the most important conveyors of information. This is characteristic of capitalist economies that are dominant in the world today although there are substantial differences in the role that markets play from country to country. The United States relies more on markets than most for determining economic outcomes. At the other end of the spectrum are the Scandinavian economies of Sweden, Norway, Denmark and Finland where more services are provided by the government than in the US and other capitalist countries, often at no charge and financed from tax revenue.

Generally speaking, economists believe that markets work well, or can be made to do so through appropriate taxes and subsidies, and that the greater the role of markets in society the better. There are many 'think tanks' whose primary purpose is to promote this view. Examples include the Fraser Institute in Canada, the Cato Institute in the USA, the Institute of Economic Affairs in Britain, CEDICE in Venezuela, and Instituto Ludwig von Mises (IMB) in Brazil. One of the questions about markets of particular interest in this book is how well they regulate human interactions with the rest of nature. If they perform well then presumably concerns about limits to the growth of the whole system are misplaced since decisions about what to produce and consume, with what resources, and generating what wastes will lead to the best outcomes. Limits to growth will be avoided indefinitely because price and profit incentives will result in new technologies and changes in behavior to make the problem of limits go away.

The belief that markets have been and will be effective for avoiding limits to growth is based on the assumption that prices provide sufficient information needed to make appropriate decisions about how we interact with nature. But how reliable is this information? How complete is it? Are there reasons for thinking that market prices do not reflect or generate the best decisions? Can we do better? These are some of the questions taken up in this chapter as we examine the relationships among the economic system, information and prices. To answer them we provide a non-technical discussion of the basic theory of markets and prices, warts and all. It's more theoretical than later chapters, and may not appeal to all readers for that reason. But an appreciation of the limitations of prices for conveying information is a crucial step in understanding why it is a grave mistake to attach undue normative significance to growth in GDP. GDP is the summation of the quantities of goods and services produced in an economy multiplied by their prices. If the information content of prices is faulty so is that of GDP, providing further grounds for questioning the significance of its growth.

## 3.1   PRICES AND INFORMATION

Every time something is traded in a market economy a price is paid. Prices provide information to buyers, sellers, investors, lenders and borrowers who adjust their behavior in response to prices and by doing so determine the quantities produced and traded and the prices paid. The information conveyed by prices allows communication among vast numbers of people and organizations that remain anonymous to one another, within a system that thrives on competition. This is in stark contrast to more traditional societies where typically information is transmitted directly between people in reciprocal and often cooperative relationships.

Just how the system of markets and prices in capitalist economies works has been the subject of intense study by economists ever since Adam Smith wrote *The Wealth of Nations* (Smith 1776). The capacity of markets to utilize massive amounts of dispersed information has been celebrated in the works of many economists, most famously by Hayek (Von Hayek 1956) who believed in the supremacy of markets for organizing economic activity. Yet it's worth noting perhaps that even Hayek recognized that there is no reason

> why the state should not assist the individuals in providing for those common hazards of life against which, because of their uncertainty, few individuals can make adequate provision . . . Wherever communal action can mitigate disasters against which the individual can neither attempt to guard himself, nor make provision for the consequences, such communal action should undoubtedly be taken. (Von Hayek 1956, p. 90)

Hayek recognized that there are circumstances of common threats requiring communal action where markets alone will not suffice. So, in relation to economic growth, we can ask the question: are prices effective for maintaining a balance between the economy and the social and environmental systems in which the economy is embedded? Do they, for example, convey any information about the scale of an economy as a whole or is their information content restricted to the allocation of scarce resources only when those resources are defined as within the economy? And what are the environmental and social consequences of unsatisfactory answers to these questions? The question of the scale of economies in relation to the biosphere in which they are embedded may well generate the kind of common threats requiring communal action that Hayek had in mind.

For quite some time, economists have considered the conditions under which prices convey accurate information, accurate in the sense that prices cover all costs, no more no less, including a 'normal' profit for the marginal (that is, incremental) unit of each good or service traded. Accurate prices are essential for any conclusion to be drawn about the efficient functioning of a market economy and for deciding whether economic growth is desirable. Efficient in this context means a situation in which no one in the economy can be made better off without someone else being made worse off. This is known as 'Pareto efficiency' after the Italian economist Vilfredo Pareto who introduced the concept. Prices play an essential role in the achievement of economic efficiency since they convey the information used by participants in an economy to guide their behavior. If the prices do not correspond closely and systematically to costs, then people, companies and governments will be misinformed. They will make decisions not necessarily in their own or others' best interests. Since economic growth is measured as growth in GDP and GDP is measured using market prices, prices that misinform at the micro level also misinform when used to describe overall economic performance.

The trouble is that the conditions that must exist for prices to convey meaningful information is a list of reasons why they fail to do so. Here are the main ones:

- *Homogeneity of products:* All suppliers of each product must produce identical products so that customers only decide based on price. There are no brands.
- *Numerous participants:* Each buyer and seller must account for such a small proportion of the market transactions that none of them can affect the market price by their own actions. There can be no large companies, industry associations or trades unions. Prices are set by the market and everyone is a price taker not a price maker. Sellers cannot set their own prices without either losing all their customers if they raise prices, or operating at a loss if they lower them.
- *Freedom of entry and exit:* Firms must be able to enter or leave the market without any impediments. Companies must not be able to limit the opportunities of potential competitors through their own actions or those of sympathetic governments.
- *Perfect information:* The available products and their prices must be known to all firms and customers. Even with the Internet, that is a very tall order.
- *Equal access to technology and resources:* All firms must have access to all production technologies; resources of land, labor and capital must be perfectly mobile.
- *No externalities:* When buyers and sellers engage in a transaction there are no material impacts on third parties who are not part of the transaction. This condition is sometimes expressed in terms of a requirement for 'well-defined' property rights extending to everything that is scarce and valuable.

It is easy to think of numerous examples where each of these assumptions does not hold in the real world and very, very hard to think of examples where they all do. Large corporations which account for a very substantial proportion of the output of all advanced economies have

considerable power to set prices, limit competition, influence regulations, change people's preferences through advertising, and so on. These
behaviors, and the organizations that practice them, are incompatible with
the assumptions required for efficient markets and for prices to convey
meaningful information. The assumption of 'no externalities' is especially
relevant to how humans interact with the rest of nature through economic
activity. Clearly it does not apply to many natural features beyond the
reach of private property such as the air we breathe or fishing on the high
seas. As a result, the use of the atmosphere for disposing of wastes appears
free even though it imposes costs by causing illness and degrades water,
fisheries, land, forests, crops, buildings and structures. And open access to
any fishery, unless moderated by some other social arrangement (Ostrom
1990), leads inexorably to over-fishing.

On top of all this, an economy is only efficient in the Pareto sense if
consumers and employers are rational decision makers who always make
choices that maximize their own well-being. For people as consumers
this means making choices to maximize their utility and for companies it
means making choices to maximize their profits. Caring for other people
or animals or nature in general is not ruled out but it has to be shoehorned
in as serving a person's own interests rather than another's. Company
objectives that deviate from profit maximization, such as the 'triple
bottom line' (Elkington 1998) where companies act on environmental and
social considerations as well as financial ones, are not allowed in a Pareto
efficient economy. Cooperatives owned by their members to pursue social,
environmental as well as financial objectives do not fit into the picture
either.

An important implication of the set of conditions required for efficient
markets is that if they are all satisfied, the price of each good and service in
the economy would just equal the marginal or incremental cost of providing them and the economy would be Pareto efficient (Baumol 1977). As
noted, this means specifically that no other allocation of resources could
be to one person's advantage without making someone else worse off.
Economists attach considerable significance to this result and here's why.
If there is a willing buyer of a product at a price that exceeds its marginal
production cost, then economists understand this to mean that the buyer
values the product by more than it costs the producer to provide it. If the
buyer paid the producer an amount equal to the marginal production cost
then the producer would be no worse off because all their costs including
a 'normal' profit are covered. Meanwhile the buyer is better off after the
trade since they would have been willing to pay a price higher than the
marginal cost. Economists theorize that in an economy that meets all
the conditions for efficient markets, competition will ensure that through

changes in the behavior of consumers and producers, prices and quantities will keep adjusting until prices equal marginal costs throughout the
economy and it will be Pareto efficient.

In this idealized economy consumers are guided by market prices to
balance their selection of commodities so that the rate at which they can
substitute one for the other (say apples for oranges) according to their
prices is just equal to the rate at which they wish to do so. At the same
time, producers adjust their production decisions in response to the same
prices, that is, what they choose to produce and how much, the production
processes they employ and the various inputs they use for production –
labor, land and capital, each of which is available at a market price. The net
result is that, taking the economy as a whole, the rate at which producers
can transform one commodity into another by changing production will
equal the rate at which consumers wish this to be done.

Economics teaches that in this continual process of adjustment it is
relative prices that matter most. If one thing is priced at double another
then we should be able to say that it costs twice as much to make, but
we can't. The price of something might be inflated simply because a few
companies control supply and force the price up to increase their profits.
Advertisers may persuade us that two products that are essentially identical
are different and that we should choose one brand over another for no
good reason. Technologies are not equally available to all; there is an entire
set of legal protections in the form of patent and copyright law to keep it
that way. Access to finance might be more available to some people and
some companies than to others. Most egregious of all is the pervasiveness
of externalities, in particular, the widespread unpriced damage to the
environment caused by economic activity.

The price of any one product can affect the prices of many others
through the choices made by buyers and sellers. Consequently, the failure
of real economies to meet the conditions required for fully informative
prices has implications for the prices of all goods and services and to a different and unknown degree. It compromises the information content of all
prices. Relative prices, the price of one thing in relation to another, are dis-
torted. What seems cheap may be dear and what seems dear may be cheap.
We just do not know, and because all prices are interrelated through multiple interconnected markets, the problem is compounded. Misinformation
is spread far and wide. For example, it is not just that coal may look like
a cheap energy source if we ignore the pollution caused during mining,
transportation and combustion. Any product made using energy from
coal will also look cheaper than it really is. Since coal is commonly used to
generate electricity, there is hardly a good or service that is not affected by
a price for coal that does not cover all its costs. A similar argument applies

to other sources of energy such as nuclear power, oil, natural gas and to renewable sources as well, though generally to a lesser extent. The environmental impacts of energy, as with all such adverse effects of production, distribution and consumption, do not just contaminate the environment, they contaminate prices as well. More generally, market failures arise from the lack of fulfillment of any and all of the conditions required for efficient markets. They drive a wedge of unknown size between prices and costs so the rate at which consumers want to substitute one commodity for another does not correspond to the rate at which resources are assigned to transform commodities from one to the other. Given the proliferation of market failures in real economies, the information content of prices is seriously compromised and so we must be careful how we interpret them. We should also be aware of how this misinformation is inadvertently incorporated into calculations of GDP especially if we are intent on giving normative significance to its growth or decline.

## 3.2   THE THEORY OF THE SECOND BEST

Economists used to think that whenever there is an opportunity to set any particular price equal to marginal production cost, then in terms of efficiency, it makes sense to do so. This pricing policy principle, which follows from the market theory described earlier, took a serious knock some 60 years ago when economists Richard Lipsey and Kelvin Lancaster considered what happens when one or more of the required market conditions are not met (Lipsey and Lancaster 1956/1957). They considered a situation where the price of just one commodity did not equal its marginal cost of production and nothing could be done about it. This could be the situation when a product or service is supplied by a company with considerable market power, enabling it to set its prices in excess of marginal production costs and earn increased profits. It also arises when environmental externalities are not included in production costs so that prices only cover those costs actually paid for by producers. Costs they are able to impose on others, say by contaminating the environment legally or otherwise, are not covered by the price. In this situation, prices will be less than marginal production costs. Similar logic applies when there are environmental costs of consumption such as air pollution from the combustion of gasoline in automobiles.

Lipsey and Lancaster posed the following question. If the first best situation in which all prices in an economy are equal to marginal production costs is, for some reason, unattainable, what should be done about setting the price for some other commodity, such as electricity supplied by a public utility? Would the second best option be to set its price equal to marginal production cost? They proved that if only one price in an economy is not equal to marginal production cost, the second best situation is that other prices should also not be equal to marginal production cost. In other words, economic efficiency in the Pareto sense achieved by equating prices and marginal production costs is an all or nothing proposition. All prices have to be equal to marginal production costs or none of them should be. To complicate matters further, Lipsey and Lancaster could find no simple rule for setting prices in a second best world, which happens to be the one in which we live. In the understated words of W.J. Baumol, 'The second-best theorem is a somewhat unfortunate result from the point of view of policy applications of welfare economic theory, for it tells us that piecemeal elimination of violations of the optimality conditions [that is, the conditions noted in section 3.1] is not necessarily beneficial' (1977, p. 526).

The theory of the second best and the general failure of the assumptions for optimality conditions to be satisfied in practice strongly suggests that the information content of prices is very imperfect, so decisions based on them should not be given the normative significance they are so commonly accorded. '[N]ational income, as a candidate for a measure of social welfare, is much less supported by economic theory than is commonly assumed' (Fleurbaey 2009, p. 1030). In the idealized case where all the conditions for competitive markets and informative prices are met, prices convey reliable information about production costs including environmental costs, but not so in the real world. And there are good reasons, discussed in later chapters, for thinking that the information that they do convey is becoming increasingly unreliable.

Interestingly, many people have reached the same conclusion more directly through their own experiences rather than economic theory. The emergence of the fair trade movement where people deliberately pay higher prices for agricultural products to improve farmers' incomes, the increasing popularity of organic food, the boycott of clothing made in sweatshops and other such consumer-led initiatives, all show that people do not always buy the product with the lowest price. How they are manufactured and by whom also matter and this information is not adequately disclosed in the product price. The divestment movement which calls for pension funds and universities not to hold stocks in oil companies or arms companies, even at the risk of lower financial returns, is based on the recognition that prices alone cannot be trusted to tell us what something really costs. It is also the reason for environmental regulations and for planning restrictions imposed on businesses and developers who could make larger profits if allowed free rein to simply pursue maximum profits.

If prices contained all the information about costs then none of these regulations and restrictions would be necessary. Market decisions would be fully informed and could not be improved upon. It turns out that this is a long way from the truth.

## 3.3 THE DUAL ROLE OF PRICES

Prices perform two distinct interrelated functions in a market economy. The first is to provide revenue to producers out of which payments are made to employees, suppliers of energy, materials and equipment, for rent on land and buildings, interest on loans, and for licenses and taxes. What's left over is profit that belongs to the companies' owners. The second function of prices is to restrict access to the output that has been produced to those willing and able to pay for it. Those without sufficient funds, no matter how dire their need, are unable to buy goods and services that are priced beyond their means. Markets can be an effective social institution for determining production and consumption, though unless the distribution of income and wealth is equitable, market outcomes can be extremely inequitable.

The dual role of prices: financing production and allocating output, works well when what is being produced is scarce, in the sense that when used by one person it is unavailable to anyone else. This describes all the items that line the shelves of supermarkets, department stores and farmers' markets. Bread, cheese, detergent, kitchen utensils and clothing all share the characteristic that they are 'rival' in consumption. What one person consumes is unavailable to anyone else because of the characteristics of the product. Rivalry also applies to raw materials and other inputs used in production such as fuel and office supplies. Their use by one firm reduces what is available for others. Rivalry also applies to many services such as hairdressing or landscaping. When those who provide these services are serving customers, others must wait. Goods and services that are rival must be allocated in some way. In capitalism, this is typically done by pricing rather than by queuing or by under-the-table payments for special treatment.

But what about situations in which what is produced is non-rival, that is, their consumption by one person does not reduce the amount available to anyone else? Such is the case for many types of services such as street lighting, national defense, public parks, roads (up to the point where congestion sets in) and many other 'public goods'. Ideas are non-rival as well: 'If you use or "consume" an idea, it does not stop me from also using it.' Thomas Jefferson made a famous analogy with the light of a candle: 'If you light your candle with mine, it does not darken my flame' (Commission on Growth and Development 2008, p. 41). In all these cases, to charge a price for something that is non-rival denies some people access to it even though it is not scarce and does not require rationing. For some of these services it is very difficult, even impossible, to exclude people, street lighting being an obvious example. Without the means of excluding people, the market system cannot function for the simple reason that no one need pay a price for a beneficial service from which they cannot be excluded. In this situation, there is no income for the service provider and no financial means or incentive to provide it. This is why many services where exclusion is difficult or impossible are provided by government and paid for with taxes. Governments also provide services without charge that could be subject to exclusion, such as health care and education, but for reasons of social justice, society decides that all citizens should have the right of access regardless of their ability to pay.

There are four possible combinations of rival/non-rival and excludable/non-excludable. To work at all, markets require exclusion provided through property rights established in law and enforced by the courts. To work well, markets should deal in goods and services that are rival because there is no need to ration those that are not. Even then, as we have seen, there are numerous reasons for doubting the efficiency of markets and the information content of prices that emerge from them.

Environmental improvement, such as a reduction in air pollution, is something from which people cannot be easily excluded. Companies that voluntarily reduce their emissions of greenhouse gases, particulates and sulfur oxides cannot obtain reimbursement for the abatement costs from those who benefit. Hence, they have no financial incentive to take the necessary actions. They can try winning the loyalty of their customers by advertising their environmentally responsible behavior. However, most governments are unwilling to rely on voluntary action for a sufficient level of emissions reduction and use regulations or impose fees to limit emissions because of the failure of markets to do so.

### 3.3.1   Prices, Information and Theft

The incessant search for profits is one of the defining characteristics of capitalism. It is a powerful driver for innovation which has yielded great benefits, but it can also induce behavior that is not necessarily in the public interest. As noted above, the dual role of prices makes most sense when what is produced is rival. Prices provide income to the producers and ration the outputs, which can only happen when exclusion is possible. This is the main reason why great efforts are made through legislation and the courts to protect property rights. In this day and age when electronically transmitted information is so pervasive we see the tensions that arise when exclusion is difficult and the service is non-rival. When television was first introduced in the 1940s and 1950s the publicly broadcast signals could be received by anyone who had an antenna. Television programs had to be funded by advertising revenue, licensing (as in the UK for example), public donations, or government. The advent of cable TV and later satellite TV made it possible to exclude people who did not pay for the service. In an economic system that thrives on exclusion we should expect the development of technologies specifically designed to limit access to only those that pay, even when the service provided is non-rival. Efforts to limit access to information provided over the Internet are much in evidence today. 'Success' in this regard has the anomalous result that once priced, a previously free service, such as access to a news or information website, has a monetized value and is included in GDP. In this case GDP increases by excluding people from the non-rival service and reducing its use.

Theft has long been considered unacceptable behavior as it should be when what is stolen is truly scarce. Stealing a loaf of bread deprives its owner. Accessing an electronic signal does not prevent anyone else from using it. This distinction is understood, perhaps subconsciously, by people who use the Internet without paying for specific applications. They know that no other users suffer as a consequence, though of course the developers experience a loss in revenue. Those in the entertainment business are especially challenged. They require revenues to cover the costs of making films, videos and musical recordings, but the Internet makes it difficult to limit access. A tremendous amount of resources are being put into solving this 'problem' by finding ways to restrict access usually through some form of encryption. An alternative approach would be to find different ways of funding non-rival services so that they do not have to be priced at all. One example of an alternative approach is the payment of a salary to university professors in the expectation that the ideas they generate through research are made freely available, ideas being non-rival. But even this proven arrangement is under threat from universities that increasingly encourage their academic staff to find ways of obtaining revenues from their publicly funded research (see Verspagen 2006; Westheimer 2010; Snowdon 2015; National Science Board 2012).

### 3.3.2 A Single Role for Prices

Prices play a dual role even though sometimes, as in the above examples, it would be better if they could only play one: to provide revenue without limiting access, but prices cannot do this. When it comes to environmental protection the opposite problem can arise, that is, how to use prices to limit access without raising revenues? Revenue neutral carbon taxes are a good example of a creative response to this dilemma. A carbon tax is a price imposed by government on the emissions of greenhouse gases expressed in dollars per tonne of emissions. The main justification for a carbon tax is to discourage the emission of greenhouse gases by making it expensive, rather than to raise revenue. Once a target for the desired level of greenhouse gas emissions has been set, a tax rate or schedule is established to meet the target. When the Government of British Columbia introduced a carbon tax in 2008 it included a legal requirement that the tax would not yield any additional revenue for the Government by requiring an equivalent reduction in other taxes (Murray and Rivers 2015). This was a deliberate attempt to take advantage of only one of the two roles that prices perform: to limit access to the atmosphere for emitting greenhouse gases without generating revenue for the government. This design of a carbon tax proved popular with the electorate in British Columbia, who re-elected the Liberal government that introduced the controversial tax in the subsequent election in 2009 and again in 2013.

A carbon tax is just one way of setting a price on greenhouse gas emissions. A system of tradable emission allowances is another, leaving it to a market in these allowances to set their price as in the US market for emissions of sulfur oxides (Ellerman and Montero 1998; Schmalensee et al. 1998), the European market for greenhouse gas emissions (Ellerman and Buchner 2007), and the Western Climate Initiative, Inc., a not-for-profit organization to help member states in the US and Canadian provinces establish cap and trade programs (WCI Inc. 2017). If the allowances are distributed without charge then the system generates no revenue for the government. As long as the total allowances are less than the total emissions that would otherwise have occurred, the cap and trade market in allowances will establish a positive price for greenhouse gas emissions, which becomes a financial incentive for their reduction.

Of course, carbon taxes and emissions trading systems can both be designed to generate revenue for the government. (For example, in Ontario's cap and trade system by law, all revenues from allowance auctions must be spent on projects that reduce greenhouse gas emissions.)[1] The point here is simply to note that situations may arise when only one of the dual functions of prices is required but it may not always be possible to choose.

How the introduction of carbon prices, and emission prices more generally, affects GDP is curious. By raising market prices a carbon price can increase GDP measured in market prices even though the quantities of goods and services produced in the economy may in fact decline as a result.

This problem is avoided when GDP is measured in 'basic' prices, which exclude taxes and subsidies, but this distinction between GDP at market prices and basic prices is not widely understood, further compounding the difficulties of interpreting GDP and its growth.

## 3.4 PRICES AND TIME

So far, we have only considered prices at a point in time but there are many occasions when we use prices to guide decision-making where time is an important consideration. How much to save or spend can depend on the rate of interest, which is just another price. How much to invest in new buildings, equipment, public infrastructure, education and how fast to extract resources from the Earth depends on the rate of interest and on expectations about future prices. Just to take this last point, economists interested in natural resources have examined the conditions under which prices can be relied on to give the right information about present and future scarcities so that new supplies will be sought and found, new technologies will be developed and substitutes adopted. This is sometimes referred to as 'dynamic efficiency' (Tietenberg and Lewis 2014). However, these conditions do not apply in practice any more than the conditions for static efficiency described above. Prices may give information that is not useful, or, even worse, information that leads to counterproductive behavior. As noted in Chapter 1, expectations of abundant natural resources and lower raw material prices in the future can induce more rapid extraction today. This could cause future shortages, the opposite of what was expected.

To make a bad situation worse, when we think about what will determine the future prices of natural resources, one of the key factors is the future incomes of those who will want to buy the resources. People in the future do not participate in the economic decisions made today, at least not directly. Indirectly they do in so far as those making decisions today consider and compare opportunities to make a profit in the future with opportunities available today. Much depends on what they assume about the future, in particular what they assume about the buying power of people in the future and how it compares with that of people today. The higher they think future incomes will be, the higher they might expect the future prices of natural resources to be. However, future incomes are not independent of the decisions made today. In fact, the two are intimately related. Future incomes will depend on the future resources available. If a seriously depleted stock of resources is left to future generations, their capacity to generate high incomes will be compromised. The opposite will be true if we are more generous with what we leave to future generations.

It can all become self-fulfilling. If through economic growth people in the future are expected to be richer than people are today, then the related expectation of higher future prices for resources will justify conservation. The future will inherit more resources than otherwise and expectations will be fulfilled. The contrary is also possible. An expectation of lower incomes in the future and lower prices will justify higher rates of extraction today, leaving less for the future. With a reduced stock of resources available in the future, incomes will in fact be lower, prices will be lower and expectations fulfilled once again. This suggests that decisions about using resources today or conserving them for people in the future is as much an ethical one as an economic one, or it ought to be. Prices cannot be relied upon to guide behavior even when property rights are fully defined, exclusion is possible and the product is rival in use.

Mainstream economics has a way of converting this kind of ethical problem, that of comparing future and current values expressed in terms of prices, into a technical one. It is called discounting and works as follows. Consider a situation where a person has to choose between receiving $100 today or $105 in a year's time. Assume that prices are not expected to change during the year so the value of a dollar is expected to remain constant. Which would the person choose? Suppose the person could save the $100 for a year and receive interest greater than $5. They would then be better off to accept the $100 today, save it and end up with more than $105 in one year's time. The discounting process works in reverse. Faced with something that has an estimated value of $105 a year hence, economists apply a discount rate to determine its present value. If a discount rate of 5 percent/year is used, then $105 in one year's time is said to have a present value of $100.

Discounting estimated future values to calculate their present value is widely used in the public and private sectors when assessing alternative investments. In the private sector this might be an investment in a new piece of machinery, a building, or in the development of new software. In the public sector, it might be an investment in a new national park or a greenhouse gas reduction program. The financial streams that enter present value calculations can be very different between private and public sector investment decisions. In the private sector, the financial streams are usually restricted to actual money flows, whereas in the public sector it is not uncommon to include environmental and other impacts for which there are no observable market prices but which are valued in money terms using one of several available methods (see Chapter 4). In both cases, a discount rate is applied to flows expressed in terms of money, which are calculated based on observed and estimated future prices.

As we have seen, there are many reasons why the information content of current prices is deficient. The problems are magnified when we try to estimate future prices. Does it make sense to further manipulate price information that contains incomplete and misleading information by applying a discount rate that entails an ethical judgment about the relative significance to give to present and future generations? Since investment is a key driver of economic growth, does it make sense to rely on such a procedure to guide an economy towards the best possible future? Yes to both if there is nothing better, but having brought ourselves into the Anthropocene with all its attendant threats by investments evaluated using prices in this way, we should not be sanguine that mainstream economics and finance have all the best answers.

## 3.5 PRICES AND THE DISTRIBUTION OF INCOME AND WEALTH

Sadly, the problems with relying too much on prices to guide decisions and to measure progress as growth of price-dependent GDP do not end here. A further limitation on the information content of prices is that they reflect the prevailing distribution of income and wealth among people currently alive. Changes in the distribution of income and wealth affect the pattern of demand and hence prices, since people with different incomes and wealth buy different goods and services. Even if all the conditions specified earlier were to prevail, and that is a really big if, we could draw conclusions about the efficiency of economic outcomes but not that they are equitable. That would depend on an ethical judgment about the fairness with which incomes and wealth are distributed within a nation, among nations and over time, a judgment that is avoided when we rely exclusively on considerations of efficiency to make ethical choices. As Babe says, 'The price system, then, is both an anthropocentric system of valuation, and an exclusive system in which the wealthy are given a much louder voice than the poor, and in which future generations are accorded no direct voice at all' (Babe 2002, p. 256).

Discounting introduces further complications such as the requirement to consider if people in the future will be richer or poorer than people are today. If richer, then a high rate of discount could be justified on ethical grounds and if poorer, then a low rate of discount is preferable (Pearce et al. 2003; Stern 2006). But as we saw earlier the investment decisions made today, including decisions to leave minerals in the ground for future use and how much to invest in research and development, influence just how rich or poor people in the future will be. This circularity cannot be overcome by applying investment decision rules in a piecemeal manner. It requires a broader assessment of present and future opportunities and their interrelationships at a larger, macro scale where, for example, the rate of economic growth becomes a matter of choice rather than the outcome of individual inadequately informed decisions.

## 3.6   OTHER SOURCES OF INFORMATION

For all the reasons given, market prices provide us with information that is very partial and so can be a very poor guide to action, especially when it comes to the scale of the economy and its interactions with natural and social systems. We should not rely so much on the information conveyed by prices to determine what is best or how we are doing; yet this is precisely what we do when we use prices to calculate GDP and judge progress in terms of its growth. Nor should we rely on prices to be sensitive to all the burdens that our economy places on nature and society and automatically to anticipate and solve whatever problems may arise if these burdens increase. As Babe says, 'even in principle . . . the price system can give no indication of the limits to growth' (2002, p. 258).

Some say that what we should do is 'get the prices right' by adding a tax when a price is too low or offering a subsidy when a price is too high. In their analysis of how pricing can affect the provision of municipal services, Elgie et al. write, 'pricing is an important tool, and to use that tool well it is critical to *get the prices right*'. This means reflecting, as much as possible, a broad definition of full cost that includes environmental harm' (2016, p. 1, emphasis added). Later they acknowledge that 'the calculation of these various aspects of costs can be complicated and some aspects are very hard to quantify, and value, particularly ones not priced in the market, such as environmental quality' (ibid, p. 19). So the call to 'get the prices right' sounds more like a slogan than a well-grounded, practical solution. It is one thing to argue that pricing can be a useful policy instrument for influencing behavior in a desired direction. It's quite another to suggest that the 'right price' can be calculated such that the resulting behavior will also be 'right', especially when it comes to the question of the scale of the economy and matters of social justice. Such an approach can be helpful for dealing with the more obvious distortions, but we are fooling ourselves if we think that we know enough or could know enough to fix all the prices in such a complex, interrelated system as a modern market economy and that the decisions that would result would solve our environmental problems.

Fortunately, when it comes to our relationships with nature, we do not have to rely solely on prices to tell us how we are doing. There is lots of information that comes from other means and methods and through other channels, and we could get more if we wanted to. There

are also other metrics independent of prices that convey useful information such as the ecological footprint (Wackernagel and Rees 1996),
the Environmental Performance Index (Hsu et al. 2016), the Human
Development Index (UNDP 2015a), the Happy Planet Index (Jeffrey
et al. 2016), the Genuine Progress Indicator (Talberth et al. 2007), and
several others. Some of these incorporate prices but with adjustments,
and others are entirely non-monetary (Bleys 2012; Kubiszewski et al.
2013; Lawn 2003; Hitly et al. 2005). For example, MuSIASEM (Multi-
Scale Integrated Analysis of Societal and Ecosystem Metabolism)
has been designed specifically to analyze multiple systems relating to
human society described in different units. It 'provides a framework
for bridging heterogeneous descriptions obtained in different scientific
disciplines, in particular biophysical and conventional economic descriptions' (Giampietro et al. 2002). Whether MuSIASEM or some other
non-monetized metric can overcome the many deficiencies in increases
in GDP for measuring economic progress without introducing serious
problems of their own remains to be seen, but there can be no doubt
about the merits of finding out.

Much of the environmental literature that has raised the alarm about
what humanity is doing to the planet depends upon scientific information
and personal observation. This information is not conveyed through
prices, or only partially so. It is collected and transmitted through other
social institutions and processes, science being one, traditional knowledge
another. No one person can stay on top of it all. Since we cannot do that,
we can at least be open to a variety of information sources and values, be
they based on our direct experience as living, breathing people immersed
in nature, or through exposure to the arts both visual and literate, or to
geography, history and science. And we should ensure that the institutions
we create in our society and on which we rely support the broadest of
approaches to understanding and dealing with the increasingly obvious
problems that expanding economies are creating as we pursue economic
growth.

## 3.7 CONCLUSION

Economic growth is measured by changes in inflation-adjusted GDP.
GDP is measured using market prices. For many reasons considered in
this chapter market prices convey unreliable information, especially in
relation to the interconnections between economies and the biosphere.
It follows that growth in GDP is an unreliable measure of progress.
While it was not intended to be used for this, it has become common to

do so. Economies can be thought of as open systems dependent on the environment for flows of material and energy without which they could not function. This proposition is a fundamental principle of ecological economics. Economies are interconnected and are also nested within social and environmental systems, the largest of which for our purposes is planet Earth, which is a closed system. System behavior depends on the information that drives positive and negative feedback loops. In a market economy, prices are the single most important source of information. The conditions required for prices to convey accurate information, particularly in relation to the size of an economy and how it relates to the social and environmental systems in which it is embedded, are not satisfied in any real situation. This is not to say that prices are meaningless or that they cannot be used to inform judgments about how a business or an entire economy is performing or decisions about what to do next. But there is a real danger in over-interpreting the information content of prices when we know that the conditions required for their meaning to be clear are unmet.

When economies were small in relation to the environment, the failure of prices to convey reliable information about economy and environment interactions was less important than it is today after a century or two of economic growth. There is plenty of other information about the myriad ways in which society in general and the economy in particular depend on the environment. If this information supported the view that environmental problems were minor, we could rely more on prices to guide behavior. Taxes and subsidies could be used for adjusting prices and we could be confident that these prices would steer the economy in a good direction. But if the problems are not small, and Chapters 5–7 will show they are not, we must conclude that the information conveyed by prices is seriously incomplete, unreliable and can be dangerously misleading as can GDP, which depends so heavily on market prices for its computation.

Faced with a broad range of environmental problems of increasing scope and scale, it will often be better to set physical limits through environmental regulations and land use planning, which will affect prices and behavior, rather than to change market prices through subsidies and taxes in the hope that the resulting quantities will be an improvement. Policy can be price determining or price determined. The former can be based on a wide variety of decision aiding tools whereas the latter relies on the monetization of environmental and other adverse effects using problematic valuation methods. Yet this monetization is what occupies a significant number of economists, governments and NGOs. We discuss this popular but controversial practice in the next chapter. In subsequent chapters, we take up the question of the scale of the economy in relation to the environment and consider whether there are biophysical limits to growth that prices, observed in the market and embodied in GDP or estimated by economists, are of little help in determining.

## NOTE

1. In July 2018 the newly elected Premier of Ontario announced plans to cancel Ontario's cap and trade program.

# 4.  Pricing nature

> ... current controversies in valuing the cost of environmental changes like climate change and biodiversity loss have exposed serious flaws in standard welfare economics. Many of these arise from the assumption that social value can be calculated using the revealed or stated preferences of self-regarding, narrowly rational individuals. (Parks and Gowdy 2013, p. 1)

> In recent decades, markets and market-oriented thinking have reached into spheres of life traditionally governed by nonmarket norms. (Sandel 2012)

In the previous chapter we explored the conditions under which prices convey reliable information on which decisions can be based and outcomes assessed. Many of these conditions are not met in the real world, giving cause for concern even in the absence of environmental considerations. GDP is built from data on market prices and quantities. So, to the extent that prices fail to convey reliable information, then increases in GDP suffer as a measure of economic growth.

We also discussed how prices can be useful for inducing people and organizations to change their behavior to help meet environmental objectives, using a carbon tax as an example. In that discussion, we assumed that the environmental objective was set outside the price system, though presumably with some consideration of the broader economic implications of imposing additional expenses on those who emit greenhouse gases. Even more directly with emissions trading systems, a quantitative emissions reduction target set by government determines the price of emissions.

Another approach to meeting environmental objectives favored by some economists is to estimate the value of the environmental damages from emissions in monetary terms. These damage estimates are then used to set a price on emissions to be paid by all emission sources. In this case, the direction of causality between emissions quantity and price is reversed. The price of emissions, based on an estimate of damages they cause, determines the quantity of emissions as sources adjust their behavior in response to the emissions price. This latter approach relies on the ability of economists to provide reasonable estimates of the monetary value of environmental damages (Muller and Mendelsohn 2009). Despite a very large number of sophisticated studies that have attempted to do this for a large number of emissions in many different places and at different times, there are several reasons for doubting the ability of economists to perform these calculations with the necessary degree of accuracy. We will discuss these reasons later in this chapter. And even if the calculations were accurate, the theory of the second best (see section 3.2 in the previous chapter) provides no foundation for thinking that the 'right' correction to market prices is simply to add these calculated environmental damage costs to existing market prices. The behavioral responses to prices modified in this way may bear little relation to the desired outcome.

Many of the reasons for doubting the efficacy of estimates of the monetary value of environmental damages apply to the considerable efforts underway to estimate the monetary value of the goods and services provided freely by nature but for which there is no market and hence no market price. These ecosystem services are the topic of Chapter 6, but issues relating to their evaluation in terms of money are discussed in this chapter. Serious deficiencies in the underlying conceptual framework, estimation methods and data lead to the only reasonable conclusion that the resulting monetary valuations should be used with great caution or not at all in driving public policy, assessing economic outcomes, and modifying GDP to better measure growth.

## 4.1   THE MEANING OF MONETARY VALUATION

To appreciate the challenge of pricing nature it is necessary to dwell for a moment on the meaning of monetary valuation. A defining condition of market equilibrium is that buyers and sellers do not wish to change their buying and selling decisions given the prevailing prices. In this situation, the rate at which buyers can substitute commodities (that is, goods and services for sale) for each other by buying more of one and less of another is the rate at which they wish to do so. The money price of each commodity shows its value at the margin to people as buyers in relation to all other commodities. In this sense, commodities sold at the same price can be said to be of equivalent value at the margin to buyers measured in monetary terms, though not in total.

The valuation of unpriced ecosystem goods and services in monetary terms is built on the assumption that the values derived through surveys (for example contingent valuation), or imputed from observed behavior (for example the travel cost method), or estimated as the cost of providing them through artificial means (for example an engineered alternative) can be compared with market prices. 'In economic terms, quantifying and valuing ecosystem services is no different from quantifying and valuing goods or services produced by humans' (Pascual et al. 2010, p. 187). Indeed, the comparison of unpriced ecosystem services with commodities bought and sold in markets is the primary purpose of such valuation (Hanley and Barbier 2009, p. 3). So, an ecosystem service such as water retention by soils beneath forests, valued at say $100 per hectare per year, can be compared with a meal for two at a good restaurant. More precisely, it presumes that unpriced ecosystem services or their loss can be compared to and substituted for commodities which have market prices, in the same way as commodities that are traded in markets can be substituted for each other. In other words, estimates of the monetary value of ecosystem goods and services are meaningful if and only if there are market-based substitutes available that people consider are sources of equivalent value. If a piece of land generates ecosystem services valued at $1 million per year in an 'undeveloped' state and would generate a rent of $1.5 million per year if built on, then by this logic, 'social welfare' would be increased if the land was 'developed'.[1] At least, this is the view of mainstream economics, including environmental economics. On the other hand, if it is widely believed that no commodities available through markets are adequate substitutes for the unpriced ecosystem services, then it makes no sense to estimate a monetary value for them. And if such comparisons are to be made, then it is important to compare market prices with marginal values of ecosystem services, and not total values including consumer surplus,[2] as is all too often the case. Otherwise the comparison is biased, possibly quite severely.

Valuing market and non-market alternatives using the common denominator of money, and simulating a market-like outcome as if buyers and sellers were involved, necessarily implies that market and non-market alternatives can be substituted for one another. 'The value of ecosystem services and biodiversity is a reflection of what we, as a society, are willing *to trade off* to conserve these natural resources' (Pascual et al. 2010, p. 187, emphasis added). Who the 'we' is matters, since different people have different propensities to trade off ecosystem services for produced commodities. Monetary evaluation of ecosystem services also implies that the values can be manipulated mathematically in a way that is meaningful and helpful to decision makers. In the next section on natural capital, we consider some reasons why this may not be so.

## 4.2   NATURAL CAPITAL: CONCERNS AND CONSIDERATIONS[3]

In 1920 Alfred Marshall, one of the founders of neoclassical economics, wrote: 'a far seeing statesman will feel a greater responsibility to future generations when legislating as to land than as to other forms of wealth; and that from the economic and from the ethical point of view, land must everywhere and always be classed as a thing by itself' (Marshall 1920).

Despite Marshall's warning a century ago that land is distinct from other forms of wealth, it has become increasingly popular among some academics, governments, international organizations and NGOs to think about land (that is, the environment or nature) as 'natural capital' and to liken it to human-made capital, which is the equipment, buildings and infrastructure produced and used in an economy. A typical definition of natural capital is:

> the world's stocks of natural assets which include geology, soil, air, water and all living things. It is from this Natural Capital that humans derive a wide range of goods and services, often called ecological goods and services, which make human life possible. (World Forum on Natural Capital 2017)

Ecological goods, or ecosystem goods, include timber, minerals and food. Ecosystem services refer to functions rather than materials that are beneficial to humans, for example pollination and the sequestration of carbon in soils. Generally speaking, it is easier to form markets for ecosystem goods than for ecosystem services because exclusion is easier so property rights can be established and protected in the courts and transferred via market transactions at a price.

The main reason for the appeal of natural capital for framing discussions about how humans interact with the rest of nature is fairly obvious. In all societies in which economic growth is a priority, the word 'capital' has particular significance. For one thing, the accumulation of capital in its more conventional sense of infrastructure, buildings and equipment has been instrumental in the improvement of living standards. More people working with more capital in innovative ways, fueled by more energy, are fundamental to economic growth. But in this endeavor, nature and the many goods and services it provides *gratis* have been woefully neglected. One way, therefore, of bringing nature into the picture is to cast it as another form of capital at least as important as human made capital and to value it in equivalent terms, which means in terms of money. And why not? Isn't nature just another set of assets from which humans derive a flow of benefits? If that's so, what's wrong with valuing these flows of goods and services in terms of money even if it means using simulated prices since real market prices often do not exist? And what's wrong with discounting these monetized flows to compute the monetary value of natural capital? By valuing nature in money terms, the argument goes, we are able to include it in investment and planning decisions so that nature and our impacts on it, so often neglected when key decisions are made, will receive due consideration and nature will be better protected.

This is a powerful argument and one that should not be dismissed lightly. Despite all their deficiencies as reliable conveyors of information, prices are used in so many ways to guide public and private sector decisions, so if conceiving of nature as capital improves upon this situation why should we resist? One answer is that in normal financial calculations involving returns to capital, either the capital value is known and a rate of return is applied to compute a flow of income, or the income stream is known or can be reasonably projected, and an interest rate is used to discount the income stream to calculate an equivalent present or capitalized value. In these kinds of calculations, knowledge of any two variables (that is, the capital value, the income stream and the interest rate) determines the third. But in the case of natural capital, other than mineral deposits or biotic resources such as forests held as private property, there is no market value for stocks of most forms of natural capital or for the ecosystem goods and services they provide. Plus, the choice of discount rate is controversial (Stern et al. 2006). So, applying the same discounted cash flow evaluation method to value natural capital is highly problematic in the absence of market values of the asset *and* the flow of services and disagreement about what discount rate to use. The lack of observable information generated in markets introduces a degree of arbitrariness into the valuation of natural capital that sets it apart from present value calculations based on observable prices.

On top of these problems there are conceptual, methodological and ethical problems in valuing nature in terms of money (Nadal 2016). Key among these is that the concept of capital as it is normally understood within economics is highly problematic and has been the subject of a celebrated debate in economics known as the 'Cambridge capital controversy'. Nadal explains the controversy as follows:

> The centre of the debate is simple. The word 'capital' has two different meanings in economic theory: it denotes a sum of money and it also serves to designate a set of machines, tools, and other heterogeneous production instruments . . . Machine tools, blast furnaces, trucks and shuttle-less looms are heterogeneous objects that cannot be added in any simple manner. In other terms, there is no physically homogeneous and malleable substance called 'Capital' that can be applied to the production of all kinds of goods. However, neoclassical economists assume that the two notions of capital can be used interchangeably: the money value of machine tools and buildings is assumed to be a good proxy for the physical quantities of these production goods. (2016, p. 67)

He might have added a third meaning of capital within the broad frame of economics and that is the one from Marx, who stressed that capital represents a social relationship between the owners of capital and their employees. From this perspective, the interests of the owners of capital lie in the pursuit of profit and only incidentally in the production of something that is useful.

Nadal goes on to explain the several difficulties in valuing the stock of conventional produced capital in monetary terms entailing problems arising from the fact that machines and tools are produced commodities, that their prices depend on the rate of profit and the distribution of income, and that there are no measures of the quantity of capital that are independent of prices, in particular the rate of interest. He implores 'advocates of the natural capital metaphor . . . to stop living in a world of parables and metaphors' (Nadal 2016, p. 72).[4] Unfortunately, proponents of natural capital and its valuation in monetary terms seem oblivious to the Cambridge capital controversy, which is all about the measurement of capital in the presence of market prices. In their absence, the problems are greatly compounded and it doesn't do to ignore them.[5]

### 4.2.1 Valuation Methods

Many different ways of valuing nature and its services have been proposed (Millennium Ecosystem Assessment 2005a; Hanley and Barbier 2009; Pascual et al. 2010). They are drawn from the extensive literature on benefit–cost analysis. Benefit–cost analysis can be understood as a way of answering the following question: if a policy, program or project were for sale in a well-functioning market, what would be the outcome? Would those who will gain be willing to pay enough to compensate those who will suffer so that, if payment was made (as it would be in a real market transaction), everyone would come out ahead, or at least no one would think themselves worse off?

When applying the valuation methods of benefit–cost analysis to nature and its services, the valuations will depend on the method used. The value that is estimated could be: (1) the money that people are willing and able to pay to retain services from nature that are already available or could be available, that is, willingness to pay; or (2) the financial compensation that people would require for giving up such services, that is, willingness to accept; or (3) the cost of obtaining equivalent services through human-made technologies. The selection of the estimation method can dramatically affect the estimated value or price of nature and its services and there may be no obvious rationale for selecting one method over the other. One approach is to assume an assignment of property rights, then use willingness to pay to value services to which a person has no prior right, and willingness to accept for those who do have a prior property right. The problem is that the assumed assignment of property rights for the purpose of valuation can be completely arbitrary. A different assignment would yield a different evaluation and neither could be deemed correct.

A further problem is that both willingness to pay and willingness to accept reflect the prevailing distribution of income and wealth, though in different ways. Willingness to pay is constrained by a person's financial resources and other demands on them, which means that estimates of willingness to pay for ecosystem services favor those with a greater ability to pay, even though no actual payment is or will be made. It is just a way of valuing unpriced environmental services as if they were for sale. You may wonder why anyone would use willingness to pay, a concept that reflects the inequities that exist in the economy, to value something precious that is beyond the boundaries of the market system. Doing so assumes that public policy should be based on a simulation of how a market, were one to exist, would decide whether to protect or destroy an ecosystem and the services it provides. This extension of market thinking and market valuation into spheres outside the market is precisely what Michael Sandel warns against in *What Money Can't Buy* (Sandel 2012).

To some extent, estimates of the willingness to accept compensation for losing an environmental service overcome the problem of built-in inequity since they do not depend so directly on a person's financial resources. Nevertheless, poorer people might well be willing to accept a smaller amount of monetary compensation for an environmental loss than a richer person simply because of the reasonable assumption that the same amount of money means more to the poor than the rich. Measures of value based on willingness to accept compensation are not entirely free of bias that favors those with higher incomes and more wealth.

Most natural capital and ecosystem service valuations that use the monetary valuation tools of benefit–cost analysis rely on willingness to pay rather than willingness to accept. One reason for this is that estimates of willingness to accept are completely confounded when respondents to questionnaires designed to elicit such estimates give 'no amount of money would compensate' as their valuation of an environmental loss. Such responses are generally discarded or reduced to some arbitrary upper limit to avoid a valuation of the total cost of the loss that is infinite, outweighing any measure of benefits. This may seem 'practical' but it lacks a satisfactory theoretical foundation. Not everything is or should be for sale.

The income and wealth constraint that favors the well off in estimates of willingness to pay for ecosystem services also affects how the estimates can be used. A person's separate expressions of willingness to pay cannot be summed to give a meaningful total. Willingness to pay is a microeconomic concept that makes sense when applied to a small change in circumstances such as the construction of a modest sized dam on a river. The same person can express a willingness to pay for many such changes, in each case assuming everything else remains the same. For example, they may be willing to pay to preserve a wetland, or to protect each of a multitude of species, or to reduce air pollution. But this does not mean that you can simply add these separate expressions of willingness to pay to estimate a person's willingness to pay for all these changes simultaneously because to do so could exceed their income. This is an example of the well-known but often ignored fallacy of composition where what is true of the *whole* cannot be inferred from the sum of its *parts*. The fallacy of composition strictly limits how estimates of willingness to pay can be used. They should be summed with great care or not at all.

Quite often the choice of method used for valuing natural capital and ecosystem services is based on the availability of data gathered for other purposes, or of valuation estimates made elsewhere in different circumstances and 'transferred' for use because collecting new data would be too expensive. It is also not uncommon for estimates derived from different methods to be added together, which further complicates the interpretation of what the resulting total means. Just because different valuation methods yield a measure of value in terms of dollars, it does not follow that they can be summed to produce a meaningful total, quite the opposite in fact. The addition of a value in dollars based on willingness to pay with one based on willingness to accept, results in a dollar amount that means neither. The information such a dollar sum conveys is unclear. If we also include in the sum an estimate of the cost of obtaining an environmental service through an engineering project, the total in dollars has no specific meaning as the information it contains is incoherent and of questionable use as an aid to decision-making.

In the end, decision-making is what this is all about. It is worth considering what kinds of decisions can be usefully informed by estimates of the monetary value of ecosystem services and, using discounting, the monetary value of the natural capital that provides them. As noted, the methods used for arriving at these values come from benefit–cost analysis (Hanley and Barbier 2009). Benefit–cost analysis is essentially an evaluation method derived from microeconomics designed originally to aid decisions about relatively small-scale projects such as whether to build a new dam or establish a new park (Eckstein 1961). One of the main assumptions in benefit–cost analysis is that prices in the economy, other than for the output of the project itself, will be unaffected by the decision to proceed or not with the project. So, if a proposed hydroelectric dam is being evaluated with benefit–cost analysis, the price of electricity might be reduced by the increased supply if the dam is built, but all other prices in the economy are assumed to remain the same with or without the project. This assumption is only reasonable for small projects or programs but not for large ones such as evaluating an economy-wide carbon tax intended to influence prices throughout the economy (Spash 2007).

There are other problems in using benefit–cost analysis for valuing ecosystem services that are less consequential for small projects than for large ones. The assumption, for example, that people understand and are informed about the implications of changes in the environment is less plausible for environmental changes that are far-reaching and distant in space and time than it is about changes that are short term and limited to the local environment with which people are more familiar. But here's the rub. Local projects require local data especially when it comes to the environment. The value of an ecosystem service varies considerably depending on how many people are or might be affected, the availability of similar goods or services such as the sport of fishing from other sources, and socio-economic and cultural factors specific to the location. Yet when projects are small it can be too expensive to obtain the necessary data. Instead, value estimates obtained from elsewhere that do not adequately reflect these local conditions are used. In such cases, it is difficult to be confident that the resulting decision is well-informed reflecting as it does the incomes, preferences and opportunities available in communities other than the one for which a decision is to be made.

At the other end of the scale are studies that purport to show the value of natural capital for very large regions, and even for the entire planet (Costanza et al. 1997; 2014; Wilson 2008; Kubiszewski et al. 2017). Not only do these studies run afoul of all the methodological pitfalls already mentioned, they also run the risk of aggregating values estimated for marginal changes in the provision of ecosystem services to arrive at the value of their total loss.

> Value thus is a marginal concept insofar that it refers to the impact of small changes in the state of the world, and not the state of the world itself . . . As ecosystems reach thresholds, marginal human impacts on the system will lead to increasingly uncertain non-marginal effects. Under these conditions, the reliable estimation of TEV [total economic value] becomes increasingly difficult – if not impossible. (Pascual et al. 2010, pp. 190, 220)

A related concern is that problems of climate change, biodiversity loss and deforestation are examples of global environmental problems where thresholds have been crossed or loom large (Farley 2008; 2012). Farley notes that specific ecosystems and individual species are threatened by ecological thresholds, the presence of which is inherently uncertain, making monetary valuation highly problematic.

For all these reasons, ambitious studies that yield value estimates based on simulated prices are of questionable value for decision-making. The large numbers generated underline the importance of nature and this can be salutary in this day and age, but it is not at all clear what decisions such valuations are intended to inform. Unless someone is contemplating removing all ecosystem services from a region or from the entire planet, what use can be made of value estimates at this level, and what decisions could be informed by them? They can be useful for emphasizing the importance of nature in general in a culturally relevant way within capitalism, though to do this by using methodologies that assume it can be traded away is less than satisfactory. Again, quoting Nadal:

> The valuation techniques used in the context of the natural capital approach yield monetary values or prices. But, once again, these are not equilibrium prices: they are affected by distortions, rigidities and imperfections existing in the real economy. Because they are disequilibrium prices, it is not possible to assume that they embody accurate information about scarcity or efficiency. The data they generate may lead to gross misallocation of resources and cannot provide reliable guidance for environmental policy making. (2016, p. 75)

This is a sobering assessment of the monetary valuation of ecosystem services and the natural capital from which they are derived. It should give us pause when considering yet another way in which these valuations are being promoted and implemented by national and international statistical agencies.

There is considerable enthusiasm in some quarters (for example OECD 2011b; Smith 2016; IISD 2016) for incorporating natural capital within the established framework of the system of national accounts from which GDP is derived. Insofar as these initiatives provide information on the biophysical dimensions of nature, they perform a useful service, leaving it open to users to apply their own value set to the data. But the impulse to go beyond the biophysical and to value the various flows of ecosystem goods and services and the 'natural capital' that generates them in monetary terms seems irresistible. It invites all of the caveats and criticisms mentioned so far as well as those that follow.

One problem of comparing monetary values of natural and produced capital arises from the different ways in which produced capital and natural capital are valued. Statistical agencies use the perpetual inventory method for estimating the stock of produced capital. 'The essence of the perpetual inventory approach is to add investment estimates to the capital stock each year and to subtract depreciation' (Statistics Canada 2016a). This measure, adjusted for inflation and aggregated over all produced capital, is described as a 'nearly ideal indicator of the sustainability of well-being' for produced capital (IISD 2016, p. 20). The same report recommends that the value of natural capital that generates marketed outputs such as timber from forests or oil from reserves be calculated as the discounted value of projected resource rents. Resource rents are defined as the difference between the annual revenues earned from extraction and the costs of the extraction, which includes materials, energy, labor, and produced capital inputs. The application of this method requires a forecast of resource rents, which is a challenge for statistical agencies that prefer to report on what has happened rather than to predict what will. 'Various assumptions can be made regarding the evolution of revenues and costs over time. The simplest assumption is constancy, meaning that resource rent remains constant over the life of the asset' (IISD 2016, p. 165). This assumption may be simple but it does not avoid the problem of predicting future resource prices and extraction costs. Constancy is still a prediction.

If the quantity of reserves measured in physical units remains the same from one year to the next but the rent rises as a result of a price increase, then it will be reported that the value of the nation's natural capital has increased. It is quite possible for the value to increase even though the physical quantity of the stocks declines. And if a discount rate is used in the valuation then it will be sensitive to the choice of the discount rate which may change over time, further complicating measurement. These issues do not arise with the perpetual inventory approach used for measuring produced capital because changes in the prices of outputs from the processes in which the produced capital is used do not enter the calculation, neither does a discount rate. The perpetual inventory approach uses the inflation-adjusted value of investment which, once added to the existing capital, is never revised.

This asymmetry in the treatment of price changes seriously compromises the comparison of the monetary values of produced and natural capital even when the natural capital produces a flow of minerals or timber that have market prices. Implicit in the perpetual inventory approach is the assumption that the purchase price of new produced capital equals the discounted value of the additional profit that its purchase makes possible. There is no subsequent attempt made in the perpetual inventory approach to adjust the value of accumulated produced capital based on changing economic conditions not anticipated at the time of purchase. The contrary is the case with natural capital. As explained, over time the value of natural capital out of which marketed products are obtained is continually revised as current real net rents change.

One example of the contradictions that can arise from these two different valuation approaches concerns stranded assets. Stranded assets are 'assets that have suffered from unanticipated or premature write-downs, devaluations or conversion to liabilities' (Caldecott et al. 2015). There is growing recognition of the possibility that reductions in the demand for fossil fuels resulting from a transition to renewable sources of energy could dramatically reduce the value of fossil fuel reserves (Fullerton 2013). Canada's oil sands are a prime example. They are a comparatively high cost source of oil and are likely to be among the first to be taken out of production if the demand for oil declines. Their value as natural capital will effectively become zero or even negative if residual costs of site remediation remain. These changes will be captured by the formula used to value this form of natural capital based on rents. However, the value of the produced capital that has been created to exploit the oil sands will also lose most, if not all, of its value but this will not be captured by the perpetual inventory approach. Clearly, something is amiss. This example of a problem in comparing monetized values of natural and produced capital arises for a sub-component of natural capital that is relatively easy to value since its output has a market price output. When natural capital is valued based on projected values of non-marketed ecosystem services the problems are compounded and the meaning of any comparisons and aggregations of capitals are even harder to grasp.

### 4.2.2  Natural Capital, an Inadequate Conceptualization of Nature

Even without the serious methodological problems already mentioned, there are reasons for thinking that conceptualizing nature as capital is a mistake. The essence of produced capital is the capacity of human action to change it in various ways: to increase it through investment, to make it more productive through technological change, and to substitute it for other inputs in the economy. To apply the same assumptions to nature is quite a stretch. Produced capital is made from nature, not vice versa, and it depreciates if not maintained by humans, whereas nature flourishes if left alone. If natural capital can be made more productive through technology, say through GMOs (genetically modified organisms), and if scarce, produced capital can be substituted for it, as with theme parks and synthetic grass, then why bother to preserve it at all? And if substitution is not possible then it doesn't make sense to use a valuation method that assumes otherwise.

There is a more subtle distinction between produced capital and natural capital, but one that is important to grasp. It is based on the difference between 'stock-flow' resources and 'fund-service' resources (Georgescu-Roegen 1971). As defined by Daly and Farley (2011), *stock-flow* resources such as mineral deposits are: 'materially transformed into what they produce . . .; can be used at virtually any rate desired . . .; their productivity is measured by the number of physical units of the product into which they are transformed; can be stockpiled; are used up rather than worn out' (2011, p. 492). Daly and Farley define *fund-service* resources such as equipment and built infrastructure as resources that are: 'not materially transformed into what they produce . . ., can be used only at a given rate, and their productivity is measured as output per unit of time; cannot be stockpiled; and are worn out, rather than used up' (2011, p. 485).

Produced capital consists exclusively of funds that provide services. A chair is a fund that provides the service of support to the person sitting on it. A lathe is a fund that provides the service of turning a material to be fashioned into different shapes. A road is a fund that provides the service of mobility. These services do not deplete the funds from which they are derived in the way that extraction of a mineral depletes the stock. If the services are not used for a day, an hour or a moment, the unused services cannot be saved for future use. Time not spent sitting on a chair one day cannot be used the next day. The service provided by the chair cannot be stored for future use. Funds wear out, they are not used up.

The definition of natural capital from the World Forum on Natural Capital given at the start of this section includes 'geology, soil, air, water and all living things'. In this context geology refers to minerals obtained from the Earth's crust which are stock-flow resources. Soil is more difficult to categorize since it performs multiple functions. In some respects, such as when soil supports plant growth, it acts as a stock-flow resource: the minerals in the soil can be used at various rates and can be exhausted. In other respects, soil acts as a fund-service resource, for example when it stores water and prevents flooding or when it provides habitat for living organisms. Air is a fund-service resource when its movement drives wind turbines and a stock-flow resource when used as a sink to absorb emissions from human activities. The same is true of water which supports boats as a fund-service resource, and a stock-flow resource when used to supply drinking water from aquifers. Living things, such as cattle, are stock-flow resources that supply meat and fund-service resources when they help improve soil conditions.

Produced capital is a fund that provides services. When these are the services of production then produced capital is a fund that acts on the stock-flow resources provided by nature. Refineries process crude oil, blast furnaces smelt iron ore. In contrast, natural capital can be stock-flow resources, fund-service resources or a combination of the two, whereas produced capital is always a fund that provides services.

The dual role of natural capital and the single role of produced capital explains why it can be so difficult to find produced substitutes for natural capital. This has implications for valuation. The concept of 'critical' natural capital has been introduced to deal with instances where there is no produced substitute for what nature has to offer. Critical natural capital is 'defined as natural capital which is responsible for important environmental functions and which cannot be substituted in the provision of these functions by produced capital' (Ekins and De Groot 2003, p. 169). The impossibility of substituting produced capital for critical natural capital rules out the possibility of developing meaningful monetary values using methods that assume substitutes are available. This is a step forward but it raises the question of whether critical natural capital is the exception or the rule. Taken in small enough steps, very little natural capital might be considered critical. What harm can one more tonne of greenhouse gas emissions do? What is the value of losing just one more hectare of old growth forest? But the fallacy of composition raises its head again. It would be quite wrong to apply a monetary evaluation estimated for a single tonne of greenhouse gases to the release of thousands of megatonnes or the monetary valuation of a single hectare to a forest of millions. Conceiving of nature as natural capital and valuing it in terms of money, as attractive as it might be for simplifying the complicated, leaves too much to be desired.

### 4.2.3 Natural Capital, an Instrumental Approach to Nature

A final and perhaps the most important reason why conceptualizing nature as capital is unwise is that it invites an exploitative attitude towards the rest of nature, its ecosystems and the countless living organisms with which humans share the planet. Numerous cultures speak of 'Mother Earth'. We are supposed to respect our mothers, not exploit them for our own personal benefit. If we think that the rights of other species to co-exist with humans matter, or put differently, that non-human nature has ethical standing, then we should resist the temptation to conceive of nature as just another form of capital, the sole purpose of which is to serve humanity.

That the concept of natural capital entails an exploitative attitude is illustrated in reports of the UK's Natural Capital Committee (NCC). The NCC was established in 2012 as an independent advisory body to the UK Government. The Chairman of the Natural Capital Committee made his view of the relationship between the economy and the environment absolutely plain when he said '*the environment is part of the economy* and needs to be properly integrated into it so that growth opportunities will not be missed' (Natural Capital Committee 2013, p. 4, emphasis added). The first report of the NCC makes numerous references to how better management of natural capital can help promote economic growth. For example: 'there are a number of ways in which the better management of natural capital *can drive growth* and boost wellbeing . . . natural environment is the source of many goods and services that are not currently being fully utilised. Recognising the value of these *could unlock opportunities for growth*' (Natural Capital Committee 2013, pp. 43–4, emphasis added). Clearly, any features that might distinguish nature from human-made capital have been overlooked in this fundamentally instrumental approach to the natural world.

Human-made capital has value only because of the goods and services it provides in the human economy. Describing nature as capital implies that nature has value for a similar reason: only to provide goods and services to humans. Nature as capital is an object, not a subject or collection of subjects, with which humans co-exist. As such it denies, or minimizes, the ethical value of nature itself, of individual and connected ecosystems, of non-human species and their members. These are all just capital to be valued for their utility to humans (Sullivan 2012). And if nature as capital turns out to be worth less than the value derived from its destruction, what then will proponents of natural capital say? Paving paradise and putting up parking lots can be very profitable.

These conceptual, methodological and philosophical concerns have led some to oppose the 'financialization of nature' for fear that it will lead to further incursions rather than more protection (Friends of the Earth International 2015). Writing about *buen vivir* (good living), a popular social philosophy in Latin America, Oliver Balch (2013) refers to the views of Eduardo Gudynas, the executive secretary of the Latin American Centre for Social Ecology in Uruguay. Balch explains that,

> according to buen vivir, humans are never owners of the earth and its resources, only stewards. This plays against the idea of natural capital, now used widely in business circles. Ecosystem services, for example, where a monetary value is given to environmental goods such as the water provision of rivers or carbon sequestration of forests, is anathema.

Quoting Gudynas, 'if you put a price on nature, then you're suggesting an ownership of the planet . . . Furthermore, capital is something that is interchangeable between people. But if you destroy the environment, then it's difficult to rebuild it, which undermines it being interchangeable' (Balch 2013).

The declaration in 2010 by the members of ALBA (Bolivia, Cuba, Ecuador, Nicaragua and Venezuela) goes even further by claiming that putting a price on nature is a step towards its privatization and exploitation for the benefit of the few at the expense of the many.

> There is within the United Nations a push to promote the concept of a 'green economy' . . . in order to extend capitalism in the economic, social and environmental arenas, in which nature is seen as 'capital' for producing tradable

environmental goods and services that should be valued in money terms and assigned a price so that they can be commercialized with the purpose of obtaining profits. (ALBA-TCP 2010)

Clearly, valuing nature and its services in terms of prices is far more controversial than it appears from most academic, governmental and NGO sources that promote the approach. In a culture in which monetary values have such a dominating presence, assigning large monetary values to nature can have considerable rhetorical power, which is important, given the precarious state of nature and the overriding importance of attracting attention to possible solutions: 'our point in making this admittedly crude estimate: to demonstrate that ecosystem services were much more important to human wellbeing than conventional economic thinking had given them credit for' (Costanza et al. 2017, p. 3). But that does not make it good economics nor does it make it ethically sound. As Ursula Franklin wrote some years ago when contemplating technology in the real world, 'there is also the urgent task of cleaning up the technocratic and egocentric mindset, to get rid of the notion that nature is just one more infrastructure in the real world of technology' (Franklin 1990, p. 88).

## 4.3   CONCLUSION

If we can't rely on prices, market or simulated, to guide decision-making especially at the interface between the economy and the environment, what should we do? A pragmatic approach not without its merits is to regulate the market through political institutions. Such regulations developed over centuries and always in flux, have limited the worst abuses of children, adults and the environment that market processes allow and encourage in the name of competition and the pursuit of profit. Inequities in distribution can be ameliorated through the system of taxes and transfers and by the direct provision of some goods and services by government agencies. All of this is common, to a greater or lesser degree, in countries around the world. The issue here is whether and to what extent valuing nature and the goods and services it provides to people in monetary terms can improve decisions relating to interactions between human economies and the biosphere.

For reasons given in this and the previous chapter, the information conveyed by market prices, and even more so by simulated prices where market prices do not exist, is more unreliable than is often assumed, especially by economists. Unreliable in this sense means that prices do not convey as much useful and readily interpretable information as economic theory might suggest for the simple reason that the conditions required for them to do so do not prevail in the real world. It's not so much their practical value for coordinating economic activity that is in question here. Rather it is their normative significance for guiding decisions, especially those relating to human interactions with the rest of nature.

One response to this problem is to place less emphasis on traditional procedures used in economic valuation such as benefit–cost analysis and more emphasis on improving the processes by which decisions are made. Even Pascual et al. say in their generally favorable review of methods for valuing ecosystem services and biodiversity, 'This [economic] valuation approach . . . should be used to complement, but not to substitute for, other legitimate ethical or scientific reasoning and arguments relating to biodiversity conservation' (Pascual et al. 2010, p. 189). But as Pascual et al. acknowledge, 'biophysical and the preference-based approaches stem from different axiomatic-frameworks and value theories, and therefore are not generally compatible' (2010, p. 194).[6] Multi-criteria decision analysis (MCDA) has been proposed as a systematic way of considering and combining several separate evaluation approaches. Relative weights are assigned to values expressed in different metrics to develop a ranking of alternatives (Munda 2004). In MCDA, the selection of the weights can be critical in determining the overall ranking of the alternatives and is best done through a process involving those most affected by the various outcomes. There is a substantial body of literature on alternative modes of decision-making involving a variety of participatory opportunities. These include deliberative monetary valuation, environmental assessment, technology assessment, mediated modeling and integrated modeling – where the outcome of alternative decisions is described and discussed and a wider range of ethical frameworks than underlies economic valuation is admitted (Zavadskas and Turskis 2011; Balasubramaniam and Voulvoulis 2005; Wang et al. 2009; Costanza et al. 2017).

In this and the previous chapter I have argued that market prices and simulated prices using the tools of benefit–cost analysis convey information that is less meaningful than generally believed. This is all too apparent in the enthusiasm with which natural capital has been embraced as a conceptual framework for understanding and managing the interactions between humans and the rest of nature, often in the pursuit of economic growth. As Pascual et al. say:

> In cases where markets do exist but are distorted, for instance because of a subsidy scheme . . . or because the market is not fully competitive, prices will not be a good reflection of preferences and marginal costs. Consequently, the

estimated values of ecosystem services will be biased and will not provide reliable information to base policy decisions on. (2010, pp. 200–201)

But these cases are not exceptional, far from it, with ramifications for economic and environmental policy that go beyond the efficacy of the economic valuation of ecosystem goods and services and the natural capital that generates them. Pascual et al. go on to say:

> these valuation techniques, which assume smooth and small system changes, may produce meaningless results in the context of ecosystems characteristics and dynamics such as ecological thresholds, resilience and regime shifts. At the policy level, it is better to address this uncertainty and ignorance by employing a safe minimum standard approach and the precautionary principle. (2010, p. 243)

Whatever one thinks of the concerns expressed in this chapter about pricing nature it is clear that the enthusiasm for it is due, at least in part, to the contribution it can make to economic growth. The UK Natural Capital Commission is quite explicit about this but others express a similar position. 'What role does nature play in economic growth?' asks the World Economic Forum (2014). 'Wealth accounting, including natural capital accounting is needed to sustain growth', says the World Bank (2016d). 'The private sector, governments, all of us, must understand and account for our use of natural capital and recognise its true value in maintaining economic growth', claims the Natural Capital Finance Alliance (2012).

There's no question that economic growth depends crucially on what nature provides for human economies to function and grow. And as the following three chapters show, there's compelling evidence that economic growth is stressing nature's capacity beyond its limits. What is in question here is how we think about our relationship to the rest of nature and to other species that inhabit the biosphere, and whether thinking of the rest of nature as another form of capital whose 'true value' can be captured in terms of money and money equivalents is just a step too far.

## NOTES

1. The terms 'undeveloped', 'developed', and 'social welfare' are in quotation marks to indicate that they are widely used terms in economics with contested meanings.
2. Consumer surplus is the difference between the total amount that buyers are willing and able to pay for a good or service and the total amount that they actually do pay, which is the market price.
3. Some of the issues raised in this section appear in Victor (2007).

4.  Similar arguments can be found in Victor (1991) and Sandel (2012).
5.  In a similar vein, Hodgson (2014) questions how economists and sociologists have changed the meaning of capital.
6.  The biophysical approaches they are referring to 'include embodied energy analysis . . . emergy analysis . . . exergy analysis . . . ecological footprint . . . material flow analysis . . . land-cover flow . . . and Human Appropriation of Net Primary Production (HANPP)' (Pascual et al. 2010, p. 194).

# 5.  Limits to growth – sources

We are not victims of natural constraints, but beneficiaries of natural conditions. (Peter Timmerman 2017)

Concern about the capacity of the biosphere to support endless economic growth is not new. Some previous warnings about threats of resource shortages have not materialized, at least to the extent anticipated. Why is this? The inventiveness, ingenuity and adaptability of humans have all contributed. New technologies, the substitution of more plentiful materials for scarce ones, a shift away from goods to services, all help explain why forecasts of impending resource shortages and environmental decline have not always been borne out. And this is no accident. It is what we might expect from price adjustments and enlightened government policies without which more adverse circumstances might have transpired. We make the future; it does not just happen.

Although the starting point has moved and the scale of the human enterprise is larger than ever before, the fundamental question remains. Will the capacity of Earth to provide and accommodate the flows of material and energy on which economies depend constrain future economic growth? Is it just a question about future economic growth, or are there signs that growth is already being constrained by planetary limits? We address these questions in this and the following two chapters. Any answer other than a straightforward 'no' to both questions obliges those of us especially in rich countries, to think about managing without growth. If we do not address this issue now, the next generation or two may have to do it anyway without any preparation for the task whatsoever. That is not a legacy for which they will thank us.

## 5.1  THE ECONOMIC CYCLE AND THE BIOSPHERE

Economies are open systems that rely on the natural environment to supply materials and energy and to provide for their disposal. The natural environment also provides the geographical space in which economic activity takes place. All the material and energy that is extracted from the environment is eventually disposed of as waste, some almost immediately and some after many years, but all eventually, except perhaps for some precious metals, gem stones and some reused building materials that stay in the economy indefinitely. This 'metabolism' of the economy has become the subject of numerous studies (Ayres 1989; Fischer-Kowalski and Hüttler 1999; Schaffartzik et al. 2014). Historically the material and energy flows on which economies depend have increased with economic growth. Now the global flows are so large that there are concerns over future supplies of resources such as oil and lithium, over contamination of the environment from the disposal of waste energy and materials, and an awareness that life-support, habitat and amenity services provided by the environment are being damaged beyond repair. In this chapter and the next we will examine a selection of these issues.[1]

The conception of the global economic system embedded in the biosphere is depicted in Figure 5.1.

The 'economic cycle' is located in the center of Figure 5.1. This cycle links firms and households and is the bare bones of market economies. A diagram showing this cycle sometimes in more detail, but out of its planetary context, can be found in most introductory textbooks on economics. In the economic cycle members of households are the ultimate owners of land, labor and capital, which they make available to firms for a price.

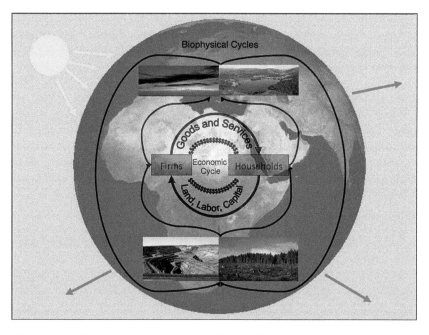

*Figure 5.1   The economy is embedded in the biosphere*

Firms use them to produce the goods and services sold to households. Land, labor and capital and goods and services flow in one direction, money flows in the other. Households provide their labor to firms in return for wages. Some households own capital and land. They provide capital to firms through equity finance in return for dividends and as loans in return for interest. They use some of these revenues to buy goods and services and save the rest. Land rent is also a source of income to those who own land and can be spent on goods and services or saved. Savings typically find their way to firms through the purchase of new equities and loans. The economic cycle can be represented in much more detail than it is in Figure 5.1, for example by the inclusion of government which taxes, borrows and spends, and the banking system, which provides a suite of financial services including the creation of money, all of which we consider in later chapters.

The representation of the economic cycle in Figure 5.1, simple though it is, is sufficient to illustrate the fundamental and inescapable dependency of the economy on the biosphere.[2] One of the main arguments in this book is that it is only by neglecting this fundamental dependency that it is possible to think that economic output can increase without limit, that there are no limits to growth. And yet neglect is the norm in most economics textbooks where the economic cycle is presented and described in various levels of detail without showing how it is embedded in the biosphere. The inadequate treatment of the dependency of the economy on the environment in the most widely used economics textbooks is proving to be a tragic error (Green 2012; Raworth 2017).

At the bottom of Figure 5.1 are two images, one of an open pit mine and the other of a forest from which materials are extracted and supplied to the economy. The materials include fossil fuels which, once within the economy, are combusted to generate energy. Other energy flows, such as solar and wind, are provided directly to the economy, unmediated by a market transaction. The photovoltaic cells and wind turbines required to make use of these free sources of energy are produced within the economy and traded, but not the primary energy sources that they transform into electricity.

Figure 5.2 shows the astonishing increase in the global use of materials from 1900 to 2015. It is an example of the Great Acceleration referred to in Chapter 2 in the discussion of the Anthropocene. Between 1900 and 1950 total global materials extraction doubled, from 7.3 billion tonnes/year in 1900 to 15 billion tonnes/year in 1950 at an annual average rate of growth of 1.5 percent. These materials consisted of biomass, fossil fuels, ores and industrial minerals and construction materials, all of which increased over the first half of the 20th century. From 1950 to 1970 the rate of growth of

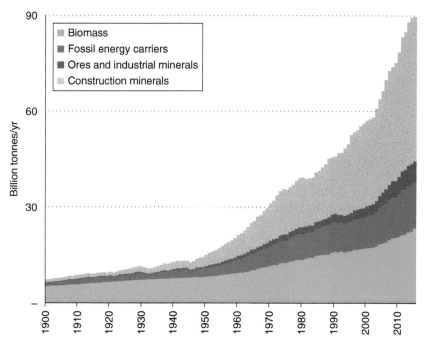

*Source:* Data from Kraussmann et al. (2009), updated in 2017.

*Figure 5.2    Global materials extraction 1900–2015 in billion tonnes*

global materials extraction increased sharply to an average of 3.7 percent/ year and extraction doubled in only twenty years. Between 1970 and 2000 the average rate of increase in extraction slowed to 2.0 percent then picked up after 2000 to 3.0 percent. At this rate, global materials extraction will double again between 2000 and 2023.

> [t]he world economy has experienced a great acceleration in material use since 2000, strongly related to the industrial and urban transformation in China, which has required unprecedented amounts of iron and steel, cement, energy and construction materials . . . global material productivity has declined since about the year 2000 and the global economy now needs more materials per unit of GDP than it did at the turn of the century. (UNEP 2016a, pp. 14, 16)

This statement from UNEP attests that since the turn of the century global materials extraction has been rising faster than global GDP despite concerted efforts to increase recycling rates, which has no direct impact on fossil fuel use and only a very delayed impact on construction materials.

As noted in Chapter 2, the laws of thermodynamics apply to economic processes which all rely, to a greater or lesser extent, on these inflows of materials and energy. The materials and energy brought into the economy are transformed through economic activity where they are inevitably degraded and eventually discarded back into the environment, some having been reused and recycled before disposal. The unavoidable degradation of materials and energy used in the economic system means that new supplies are always required to replace old ones. Like any perpetual motion machine, a completely 'circular economy' running entirely on its own wastes is unattainable, though it can provide a useful image for the direction in which economies ought to go even if it is a journey that can never be completed.

The flows of waste materials and energy out of the economy are shown in Figure 5.1 by the two arrows leaving the economic cycle with illustrations of the air and water 'sinks' into which they are emitted. In the event that these sinks become overloaded, which is increasingly common these days, the cycles in the biosphere on which all life depends become disrupted. From a human perspective, this disruption can reduce the capacity of the biosphere to provide goods and services used by the economy and by people directly, and if severe enough, can limit economic growth. Acid rain is a good example. The smelting of ores and the combustion of fossil fuels release sulfur gases that increase the acidity of rain and snow. When this precipitation falls on forests it can inhibit tree growth, adversely affecting the forests, the habitat of the wildlife that dwells there and the economic activities that depend on them (Miller 2004, pp. 430–32). When lakes acidify, fish populations can be adversely affected, and sport and commercial fishing suffer. The acid rain problem was widely recognized in the early 1980s in Europe and North America and steps were taken to reduce the emission of these acid gases. Acid rain was mitigated but still remains a matter of considerable concern (Burns et al. 2016).

The connections between materials extraction, processing, use, disposal and ecological impacts have not always been obvious and to a considerable extent are still neglected. Figure 5.1, which makes plain the dependency of the economy on the biosphere, is a perspective not shared by mainstream economists, who typically conceive of the economy as a self-contained system completely removed from and independent of the biosphere (Green 2012). Those that do pay attention to these economy–environment linkages within the mainstream do so under the rubric of two sub-specializations: natural resource economics and environmental economics. The fact that these are considered two separate sub-specializations with their own academic journals further illustrates the lack of appreciation of the intimate relationship that exists between the materials and energy that enter the economy as resources – the focus of natural resource economics – and the impacts of their disposal on the environment – the focus of environmental economics. In contrast, the perspective of ecological economics illustrated in Figure 5.1 uses the concept of throughput and metabolism to unite material and energy inflows and outflows, plus all intermediate uses in between. Ecological economists also consider the economic implications of the first and second laws of thermodynamics, such as the impossibility of 100 percent recycling, and design practical metrics for measurement and accounting not subject to the limitations of price-based information as described in the previous chapter (Wackernagel and Rees 1996; Giampietro et al. 2010).

There are a vast number of studies, pro and con, that are relevant to questions about the capacity of Earth to provide and accommodate the throughput of materials and energy on which economies depend. There is also a healthy debate about whether this capacity is an increasingly stringent limit on economic growth. In an attempt to present a reasonable and informed assessment of the situation, wherever possible we rely on and cite comprehensive, peer-reviewed articles, books and reports, including some that present contrary views to provide perspective, if not balance. For convenience, the overview of these possible biophysical limits to growth is divided into four main categories: sources, sinks, services and synthesis. 'Sources', the focus of this chapter, means the supply of materials and energy. 'Sinks' refers to their disposal, and 'services' relates to how we are transforming nature in ways that deprive us of essential ecological services such as clean air and water and that destroy the habitat of countless species. We also look at the extent to which the search by humans for sustenance to support the expanding populations of people and our artifacts are depriving our fellow creatures of habitat and nourishment. Sources, sinks and services are all interrelated. In Chapter 7, on synthesis, we consider some different ways of examining all of these potential limits to growth simultaneously for a more complete and integrated picture.

## 5.2   SOME LESSONS FROM THE PAST

Anyone credited with being the first to think of an idea usually got it from someone else who was not the originator. Thomas Malthus is usually recognized as starting the debate about the capacity of the Earth to support a rapidly growing population (Malthus 1798). Malthus's argument was anticipated by Condorcet, a French intellectual of the Enlightenment. Condorcet was more optimistic than Malthus. He believed that people would use their powers of reason to control their fertility voluntarily, avoiding the grinding poverty and rising mortality that Malthus predicted (Sen 2001). The history of the past two centuries has been kinder to Condorcet than Malthus on this point, yet it is the pessimistic Malthus who has made the more lasting impression. Perhaps this is because we gravitate more readily to bad news than to good. Or perhaps it's because we have a nagging belief that Malthus may have been wrong so far but eventually he will be proven right.[3]

Another possibility, more generous to Malthus, is that in fact he was at least partially correct and the evidence is already before us. Many commentators note the decline in the percentage of people living in extreme poverty worldwide, where extreme poverty is defined as an income of less than US$2/day (or more precisely as $1.90 in 2011 purchasing power parity terms (World Bank 2016b, p. 3)). Yet pain, suffering and early death are felt by people, not by percentages, so it is the number of people living in abject poverty that really matters as much if not more than the percentage. The world's population has increased more than seven-fold since Malthus wrote the first edition of his *Essay on the Principle of Population*, and the percentage of people living in extreme poverty has certainly declined. This is laudable and is the case against Malthus. From 1990 to 2015 the number of people living in extreme poverty declined from 1.9 billion in 1990 to 836 million (United Nations 2015b, p. 4), a major achievement indeed. Yet not all of the roughly 1 billion people alive in Malthus's time were living at subsistence level, so over the long haul, the number of people living at the barest subsistence level has not declined much in more than two hundred years. No wonder Malthus's dismal outlook still resonates. What is even less encouraging is that after this, the number of chronically undernourished people in the world actually increased from 777 million in 2015 to 815 million in 2016 (FAO 2017, p. ii), including almost one in four children under the age of five with stunted growth and a greatly heightened risk of cognitive damage and susceptibility to infection. The FAO report states that this upturn 'could signal a reversal of trends' (2017, p. ii) partly as a result of climate change. Looking ahead to 2030, the FAO estimates an increase of between 35 and 122 million people by 2030 living in extreme poverty due to the effects of climate change on agricultural productivity (FAO 2016c, p. 13).

Unfortunately, the welcome decline in extreme poverty and the number of undernourished people to 2015 was accompanied by a significant increase in the number of obese and overweight people. 'Overweight and obesity are defined as abnormal or excessive fat accumulation that may impair health' (World Health Organization 2017). The World Health Organization reports that worldwide obesity has more than doubled since 1980. In 2014 more than 1.9 billion adults were overweight and of these over 600 million were obese. Although overweight and obesity are on the rise in low- and middle-income countries, particularly in urban areas (World Health Organization 2016), it is in some of the richest countries where the problems are the greatest. In the USA for example, 36 percent of adults are obese (Cohen 2016). So while economic growth has brought a massive expansion of agricultural output, unequally shared both within and among countries, it has also brought nutritional problems associated with excess, where further economic growth is not the answer.

Malthus predicted that population growth would outpace growth in the food supply. He did not consider other resources but some writers did and they faced much the same fate as Malthus – dismissed by many as having been proven wrong yet remembered for having touched a nerve that remains exposed today. W. Stanley Jevons (1835–82) is a good example. He was a major contributor to the late 19th-century 'marginal revolution' in economics and is recognized as one of the founders of neoclassical economics, yet in his time Jevons was more widely known for his work on 'the coal question'. He published a book with that title in 1865 in which he expressed concern about the declining supply of cheap coal in Britain (Jevons 1865). Jevons forecast that Britain would lose its position as the world's most prosperous economy because of an emerging shortage of cheap coal from British mines. His work on coal anticipated the modern concern about peak oil – the impending decline in the production of oil worldwide, which we will discuss later in this chapter. Some writers, noting that there is still plenty of coal left in the world, suggest that because Jevons was wrong about coal, those concerned about peak oil are wrong as well (Smil 2003a).

But was Jevons wrong? It is true that he underestimated the amount of coal that could be mined economically in Britain. According to Beckerman this was a 'decisive falsification of Jevons' predictions' (Beckerman 2003). This is incorrect. Jevons's predictions concerned the future of the British economy whose dominance in the world economy depended on its access to cheap coal which Jevons believed would not last: 'so far as cheap fuel and power is the exciting cause of manufactures, these must pass to where fuel is cheapest, especially when it is in the hands of persons as energetic and ingenious as ourselves' (Jevons 1865, p. xxxvi). 'England's manufacturing and commercial greatness, at least, is at stake in this question' (Jevons 1865, p. 3).

Jevons did not think that Britain would ever 'run out' of coal, only that it would become more difficult to mine and hence more expensive: 'It is almost needless to say, however, that our mines are literally inexhaustible. We cannot get to the bottom of them; and though we may some day have to pay dear for fuel, it will never be positively wanting' (1865, p. xxx).

To confirm this understanding of what Jevons intended, the following 'excellent' remarks by Sir W. Armstrong in an Address to the British Association at Newcastle in 1863 are quoted by Jevons in his book:

> It is clear that, long before complete exhaustion takes place, England will have ceased to be a coal-producing country on an extensive scale. Other nations, and especially the United States of America, which possess coal-fields thirty-seven times more extensive than ours, will then be working more accessible beds at a smaller cost, and will be able to displace the English coal from every market. The question is, not how long our coal will endure before absolute exhaustion is effected, but how long will those particular coal-seams last which yield coal of a quality and at a price to enable this country to maintain her present supremacy in manufacturing industry. (Jevons 1865, Chapter 2, paragraph II.28)

This concern proved well founded. In 1870, Britain accounted for 31.8 percent of world manufacturing. By 1913, despite considerable economic growth in the intervening years, Britain's share had fallen to 14 percent, having been surpassed by the USA (35.8 percent) and Germany (15.7 percent) (Halsall n.d.). These countries had found cheaper supplies of coal. By 1905, coal production in the USA was already 50 percent greater than in the UK and Germany was gaining fast (Bauermann and Ross 1910). In transportation and some industrial uses oil started to replace coal as a more convenient form of fossil fuel energy. Britain did not discover oil on its own territory until the 1960s under the North Sea. There were other factors besides dependence on cheap coal that caused Britain's decline as the world's largest economy, but when placed in context, Jevons's analysis of the coal question, despite its underestimate of British coal deposits, remains relevant to understanding the dependence of economic growth on abundant and cheap supplies of energy.

After World War II, when full employment and then economic growth became important objectives of government policy, the same sort of questions that Jevons asked in the 19th century in Britain were being asked in the United States. The President's Materials Policy Commission, known as the Paley Commission after its chairman William S. Paley, was set up to inquire 'into all major aspects of the problem of assuring an adequate supply of production materials for our long range needs' (quoted in Barnett and Morse 1963, p. 20). The Commission concluded that:

> There is evidence of recent moderate increase in costs of raw materials and prospects of further rises. But there is no serious threat to economic growth during the next generation . . . . (2) . . . foreign natural resources should be increasingly relied upon as a source for the US consumption of raw materials. (Barnett and Morse 1963, pp. 44, 45)

The report of the Paley Commission was just one of several on the relation between resources and growth that were published around this time, reflecting a concern that was largely dispelled in the minds of many by economists Barnett and Morse through their influential study *Scarcity and Growth* (1963). Barnett and Morse examined the inflation-adjusted prices and costs of natural resources traded in the United States from about 1870 to 1957. With few exceptions, these prices and costs declined, even though in that 87-year period the population of the United States quadrupled and economic output increased roughly twenty-fold. By these measures of prices and costs Barnett and Morse concluded that the scarcity of natural resources had not been a constraint on economic growth and was unlikely to be in the future. This conclusion has permeated the thinking of most economists and those they advise for more than half a century.

In 1979, a second book, *Scarcity and Growth Reconsidered* (Smith and Krutilla 1979), was published. This was a set of papers written by multiple authors presenting a variety of views. Generally speaking, Barnett and Morse's conclusions about natural resources and growth were reiterated though more cautiously and more circumscribed. Notably the book's editors, economists V. Kerry Smith and John Krutilla, questioned the statistical methods used by Barnett in an update of his earlier analysis (with Morse) that is included as a paper in the later volume. They said, 'the rejection of a hypothesis of increasing natural resource scarcity that is based on the results of simple statistical tests using these data alone must be viewed as not substantiated' (Smith and Krutilla 1979, p. 28). This was a polite way of saying that Barnett's proposition about the declining scarcity of natural resources in the United States was not proven.

The scope of *Scarcity and Growth* was limited to minerals, agriculture, forestry and fishing. Smith and Krutilla broadened the definition of natural resources to include 'all the original endowments of the earth whose services may bear directly or indirectly on our ability to produce and consume utility-yielding goods and services while maintaining ambient conditions supportive of life' (Smith and Krutilla 1979, p. 277). They acknowledged that markets may do a reasonable job of signaling scarcity and inducing appropriate responses for specific market-controlled natural resources, but they also argued that markets cannot be relied on for managing 'the services of common property environmental resources not exchanged or organized [in] markets' (Smith and Krutilla 1979, p. 278).

This theme is taken much further in *Scarcity and Growth Revisited* (Simpson et al. 2005), yet another retrospective on the still influential *Scarcity and Growth* published 42 years earlier. Barnett and Morse had identified two exceptions to their general finding that the costs and prices of raw materials had declined in the United States. These exceptions were commercial fish and forest products. Unlike non-renewable resources where use necessitates depletion, these two renewable resources can last indefinitely as long as the rate of use does not exceed the rate of regeneration. If use does exceed regeneration then the stock of a renewable resource, say a forest or a fishery, is depleted and supply must eventually decline. This circumstance can easily happen when property rights over such resources are poorly defined or non-existent or in the absence of effective control by government or some other collective arrangement for regulating access and use.

In *Scarcity and Growth Revisited* the editors, economists R. David Simpson, Michael A. Toman and Robert U. Ayres, distinguish between the 'Old Scarcity' that dealt with 'resources traded in markets' and the 'New Scarcity' of global public goods. These public goods include biological diversity, changes in atmospheric chemistry causing climate change, and in general, 'the ecological services that diverse natural ecosystems provide' (Simpson et al. 2005, p. 11). The labels 'old' and 'new' scarcity help to capture the evolving concerns in society at large over the 42 years that separate *Scarcity and Growth* from *Scarcity and Growth Revisited*. The earlier focus was almost exclusively on the scarcity of sources of traditional raw materials. That concern has not gone away but it has been overshadowed in more recent years by awareness of threats to the supply of ecological goods services provided free by nature and especially those unmediated by markets.

The transition from a concern about the ongoing supply of raw materials to the diminishing provision of ecological goods and services should not be a surprise since responses to the Old Scarcity have, to a large extent, caused the New Scarcity. Exploration, extraction, processing, transportation, manufacture, use and disposal of materials and energy have generated the environmental impacts underlying the New Scarcity. Resource-related air and water contamination can be found almost everywhere around the globe. The enormous tailings ponds created by the exploitation of Alberta's oil sands (Kurek et al. 2012) and the multitude of environmental and social impacts from mining (Working Group on Mining and Human Rights in Latin America 2013) are just two examples of how increasing efforts to supply the economy with energy and materials are causing environmental disruption on a grand scale. As the Earth is disturbed in ever more aggressive ways in the search for new supplies of materials and energy, ecosystems are disrupted that provide valuable and often unpriced ecological goods and services. What we gain in GDP is offset, partially or completely, by what we lose in values not captured by the market. In this process, the market values themselves, that is, the prices that convey the information on which markets and governments depend, become increasingly unreliable. As a substantial and growing component of production and transportation costs – the environmental costs – are excluded from the calculations, the prices and costs actually paid for resources become less and less useful indicators of scarcity. They can even decline, as have the prices of fossil fuels starting in 2014, while greenhouse gases from their combustion continue to accumulate in the atmosphere, so scarcity in its fullest sense is increasing. But we will not see this if we only look at market prices or at GDP, which relies so heavily upon them.

### 5.2.1   Betting on the Future

Paul Ehrlich should have known better than to take a bet with Julian Simon. Until his death in 1998 Julian Simon was a Professor of Business Administration at the University of Maryland, with plenty of experience and success in business. As a student, he worked as an encyclopedia sales-man, caddy, cost accountant, drugstore clerk, self-employed sign painter, brewery worker, tin-can factory worker, technical writer, freelance maga-zine writer, grass-seed factory worker, and cab driver (Simon 1998). Simon was a man of the world and an optimist about the future of humanity.

Paul Ehrlich 'grew up chasing butterflies and dissecting frogs' (Whitney R. Harris World Ecology Centre). He joined Stanford University as an Assistant Professor of Biology in 1959 and progressed through the ranks to become a full Professor of Biology. Ehrlich has enjoyed a successful career as an academic and public figure. He is most well known outside academia for his publications and speeches on population and the environment. Ehrlich is a man of the natural world and a pessimist about the future of humanity (Ehrlich 1968).

In 1980 Simon and Ehrlich bet on the prices of five metals. Simon bet that the prices of these metals would fall by 1990 and Ehrlich bet they would rise. Simon allowed Ehrlich to choose the metals. He chose copper, chromium, nickel, tin and tungsten. Together they calculated how much of each of these metals could be bought in 1980 for $200 per metal, for a total budget of US$1000. They were to check again in 1990. If it cost more in 1990 than US$1000 (allowing for inflation) to buy the same quantities of the metals as in 1980 Simon would pay Ehrlich the difference. If it cost less, Ehrlich would pay Simon the difference (Ehrlich 1981). Ehrlich lost the bet and paid Simon US$576.07.

What does this bet tell us? First of all, that both Ehrlich and Simon believed that increases or decreases in the market price of metals are a reliable indicator of their scarcity or abundance. We saw in Chapter 3 the extraordinary range of assumptions that are required to support this belief. Richard Norgaard has examined this issue with particular reference to non-renewable natural resources and says that the view that prices of non-renewable resources reflect their scarcity is based on a simple syllogism:

First premise: If resources are scarce;
Second premise: If resource allocators (i.e. those who make decisions about rates of extraction) know they are scarce;
Conclusion: Then resource costs (or prices or rents) will increase.

Norgaard says that looking at resource costs, rents or prices to establish whether resources are scarce (or whether they are becoming increasingly scarce) neglects the second premise. Trends in these economic measures reflect beliefs about scarcity, not necessarily the scarcity itself, and it is impossible to tell from the data which it is (Norgaard 1990; 2002). So if Norgaard is correct, which I think he is, we should not read very much into the time path of the prices of five non-renewable resources about resource scarcity even in the absence of any environmental costs associated with their extraction.

That said, had Ehrlich and Simon made the same bet in 1985, 1986, and in any year from 1994 to 2004 rather than 1980, Ehrlich would have won (based on 1998 constant dollar prices; United States Geological Survey 2006). The number of wins would have been almost equal, with Ehrlich victorious, winning 13 of 25 bets from 1980 to 2004 (the last year for which 10 years of future price data are available at the time of writing). But the value of Ehrlich's wins would have far exceeded his losses, such that had they bet in each year from 1980 to 2004, Simon would have had to pay Ehrlich a total of US$11 365, which is equivalent to US$15 847 in 2016 prices.

These lessons from the past illustrate the challenges of making confident predictions about the future, in particular in relation to sources of materials and energy required for economic growth. The remainder of the chapter looks at the current situation regarding supplies of materials and energy on which all economic activity depends, and the outlook in the decades ahead.

## 5.3 MATERIALS

One of the arguments often made as to why concern about the material and energy basis of economic growth is misplaced is that advanced economies have 'decoupled' economic growth from their material and energy requirements. Decoupling refers to the proposition that economies can grow and yet reduce their use of materials and energy through a combination of technological change and a switch from goods to services. (See section 2.3 in Chapter 2.) This is what is meant by a 'knowledge based economy', a term coined by Peter Drucker (1969) and which became widespread by the turn of the century, although falling out of fashion more recently.

With so many economies and so many different kinds of material and energy inputs and waste outflows, examples can be found to support or counter the decoupling proposition. Even if decoupling is occurring when measured per unit of economic output, it may not be happening fast enough to overcome increases in the total size of GDP. This is the difference between 'relative' and 'absolute' decoupling. Relative decoupling of materials from GDP occurs when, over time, material use per dollar of GDP declines (that is, material intensity) but total material use does not. Absolute decoupling occurs when material intensity declines faster than GDP grows, so that total material use also declines.

Although absolute decoupling must also involve relative decoupling, there are several reasons why relative decoupling does not automatically lead to absolute decoupling. The first reason is known as the Jevons paradox, an insight put forward by William S. Jevons in his study of Britain's coal industry. Jevons found that improvements in the efficiency of steam engines which reduced operating costs induced increases in coal consumption. '*It is a confusion of ideas to suppose that the economical use of fuel is equivalent to diminished consumption. The very contrary is the truth*' (Jevons 1865, Chapter VII.3, italics in the original). The Jevons paradox, or 'rebound effect' as it is now called, is a pervasive relationship that explains much of the disconnect between relative and absolute decoupling. Improvements in efficiency brought about by technological advance that reduce material requirements per unit of output can result in lower prices. If the lower prices induce a sufficient increase in sales, the overall effect of the improved efficiency can be to *increase* the total use of the materials affected by the efficiency improvements. At the very least, this response to efficiency improvements can substantially reduce the expected reduction in materials use if they are calculated without considering the rebound effect. In some circumstances when price elasticities are high, the rebound effect can eliminate the resource savings from efficiency improvements or even result in an absolute increase in resource use, as Jevons discovered 150 years ago (Sorrell 2007; Buhl 2014; Magee and Devezas 2017).

In addition to the rebound effect, two other factors explain the disconnect between efficiency improvements and absolute reductions in throughput over time: increases in population and increases in consumption per person. Taken together they can increase total materials and energy use even while improvements in efficiency reduce material and energy intensities. This is apparent at the global level from Figure 5.3, which shows that between 1970 and 2015 world real GDP increased 250 percent and population doubled. Prior to 2000 global material intensity declined by 25 percent, reflecting a modest level of relative decoupling of material extraction from growth in GDP measured in physical units per dollar and comprising minerals, fossil fuels, metal ores and biomass. But after 2000 global material intensity began to increase, and since then the

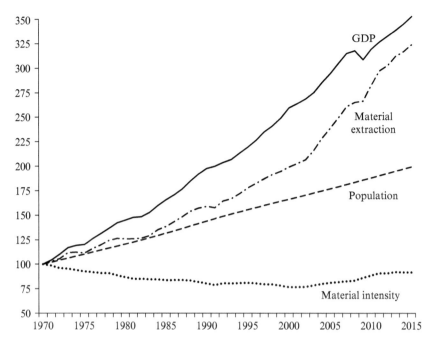

*Source:*   UNEP IRP Global Material Flows Database, available at http://www.resourcepanel.
org/global-material-flows-database.

*Figure 5.3     Trends in global resource extraction (minerals, fossil fuels,
                metal ores and biomass), GDP and material intensity
                1970–2015 (1970 = 100)*

rate of growth in material extraction has been rising faster than the rate
of growth of global GDP. Not only did relative decoupling cease at the
turn of the century, it reversed direction. So far, rather than decoupling
materials from economic growth, the 21st century has witnessed an
unprecedented period of relative and absolute *re-coupling* of material
extraction and global GDP.

> [G]lobal material productivity has declined since about the year 2000 and the
> global economy now needs more materials per unit of GDP than it did at the
> turn of the century. What may seem counter-intuitive has been caused by a large
> shift of economic activity from very material-efficient economies such as Japan,
> the Republic of Korea and Europe to the much less material-efficient economies
> of China, India and Southeast Asia. This has resulted in growing environmental
> pressure per unit of economic activity and works against the hypothesis of
> decoupling – achieving more with less. (UNEP 2016a, p. 26)

Taking an even longer historical perspective in the relationship between resource extraction and global economic growth, Vaclav Smil (2014) provides a comprehensive, detailed account of decoupling resource extraction starting with the first industrial revolution to the present day. Smil provides plenty of evidence and numerous examples of relative decoupling and he expects it to continue well into the future. However, he is very skeptical about the prospects for absolute decoupling, and yet this is what those who maintain that growth can continue indefinitely rely on. Concluding his book, Smil writes: 'to stress the key point for the last time, these impressive achievements of relative dematerialization have not translated into any absolute declines of material use on the global scale' (2014, p. 180).[4]

He goes on to say that:

> the global gap between the haves (approximately 1.5 billion people in 2013) and the have-nots (more than 5.5 billion in 2013) remains so large that even if the aspirations of the materially deprived four fifths of humanity were to reach only a third of the average living standard that now prevails in affluent countries, the world would be looking at the continuation of aggregate material growth for generations to come. (2014, p. 180)

So much for global decoupling that sees material use declining while economic growth continues. It's a seductive idea but one that remains a future possibility rather than an historical fact. The record at the national level is more encouraging. Smil observes that, 'Clearly, there is no recent evidence of any widespread and substantial dematerialization – be it in absolute or . . . per capita terms – even among the world's richest economies' (2014, p. 142). However, he does point to Germany and the United Kingdom as examples of a few countries where 'overall material inputs have stabilized or have even slightly declined' (2014, p. 142). Smil acknowledges that this promising result may be due to changes in trade patterns without further exploring this possibility, yet this is exactly what other research studies have shown. The shift in manufacturing from industrialized to developing countries has entailed a shift in the location of where materials enter the interconnected economies of the global economic system, rather than any absolute reduction in global quantities.

Tommy Wiedmann and colleagues (Wiedmann et al. 2015) traced the material inputs (that is, biomass, construction minerals, fossil fuels and metal ores) embedded in the consumption of 186 countries from 1990 to 2008. Their findings highlight the connection between international trade and the absence of absolute decoupling: 'As wealth grows, countries tend to reduce their domestic portion of materials extraction through international trade, whereas the overall mass of material consumption generally increases. With every 10% increase in gross domestic product, the average national MF[5] increases by 6%' (Wiedmann et al. 2015, p. 6271).

Wiedmann and colleagues observe that:

> The EU-27 [27 member countries of the European Union], the OECD, the United States, Japan, and the United Kingdom have grown economically while keeping DMC [direct material consumption] at bay or even reducing it, leading to large apparent gains in GDP/DMC resource productivity. In all cases, however, the MF has kept pace with increases in GDP and no improvements in resource productivity at all are observed when measured as the GDP/MF. (Wiedmann et al. 2015, p. 6273)

These findings are illustrated in Figure 5.4, where from 1990 to 2008 the material footprint of OECD countries in total moved in step with GDP, while their direct material consumption showed relative decoupling (and absolute decoupling during recessions).

The most reasonable conclusion to draw from studies such as those of Smil and Wiedmann et al. is that since there is very little precedent for absolute decoupling there is no foundation of experience on which to base

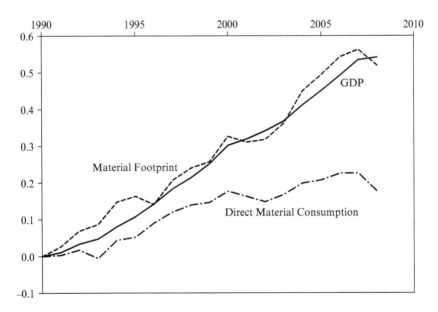

*Source:* Wiedmann et al. (2015).

*Figure 5.4 Relative change in GDP, direct material consumption and material footprint in OECD countries 1990–2008*

a realistic expectation that absolute decoupling of material use over the long term is compatible with global economic growth.

But does it matter if reductions in material use per unit of GDP have failed so far to reduce the absolute levels of material inputs to the economy? This can be true while at the same time the quantities of material moved by humans remains insignificant in relation to what happens naturally, without human intervention. If this were true it might reduce concern about the environmental impacts of resource extraction though not about overall resource supply. And at this aggregate level of analysis it is the environmental impacts of resource extraction that are of greater concern than the availability of materials (with the possible exception of fossil fuels, which we will examine in a moment). A study by Klee and Graedel (2004) provides some perspective on this issue. They examined information on the cycles of 77 of the 92 elements in the periodic table and found that 'human activities dominate 54 elements, and nature dominates 23 elements' (2004, p. 77). 'Human action dominates the cycles of the elements whose usual forms are highly insoluble, nature those that are highly soluble' (2004, p. 69). This is a remarkable finding and shows that humans move greater quantities of a majority of elements than nature. As Klee and Graedel correctly observe, 'An important caveat with respect to our dominance determinations is that they apply only to flows, not to impacts' (2004, p. 80). Nonetheless, it would be foolhardy to remain complacent about material flows in light of these remarkable quantitative estimates of human-induced material flows, especially since the environmental impacts associated with obtaining increasing quantities of materials, sometimes from difficult and/or environmentally significant locations, may restrict their supply.

### 5.3.1 Critical Materials

So far, we have considered materials (including fossil fuels) in the aggregate without paying much attention to specific minerals and metals. We will leave fossil fuels until the next section. Here we consider materials other than fuels that have been identified as critical for continued economic growth in developed economies.

Critical materials are defined as 'minerals for which the risk of disruptions in supply is relatively high and for which supply distortions will be associated with large economic impacts' (Coulomb et al. 2015, p. 3). The study from which this definition is taken analyzed information on supply risks to OECD countries for 51 minerals. Supply risks were measured in terms of the substitutability of each mineral in specific uses, recycling rates, and the concentration of production in countries considered to be relatively politically unstable. Minerals used heavily in a sector that constitutes a large part of the economy are considered economically important. Geological constraints leading to physical scarcity were not considered a source of supply risk either at present or projecting forward to 2030, though it was noted that 'the exhaustion of economically competitive minerals deposits in industrialized countries has made supplies increasingly dependent on the political stability of mineral-rich emerging economies' (Coulomb et al. 2015, p. 8). The OECD study did not look beyond 2030 when more generalized physical scarcity resulting in escalating supply costs could become a more significant factor. Potential disruptions in supply were attributed to a combination of production concentration and geopolitical risks, which is typical of these kinds of studies (European Commission 2010; 2014; Graedel et al. 2012).

Figure 5.5 shows the 51 minerals examined in the Coulomb et al. study classified according to economic importance and supply risk. The 21 minerals scoring above 1 on the supply risk index and above 0.05 on the economic importance index were identified as critical as of 2015. They are

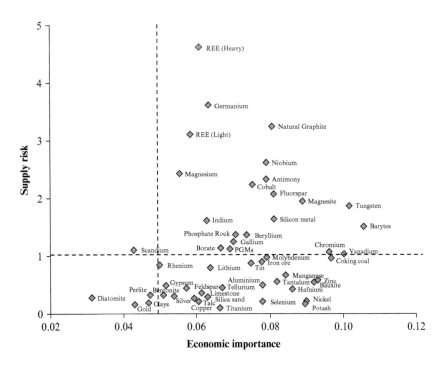

*Source:*   Coulomb et al. (2015, p. 23).

*Figure 5.5   Critical minerals in OECD countries in 2015*

located in the top right quadrant in Figure 5.5. The ten minerals with the highest supply risk in order are: rare Earth elements (heavy), germanium, natural graphite, rare Earth elements (light), niobium, magnesium, cobalt, fluorspar, magnesite, tungsten (see Coulomb et al. 2015, Table 4 for more details). The top ten most economically important minerals to OECD countries in 2015 were: barytes, tungsten, vanadium, coking coal, chromium, zinc, bauxite, nickel, potash, magnesite. Of these, only magnesite lies within the top ten on supply risk.

Some examples of where these economically important minerals are used include barytes, of which over three-quarters is used in drilling fluids in oil and gas exploration; tungsten is a metal with a wide range of uses, the largest of which is as tungsten carbide in cemented carbides, which are wear-resistant materials used by the metalworking, mining and construction industries; vanadium is used in automobiles and machinery as an alloy. It is also used together with aluminium in jet engines and high-speed airframes (Coulomb et al. 2015, p. 22).

Within the group of OECD countries there is some variation among the situation facing individual members, particularly with respect to the economic importance of minerals. Apart from barytes, which is heavily used in the US in oil and gas drilling fluids, the economic importance of the materials considered in the Coulomb et al. study is very similar in the USA and the OECD as a whole, reflecting the large size of the US economy relative to the rest of the OECD (Coulomb et al. 2015, p. 24). Japan is different in that most minerals are more economically important in Japan than for the OECD in total. The same is true, though less so, for the EU countries compared to the OECD (2015, p. 25).

Of considerable concern to the OECD and the EU is their dependence on emerging and developing countries for supplies of these critical minerals and the risks of supply interruptions for political reasons. Figure 5.6 shows the percentage of global supply of critical materials identified in the Report to the European Commission (European Commission 2014), which corresponds very closely to the critical minerals identified by Coulomb et al. for the OECD countries. China stands out as a supplier of 18 of 20 critical materials identified in the EU study, accounting for 49 percent of global supplies. The USA lies in second place, with only 9 percent of global supplies of these critical materials.

It is not easy to assess how the situation will change in the future with respect to critical materials for advanced economies. Much depends on development and deployment of new technologies, new discoveries of mineral deposits, the prices of minerals and the extent to which new reserves are established and new extraction technologies are introduced in response to rising prices. By making assumptions about these and other

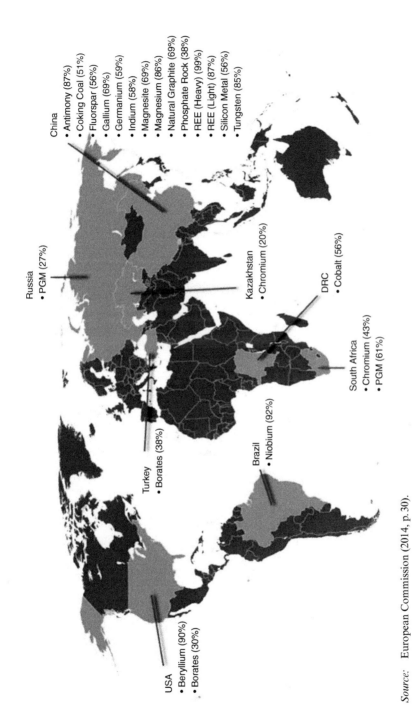

*Source:* European Commission (2014, p.30).

*Figure 5.6   Major suppliers of EU critical materials*

factors, including a stronger role for the physical availability of reserves, the OECD study considered the situation in 2030 for critical materials. It was 'found that the supply risk attending to barytes, borate, phosphate rock and molybdenum . . . increases' and that '. . . economic development along a baseline scenario that assumes continued reliance on fossil fuels for energy does not change significantly the pattern of economic importance of the various minerals concerned' (Coulomb et al. 2015, p. 45). The report goes on to say that, 'future work should evaluate whether this also holds true for a pathway towards green, low-carbon growth . . . since many environmental technologies depend crucially on rare minerals' (Coulomb et al. 2015, p. 3).

Two conclusions emerge from these studies of critical materials as seen from the perspective of developed countries. One is that the supply situation for materials critical to economic growth in OECD countries is not of immediate concern, though circumstances could change in the future. The other is that there is a degree of unease in these countries about the possibility of supply interruptions that stimulated the studies referred to here and others in the literature. The inclusion of environmental risk in the earlier EU study (European Commission 2010) but omitted in the later one in 2014 is telling. Environmental risk does not, in this case, refer to possible impacts on the environment and human health from the extraction, processing, use, recycling and disposal of materials as it normally does. Instead it refers to 'the risks that measures might be taken by countries with the intention of protecting the environment and by so doing endangering the supply of raw materials to the European Union' (European Commission 2010, p. 29). Whether this kind of intervention designed to protect the environment and health in the poorer exporting countries is captured by the term 'supply distortion' as used in Coulomb et al.'s definition of critical minerals is hard to say. But it's a disturbing possibility if it means that developed countries were to take steps to impede efforts by developing countries to protect their environment by claiming to the World Trade Organization, for example, that such measures are protectionist policies in disguise (Kogan 2004). This could be a real possibility given the conclusion reached by Graedel and colleagues that 'for a dozen different metals, the potential substitutes for their major uses are either inadequate or appear not to exist at all. Further, for not 1 of the 62 metals are exemplary substitutes available for all major uses' (Graedel et al. 2015, p. 6295). If this is correct, then the prospect is very real that supplies of some critical materials will become a significant constraint on economic growth if they are not already.

## 5.4   THE SPECIAL CASE OF ENERGY

In Chapter 2 we explained that unlike materials, which can be reused and recycled, though with some losses along the way, energy cannot. Energy can be used more or less efficiently such as when LED lights replace incandescent lights converting a much greater proportion of electricity into light rather than heat. But once used, the energy cannot be captured and reused to perform the same task. The quantity of energy used in any process remains unchanged, but its capacity to do work necessarily declines. This is an unavoidable implication of the second law of thermodynamics. Consequently, just to sustain a constant level of any economic activity with a given technology requires a continuous supply of new energy. Improvements in technology can lessen the requirement for energy to provide the same service but cannot eliminate it altogether. Also, the rebound effect can reduce, eliminate or more than negate the energy savings from improved technology, but no matter the efficiency of a technology, its continuing operation will require energy from new sources.

Throughout almost all of human history people have relied exclusively on renewable sources of energy: wood, wind, water and draft animals. It was not until about 1880 that coal overtook wood as the single most important source of energy globally although most of the coal used was concentrated in a few countries, with Britain being the leader. The age of fossil fuels began with coal and coal remained the single most important source of fossil fuel energy worldwide until the mid-1960s when it was surpassed by oil. This was 100 years after the first successful oil well was drilled in Pennsylvania by Edwin Drake, which shows how long a transition from one form of energy to another can take. Today coal is still used in large amounts for smelting and for generating electricity. Its use in generating electricity, though expected to decline in proportional terms, is still projected to increase in absolute terms at 0.8 percent/year to 2040 for electricity generation and slightly more slowly in total (US Energy Information Administration 2016b).

We are living in the age of fossil fuels, with nearly 90 percent of energy coming from oil, coal and natural gas (US Energy Information Administration 2016b, Table A.2). We are also living in the electricity age but much of the electricity we use is generated from the combustion of fossil fuels, mostly coal, and is considered secondary energy. Nuclear and hydroelectric power plants generate electricity as primary energy comparable with fossil fuels, but in 2014, they contributed only 7.2 percent of global primary energy (International Energy Agency 2016a). Electricity from wind and solar also counts as primary energy but their contribution worldwide, while growing fast, is still very small (International Energy Agency 2016a).

The transition from wood to coal to oil and natural gas, coupled with the generation of electricity, was driven by a number of factors, with price, convenience and versatility as the most important. The shortage of wood for making charcoal led to the discovery and use of coal for smelting in early 18th-century Britain. Coal proved cheaper and more convenient than wood, and the age of steam power was based on it. Oil is easier to extract from the Earth than coal and it is more convenient to use, especially in transportation. It made possible a completely new range of transport technologies from the automobile, where there were alternative fuels, to the jet plane, where there were none. Natural gas is even better than oil in some uses such as space heating, where it is more compatible with air conditioning, and as an alternative to coal for generating electricity, especially when variable supply is required. Coal remains important particularly for generating base-load electricity, especially in the USA and China, largely because of its availability and low price.

The early promise of nuclear energy as a cheap source of electricity has not been fulfilled. Nuclear energy continues to be promoted as clean, reliable and affordable, and part of the solution to reducing greenhouse gas emissions (World Nuclear Association 2016), but these claims are disputed (Smith 2006). Nuclear energy is not cheap and, in view of the Fukushima Daiichi nuclear disaster in 2011, doubts about its safety continue to impede its widespread adoption. As of 2016, Australia, Austria, Denmark, Greece, Malaysia and New Zealand have no nuclear power stations and remain opposed to nuclear power. Germany, Italy, Spain and Switzerland are phasing out nuclear power (Wikipedia 2016). The problem of safe, very long-term disposal of high-level radioactive waste has not been solved, and the deep geological repositories that are at various stages of planning, design and construction in different countries remain controversial. The links to weapons production and the threat of terrorism to nuclear facilities and the movement of used nuclear fuel are further obstacles to the expanded use of nuclear energy (Pembina Institute 2007). Also, the potential for electricity from nuclear generating stations to replace fossil fuels in transportation directly or in the production of hydrogen is limited by the requirement for changes in infrastructure and energy-using equipment. Cars running on gasoline cannot switch to electricity. Entire new fleets of vehicles and delivery systems would be required, which is possible but very costly. (See Chapter 11 for more on this.)

### 5.4.1   Peak Oil

Peak oil is the proposition that global production of oil from conventional sources will cease to increase and will start declining possibly after a plateau of some years. Conventional crude oil is 'petroleum found in liquid form, flowing naturally or capable of being pumped without further processing or dilution' (Canadian Association of Petroleum Producers 2006). The idea of peak oil goes back to the 1950s when M. King Hubbert, a geologist with Shell Oil and then the US Geological Survey, analyzed oil supply from the US lower 48 states. He forecast that oil production from these states would peak in 1970 (Hubbert 1956). At the time, few people paid attention to his analysis. Not much changed for a quarter of a century even though his forecast proved remarkably accurate. Then in the 1990s, when crude oil prices started trending upwards, new voices were heard promoting the idea of peak oil based on Hubbert's earlier analysis for the USA, but this time as a global proposition.

In the first few years of this century there was a lively debate about peak oil. Some 'peakists', mostly geologists or those strongly influenced by them such as Campbell (2005), Deffeyes (2005), Kunstler (2005), Simmons (2005) and Heinberg (2006) believed that the peak had already been reached or was imminent. Still others such as the United States Geological Survey (2006) thought it was a matter of a couple of decades before peak oil would be upon us. Though differing in the timing of the peak, they all relied on data about discoveries, reserves and production measured in barrels of oil to forecast world oil production from conventional sources, concluding that it will peak in the first decades of the 21st century, and then decline. This would cause the price of oil to rise, threatening widespread economic and social disruption. The views of these 21st-century peakists were seemingly reinforced by the substantial increase in the price of crude oil that went from US$20/bbl in 2001 to US$145/bbl in July 2008, plunging sharply to US$30/bbl in December of that year as the financial markets crashed and the global economy went into a major recession from which it has still not fully recovered. Hamilton (2009) and others attributed the Great Recession of 2008/2009, though not exclusively, to the escalation of oil prices that preceded it.

The debate about peak oil has receded in the past few years because of the largely unanticipated increase in hydraulic fracturing or 'fracking' that has provided access to 'tight' oil or shale oil. Shale oil is crude oil contained in petroleum-bearing formations that must be fractured with chemicals at high pressure and brought to the surface. Also, the wider use of horizontal drilling allowing wells to be drilled at a sharp angle has increased access to oil that was previously considered uneconomic. These technologies have had a significant impact on oil production, particularly in the USA. Combined with a slowdown in economic growth and the rising popularity of renewable energy alternatives, starting in 2014 the world experienced a surplus of oil that depressed the price of crude oil, which at the time of writing is only now beginning to recover. These experiences seemed to vindicate the views of the critics of peak oil (Deming 2000; Dunkerley 2006; Lynch 1998; Watkins 2006; Beckerman 2003) who were mostly economists. They argued that any scarcity of oil, actual or anticipated, would be reflected in higher prices. The higher prices would stimulate the search for new deposits, the development of new oil exploration and extraction technologies, greater conservation and a switch to alternative sources of energy.

Both sides of the peak oil debate argued their case with great passion and ten years ago it was hard to find a balanced appraisal of the different points of view. One such appraisal came from Vaclav Smil (2003a), a leading energy analyst who had written about energy issues for many years and continues to do so. Another came from Hirsch et al. (2005) in a report sponsored by the US Department of Energy. Hirsch et al. concluded by saying that:

> the problem of the peaking of world conventional oil production is unlike any yet faced by modern industrial society. The challenges and uncertainties need to be much better understood. Technologies exist to mitigate the problem. Timely, aggressive risk management will be essential. (2005, p. 7)

They did not venture an opinion on the likelihood of such action. In the first edition of this book I wrote that:

> The debate about peak oil at the global level will continue for a few more years at least. In the end, the data will determine who is or was right. If oil production from conventional sources continues to rise into the next decade and beyond, then the peak oil alarmists who predicted a downturn some time this decade will have been proven wrong. If the peak does occur this decade then they will be proven right. (Victor 2008, p. 62)

So what do the data show? Figure 5.7 presents data on the global production of crude oil and condensates[6] from all sources from January 1994 to January 2014. It shows that global oil production from all sources plateaued at around 73 million barrels per day between 2005 and 2010, consistent with the views of the peakists who believed that peak oil production had been reached. Subsequently, global production began to rise again, surpassing 76 million barrels in January 2014, confounding the views of the peakists and confirming the views of their critics, or so it might seem. However, a closer inspection of Figure 5.7 reveals that 'all of the growth in global liquid fuel supply has come from unconventional and low grade sources of supply' (Mearns 2014). So in a sense, both sides in the peak oil debate are supported by the data. The peakists can claim

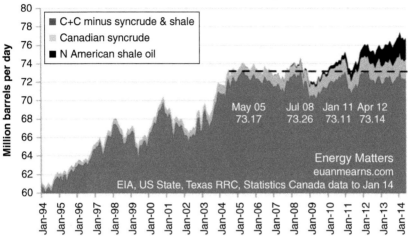

*Source:* Mearns (2014).

*Figure 5.7   Global production of oil January 1994–January 2014*

that the production of oil from conventional sources has indeed leveled off. On the other hand, the critics can point to the expansion of output from unconventional sources such as the oil sands of Alberta and fracking in the USA and elsewhere, as evidence of how higher prices help alleviate scarcity by encouraging the development and deployment of new technologies.

Commenting on the peak oil debate, Miller and Sorrell (2014) state that 'few debates are more important, more contentious, more wide-ranging' (2014, p.1). After a careful review of the different positions and the available evidence, they stand by the conclusion of an earlier review that 'a sustained decline in global conventional production appears probable before 2030 and there is a significant risk of this beginning before 2020' (2014, p.17). They go on to say that 'on current evidence the inclusion of tight oil resources appears unlikely to significantly affect this conclusion, partly because the resource base appears relatively modest' (2014, p.19).

The other main source of 'unconventional oil' is the oil sands, which already contribute a significant amount to global oil supplies. But even with optimistic assumptions about further expansion, the Canadian oil sands will deliver less than 6 percent of the IEA's projection of all-liquids produced in 2030 (Miller and Sorrell 2014). Miller and Sorrell consider the likely contribution of other sources of liquid fuels, such as biofuels and liquids from gas and coal to be even more limited as substitutes for conventional oil. For environmental reasons, as much as reasons of constrained supply, they look to demand-side measures and a transition to alternative sources of energy as the most promising way forward.

### 5.4.2   Making an Energy Transition

The rationale for making deliberate efforts to achieve an energy transition to a system based largely on supplies from renewable resources and demand-side measures to reduce energy consumption rests on three propositions:

1.   supplies of fossil fuels, especially oil, are limited and need to be replaced; and/or
2.   the environmental risks associated with fossil fuel extraction, processing and combustion pose increasingly unacceptable risks;
3.   left to itself, the market system driven by private interests will not make the transition or will make it too slowly.

Either of the first two propositions justifies the need for an energy transition though most contributors believe both are relevant. The third proposition is necessary to justify deliberate public policy to bring about an energy transition. It is based on the view that the market system as it exists in contemporary capitalism cannot be relied upon to make the transition either at all or fast enough.

Speaking of the transition away from oil, Smil comments that:

> If the proponents of early exhaustion are correct, this would be the first time in history when the world would be facing a permanently declining supply of the dominant fuel: transitions from wood to coal and from coal to oil were not brought about by global exhaustion of the substituted resource, but by lower prices and better qualities of new fuels. (Smil 2003a, p. 195)

Smil might also have added that it would be the first time that an energy transition would be away from non-renewable sources back to renewable sources, though this direction is not certain. Some see a greater reliance on nuclear energy as a viable alternative to declining supplies of oil. In addition to cost, performance, long approvals and construction times, and the environmental and terrorist risks specific to nuclear technologies, it would require a massive and expensive change in our energy-using infrastructure to substitute electricity from nuclear power plants for oil, gas and coal. The same is true for electricity generated from renewable sources such as solar, wind, small hydro and geothermal. Their environmental impacts are far less than those of fossil fuel and nuclear plants but they do not offer a viable alternative to oil used in transportation without a massive investment in equipment and infrastructure. Nor are their environmental impacts, especially if implemented on a large scale, trivial (Union of Concerned Scientists n.d.). Renewable alternatives for oil such as biofuels are easier to substitute for oil but present their own problems. For example, ethanol produced from corn can be costly and require significant inputs of energy, pesticides and fertilizers. They also divert agricultural land from food production, pitching the interests of automobile owners against poorer people in need of food (Brown 2006). Ethanol produced from corn has come under especially heavy criticism for economic and environmental reasons:

> Ethanol production in the United States using corn is heavily subsidized by public tax money. Numerous studies have concluded that ethanol production does not enhance energy security, is not an economical fuel, and does not ensure clean air. Furthermore, its production uses land suitable for crop production . . . Ethanol production using sugarcane is more energy efficient than that produced using corn; however, more fossil fuel energy is still required to produce a liter of ethanol than the energy output in ethanol. (Pimental et al. 2002)

Other sources of biofuels such as wood waste and switch grass are preferable from an environmental standpoint but they are also more costly using technologies available today (Hirsch et al. 2005).

A transition from non-renewable energy sources to renewable ones will have to confront the fact that the former are stock-flow resources and many of the latter are fund-service resources (Daly and Farley 2004, pp. 70–72). Stock-flow resources such as minerals and fossil fuels are rival in consumption and usually excludable, meaning that legal ownership is recognized and enforceable. The market system works best under these circumstances. The stocks of resources and the flows obtained from extraction can be owned and traded. Hotelling (1931) explained how, under assumed conditions of competition, the depletion of these resources would be reflected in a gradual increase in the net price (that is, price minus current extraction cost) of the resource. In the absence of competition and with imperfect foresight, very different circumstances can arise but they do not entirely undermine the role of markets in conserving stock-flow resources.

Fund-service resources such as solar energy and wind energy are for all practical purposes non-rival in consumption and non-excludable. The sun is a fund that is not itself consumed when the service it provides, that is, solar energy, is used. Neither the sun nor the solar energy it generates are excludable. They cannot be owned and traded, and the energy is non-rival in consumption. Anyone can install a solar panel or a wind turbine and capture energy from the sun or wind without paying for the energy source.

This is quite different from users of fossil fuels who must pay for the fuel if they wish to use it as well as the devices such as cars, trucks and furnaces, which convert the fuel into useful energy.

Fortunes have been made and continue to be made by private corporations and governments from the exploitation of fossil fuels. There is no money to be made out of solar energy itself, only from the devices that capture it for use, such as photovoltaic cells and wind turbines and the electricity they generate. The manufacture of these devices is a very different business from the extraction and refining of fossil fuels so it should be no surprise that corporations, whether government or privately owned, have been very slow to move into renewable energy (CBC 2016). The financial returns simply don't compare. Better to sow seeds of doubt about climate change and impede policy initiatives designed to move economies away from fossil fuels as documented by Hoggan (2009) than become major suppliers of renewable energy technologies. That will likely be left to other corporations. The transition away from fossil fuels to the large-scale use of renewable energy is not a direction that the market will easily lead us. It will require determined action by government through a combination of direct investment, financial incentives and regulations to make the transition.

There is considerable disagreement about the technical and economic feasibility of making the kind of changes outlined here. In a widely cited paper, Delucchi and Jacobson (2011) conclude that:

> a large-scale wind, water and solar energy system [WWS] can reliably supply the world's needs . . . at reasonable cost . . . the obstacles . . . are primarily political, not technological . . . With sensible broad-based policies and social changes, it may be possible to convert 25% of the current energy system to WWS in 10–15 years and 85% in 20–30 years, and 100% by 2050. Absent that clear direction, the conversion will take longer. (2011, pp. 1178–9)

In their review of the Jacobson and Delucchi paper Clack and colleagues wrote: 'We find that their analysis involves errors, inappropriate methods, and implausible assumptions. Their study does not provide credible evidence for rejecting the conclusions of previous analyses that point to the benefits of considering a broad portfolio of energy system options' (Clack et al. 2017). Jacobson and Delucchi (2017) responded to this critique and the heated debate between them is likely to continue for some time.

Smil (2014) provided an assessment of the feasibility and speed of a transition from fossil fuels to renewables by looking at previous energy transitions. Figure 5.8 shows how long it took various sources of energy to contribute a significant percentage of global demand after reaching a threshold of 5 percent. Modern renewables (excluding hydropower) contributed just less than 5 percent in 2015 and though increasing fast,

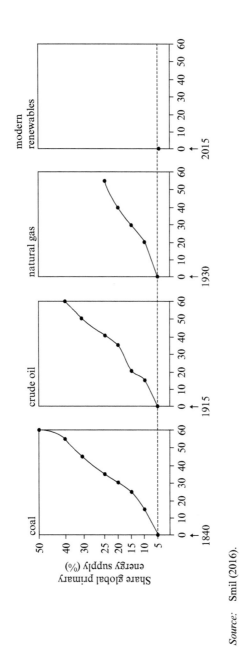

*Source:*    Smil (2016).

*Figure 5.8    Years after energy source begins supplying 5% of global demand*

have a very long way to go. Smil says that: 'perhaps the most misunderstood aspect of energy transitions is their speed ... Turning around the world's fossil-fuel-based energy system is a truly gargantuan task ... It is impossible to displace this supersystem in a decade or two – or five, for that matter' (2014, p. 52).

Sovacool (2016) provides a more positive assessment of the history of energy transitions than Smil and the possibility of a relatively speedy transition in the future. Clearly there is plenty of room for debate about the past and the future.

Another perspective on the potential for renewable energy sources to displace fossil fuels and the speed at which this can be done comes from the work of Charlie Hall and his colleagues on the energy return on energy invested 'EROI' (Hall et al. 2014). 'Energy return on investment (EROI) is a means of measuring the quality of various fuels by calculating the ratio between the energy delivered by a particular fuel to society and the energy invested in the capture and delivery of this energy' (2014, p. 142). In simple terms, EROI measures how much energy must be used in order to deliver useful energy for society. Figure 5.9 shows the relationship between the EROI of different sources of energy and percentage of energy obtained that is available for use. It is this net energy that the non-energy sectors of the economy rely on to function.

Figure 5.9, first drawn by Euan Mearns (2016), has been termed the 'net energy cliff', a phrase coined by Nate Hagens. It shows that, generally speaking, the oil and gas fields that were exploited first had EROIs as high

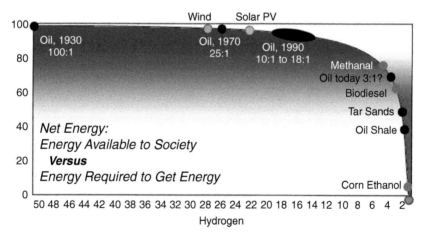

*Source:*   http://www.jpods.com/metrics.

*Figure 5.9   The net energy cliff*

as 100:1, meaning that 99 percent of the energy obtained from the fuels was net energy available for other uses. Other conventional sources of oil and natural gas have lower EROIs, but even at an EROI of 25, 96 percent of the energy from the fuels is available for other uses. As Figure 5.9 shows, the picture changes dramatically as the EROI declines beyond about 8:1. At an EROI of 8 (for example, lower efficiency photovoltaic cells), the net energy falls to 87.5 percent, at an EROI of 5, net energy is 80 percent and at 2 it is 50 percent (for example, corn-based ethanol).

Commenting on the EROI of renewable energy sources, Hall et al. (2014) write:

> Alternative renewable energies lack many of the undesirable characteristics of fossil fuels, including direct productions of carbon dioxide and other 'pollutants', but also lack many of the highly desirable traits of non-renewable fossil fuels. Specifically, renewable energy sources: are not sufficiently 'energy dense', tend to be intermittent, lack transportability, most have relatively low EROI values (especially when corrections are made for intermittency), and currently, lack the infrastructure that is required to meet current societal demands . . . It would appear that a shift from non-renewable to renewable energy sources would result in declines in both the quantity and EROI values of the principle energies used for economic activity . . . If any resolution to these problems is possible it is probable that it would have to come at least as much from an adjustment of society's aspirations for increased material affluence and an increase in willingness to share as from technology. (2014, pp. 150–51)

As with all metrics that try to condense very complex relationships into a single number there are complications that can arise from imperfect and incomplete data sources, measurement boundaries and, especially in the case of energy, differences in quality (Hall et al. 2014). However, the aggregation problems with EROI pale in comparison with those associated with GDP, which is used to measure the success of economies around the world. EROI is a convenient and easy to understand metric that reminds us that access to useful energy requires energy expenditures. Just like market prices, energy prices expressed in terms of EROI can become too expensive to afford.

### 5.4.3 The Energy–Emissions Trap[7]

The declining EROI of energy sources is a serious threat to sustained economic growth. As more and more energy is used to obtain energy, less and less is available for the rest of the economy. And since all major sources of non-fossil fuel energy (that is, solar, wind, hydro, nuclear) are capital intensive, as is carbon capture and storage, there is a real prospect that the energy sector will absorb an increasing proportion of capital investment, leaving less for other sectors of the economy. This has led some analysts to argue that declining EROI will dampen, if not entirely eliminate, economic growth (Murphy 2013). Sers and Victor (2018) refer to this as an energy trap facing advanced economies in particular with their high dependence on imported fossil fuels. But that is not all. The majority of greenhouse gas emissions that are causing climate change come from the supply and use of energy from fossil fuel. To reduce the risk of catastrophic climate change it will be necessary for cumulative global greenhouse gas emissions not to exceed 2900 gigatonnes of $CO_2$ emissions (IPCC 2014b). As of 2017 approximately 70 percent of this 'carbon budget' has been used up by emissions dating back to 1750. Staying within the carbon budget will require a more rapid transition from fossil fuels to renewable sources of energy (with a possible contribution from additional nuclear energy) than necessitated by the declining EROI of fossil fuels. This is the emissions trap.

The question arises as to whether the global economy, and its constituent national and regional economies, is capable of transitioning to renewable sources of energy slowly enough to avoid the energy trap and fast enough to avoid the emissions trap. This would be green growth, at least with respect to climate change. To address this question Sers and Victor (2018) developed EETRAP, a system dynamics model that generates internally consistent paths over 34 years for GDP, gross and net energy, investment, GHG emissions annually and cumulative based on different assumptions about: the rate of investment in renewable energy, EROIs for fossil fuels and renewables, improvements in energy efficiency, and the lead time for additions to renewable energy capacity. Based on values of these variables derived from the literature it seems very unlikely that a 3 percent rate of growth in global GDP can be sustained to mid-century while meeting the carbon budget.

A scenario that does meet the carbon budget is illustrated in the six panels of Figure 5.10. In the first panel GHG cumulative emissions rise from 2016 to 2050, peaking below the carbon budget constraint. Energy demand and supply by renewable and non-renewable generation are shown in the second panel, with overall energy demand indexed to 100. Energy from non-renewable fossil fuels is phased out by 2050. The third panel shows the EROIs for fossil fuels and variable renewables such as photovoltaic solar and wind. The EROI for fossil fuels declines slightly as more difficult sources of fossil fuels are accessed. The EROI for variable renewables declines significantly as a result of the increasing energetic costs associated with grid storage and flexibility. In this scenario, the EROI for variable renewables declines to 5 by 2050. The EROI for non-variable renewables (not shown), for example large hydro, is assumed to remain constant at 84 in accordance with the value in Hall et al. (2014). The fourth panel shows the trajectories for output (GDP) and its growth rate, with the latter falling from 3 percent to zero or less between 2030 and 2050. Panel 5 shows investment as a percentage of output in renewables, the fossil fuel sector, and the total energy investment rate, which is the sum of both. Renewable investment increases from just above zero to about 15 percent of output, drawing investment away from other activities. The sixth panel shows the ratio of net energy in the economy to total energy use in a given year; this ratio gives the fraction of total energy used in the economy that can be allocated to productive use. Panel 6 shows clearly that the long-term consequence of transitioning to lower EROI renewables is a declining fraction of net useful energy in the economy. As energy is increasingly generated by lower EROI renewables, less net energy is available. In this scenario, the energy–emissions trap is avoided at the expense of a dramatic reduction in the rate of economic growth.

The scenario illustrated in Figure 5.10 is only that, a scenario. It reflects assumptions about EROI which could well prove faulty, either too low or too high. If they are too low then the transition from fossil fuels to renewables might be accomplished without eliminating the rate of economic growth as shown in panel 4. But the opposite is also possible and the decline in the rate of growth could be even greater. The real point of the scenario is not to predict what will happen but to draw attention to the fact that there are two dimensions to the energy–emissions trap, an energy one described by EROI and the challenge of obtaining sufficient net energy to sustain economic activities, and an environmental one: the pressing need to reduce greenhouse gases emissions to avoid catastrophic climate change. Navigating between the energy and emissions aspects of the trap is no easy task and it is made even more difficult by the problem of stranded assets (Fullerton 2013; ESRB 2016). There is a very real possibility that in order to avoid the emissions trap it will be necessary to leave vast quantities of fossil fuels in the ground that could profitably be extracted. These proven reserves of coal, oil and natural gas, which energy corporations, nations and sub-national states count as financially valuable assets, would be rendered worthless, and the related extraction and transportation infrastructure too, stranded, with dramatic financial and economic repercussions. In 2012 the International Energy Agency warned that 'no more than one-third of proven reserves of fossil fuels can be consumed prior to 2050 if the world is to achieve the 2°C goal, unless carbon capture and storage technology is widely deployed' (International Energy Agency 2012, p. 35). The prospects for carbon capture and storage are perhaps less encouraging now than they were in 2012 (IEA 2016d, p. 11) so the problem of stranded assets is another dimension of the energy–emissions trap that will be difficult to avoid.

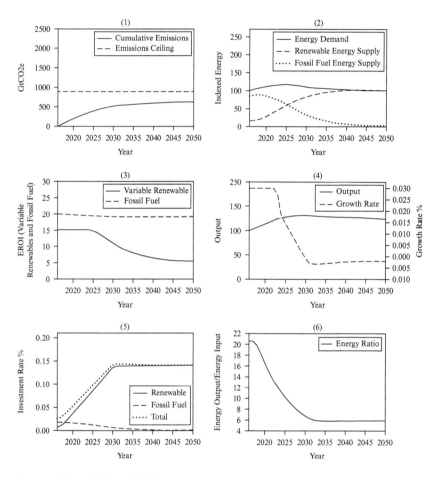

*Source:*   Sers and Victor (2018).

*Figure 5.10    A simulation of the energy–emissions trap*

### 5.4.4   Energy Planning or Energy Determinism?

When thinking about energy planning it is customary to consider the kind of economy and size of population we expect to have at some time in the future and ask how much energy will be required and where to get it from. These energy planning questions are being asked now with a sense of urgency in many rich countries that are dependent on diminishing supplies of fossil fuels from increasingly remote, unreliable, costly and environmentally risky sources. That steps must also be taken to reduce emissions of greenhouse gases only exacerbates the problem.

Forecasts of future energy requirements usually include a forecast of economic growth. The demand for energy is derived from the demand for energy services and these services depend on the future size and con-figuration of the economy. In this way, future energy demands are seen as dependent on the size, structure and functioning of the economy. Specify the latter and derive the former. Sometimes these 'top down' forecasts are coupled with 'bottom up' assessments based on detailed engineering analyses of energy requirements by industrial, commercial, residential and transportation sectors (OECD 1999; National Energy Board 2016; Trottier Energy Futures Project 2016).

Another way of looking at the issue of economic growth and energy demand, one more in keeping with systems thinking, is to recognize that the size and configuration of an economy *depend* on the available energy. In other words, it is not the economy that determines how much energy we need; it is the availability of energy that determines the kind of economy we have. Food is the most important source of energy for humans. Advances in agriculture that made it possible for some people to produce more food than they required for themselves was an essential precondition for the establishment of towns. People did not build towns and then set about assuring an adequate supply of food. Until means were discovered where some people could produce more food than they consumed themselves, significant agglomerations of people were unsup-portable. These means were not simple. They entailed the ability to make containers, to organize storage of seeds and produce, and to use manure and tools to work the land. This allowed the cultivation of the same piece of land without having to move every few years, thus instituting property that needed protecting and so on. Most importantly, it set the stage for potential planned increases in production under managerial control, that is, for growth.

Of course, it works both ways. Once a town or city becomes established the residents try to ensure that they will have sufficient food to meet their needs, just as all living beings sometimes take extraordinary measures to secure their food for the day. The same is true for other sources of energy. Cheap gasoline created suburbia, not the other way around. Suburbia is threatened when gasoline prices make it too expensive to commute, espe-cially if accompanied by road tolls, high parking fees and inadequate mass transit. Not only is suburbia threatened by the prospect of higher energy prices, entire economies are at risk, particularly those dependent on energy imports to keep going. Having built economies on cheap fossil fuels, the realization that we have to reduce their use if we are to avoid catastrophic climate change may well oblige us to confront the energy–emissions trap and its implications for economic growth.

So, as we think about managing without growth, we must remember that if the biophysical constraints which prompt this inquiry increasingly take hold, our economy will change whether we like it or not. We can consider these changes in advance and choose our future, or we can simply see what happens without any forethought or planning and face the consequences.

## 5.5   CONCLUSION

The potential for decoupling economic growth from materials and energy inputs may be considerable but the record to date is discouraging. We can expect continued economic growth in rich countries to depend on very substantial requirements for materials and energy. Potential scarcities and limits to substitution are a real concern. The transition away from fossil fuels, perhaps the biggest challenge of all in terms of sources, will not be simple, especially if it is to be done quickly. An energy transition driven by convenience, versatility and lower environmental impacts is to be welcomed. An energy transition driven by scarcity and high prices is to be avoided, even feared, if it is so abrupt that our social, economic and political institutions cannot cope with the pace of change. Learning to live without depending on economic growth will help relieve the pressure to make changes at such a speed that we cannot think carefully about the consequences and how to mitigate them. Unfortunately, too often a transition to renewable energy is seen as a way of stimulating economic growth without realizing that faster growth magnifies the scale of the transition that has to be made, making it harder to accomplish. (See Table 2.1 in Chapter 2.)

Concern about limits to growth based on inadequate sources of material and energy inputs has a long history reaching back over two hundred years to Malthus. It was revisited by Jevons in the 19th century and by Barnett and Morse (1963) in the 20th, to name just a couple of the best-known contributors. In the 21st century, the concern has again arisen, this time with a focus on oil. The world's motorized transportation systems on land, sea and air depend heavily not just on oil, but, especially in many rich countries, on cheap imported oil that many commentators, including prominent people in the oil industry, warn will not be available in increasing amounts for much longer (Hirsch 2007).

We have started an energy transition that promises to be unlike any that has preceded it because this time many of the alternatives are less attractive in some key respects than the energy sources they are expected to replace. The non-conventional sources of oil and gas – oil sands, shale, and subarctic deposits – are expensive and environmentally damaging. Nuclear energy remains costly, potentially hazardous on a scale all its own, and no satisfactory means of long-term used fuel disposal exists anywhere on the planet. Hope lies with renewable energy sources, and progress is being made, but even here there are difficulties.

It is easy to underestimate the significance of this transition for human well-being. For example, D. Gale Johnson writes very positively and authoritatively about population, food, knowledge, and the rapid improvement in well-being of the world's population since about 1800. He notes, 'fewer famines, increased caloric intakes, reduced child and infant mortality, increased life expectancy, great reductions in time worked, and greatly increased percentage of the population that is literate.' In explaining how these gains were made Johnson says, 'we have found ways to offset the limitations that natural resources imposed on the world's output in times past . . . we have found low cost and abundant substitutes for natural resources important in the production process' (Johnson 2000). Similar sentiments are expressed by the 'new optimists' (www.newoptimists.com). Yet not once does Johnson mention the critical role of cheap energy from fossil fuels in these changes; indeed, he completely overlooks the role that energy has played in the improvements that he documents. During the industrialization and modernization of the past two hundred years, fossil fuels have added enormously to the available supplies of energy. Many industries and the transportation sector in particular are dependent on oil, the continued supply of which at low prices is now seriously in question. If the era of inexpensive oil really is over, or will be soon, then much depends on our capacity to make a smooth transition to alternatives (including more efficient use of energy) if the improvements of the past two centuries are to be sustained.

Gains have been made with respect to the materials and energy per unit of GDP but not to the point where their total use is declining. For that we also have to address growth in GDP itself because increases in efficiency will not be sufficient. And it is not only the supply of materials and energy that point in this direction. In the next chapter, we examine some of the information about the fate of the materials and energy we use in our economies and find that they too impose limits to growth, arguably more pressing than limits on sources.

## NOTES

1. More comprehensive assessments than provided in this chapter can be found in Heinberg (2007) and Bryan (2015).

2.  Throughout the book biosphere is used to refer to 'the global ecological system integrating all living beings and their relationships, including their interaction with the elements of the lithosphere, geosphere, hydrosphere, and atmosphere' (http://environment-ecology.com/what-is-environment/669-environment.html).
3.  Taking the long view James Brander argues that 'Malthus was looking back on approximately 5,000 years of recorded history. In most places and at most times the world was resolutely Malthusian' (Brander 2007). Revisiting Malthus, Brander concludes that 'the most fundamental sustainability factor is demography, as originally identified by Malthus' (2007, p. 36).
4.  Dematerialization is another term for decoupling material use from GDP growth.
5.  MF refers to the 'material footprint' of nations, which includes all of the materials used to support consumption in countries, irrespective of where the materials are obtained.
6.  'Conventional Crude Oil and Condensate is the black stuff that normally flows from sub-surface reservoirs to the surface under natural buoyancy pressure. This is the stuff that flows out of the North Sea, Middle East, Texas and Nigeria. It is not always black and there is a continuum towards very light and gassy oil that is called condensate that is a clear amber coloured liquid, like gasoline, when it comes out of the ground' (Mearns 2014). Natural gas liquids are not included though some sources do.
7.  This section is based on Sers and Victor (2018).

# 6. Limits to growth – sinks and services

> The substantial contributions of ecosystem services to the sustainable wellbeing of humans and the rest of nature should be at the core of the fundamental change needed in economic theory and practice if we are to achieve a societal transformation to a sustainable and desirable future. (Costanza et al. 2017, p. 1)

> A curious thing about *H. sapiens* is that we are clever enough to document – in exquisite detail – various trends that portend the collapse of modern civilization, yet not nearly smart enough to extricate ourselves from our self-induced predicament. (Rees 2017)

In the last chapter we saw that concerns about the adequacy of sources of materials and energy to support global economic growth have a long history of claims and counter claims. Possibilities for decoupling growth from material and energy inputs exist but what evidence there is suggests that it will need to be far more effective in the future than it has been in the past if total requirements are to decline while more than 9 billion people strive for economic growth. Indeed, since 2000 global trends are in the wrong direction and there are real concerns that shortages of critical materials and available net energy will limit economic growth.

In this chapter we look at what becomes of the materials and energy used by economies after they have been discharged as wastes. How adequate is the capacity of the environment to absorb these wastes and what are the consequences for humans and other species when that capacity is insufficient? We will consider how the biosphere is used as a 'sink' and how the ability of the biosphere to support humans through the provision of 'services' can be compromised when the sinks are overloaded. The distinction among sources, sinks and services should not be overdrawn. Forests, for example, act as a sink for excess carbon dioxide and also a source of timber supply and habitat for numerous species. They are both source and sink, as are the oceans and the atmosphere. We could have discussed all of these as sources in the previous chapter rather than sinks as we do in this one but their dual role should not be forgotten. Chapter 7 on synthesis brings them back into the picture together as an interrelated system.

The implications of overloading sinks and damaging their capacity to support economic growth are not hard to see. As a UNEP report notes:

> Given the fact that the global economy, at today's level of resource use, is already surpassing some environmental thresholds or planetary boundaries, this shows that the level of well-being achieved in wealthy industrial countries cannot be generalized globally based on the same system of production and consumption. (UNEP 2016a, p. 16)

## 6.1 PLANETARY BOUNDARIES

The planetary boundaries referred to in the previous quote are a new framing concept that recently entered the environmental science lexicon (Rockström et al. 2009a). The main thesis of the planetary boundaries principle is that:

> Anthropogenic pressures on the Earth System have reached a scale where abrupt global environmental change can no longer be excluded. We propose a new approach to global sustainability in which we define planetary boundaries within which we expect that humanity can operate safely. Transgressing one or more planetary boundaries may be deleterious or even catastrophic due to the risk of crossing thresholds that will trigger non-linear, abrupt environmental change within continental- to planetary-scale systems. (Rockström et al. 2009a, Abstract)

The previous quote from the UNEP report suggests that thresholds and boundaries can be used interchangeably but there is a crucial difference between them. Thresholds are hypothesized levels of environmental parameters that, if exceeded, will cause large-scale, disruptive and likely irreversible changes to the environment. Examples of thresholds are the concentration of greenhouse gases in the atmosphere or the level of acidification of the oceans. These thresholds, or tipping points, are not known with certainty and may even be unknowable until they have been crossed, by which time it may well be too late to turn back. To avoid crossing the thresholds, Rockström et al. proposed quantitative limits or boundaries that they believed were on the safe side of the unknown thresholds. These boundary values were updated in 2015 (Steffen et al. 2015a). The thresholds are in principle purely scientific constructs based on the expected behavior of ecosystems. The planetary boundaries are precautionary limits informed by science but also based on considerations of the likelihood of exceeding a threshold, the consequences of doing so and the forgone opportunities involved. The more restrictive the boundary (for example the target level of greenhouse gas concentration in the atmosphere), the lower is the risk of crossing the climate change threshold but at greater cost than if the boundary was less stringent.

Figure 6.1 shows the planetary boundaries as illustrated in Steffen et al. (2015a).[1]

The green zone is the safe operating space (below the boundary), yellow represents the zone of uncertainty (increasing risk), and red is the high-risk zone.

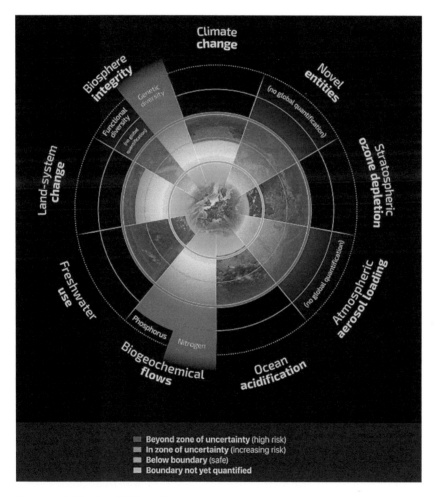

*Source:* Steffen et al. (2015a, p.6).

*Figure 6.1 A safe operating space for humanity*

The planetary boundary itself lies at the inner blue circle. The control variables
have been normalized for the zone of uncertainty (between the red and blue two
circles); the center of the figure therefore does not represent values of 0 for the
control variables. The control variable shown for climate change is atmospheric
$CO_2$ concentration. Processes for which global-level boundaries cannot yet be
quantified are represented by gray wedges; these are atmospheric aerosol load-
ing, novel entities, and the functional role of biosphere integrity. (2015a, p. 6)

Though not without its critics (for example Blomqvist et al. 2012), the
planetary boundaries framework began to influence the discourse on environmental science and policy shortly after the first paper was published
in 2009 (United Nations Secretary-General's High-level Panel on Global
Sustainability 2012).

The combination of science and imaginative graphics has been very
effective in raising awareness of the unprecedented scale and extent of
human impacts on the biosphere and the actual and potential damage
being done that affects not just humans but all species with which humans
share the planet. 'The Planetary Boundaries framework offers, for the first
time, an attempt to identify all the critical, interacting processes on Earth
that contribute to the stability and resilience of the Earth system as a
whole' (Rockström 2017).

Other analysts have built on the planetary boundaries framework and
extended the graphics. Kate Raworth, for example, hollowed out the center
of Figure 6.1, making it into a donut (Raworth 2012; 2017). In the center of
the donut she listed 10 components of 'inclusive and sustainable economic
development' and asked whether and under what circumstances they could
be provided to the entire human population on Earth while remaining
within the planetary boundaries. She has provided a thoughtful answer to
this question in *Doughnut Economics* (Raworth 2017). In Chapter 11, in a
similar vein, we use simulations to consider whether and how advanced
economies no longer reliant on economic growth can meet a number of
key economic, social and environmental objectives simultaneously.

## 6.2   SINKS

What goes into an economy must come out sooner or later. Such is the
nature of economies as open systems. The vast quantities of wastes that
modern economies produce must go somewhere: on or under land, into
water or into the air. We refer to these as 'sinks', though that could give the
impression that once deposited a waste stays where it is put. This is seldom
the case. Very often, a waste released into an environmental sink is transported and transformed by natural processes so that the impacts are felt

somewhere quite distant from the original release and even in a different sink. Acid rain is a good example. Sulfur and nitrogen oxides from combustion and smelting mineral ores undergo physical and chemical changes in the atmosphere, acidifying rain, snow and dust and causing damage to freshwater fish, forests, agriculture and buildings. What starts out as air pollution ends up polluting fresh water lakes and rivers and damaging virtually anything touched by acidified precipitation and dust. The impacts of greenhouse gases are even more wide-ranging and the main greenhouse gas, carbon dioxide, is not really an air pollutant at all in the conventional sense. It is not toxic except in concentrations many times greater than the levels that cause climate change. When greenhouse gases accumulate in the atmosphere they trap heat radiating from Earth, which affects the climate. Much of the excess carbon dioxide is absorbed by the oceans, acidifying them and disrupting the growth of fish and plant life.

Nature is very helpful in dealing with the wastes generated by humans. Some of the wastes decompose and become nutrients for other forms of life in continuous cycles. Some are simply diluted in air and water in concentrations so low that there are no harmful effects to humans or other species. As long as the capacity of natural systems to degrade our wastes is not exceeded, we can worry about other more pressing concerns. The problem is that we often do exceed this capacity locally, regionally and globally. For example, urban air pollution is caused mainly by excessive emissions of a few common pollutants (sulfur oxides, nitrogen oxides, particulates, carbon monoxide and volatile organic compounds). Some of these emissions come from local sources. Others may come from far away. In Southern Ontario about 50 percent of the air pollution comes from sources in the United States (Yap et al. 2005) and Japan and China are exploring ways to reduce transboundary air pollution drifting from China to Japan (Tanabe 2013). Water pollution is also frequently caused by too much waste, such as suspended solids and biochemical oxygen demand, going into rivers and lakes that have insufficient capacity to degrade them without hurting other species in the process. Until quite recently, few people worried about the carbon dioxide emitted by the combustion of fossil fuels (Weart 2012). Now we know it is a serious problem. The widespread use of fossil fuels results in emissions of carbon dioxide that are exceeding the capacity of natural processes to recycle the carbon. Carbon dioxide and other greenhouse gases are accumulating in the atmosphere, changing the heat balance of the planet and threatening dire consequences (IPCC 2013).

All of these examples have one thing in common. Nature has a significant capacity to assimilate and degrade many of the wastes that we produce. Problems come when we exceed that capacity. But there are many types of wastes produced by modern economies that nature has no capacity to handle without adverse consequences. Most of these are synthetic materials deliberately produced by the chemical industry, one of the backbones of industrialization. Synthetic materials were and are celebrated for their ability to perform better than natural products in terms of durability, strength, flexibility and functionality. In addition, they are often cheaper to manufacture than a natural alternative. The problem is that the very features that make synthetic materials so attractive are the same ones that sometimes make it difficult, even impossible, for nature to cope with them. This issue was examined by Rachel Carson in 1962 who looked specifically at pesticides in the environment (Carson 1962) and by Barry Commoner in 1971 who looked at the problem more generally (Commoner 1971). Since then the situation has become more complicated with the introduction of genetically modified organisms (GMOs), and many new materials such as nanoparticles with properties that are poorly understood (Stander and Theodore 2011). The nutritional value of genetically modified animals, plants and microbes is a subject of much debate (World Health Organization Food Safety Department 2005; Hilbeck et al. 2011; Buiatti et al. 2013). What happens and what could happen if they escape into the environment or when they end up as waste is possibly an even greater threat (Altieri 2009; Giunta 2006; Pavone et al. 2011).

In many ways we expect too much of nature. We have an out of sight, out of mind mentality that is no longer viable. To illustrate the seriousness of this problem let us look more deeply into a few examples of what happens when we over-use nature as a sink for our wastes.

### 6.2.1 Lead and CFCs (Chlorofluorocarbons)

Lead and CFCs do not have much in common. Lead is a naturally formed element that has been used by humans for thousands of years. It is a very versatile material. The Romans made water pipes out of lead and it has been used to make roofing, glass, ammunition, batteries and paint. It has also been used as an additive in gasoline to make internal combustion engines run more smoothly. CFCs do not occur naturally. They are a group of synthetic compounds of carbon, hydrogen, chlorine and fluorine that were invented in the 1920s. CFCs have many desirable properties: low toxicity, nonflammable, non-corrosive, and they do not easily react with other chemicals. All sorts of uses for CFCs were found, including as a refrigerant, an aerosol propellant, a cleaning agent for electronic components, and a foam blowing agent (Bryson 2003). So, what do lead and CFCs have in common? The answer is Thomas Midgley Jr, an employee of General Motors, who discovered that lead, in the form of tetra-ethyl lead, was an effective anti-knock agent in engines. He also discovered that a particular type of CFC (dichlorofluoromethane, more commonly known as Freon) was a better refrigerant than sulfur dioxide or ammonia that were being used in the 1920s. Both of Midgley's discoveries were hailed as great achievements. He received many prestigious awards during his lifetime, which came to an abrupt end when he was strangled by a device he designed to help him cope with the debilitating effects of polio (Giunta 2006).

Lead and CFCs in multiple uses share something else in common apart from Thomas Midgley Jr. Lead in gasoline and CFCs became widely used for good economic reasons. They both offered improved performance and they were cheap, just the kind of technological development that has contributed to economic growth. But they were introduced with little or no regard to their environmental fate. It was assumed that the environment could cope with them, that there were adequate sinks. The full life cycle of these products was not considered in advance and many people suffered as a consequence. In 2010 *TIME* magazine included CFCs and lead in gasoline among the top 50 worst inventions of all time (Fletcher 2010). Of course, this lack of foresight is not limited to lead and CFCs. It is typical of what happens in economies that adopt new technologies without first thinking through their broader environmental and social implications. This is not wise but it is to be expected in a world in which the pursuit of economic growth is the primary aim and time costs money.

In the case of lead, the health effects of lead poisoning had been known for decades but for a long time the car industry and the oil industry resisted efforts to eliminate lead in gasoline (Warren 2000). Lead also poisons the catalytic converters installed by car manufacturers to reduce emissions of other pollutants. This realization, combined with rising public concern about lead's health effects, led to a phase down and then elimination of lead in gasoline, first in North America then in other countries. The Earth Summit in 2002 advocated for the total elimination of lead in gasoline by 2006. Yet in 2007, as many as a quarter of a billion people in developing countries were still exposed to lead from gasoline (O'Brien 2007). Progress in the removal of lead in gasoline has continued but there are still reports of its use in several countries (Lead Group Inc. 2011a; 2011b; Sawe 2017). The decline and fall of CFCs is similar. Some 40 years after CFCs were invented, M.J. Molina and F.S. Rowland published a paper in *Nature* suggesting that CFCs were breaking down the stratospheric ozone layer (Molina and Rowland 1974). This was such an important finding that in 1995 they were awarded the Nobel Prize for chemistry. The stratospheric ozone layer reduces the exposure of living things to ultra violet radiation which can damage cell structure and cause skin cancer in humans. In 1984, conclusive evidence was found that the ozone layer was thinning. The number of humans suffering from skin cancers of various levels of severity has increased because of CFCs and will continue to do so for some time (Van Dijk et al. 2013). CFCs have also caused adverse effects on fisheries, agriculture, wildlife and building materials. This was such bad news that it galvanized the countries of the world into action.

Through a series of international agreements starting with the Montreal Protocol in 1987, production of the five main CFC gases was reduced then almost eliminated. The relative speed with which the international community responded to the CFC problem was encouraging. A study commissioned by Environment Canada estimated that this preventative action resulted in about 19.1 million avoided cases of non-melanoma skin cancer worldwide by 2060; about 1.5 million avoided cases of melanoma skin cancer; about 333 500 avoided skin cancer deaths; about 129 million avoided cases of cataracts; and a significant reduction in illnesses and deaths from infectious diseases. The study also estimated that the measures to reduce the production and use of CFCs will avoid damages to the world's fisheries worth US$238 billion, to agriculture worth US$191 billion, and to PVC used in buildings worth US$30 billion (Environment Canada 1997; all values in 1997 constant US dollars).

Several factors led to this unusually rapid response from the international community to the problem of CFCs once it was discovered. These included the scientific consensus on the chemistry of CFCs in the stratosphere, heightened public awareness, the availability of profitable and less harmful substitute chemicals such as HFCs and HCFCs, but which are potent greenhouse gases (Andersen et al. 2014), and the small number of producers, making regulations easy to enforce, though a black market in CFCs developed, undermining for a time the new regulations. Yet even with the dramatic decline in the production and use of CFCs, it will take more than half a century for stratospheric ozone to return to pre-CFC levels. In the meantime, people will continue to suffer excessive rates of skin cancer and generations of children are being taught to be afraid of the sun.

### 6.2.2 Climate Change

Climate change caused by greenhouse gases and land use changes has much in common with the depletion of the ozone layer by CFCs, though in an exaggerated form. It too was identified as a possibility by a distinguished scientist who received the Nobel Prize for chemistry but not for his work on climate change. In 1896, Servante Arrhenius published his calculations of the impact on global temperatures of a doubling of the concentration of carbon dioxide in the atmosphere. He estimated that it would cause an increase in temperature of 4.95°C at the equator averaged over the year, rising to an increase of 6.05°C averaged over the year in more northern latitudes (Arrhenius 1896). These estimates are just outside the upper end of the 2 to 4.5°C range estimated over 100 years later by the Intergovernmental Panel on Climate Change (IPCC), with a best estimate of about 3°C (IPCC 2007). The IPCC adds that 'values substantially higher than 4.5°C cannot be excluded' (2007, p. 12). Similar conclusions were expressed in the subsequent report of the IPCC (2013), as documented in Box 6.1b below.

Many others contributed to the science of climate change during earlier decades of the 20th century. Much of this work was summarized in a publication in 1972 prepared by over 100 scientists as input to the Stockholm Conference on the Environment (SCEP 1970). The warnings were largely ignored until 1988 when an international conference on climate change held in Toronto caused a stir, leading eventually to the UN Framework Convention on Climate Change, adopted in May 1992 and signed by 166 countries when it came into force on 21 March 1994. By 2016 it had been signed by 197 parties consisting of 196 states and one regional economic integration organization.

> The ultimate objective of this Convention and any related legal instruments that the Conference of the Parties may adopt is to achieve, in accordance with the relevant provisions of the Convention, stabilization of greenhouse gas concentrations in the atmosphere at a level that would prevent dangerous anthropogenic interference with the climate system. Such a level should be achieved within a time-frame sufficient to allow ecosystems to adapt naturally to climate change, to ensure that food production is not threatened and to enable economic development to proceed in a sustainable manner. (United Nations 1992, Article 2)

Under the Convention, governments agree to gather and share information on greenhouse gas emissions, national policies and best practices, launch national strategies to address greenhouse gas emissions and adapt to expected impacts, including the provision of financial and technological support to developing countries, and cooperate in preparing for adaptation to the impacts of climate change. In 1997, the Convention was followed by the Kyoto Protocol, with its country-specific targets and compliance mechanisms. The Kyoto Protocol became international law, effective 16 February 2005, after 55 countries producing at least 55 percent of the world's output of greenhouse gases in 1990 had ratified it.

Compared with CFCs, the world has been slow to act on climate change. Powerful interests and professional nay-sayers deliberately exaggerate the uncertainties inherent in the science. They want to delay any action to deal with climate change that might hurt the economy, but especially their own profits (Monbiot and Matthew 2006; Hoggan 2009). Responding to the inertia, the Presidents of the Academies of Science from 11 countries – the United States, Russia, China, India, Canada, Brazil, France, Germany, Italy, Japan and the UK – felt it necessary to throw their considerable weight clearly on one side of this debate. They released a joint statement saying that 'there is strong evidence that significant global warming is occurring . . . It is likely that most of the warming in recent decades can be attributed to human activities. This warming has already led to changes in the Earth's climate.' The Presidents urged all nations 'to take prompt action to reduce the causes of climate change' (Joint Science Academies 2005).

In support of their position, the Presidents of the National Science Academies said they 'recognise the international consensus of the Intergovernmental Panel on Climate Change (IPCC)' (Joint Science Academies 2005). They were referring specifically to the Third Assessment report of the IPCC published in 2001. In 2007, the IPCC spoke again, this time with even more confidence:

> Global atmospheric concentrations of carbon dioxide, methane and nitrous oxide have increased markedly as a result of human activities since 1750 and now far exceed pre-industrial values determined from ice cores spanning many thousands of years . . . The global increases in carbon dioxide concentration are due primarily to fossil fuel use and land use change, while those of methane and nitrous oxide are primarily due to agriculture. (IPCC 2007)

In 2014 the US National Academy of Sciences and the UK Royal Society endorsed these views, describing climate change as 'one of the defining issues of our time' and saying that, 'It is now more certain than ever, based on many lines of evidence, that humans are changing Earth's climate. The atmosphere and oceans have warmed, accompanied by sea-level rise, a strong decline in Arctic sea ice, and other climate-related changes. The evidence is clear' (Wolff and Fung 2014, p. 1).

Between 1995 and 2014, the IPCC has taken successively stronger and more confident positions on the causes and consequences of climate change. Boxes 6.1a–d provide excerpts from the 2nd to 5th assessments of 1995, 2001, 2007 and 2014 that show the increasingly assured views of the IPCC on:

- the occurrence of climate change;
- predictions of future average global temperatures;
- human causes of climate change;
- the consequences of climate change.

## BOX 6.1A THE OCCURRENCE OF CLIMATE CHANGE

1995 'Global mean surface temperature has increased by about 0.3 and 0.6°C since the late 19th century.' (IPCC 1995, p.5)

2001 'The global average surface temperature has increased by 0.6 ± 0.2°C since the late 19th century.' (IPCC 2001, p.26)

2007 'Warming of the climate system is unequivocal, as is now evident from observations of increases in global average air and ocean temperatures, widespread melting of snow and ice, and rising global average sea level ... The total temperature increase from 1850–1899 to 2001–2005 is 0.76 [0.57 to 0.95]°C.' (IPCC 2007, p.5)

2014 'Each of the last three decades has been successively warmer at the Earth's surface than any preceding decade since 1850. The period from 1983 to 2012 was *very likely* the warmest 30-year period of the last 800 years in the Northern Hemisphere, where such assessment is possible (*high confidence*) and *likely* the warmest 30-year period of the last 1400 years (*medium confidence*). The globally averaged combined land and ocean surface temperature data as calculated by a linear trend show a warming of 0.85 [0.65–1.06]°C ... over the period 1880 to 2012, when multiple independently produced datasets exist . . . .' (IPCC 2014b, p.40)

## BOX 6.1B PREDICTIONS OF AVERAGE GLOBAL TEMPERATURES

1995 'For the mid-range IPCC emission scenario, IS92a, assuming the "best estimate" value of climate sensitivity and including the effects of future increases in aerosol concentrations, models project an increase in global mean surface temperature relative to 1990 of about 2°C by 2100.' (IPCC 1995, p.5)

2001 'Projections using the SRES emissions scenarios in a range of climate models result in an increase in globally averaged surface temperature of 1.4 to 5.8°C over the period 1990 to 2100 ... Temperature increases are projected to be greater than those in the Second Assessment Report (SAR), which were about 1.0 to 3.5°C based on six IS92 scenarios.' (IPCC 2001, p.8)

2007 'global average surface warming . . . is likely to be in the range 2 to 4.5°C with a best estimate of about 3°C, and is very unlikely to be less than 1.5°C. Values substantially higher than 4.5°C cannot be excluded, but agreement of models with observations is not as good for those values.' (IPCC 2007, p.12)

2014 'Relative to 1850–1900, global surface temperature change for the end of the 21st century (2081–2100) is projected to *likely* exceed 1.5°C for RCP4.5, RCP6.0 and RCP8.5 (*high confidence*). Warming is *likely* to exceed 2°C for RCP6.0 and RCP8.5 (*high confidence*), *more likely than not* to exceed 2°C for RCP4.5 (*medium confidence*), but *unlikely* to exceed 2°C for RCP2.6 (*medium confidence*). {2.2.1}

Warming will continue beyond 2100 under all RCP scenarios except RCP2.6.' (IPCC 2014b, pp.10, 16)

## BOX 6.1C   HUMAN CAUSES OF CLIMATE CHANGE

1995   'The balance of evidence, from changes in global mean surface air temperature and from changes in geographical, seasonal and vertical patterns of atmospheric temperature, suggests a discernible human influence on global climate.' (IPCC 1995, p. 5)

2001   'There is new and stronger evidence that most of the warming observed over the last 50 years is attributable to human activities.' (IPCC 2001, p. 5)

2007   'Most of the observed increase in globally averaged temperatures since the mid-20th century is very likely due to the observed increase in anthropogenic greenhouse gas concentrations. This is an advance since the TAR's conclusion that "most of the observed warming over the last 50 years is likely to have been due to the increase in greenhouse gas concentrations". Discernible human influences now extend to other aspects of climate, including ocean warming, continental-average temperatures, temperature extremes and wind patterns.' (IPCC 2007, p. 10)

2014   'The Synthesis Report confirms that human influence on the climate system is clear and growing, with impacts observed across all continents and oceans. Many of the observed changes since the 1950s are unprecedented over decades to millennia. The IPCC is now 95 percent certain that humans are the main cause of current global warming.' (IPCC 2014b, p. v)

## BOX 6.1D   THE CONSEQUENCES OF CLIMATE CHANGE

1995   'Human health, terrestrial and aquatic ecological systems, and socio-economic systems (e.g., agriculture, forestry, fisheries and water resources) are all vital to human development and well being and are all sensitive to both the magnitude and the rate of climate change . . . Although our knowledge has increased significantly during the last decade and qualitative estimates can be developed, quantitative projections of the impacts of climate change on any particular system at any particular location are difficult because regional-scale climate change projections are uncertain.' (IPCC 1995, p. 6)

2001   'An increase in climate variability and some extreme events is projected. (SPM: 14) . . . Greenhouse gas forcing in the 21st century could set in motion large-scale, high-impact, non-linear, and potentially abrupt changes in physical and biological systems over the coming decades to millennia, with a wide range of associated likelihoods.' (IPCC 2001, p. 14)

2007   'There is now higher confidence in projected patterns of warming and other regional-scale features, including changes in wind patterns, precipitation, and some aspects of extremes and of ice.' (IPCC 2007, p. 15)

2014   'Climate change will amplify existing risks and create new risks for natural and human systems. Risks are unevenly distributed and are generally greater for disadvantaged people and communities in countries at all levels of development . . . A large fraction of species faces increased extinction risk due to climate change during and beyond the 21st century, especially as climate change interacts with other stressors (*high confidence*) . . . Climate change is projected to undermine food security . . . Climate change is projected to reduce renewable surface water and groundwater resources in most dry subtropical regions (*robust evidence, high agreement*), intensifying competition for water among sectors (*limited evidence, medium agreement*) . . . Until mid-century, projected climate change will impact human health mainly by exacerbating health problems that already exist (*very high confidence*). Throughout the 21st century, climate change is expected to lead to increases in ill-health in many regions and especially in developing countries with low income, as compared to a baseline without climate change (*high confidence*). By 2100 for RCP8.5, the combination of high temperature and humidity in some areas for parts of the year is expected to compromise common human activities, including growing food and working outdoors (*high confidence*).

In urban areas climate change is projected to increase risks for people, assets, economies and ecosystems, including risks from heat stress, storms and extreme precipitation, inland and coastal flooding, landslides, air pollution, drought, water scarcity, sea level rise and storm surges (*very high confidence*). These risks are amplified for those lacking essential infrastructure and services or living in exposed areas.

Rural areas are expected to experience major impacts on water availability and supply, food security, infrastructure and agricultural incomes, including shifts in the production areas of food and non-food crops around the world (*high confidence*).

Aggregate economic losses accelerate with increasing temperature (*limited evidence, high agreement*), but global economic impacts from climate change are currently difficult to estimate. From a poverty perspective, climate change impacts are projected to slow down economic growth, make poverty reduction more difficult, further erode food security and prolong existing and create new poverty traps, the latter particularly in urban areas and emerging hotspots of hunger (*medium confidence*). International dimensions such as trade and relations among states are also important for understanding the risks of climate change at regional scales.

Climate change is projected to increase displacement of people (*medium evidence, high agreement*). Populations that lack the resources for planned migration experience higher exposure to extreme weather events, particularly in developing countries with low income. Climate change can indirectly increase risks of violent conflicts by amplifying well-documented drivers of these conflicts such as poverty and economic shocks (*medium confidence*).

Many aspects of climate change and associated impacts will continue for centuries, even if anthropogenic emissions of greenhouse gases are stopped. The risks of abrupt or irreversible changes increase as the magnitude of the warming increases.' (IPCC 2014b, pp. 13, 15, 16)

The quotations from successive reports of the IPCC in Box 6.1a show that the consensus view of climate scientists is that the average combined land and ocean surface temperature is approaching 1°C above its level in the mid-19th century.

Predictions highlighted in Box 6.1b of future increases in global surface temperatures depend on the scenarios regarding economic growth and energy use against which they are compared. In the 2014 report the predicted increase varies from 1.5°C by 2011 to more than 2.0°C, depending on the scenario.

The adverse consequences of climate change have become increasingly well understood. The quotes in Box 6.1c make clear that as the evidence has accumulated the IPCC has become increasingly confident that since the mid-20th century, human activities have become the dominant cause of the observed warming trend.

Box 6.1d shows that the variety and severity of the anticipated consequences of climate change have also been brought into sharper relief over the years.

Preparation for the 6th assessment report began in 2016. The working group reports are expected in 2020/2021 and a Synthesis Report in 2022 (IPCC 2016). Meanwhile, ongoing research and reporting on climate change by scientific organizations such as NASA in the USA (http://climate.nasa. gov/) and the Tyndall Centre in the UK (http://www.tyndall.ac.uk/) and the myriad of scientists around the world strongly suggests that unless there is a dramatic and expeditious reduction in greenhouse gas emissions, net of any increases in natural or engineered sequestration, the situation will go from bad to worse to catastrophic. After surveying the most recent evidence, the US Global Change Research Program concluded that:

> it is extremely likely that *human activities, especially emissions of greenhouse gases, are the dominant cause of the observed warming since the mid-20th century.* For the warming over the last century, there is no convincing alternative explanation supported by the extent of the observational evidence.
>
> In addition to warming, many other aspects of global climate are changing, primarily in response to human activities. *Thousands of studies conducted by researchers around the world have documented changes in surface, atmospheric, and oceanic temperatures; melting glaciers; diminishing snow cover; shrinking sea ice; rising sea levels; ocean acidification; and increasing atmospheric water vapor.* (Wuebbles et al. 2017, p. 12, emphasis in original)

There are some positive signs that catastrophe may be avoided. In 2009 world leaders met in Copenhagen at COP 15.[2] The Copenhagen Accord, which came out of this meeting, expressed clear political intent at the highest level to limit greenhouse gases to meet the long-term goal of an average temperature increase of no more than 2°C. However, it did not include a commitment to practical steps and national targets required to meet this goal and so the meeting was widely regarded as a failure. In October 2018 the IPCC released a Special Report on Global Warming of 1.5°C (IPCC 2018): 'The world stands on the brink of failure when it comes to holding global warming to moderate levels, and nations will need to take "unprecedented" actions to cut their carbon emissions over the next decade, according to a landmark report by the top scientific body studying climate change' (Mooney and Dennis 2018).

The difficulty of obtaining agreement from nearly 200 independent countries, with their different economic, political, social, cultural and environmental circumstances should not be underestimated. Following the Copenhagen meeting the idea began to emerge that faster progress might be made if a small number of powerful, influential countries took the lead by committing themselves to action on greenhouse gases, motivating others to follow. In November 2014, during a meeting in China of the Asia-Pacific Economic Cooperation forum, US President Barack Obama announced a target to cut US greenhouse gas emissions between 26 to 28 percent below 2005 levels by 2025. At the same time Chinese President Xi Jinping announced targets for Chinese carbon dioxide emissions to peak round 2030 and the share of non-fossil fuel energy to rise to around 20 percent by 2030 (WRI 2014). By doing so they joined the European Union in setting ambitious targets without requiring the agreement of other countries. Since their combined greenhouse gas emissions represent about 50 percent of the global total, these are significant commitments.

Subsequently, in 2015 COP 21 was held in Paris with somewhat better results than in Copenhagen six years earlier. Prior to the Paris meeting countries submitted their indicated nationally determined contributions (INDCs) to reducing greenhouse gas emissions starting in 2020. These INDCs become NDCs (nationally determined contributions) when countries formally join the Paris Agreement. A distinguishing feature of the unanimously supported Paris Agreement is reliance on these national contributions and the absence of any international system of enforcement, as was attempted under the Kyoto Protocol, which expired in 2012. The Paris Agreement came into effect on 4 November 2016 after ratification by 55 Parties to the Convention, accounting for at least 55 percent of the total global greenhouse gas emissions. It remains in effect despite the announcement by US President Trump in June 2017 that the US will withdraw from the Agreement.

The aggregate effect of the INDCs as of 4 April 2016 on global GHG emissions is shown in Figure 6.2. Historical emissions shown in solid gray are trending upwards and are projected to continue to increase in the absence of the INDCs (pre-INDC scenarios line). The effect of the INDCs on global emissions, assuming they are all fulfilled, is shown by the shaded

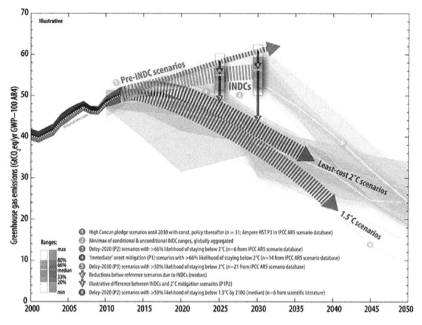

*Source:*   Adapted from UNFCCC (2016).

*Figure 6.2*   *Comparison of global emission levels in 2025 and 2030 resulting from the implementation of the intended nationally determined contributions and under other scenarios*

band just beneath the pre-INDC scenarios line. The band is quite wide, reflecting various assumptions and conditions specified by the Parties and uncertainties in the information provided. It is clear from Figure 6.2 that even if all the INDCs are fulfilled, global emissions will remain far in excess of the trajectories indicated by the line for a 66 percent chance of not exceeding a temperature increase of 2°C and even more so for a 50 percent chance of not exceeding a 1.5°C increase. It is sobering to read that 'At the time of publication of this document [April 2016], no scenarios were available in the literature in which warming was limited to below 1.5°C considering global emission levels in 2030 resulting from the implementation of the INDCs' (UNFCCC 2016, p. 13). A subsequent report on the 'emissions gap' states that 'the overarching conclusions . . . are that there is an urgent need for accelerated short-term action and enhanced longer-term national ambition, if the goals of the Paris Agreement are to remain achievable' (UNEP 2017, p. xiv).

Although the Paris Agreement provides a useful framework for making significant progress in containing global GHG emissions, including as it does provisions for monitoring, reporting, mitigation, adaptation and finance starting in the year 2020, the reductions in GHG emissions will have to be considerably greater than those to which the Parties are currently committed.

There is some debate about how long emissions of GHGs stay in the atmosphere. Take $CO_2$ for example. The IPCC estimates that 'about 15 to 40% of $CO_2$ emitted until 2100 will remain in the atmosphere longer than 1000 years' (Ciais et al. 2013, p. 472). Harde (2017) takes a very different view and estimates the average residence time of anthropogenic sources of $CO_2$ to be four years. The US EPA's position is that '$CO_2$ remains in the climate system for a very long time: $CO_2$ emissions cause increases in atmospheric concentrations of $CO_2$ that will last thousands of years' (US EPA n.d.). The longer residency time also means that most of the GHGs currently resident in the atmosphere today were put there by the developed economies even though developing economies now account for nearly two-thirds of current global emissions (Center for Global Development 2015). It is cumulative emissions that determine the impact of GHGs on the climate. 'Greenhouse gases such as methane, chlorofluorocarbons, that linger in the atmosphere for just a year to a few decades, can cause sea levels to rise for hundreds of years after the pollutants have been cleared from the atmosphere' because of their lasting effect on ocean temperatures (NASA 2017). These long-term effects of historical emissions of GHGs raise complicated ethical issues of a fair allocation of future GHG emissions among the countries and people of the world.

A useful way to think about this is to consider a carbon budget, that is, the total quantity of additional $CO_2$ in the atmosphere consistent with an increase in the global average temperature of less than 2°C above pre-industrial levels.[3] The IPCC has estimated that to achieve this target with a greater than 66 percent probability, cumulative $CO_2$ post-2011 should not exceed approximately 1000 Gt (NASA 2017, p. 13). Some of this has already been emitted. How should the rest be shared? Should each country's historical emissions be taken into account or only current emissions, or some combination of both? The answer to this question will have very different implications for developed and developing countries and will be the topic of difficult and fractious negotiations for years to come. Unless this is settled soon, and there is not much chance of that, with the passage of time the size of the unused portion of the global carbon budget will shrink and arguments about the fair allocation of the remaining global carbon budget will become increasingly irrelevant.

Looking ahead, what combination of reduction in greenhouse gas emissions and increases in biological sequestration (long-term carbon capture through photosynthesis) and underground storage will be necessary to avoid catastrophic climate change? Clearly, much more will be required than the INDCs. And since meeting them is up to each country without any kind of international sanction for falling short, it is hard to be confident that the INDCs will in fact be achieved. As noted in an assessment of their aggregate contribution when contemplating opportunities in the medium and longer terms:

> The extent to which efforts to reduce emissions will be sufficient to limit the global average temperature rise to less than 2 or 1.5°C above pre-industrial levels strongly depends on the long-term changes in the key economic drivers that will be induced by the implementation of the communicated INDCs, as well as on the determination of Parties to increase their level of ambition before and after 2030. (UNFCCC 2015)

So, the UNFCCC recognizes that implementation of the INDCs might affect key economic drivers but not that deliberate changes to the economic drivers, in particular reduced rates of economic growth, might also be necessary to prevent the target levels of average global temperature increase from being exceeded. We will consider this possibility in some detail in Chapter 8.

### 6.2.3   Nuclear Wastes

'Our children will enjoy in their homes electrical energy too cheap to meter', said Lewis L. Strauss, chairman of the US Atomic Energy Commission in a speech to the National Association of Science Writers on 16 September 1954. Well, we certainly did not get that. What we did get was a highly complex technology that uses the heat from atomic fission to produce steam that drives turbines to generate electricity. We also get radioactive wastes, some of which, the high-level wastes, must be stored for tens of thousands of years and prevented from coming into contact with anything alive. Even low-level radioactive waste such as contaminated clothing and equipment that 'loses most or all of its radioactivity within 300 years', or 'intermediate-level radioactive waste [such as waste from station refurbishment] that requires isolation and containment for periods beyond several hundred years' (Canadian Nuclear Safety Commission 2016) present extremely challenging technical, environmental and social problems (Butler et al. 2011). But the most daunting problems of nuclear waste disposal relate to high-level nuclear waste, which is mostly used fuel that must be isolated from the environment for hundreds of thousands of years or longer.

The problem of the long-term disposal of high-level nuclear wastes is a classic example of a technology that produces a waste material that nature cannot digest. There is no assimilative capacity for this kind of waste. The best we can hope for is a means of storing it securely for a time so far into the future that we have to assume a complete breakdown in society and its institutions. In other words, we must dispose of the waste in a place that we should assume no one will remember, for which all records will be lost, and where the chances of it being disturbed are virtually zero. That is a very tall order. Do we put it somewhere so far out of reach that it would be virtually impossible to retrieve, even if someone, some time, wanted to? Deep in a stable geological stratum might work, but what if something should go wrong and what once seemed safe turned out not to be? If we make it so very hard to get at there may be no way to solve this problem should it arise (Nuclear Waste Management Organization 2005; 2017; Alley and Alley 2014).

An alternative is to place it somewhere and in some form that those who come later can access if they wish. They may want to do so for safety reasons or to reprocess the material to generate more energy. Such storage is less than completely secure because access is designed in from the start. And what if the records of the stored material are lost or their meaning no longer understood? In the past 10 000 years civilizations came and went many times and will likely do so again (Tainter 1988; Wright 2004; Diamond 2005). Is it responsible to knowingly create such a hazardous material and store it in a way that it poses a threat to people and other living organisms in the future who may not even know it is there, let alone have the means to deal with it?

No country where electricity is produced using nuclear energy has established a facility for long-term disposal of used radioactive fuel. Some have opted for a deep geological repository and are at various stages of site selection and approval. Others have postponed the decision.

> implementing geological disposal of high level waste and spent nuclear fuel has proven to be more challenging than originally anticipated. No countries have fully implemented deep geological disposal facilities to date ... RWMOs [Radioactive Waste Management Organizations] in the United States, Sweden and Finland have submitted a license application to construct repositories, while the French waste management organization is currently preparing its application. (Kollar and Mayer 2015)

The situation in Canada is fairly typical. In 2002, over 30 years after the first Canadian nuclear generating station went into operation, the government of Canada established the Nuclear Waste Management Organization (NWMO). The Board of Directors of the NWMO consists of representatives of the electric power companies with nuclear generating stations who are the owners of the used nuclear fuel. The first main task of the NWMO is to recommend a long-term approach for managing used nuclear fuel produced by Canada's electricity generators. The NWMO submitted its final report in 2005, recommending that:

> Centralized containment and isolation of the used fuel in a deep geological repository in a suitable rock formation . . . [and] potential for retrievability of the used fuel for an extended period, until such time as a future society makes a determination on the final closure, and the appropriate form and duration of post-closure monitoring. (NWMO 2005)

The NWMO's recommendation is for 'adaptive phased management'. This approach is intended to allow learning to take place over a very long time, and for adjustments to be made as new knowledge is gained or as problems arise. Whether such an approach can in fact be implemented over time scales far, far longer than Canada has existed as a country, or any nation state for that matter, is impossible to tell. It will require a continuity of institutional arrangements that are unprecedented. Unless something goes terribly wrong in short order, none alive today will know if 'used fuel will . . . be contained and isolated from people and the environment essentially indefinitely' (NWMO 2005, p. 15). In 2007 the federal government of Canada accepted the NWMO's recommendation of adaptive phased management and the search for a suitable site for a repository in Canada is under way. Since 2010, the NWMO has been 'engaged in a multi-year, community-driven process to identify a site . . . where Canada's used nuclear fuel can be safely contained and isolated in a deep geological repository . . . The process . . . is designed to ensure, above all, that the site selected is safe and secure, and has an informed and willing host . . .' (NWMO 2017).

We cannot turn the clock back. Nuclear power plants are up and running. A considerable quantity of used fuel has been produced and some method of long-term containment is essential. We could take comfort from statements such as that of the International Atomic Energy Agency which says, 'the scientific and technical basis for safe geological disposal of high level waste and spent nuclear fuel has been well established in several national programmes' (Kollar and Mayer 2015) or from Canada's NWMO that 'there is also consensus among major nuclear regulatory and monitoring organizations that deep geological repositories are the responsible way forward' (NWMO 2017). However, there are several considerations that should give us pause about the prospects for the safe disposal of high-level radioactive waste. Geology, on which assurances of the safety of deep disposal are based, is a relatively new science. The theory of plate tectonics only became generally accepted by geologists in the mid-20th century (Blackett et al. 1965). Do we really know enough to be confident about the indefinite isolation of highly radioactive waste underground? Will adaptive management work as prescribed? Very little is known about life that lives far beneath the surface and how it affects geological processes. Microbes can live many miles underground (Hadhazy 2015). How might this affect the movement of radioactive materials over very long time periods?

Another concern is the potential conflict between the desire of radioactive management organizations to find a 'willing host' – a community that has indicated that it would favor the location of a deep geological repository close by – and the importance of finding the best site from a scientific, technical and environmental perspective. The debate about siting a repository for low- and intermediate-level radioactive waste on the site of the Bruce nuclear plant, only 1.2 kilometers from Lake Huron, is an example where – at least to some – the willing host trumped the potential risk to the drinking water supply of 40 million Canadians and Americans (see Blackwell 2015; CBC News 2015; Simpson 2015; 2016). And finally, the risk of highly radioactive waste with bomb-making potential of finding its way into the wrong hands remains a concern, all the more so as pressure builds to include the expansion of nuclear generating stations as part of a program for reducing GHG emissions (Rowe 2009; Teräväinen et al. 2011).

If new nuclear plants are built in Canada or in any other rich country, it will be in pursuit of economic growth. More growth requires more energy. Electricity is the most versatile and convenient form of energy available. If we were content to rely on renewable sources of electricity, we could still increase the supply in smaller and more dispersed increments rather than with a few very large reactors. It may take more time and money, though that is disputed, but it would not leave future generations with a problem that we ourselves do not know how to solve (Hooker et al. 1981; Scheer 2007; Taebi 2011).

Lead, CFCs, greenhouse gases and nuclear waste are just a few examples of situations where the assimilative capacity of the environment has been exceeded. It is a widespread problem arising from the increasing throughput of materials and energy in our growing economies. Some progress has been made in dealing with excessive use of assimilative capacity such as the reduced contamination of some lakes and rivers and improved air quality in urban areas, especially in advanced economies (Zhang et al. 2010; Onda et al. 2012; United Nations 2015b). At larger geographic scales all the way up to the global, and in most poorer countries, the record is much worse. The overuse of assimilative capacity diminishes the supply of services that nature provides and on which we depend. It is to this loss of services that we now turn.

## 6.3   SERVICES

We rely on nature for our very existence. We are part of nature, albeit a part that has become self-conscious and self-aware. We are also apart from nature, having separated ourselves, or the way we think of ourselves, from the rest of nature. This separation is an illusion as you can quickly discover if you try going without food for a few weeks, without water for a few days, or without air for a few minutes. Karl Marx expressed our relationship to the rest of nature very well when he said:

> Man opposes himself to Nature as one of her own forces ... in order to appropriate Nature's productions in a form adapted to his own wants. By thus acting on the external world and changing it, he at the same time changes his own nature. (Marx 1887[2003], p. 177)

We have already looked at our reliance on nature for sources of materials and energy and for sinks to dispose of our wastes. Without these sources and sinks neither we, nor our economies, could function. They are the most obvious ways in which nature provides for us. There is also a range of other services on which we depend and which nature supplies, if not in abundance, in substantial amounts. As our numbers grow and as affluence increases, we place increasing demands on nature for sources, sinks and places to live, work and play. All too often, these demands reduce the productivity of the ecosystems on which we rely and hence the provision of essential and important ecological services.

In the past two decades there have been several detailed assessments of the impacts of human activity on global ecosystems. National studies have also been undertaken, for example the UK National Ecosystem Assessment Follow-on (2014). Two stand out because of their comprehensiveness and authorship: *World Resources 2000–2001: People and Ecosystems* (Rosen 2000), and the five-volume *Millennium Ecosystem Assessment* (Millennium Ecosystem Assessment Board 2005a) written by 1360 experts from around the world under the supervision of a governing board drawn from UN organizations, governments, academia, business and indigenous peoples. More recent reports carry similar messages (see for example Halpern et al. 2008; Ellis 2011; Barnosky et al. 2012; Goldewijk et al. 2012). These reports tell much the same story. *People and Ecosystems* examined the capacity of five major categories of ecosystem (agriculture, coast, forest, fresh water and grasslands), to provide eight types of ecosystem service: food/fiber production, water quality, water quantity, biodiversity, carbon storage, recreation, shoreline protection, and wood fuel production. Not every category of ecosystem provides each ecosystem service. For example, fresh water does not provide wood fuel production. Out of the 40 possible combinations of ecosystem category and ecosystem services, *People and Ecosystems* analyzed 24, noting whether they were improving, declining or staying the same (Rosen 2000, p. 47). They found that 18 showed a decline, three showed both decline and improvement, two showed insufficient information to decide, and only one (food/fiber production from forests) showed improvement. In sum, as of 2000, 75 percent of the ecosystems providing services worldwide were in decline.

In the later and more detailed Millennium Ecosystem Assessment reports prepared at the instigation of the United Nations Secretary General, the authors adopted a similar approach. They reached three main conclusions:

> First, approximately 60% (15 out of 24) of the ecosystem services examined during the Millennium Ecosystem Assessment are being degraded or used unsustainably, including fresh water, capture fisheries, air and water purification, and the regulation of regional and local climate, nature hazards, and pests. The full costs of the loss and degradation of these ecosystem services are . . . substantial and growing . . . Second, there is established but incomplete evidence that changes being made in ecosystems are increasing the likelihood of nonlinear changes in ecosystems (including accelerating, abrupt, and potentially irreversible changes) that have important consequences for human well being . . . Third, the harmful effects of the degradation of ecosystem services . . . are being borne disproportionately by the poor, are contributing to growing inequities and disparities across groups of people, and are sometimes the principal factor causing poverty and social conflict. (Millennium Ecosystem Assessment Board 2005b, pp. 16–17)

Clearly, the ecological systems that provide services on which we and our economies depend are in distress. Let us consider three of the most serious: forests, oceans and fresh water.

### 6.3.1   The Forests

In Chapter 4 we introduced the distinction between stock-flow and fund-service resources. Stock-flow resources such as minerals can be stockpiled and used at any rate, providing the necessary capital equipment, energy and labor are available. The flows obtained from the stocks, iron ore and timber for example, deplete the stocks and are transformed into products. In contrast, with fund-service resources such as a piece of equipment, the fund is not transformed into the product. It provides a service that cannot be stored, and the rate at which it can be used is strictly limited. For example, if the shade offered by a tree in leaf is not used today, it cannot be stored for future use. The amount of shade it provides at any time is fixed. We also noted that whereas produced capital is always a fund-service resource, the assets provided by nature can be both stock-flow and fund-service resources at the same time. One such example is forests.

Forests as a stock of biomass can yield a supply of wood used in a variety of ways to produce furniture, fuel, and lumber and pulp for making paper products. Forests as a fund provide habitat for humans and wildlife, clean air and water, flood control and carbon sequestration. Because of their physical characteristics, the flows of wood from forests are more easily owned, controlled and sold than the services. The result is that financial incentives provided by markets favor the use of forests for generating flows, often at the expense of the services that they also provide. It is more difficult, if not impossible, to sell the service of flood control than it is to cut trees and sell them for fuel or timber. Yet cutting trees can result in flooding. The single most important cause of deforestation, especially in the tropics, is the conversion of forests to agriculture (FAO 2015, p. 20). When the expected profitability of cash crops or meat exceeds that of wood products there is a strong incentive to transform forests into farmland regardless of what forest services are lost. This happened over centuries in Europe, took less time in North America and is moving ahead faster still in many parts of the southern hemisphere today where population growth rates are the highest and incomes are rising (FAO 2016a).

Deforestation takes many forms. It can result from clear-cutting of large areas for timber or to gain access to underground minerals, or by fragmentation due to road and pipeline construction. Potapov et al. (2017) define an intact forest landscape (IFL) as:

> a seamless mosaic of forests and natural treeless ecosystems that exhibit no remotely detected signs of human activity or habitat fragmentation and are large enough to maintain all native biological diversity including viable populations of wide-ranging species ... IFLs are critical for stabilizing terrestrial carbon storage, harboring biodiversity, regulating hydrological regimes, and providing other ecosystem functions. (Potapov et al. 2017, p. 1)

Their global mapping of IFLs reveal a loss of 7.2 percent in coverage between 2000 and 2013 with the annual rate of loss rising (2017, p. 1). Forests cover approximately 44 percent of the Earth's ice-free land area and of this 22 percent was covered by IFLs in 2000, two-thirds of which were in Russia, Brazil and Canada. It is these three countries that accounted for over half of the loss of IFL area between 2000 and 2013 (Potapov et al. 2017, p. 2). Commenting on an earlier study by Potapov et al. and related studies of deforestation, Leahy (2014) writes that 'it is Canada that has been leading the world in forest loss since 2000, accounting for 21 per cent of global forest loss.' He attributes Canada's poor record to 'massive increases in oil sands and shale gas developments, as well as logging and road building' (Leahy 2014, p. 1).

Figure 6.3 shows how the transformation of the planetary landscape brought about by the expansion of the human population, coupled with

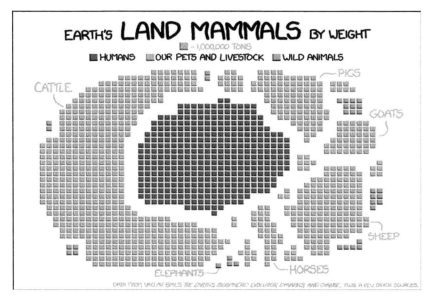

*Source:*  https://XKCD.Com/1338/.

*Figure 6.3    Earth's land mammals by weight*

economic growth and the spread of agriculture at the expense of wildlife habitat, has affected the Earth's land mammal populations. Each square represents 1 million tons of body mass. The darker squares in the center show the tonnage of humans. Surrounding these are lighter squares representing the tonnage of animals in the service of humans as pets and livestock. The few green squares show the tonnage of wild animals, the astonishing demise of which, along with numerous other species of flora and fauna, has been dubbed the 'sixth extinction', of which humans are the primary cause (Kolbert 2015). 'We have unleashed a mass extinction event, the sixth in roughly 540 million years, wherein many current life forms could be annihilated or at least committed to extinction by the end of this century' (Ripple et al. 2017). The impending extinction crisis of the world's primates is especially disturbing, not just because they are our closest biological relatives (Estrada et al. 2017).

Perhaps even more disturbing, though unglamorous to all but entomologists, is the decline in insect species and populations on which the rest of terrestrial life depends. Most of these insects live in forests, especially in the tropics. 'Loss of insects is certain to have adverse effects on ecosystem functioning, as insects play a central role in a variety of processes, including pollination . . ., herbivory and detrivory . . ., nutrient cycling . . . and providing a food source for higher trophic levels such as birds, mammals and amphibians' (Hallman et al. 2017, p. 1). The study from which this quote is taken measured the number of flying insects in 63 protected areas in Germany over 27 years and found a decline of 76 percent.

There are several approaches to preventing and reversing deforestation, including stronger and better-enforced regulations, financial incentives to promote management practices that favor the provision of forest services, and more secure forest tenure that permits exclusion but which may have undesirable implications for social justice. Regulations can be used to limit what can and cannot be done to a forest and what should be done to regenerate it. Regulatory regimes and enforcement practices vary considerably from country to country. They cover harvesting and replanting practices as well as the designation of large areas for conservation. In recent years, these regulations have been complemented by certification systems such as those of the Forest Stewardship Council and the Programme for the Endorsement of Forest Certification. Voluntary certification systems inform those who buy forest products that the supply comes from sustainably managed sources. In 2015 certification covered 11 percent of global forest area (FAO 2015, p. 22).

A second approach is to pay landowners for the unpriced services of forests. Costa Rica has been a leader in this approach since the late 1990s (Porras et al. 2013).

> Since 1997, nearly one million hectares of forest in Costa Rica have been part of these 'payments for ecosystem services (PES)' schemes at one time or another. Meanwhile, forest cover has returned to over 50 per cent of the country's land area, from a low of just over 20 per cent in the 1980s. (Barton 2013)

How much of this reforestation in Costa Rica can be attributed to payments for ecosystem services is a matter of debate. Ostrom (2008) reports that a study by Sánchez-Azofeifa et al. (2007) using GIS found that 'deforestation was not significantly less in regions where large allocations of PES payments had been invested' (Ostrom 2008, p. 16). She also referred to the finding of another study by Zbinden and Lee (2004) of the Costa Rican experience with payments for ecosystem services which reported that the payments tended to be allocated to large landowners with high incomes. A more recent assessment of 20 years' experience of payments for ecosystem services in Costa Rica concludes that from 1997 to 2016 the payments combined with regulations and despite political changes have contributed to the conservation of nearly 1 million hectares of forest (Porras et al. 2013).

With increased attention being given to climate change, a determined effort has been by the UN through REDD+ to create:

a financial value for the carbon stored in forests by offering incentives for developing countries to reduce emissions from forested lands and invest in low-carbon paths to sustainable development . . . REDD+ goes beyond simply deforestation and forest degradation, and includes the role of conservation, sustainable management of forests and enhancement of forest carbon stocks. (UN-REDD 2017)

Security of forest tenure can be important for capital investment by government and the private sector and it can motivate the sustainable use of forest resources (FAO 2015, p. 38). Between 1990 and 2010 forest areas under public ownership worldwide decreased by about 120 million ha, while privately owned forests increased by about 115 million ha, primarily in upper middle-income areas, with China accounting for 85 million ha of the additional privately owned forests (FAO 2015). In some countries, notably Brazil and Colombia, publicly owned forests are under community management rather than public administration though the proportion owned by communities is in decline (FAO 2015, p. 39).

Ostrom, whose work on the management of the commons earned her the Nobel Memorial Prize in Economic Sciences in 2009, observed that: 'The most important lesson that needs wide dissemination is that simple panaceas offered for solving problems related to the commons – whether they are for government, private, or community ownership – may work in some settings but fail in others' (Ostrom 2008, p. 4).

Through regulation, financial incentives and more secure forest tenure there has been a reduction in the rates of deforestation from 1990 to 2015. During that period the world's forests declined from 4.128 million ha to 3.999 million ha, a loss about equal in size to the area of South Africa. The good news is that the rate of net loss has declined from 0.18 percent per year in the 1990s to 0.08 percent per year between 2010 and 2015. The greatest losses occurred in South America and Africa although there too, the rate of loss has decreased in the past five years (FAO 2015, p. 3). At the same time, there was some displacement of natural forests by planted forests, with natural forests declining at 6.5 million ha/year between 2010 and 2015, somewhat more slowly than in the previous 20 years (FAO 2015). As the FAO notes, 'natural forest area change is perhaps a better indicator of natural habitat and biodiversity dynamics' than total forested area (FAO 2015, p. 3). If the planted species are chosen because of their capacity to produce high fiber yields at the expense of valuable services provided by natural forests, there is still a loss of services. And when the replanting results in monocultures more susceptible to fire and disease than the forest it replaces, then new problems arise (Altieri 2009; Reich et al. 2012).

Clearly, deforestation remains a matter of considerable concern especially in the southern hemisphere. Although the rate of deforestation in the Amazon rainforest is slowing, mostly due to the sharp drop in forest clearing in Brazil since 2004, it appears to have stabilized at around 5000 to 6000 sq km/year in the Brazilian Amazon (Butler 2016). However, there is research showing that tropical forests, the lungs of the world, have become a net source of carbon emissions, which is extremely disturbing and illustrates how degradation of one sink – the forests – can overwhelm another – the atmosphere (Baccini et al. 2017). There are ongoing significant declines in forests in Asia and Africa as well (FAO 2015, p. 20). These declines can all be attributed, at least in part, to the demands of increased consumption in many parts of the world generated by more people with rising incomes coupled with expanding global trade. It remains to be seen if continued improvement in forest management practices will be sufficient to halt and reverse deforestation everywhere, much as it has done in Europe and North America (FAO 2015, p. 20), so that a process of recovery can begin.

### 6.3.2   The Oceans

The oceans which cover 70 percent of the planet are so vast and complex that it is difficult to assess their condition, how it is changing and why. There are numerous studies on aspects of the oceans, but very few that attempt an overall assessment. One that does is the UN's first World Ocean Assessment (United Nations 2016b). The *Living Blue Planet Report: Species, Habitats and Human Well-being* (WWF 2015) provides a comprehensive assessment of life in the oceans and its relation to human well-being. Taken together, these reports paint a very disturbing account of the impacts of human activity on the oceans on which, to a greater or lesser extent, we all depend.

The UN report concentrates on the four main ocean basins that form an interconnected system: the Arctic Ocean, the Atlantic Ocean, the Indian Ocean and the Pacific Ocean. The physical and chemical composition of ocean water varies by geography. For example, salinity (dissolved salts) is affected by inputs of freshwater and evaporation. Stratification (layers of water with different physical and chemical properties) is caused by differences in salinity and temperature, and can affect the distribution of oxygen and nutrients, and the penetration of light and hence photosynthesis by ocean-dwelling plants that produce 50 percent or more of atmospheric oxygen (Roach 2004). The oceans are home to an enormous variety of marine species, the density and distribution of which depends on the interplay of 'geological forms, ocean currents, nutrient fluxes, weather, seasons and sunlight' (United Nations 2016b, p. 3).

The oceans are not an isolated system – they interact with the atmosphere through the two-way transfer of gases, heat and surface movements. For example, the very troubling increase in ocean acidity is due to the absorption of about 26 percent of the anthropogenic carbon dioxide released into the atmosphere (United Nations 2016b, p. 3). The oceans have 'absorbed about 93 per cent of the combined extra heat stored by warmed air, sea, land and melted ice between 1971 and 2010' (United Nations 2016b, p. 10). The changes in ocean temperature and salinity are causing great concern as the circulation of ocean water driven by temperature and salinity differences – thermohaline circulation – may be altered, with serious adverse consequences, the likelihood of which is not well understood (Osborn and Kleinen 2008).

The UN assessment of the world's oceans identifies and describes in some detail ten main themes. Table 6.1 provides a summary of this assessment. In the account provided of these themes in the UN's report, the following observations directly relevant to the main theme of this book are made:

Human impacts on the sea are no longer minor in relation to the overall scale of the ocean . . . Even if discharges of industrial effluents and emissions were restrained to the lowest levels in proportion to production that are currently practicable, continuing growth in production would result in increased inputs to the ocean. (United Nations 2016b, pp. 8, 9)

The UN assessment of the state of the world's oceans paints a dismal picture indeed and, with few exceptions, one that is deteriorating.

Oxygen concentrations in both the open ocean and coastal waters have been declining since at least the middle of the 20th century. This oxygen loss, or deoxygenation, is one of the most important changes occurring in an ocean increasingly modified by human activities that have raised temperatures, $CO_2$ levels, and nutrient inputs and have altered the abundances and distributions of marine species. (Breitburg et al. 2018)

The *Living Blue Planet Report* (WWF 2015), with a focus on species, habitats and human well-being, tells much the same story with the effective use of indices, graphically represented. The Living Planet Index (LPI) for marine populations is based on trends in 5829 populations of 1234 mammal, bird, reptile and fish species (WWF 2015, p. 6). As Figure 6.4 shows, the global marine LPI declined 49 percent between 1970 and 2012. This is close to the 58 percent decline in the LPI for vertebrates, which measures trends in 14152 populations of 3706 mammals, birds, fishes, amphibians and reptiles from around the world. 'Population sizes of vertebrate species have, on average, dropped by more than half in little more than 40 years' (WWF 2016, p. 18). These declines point to the sixth extinction (Kolbert 2015).

In Figure 6.4 the white line shows the LPI for marine populations and

*Table 6.1   Summary of an assessment of the world's oceans*

| Theme | Assessment |
| --- | --- |
| Climate change | Serious implications: rising sea levels, increased acidity, reduced mixing, increased deoxygenation. |
| Marine resources | Exploitation has exceeded sustainable levels in many regions causing declining biological resources. |
| Food security and safety | Global capture of 80 million tons/year is near the oceans' productive capacity. Contribution of aquaculture growing rapidly but brings new pressures on marine ecosystems. |
| Biodiversity | Pressures on marine biodiversity are increasing. |
| Ocean space conflicts | Increased conflicting demands especially in coastal areas from fishing, shipping, hydrocarbon extraction, mining, generation of renewable energy offshore. |
| Material and excess nutrients | Increased population, industrial and agricultural production result in increasing inputs of harmful material (e.g. plastics) and excess nutrients. |
| Cumulative impacts | Adverse impacts on marine ecosystems and a loss in ecosystem services come from the cumulative impacts of a number of human activities. |
| Distribution of benefits | Very uneven distribution of the benefits from the ocean due to differences in the natural distribution of resources and management capacity. |
| Management | A coherent approach to management is required for sustainable use of the ocean. Gaps in knowledge and capacity building are considerable. |

*Source:*  Based on the summary of the 10 main themes in The First Global Integrated Marine Assessment (UN 2016b).

the shaded blue areas show the confidence limits. Most of the decline in the index occurred between 1970 and 1988, with the index staying roughly constant since then. This general pattern is repeated in the sub-indices for fish, Scrombidae (tuna, mackerel, bonito), reef associated fish species, fish in seagrass habitats, deep-sea fish, and Antarctic toothfish in the Ross Sea. 'Overfishing is a global problem but there is evidence that effective management can rebuild stocks' (WWF 2015, p. 28).

The tonnage of fish caught annually remained virtually unchanged at around 90 million tonnes between 1990 and 2014 despite a huge increase in fishing effort (FAO 2016b, p. 53). As fleets move around the globe deplet-

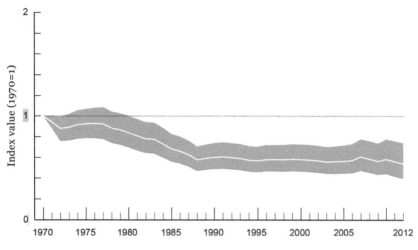

*Source:* WWF (2015, p. 6).

*Figure 6.4*    *Global marine Living Planet Index*

ing fish stocks as they go, they have also had to catch less favored species at increasing depths working down the food chain. With nearly 3 billion people relying on fish as a major source of protein (WWF 2015, p. 2), considerable effort has been made through the expansion of aquaculture to maintain the increase in total fish supplied to markets, reaching 167 million tonnes in 2014 (FAO 2016b).

But farming fish is not always a sustainable alternative. In many countries, aquaculture production has depleted key ecosystems like mangroves, polluted aquatic environments and potentially reduced climate change resilience for coastal communities. Poor management, a lack of capacity and access to technical knowledge, or irresponsible practices have also led to large-scale disease outbreaks, such as early mortality syndrome for shrimp in Asia (WWF 2015, p. 29).

This brief overview of the declining state of the oceans and the precariousness of the world's saltwater fisheries is a shocking abuse of what not so long ago was considered an infinite resource. It can be attributed in large part to the inadequate systems of governance to which they are subject. The quality of waste management systems as well as population size are identified by Jambeck et al. (2015) as the main causes of 4.8 to 12.7 million tonnes of plastic waste entering the ocean in 2010 adding to the much publicized 'Great Pacific Garbage Patch' (Montanari 2017). There are more than 5 trillion plastic pieces weighing over 250 tons floating in the oceans (Eriksen et al. 2014) contaminating and killing wildlife. The United Nations Law of the Sea confers special rights to nations for the exploration and use of marine resources within 200 nautical miles of their coast. This gives nations some capacity to place restrictions on these activities that are essential for conservation. Beyond the 200-mile limit the oceans are open to anyone to exploit as they wish. Experience shows that unregulated open access is a formula for over-exploitation since there is no financial gain to be had from conserving resources, be they fish in the ocean or minerals under the seabed, if someone else can extract them for short-term profit. At the same time, the rapid expansion of aquaculture is just one more example of how we rush into new technologies before adequately assessing all the risks. Depletion of the ocean fisheries may be the immediate cause of the increasing reliance on farmed fish, but it is the pursuit of economic growth, if not at all costs, at very considerable costs to the environment and the consumer, that is the underlying driving force.

### 6.3.3 Fresh Water

Water has been described as 'the issue for the 21st century' by such high profile figures as Mikhail Gorbachev, Shimon Peres and Crispin Tickell (Peres and Gorbachev 2000; Tickell 2003). Their concern is political, because they anticipate violent conflict over the growing scarcity of fresh water. At a more subtle level, Smakhtin et al. (2004) have looked at water basins around the globe and assessed the extent to which water that is used to satisfy domestic, industrial and agricultural needs leaves too little to provide ecosystem services such as fisheries, flood protection and wildlife. They conclude that 'basins where the current water use is already in conflict with the EWR [environmental water requirements for ecosystem services] cover over 15 per cent of the world land surface and are populated by over 1.4 billion people in total', a situation they expect to get only worse as water withdrawals increase (Smakhtin et al. 2004, p. 315) with economic and population growth.

Water scarcity is becoming increasingly severe. In 2017 the United Nations reported that 'about two thirds of the world's population currently live in areas that experience water scarcity for at least one month a year . . . about 50% of the people facing this level of water scarcity live in China and India . . . About 500 million peoples live in areas where water consumption exceeds the locally renewable water resources by a factor of two' (WWAP 2017, pp. 10–11). The socio-economic and health implications of drought are extremely troubling. The civil war and migration out of Syria have been attributed in part to the extreme drought in 2007–10, which ruined agriculture on 60 percent more of Syria's farm land (WWAP 2017) forcing people to move. In its assessment of global risks over the next 10 years, the

World Economic Forum placed the freshwater crisis at the top for people and economies (WEF 2016, p. 13).

## 6.4   CONCLUSION

Towards the end of the 20th century human impacts on the environment, climate change and biodiversity loss in particular, emerged as more pressing and more threatening limits to economic growth than shortages of raw materials. This assessment could turn around very quickly if the worst predictions of peak oil come to pass or if shortages of critical materials are realized. Then, in pursuit of economic growth, the world's appetite for cheap oil and the materials required for new technologies, most deeply felt in the rich countries, will likely override efforts to protect the environment from further human excess and the already troubling loss of ecosystem services will accelerate.

It will not be easy to work through this. We are dealing with a complicated highly integrated system in which human economies thrive by extracting materials from the biosphere, and use energy primarily from fossil fuels, for processing, transporting, using and disposing of material and energy wastes in ever increasing amounts. Though they can be described separately, sources, sinks and services must be understood as a system or set of systems driven very much by the human economy, where what happens in one has implications for the others. Economic growth relies upon these sources, sinks and services, benefiting some people often at the expense of others and almost always to the detriment of other species. In the next chapter we will look at several attempts to understand and measure the interconnections of sources, sinks and services and the human systems with which they are intimately related.

## NOTES

1.   The version of Figure 6.1 in the online version of Steffen et al. (2015a) uses different colors than the version shows here, which is from Rockström (2017).
2.   COP refers to the conference of the parties to the UN Framework Convention on Climate Change. This was their 15th meeting since the Convention was signed in 1994.
3.   Many analyses of greenhouse gases include several gases such as water vapor, carbon dioxide, methane, nitrous oxide, ozone and chlorofluorocarbons. They each have a different 'global warming potential' (GWP). The GWP of $CO_2$ is set at 1 and the GWP of all other gases is calculated relative to that so the GWP of all greenhouse gases combined can be calculated in terms of $CO_2$ equivalent or $CO_2^e$. Discussion in UNFCCC 2016 of a carbon budget is restricted to $CO_2$.

# 7. Limits to growth – synthesis

> Economic theories that endorse limitless growth are based on a model of the economy that, in essence, does not account for the resource inputs and waste-absorption capacities of the environment, and the limitations of technological progress and resource substitutability. (Motesharrei et al. 2016)

It is convenient for expositional purposes to distinguish among sources, sinks and services but we should not overlook the fact that they are highly connected. The Western intellectual tradition places great emphasis on reductionism: breaking complicated problems into their component parts in the belief that if we understand the parts we will understand the larger problems. Often this works well, but not always. The specialization of human knowledge has led to the creation of numerous distinct academic disciplines, each with its own way of seeing the world, identifying issues, describing and analyzing them, and reaching conclusions. Even within the broad groupings of natural science, social science and the humanities, there are major differences in the way their practitioners think and work. The rise of interdisciplinary studies in Western universities that began in the 1960s can be understood as a response to the limitations of reductionism, though not an entirely satisfactory one, at least not yet.

We have to find a way of considering and measuring sources, sinks and services together if we are to grasp the big picture of the dependence of economies on the environment and to assess concerns about biophysical limits to growth. There is no fully satisfactory way of doing this but there are several promising approaches. The ones we shall consider here are: system dynamics, human appropriation of net primary production, and the ecological footprint.

## 7.1 SYSTEM DYNAMICS

In Chapter 2 we described economies as open systems, their structures and functions dependent on the throughput of energy from the environment. System dynamics, which was developed by Jay Forrester of MIT in the 1950s and 1960s initially for industrial applications, is a way of modeling systems that emphasizes stocks, flows, feedbacks, lags and non-linearities. It is very useful for examining the behavior of systems over time. Modelers identify patterns of behavior of key system variables (the stocks and flows), and build models to mimic system behavior. The models are then used to examine possible interventions to achieve a desired outcome (Radzicki 1997).

Forrester became interested in urban problems and in 1969 published *Urban Dynamics*, which featured a system dynamics model of urban areas (Forrester 1969). He showed how well-intentioned actions can have 'counterintuitive' results, that is, unexpected reactions, because of non-linear feedback loops and time delays in the urban system. He examined four programs for improving depressed areas of central cities and found the programs ranged from ineffective to harmful (Forrester 1971a). Two years later Forrester applied system dynamics to the entire world (Forrester 1971b). This book went largely unnoticed at first but became widely reviewed after publication of *The Limits to Growth*, which built on Forrester's work and was published only a year later, making headline news around the world (Meadows et al. 1972).

Perhaps it was the title *The Limits to Growth* that caused such a stir. After 25 years of uninterrupted economic growth this was not a message for which there was much appetite among political and business leaders or economists. The book was a critical appraisal of the future prospects for economic and population growth at the global level. It questioned the sustainability of the track that the world was on. The startling reaction to such a small book may also have had something to do with the fact that the research it described had been commissioned by a mysterious sounding group called the Club of Rome. This was an informal group of individuals, none of whom held public office, drawn from many countries and united 'by their overriding conviction that the major problems facing mankind are of such complexity and are so interrelated that traditional institutions and policies are no longer able to cope with them' (Meadows et al. 1972, pp. 9, 10). The high degree of public interest may also have been influenced by the research team's use of a computer to produce their results. In 1972, this was considered newsworthy.

Meadows et al.'s system dynamics model included stocks and flows for industrial production, natural resources, environmental pollution connected by multiple, non-linear, feedback loops. The main conclusions of *The Limits to Growth* were:

1.  If the present growth trends in world population, industrialization, pollution, food production and resource depletion continue unchanged, the limits to growth on this planet will be reached some time within the next one hundred years. The most probable result will be a rather sudden and uncontrollable decline in both population and industrial capacity.

2. It is possible to alter these growth trends and to establish a condition of ecological and economic stability that is sustainable far into the future. The state of global equilibrium could be designed so that the basic material needs of each person on earth are satisfied and each person has an equal opportunity to realize his individual human potential.
3. If the world's people decide to strive for this second outcome rather than the first, the sooner they begin working to attain it, the greater will be their chances of success. (Meadows et al. 1972, pp. 23–4)

*The Limits to Growth* came under heavy criticism, which it still does, rather like Malthus's *Essay on the Principle of Population*, in which tradition it follows. Some of the criticism was generally supportive and constructive (University of Sussex Science Policy Research Unit 1973), but most was negative and dismissive. Economists in particular were critical because Meadows et al., and Forrester before them, did not include the price mechanism among the feedback mechanisms in their models:

> one notes that there is no explicit mechanism for allocating resources over time and between sectors. Economists usually introduce prices as an allocating mechanism. This is a crucial omission in Forrester's system, for prices are one obvious adaptive mechanism by which economic man does adjust to changes in relative scarcities such as those Forrester describes. If there is sufficient substitutability between producible and non-producible resources and if the price system is functioning adequately, the inevitable collapse predicted by Forrester will be avoided. (Nordhaus 1973[1])

Nordhaus's critique included two key assumptions: sufficient substitutability between producible and non-reproducible resources and an adequately functioning price system. Presumably, if one or both of these assumptions are not satisfied, as previous chapters in this book suggest they are not, then Nordhaus would have agreed with the conclusions of *The Limits to Growth*. In fact, Meadows et al. did allow for enhancements in technology and more abundant reserves of natural resources, features that can be used, at least partially, to simulate price effects, but not their assumed ongoing potential to steer the world system away from its limits. We saw in Chapter 3 that such effective and informed steering may be beyond the capacity of the price mechanism, lacking as it does some of the information essential to perform this function. And in Chapter 4 we saw the limitations of pricing nature as a way of fixing the problem, especially when substitution of produced capital for nature (Nordhaus's producible and non-producible resources) is not feasible.

The conclusions of *The Limits to Growth* have also been criticized:

About thirty [sic] years ago, in the infancy of the computer era, there was a rather extensive effort, known as *limits to growth*, that had the goal of making global predictions. The hope was to be able to forecast, among other things, the growth of the human population and its impact on the supply of natural resources. The project failed miserably because the outcome depended on unpredictable factors not explicitly incorporated in the program. (Bak 1996)

Friedman, extolling the virtues of economic growth, combines both criticisms: '*The Limits to Growth* authors made such faulty predictions because they underestimated the power of technological advance, and ignored altogether the role of initially higher prices both in encouraging substitution by users and in stimulating new supplies' (Friedman 2005). No model is immune from criticism and there is some validity to the points that critics made when *Limits to Growth* was published and still make. The model was extremely aggregated. For example, it did not differentiate among regions of the world. The inclusion of time (from 1990 to 2100) in the diagrammatic results did suggest they were making predictions about when the world system might encounter limits to growth, but Meadows et al. were careful to explain the sense in which they were making such predictions. Their interest was much more in the tendency of the system to overshoot its limits rather than in predicting when that would happen.

[W]e are interested only in the broad behavior modes of the . . . system. By *behavior modes* we mean the tendencies of the variable in the system (population or pollution for example) to change as time progresses . . . this process of determining behavior modes is 'prediction' only in the most limited sense of the word. (Meadows et al. 1972, pp. 91, 92)

Incidentally, the 'standard run' of the original limits to growth model in which 'no major change [occurs] in the physical, economic, or social relationships that have historically governed the development of the world system' (Meadows et al. 1972, p. 124) shows the system peaking and then collapsing well into the 21st century. When comparing what actually happened in the world since the publication of *The Limits to Growth* with the scenarios described in the book, Turner (2008) observes '30 years of historical data compare favourably with key features of . . . the "standard run" scenario, which results in collapse of the global system midway through the 21st century'. This finding was reinforced in Turner's subsequent analysis of the data extending over 40 years (Turner 2014) and further amplified in Jackson and Webster (2016). So, in light of what has happened in the world since *The Limits to Growth* was published, it is obviously premature to say, as Bak did and others continue to claim, 'they failed miserably'.

There have been two sequels to the original book, *Beyond the Limits*

(Meadows et al. 1992) and *Limits to Growth: The 30-Year Update* (Meadows et al. 2004). Both books employ much the same model and analysis as in the 1972 version, with some updating to account for new data. The main conclusions remain substantially the same, as do the criticisms (Nordhaus 1992a; 1992b). In 2012 Jorgen Randers, one of the authors of *The Limits to Growth* and the two sequels, offered a 'status report' and an assessment of whether 'humanity will rise to the occasion and effectively address the global unsustainabilities we still face' (Randers 2012, p. 354). His global forecast out to 2052 is not pretty, including as it does increased social strife, increased risk of self-reinforcing global warming, significant biodiversity loss and continuing gross inequalities.

More profound than the 'technical' critique of the limits to growth was the deeply felt objection to any suggestion that growth might have limits. Economic growth has become the primary policy objective of governments and political parties of all stripes. It is widely believed that economic growth is a pre-condition for meeting all other economic and social objectives. In some quarters, economic growth has gone from being regarded as a necessary condition for the fulfillment of other objectives, to being viewed as sufficient. For example, anti-poverty programs have been weakened and even abandoned on the assumption that the fruits of growth will trickle down. Likewise, it is often argued that while economic growth may not automatically improve the environment and that government intervention is necessary, it is a necessary condition for environmental improvement: 'environmental development [sic] often stems from economic development – only when we get sufficiently rich can we afford the relative luxury of caring about the environment' (Lomborg 2001, p. 33). Others note the contribution of technology and prices in mitigating resource depletion and damage to the environment (Friedman 2005, p. 377) but even Friedman qualifies his observations on economic growth and the environment by saying that 'it would be a mistake, however, to conclude from this rise-and-fall pattern that environmental concerns somehow "take care of themselves" as part of the economic growth process, leaving no need for public policy' (2005, p. 383).

Despite the criticisms, *The Limits to Growth* had quite an impact on how we think as well as on what we think about. The use of system dynamics highlighted the importance of systems thinking with its emphasis on positive and negative feedbacks, non-linear relationships and the difficulty of making predictions about the state of the world. If Meadows and colleagues paid too little attention to the self-adjusting capacity of the market in their models of the world system, their critics paid too much. Prices can mislead and decisions based on them can be shortsighted. As argued in Chapter 3, we need more information than is contained in prices to manage an economic system that is operating on such a scale as to affect the environment in so many deleterious ways. And in any case, to rely on technology to provide the solution, whether or not driven by price signals, is unwise as Huesemann and Huesemann (2011) argue in their comprehensive account of 'why technology won't save us or the environment'.

*The Limits to Growth* stimulated interest in long-term prospects and possibilities at the global level among the public, academics and, for a time, at the highest political levels. USA President Jimmy Carter commissioned a report from the Council on Environmental Quality to look at possible limits to growth and how the USA might be affected. The Commission concluded by saying that:

> If present trends continue, the world in 2000 will be more crowded, more polluted, less stable ecologically, and more vulnerable to disruption than the world we live in now. Serious stresses involving population, resources, and environment are clearly visible ahead. Despite greater material output, the world's people will be poorer in many ways than they are today. (Barney and US Council on Environmental Quality 1980)

Such prognostication does not seem as far off the mark as the more optimistic commentators such as Nordhaus, Lomborg and Friedman, relying on a belief in the efficacy of price signals and technology, would have us believe.[2]

*The Limits to Growth* also stimulated the development of improved global simulation models able to take advantage of the more comprehensive data sources than were available in the early 1970s. Integrated assessment models (IAMs) study human feedbacks and influences on climate change by coupling different models with each other, such as a climate model, a land use model, an energy model, often driven by forecasts of population and economic growth (Schwanitz 2013). IAMs have been extensively used by the Intergovernmental Panel on Climate Change (IPCC) to inform international negotiations on climate change. One criticism of these models is the rather limited feedbacks typically included between the climate and human systems. 'Common to these models is their deficiency in capturing dynamic bidirectional feedbacks between key variables of the Human System and the Earth System; instead, they simply use independent projections of Human System variables in Earth System Models' (Motesharrei et al. 2016, p. 478). Motesharrei et al. propose more comprehensive Earth System Models in which Earth and human systems are coupled more comprehensively, as illustrated in Figure 7.1.

Earth system models have very demanding requirements for data but the development of massive, real time data bases from various sources has made 'data assimilation' a practical proposition. They also give rise to the need for synthetic metrics that describe, measure and communicate

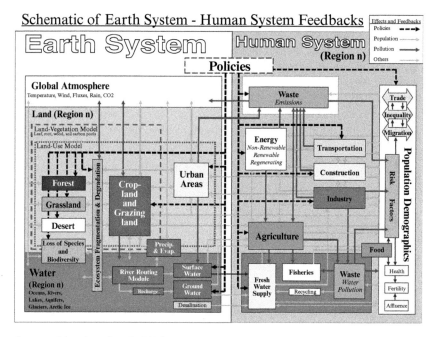

*Source:*   Motesharrei et al. (2016).

*Figure 7.1    Schematic of Earth system–human system feedbacks*

the performance of the coupled systems. Two that were first introduced in the 1990s are HANPP (the Human Appropriation of Net Primary Production) and the ecological footprint, which are described below.

## 7.2  HUMAN APPROPRIATION OF NET PRIMARY PRODUCTION

One of the barriers to enhancing our understanding and measurement of these systemic interactions and taking appropriate action is the lack of credible, informative indicators of the overall human impact on the environment. A promising approach was suggested by Vitousek and colleagues, who developed estimates of the extent to which humans draw upon the net products of photosynthesis (NPP), which are the basic foodstuff of all herbivores, carnivores and omnivores (Vitousek et al. 1986). Haberl and colleagues address the same issue using HANPP, 'an integrated socioecological indicator quantifying effects of human-induced changes in productivity and harvest on ecological biomass flows' (Haberl et al. 2014, p. 363). In the mid-1980s, Vitousek et al. (1986) estimated that humans were appropriating 'nearly 40% of potential global terrestrial NPP . . . or 25% of the potential global terrestrial and aquatic NPP . . . humans also affect much of the other 60% of terrestrial NPP, often heavily' (p. 372). This was an astonishing finding. It highlighted the pressure that our single species is placing on the Earth's ecosystems, which is fully consistent with the subsequent detailed analysis in the Millennium Ecosystem Assessment (2005) and with the estimates of more than 16 000 species at risk of extinction and rising (IUCN 2007; see also WWF 2016) as the sixth extinction takes hold. Vitousek et al.'s paper raised questions about possible ecological limits to growth. If in the mid-1980s, humans were appropriating nearly 40 percent of the net products of photosynthesis, how much more would we and could we take, with twice the population living at a much higher material standard of living?

Other scientists have estimated HANPP ranging from 3 percent to 55 percent (Haberl et al. 2014, p. 367). The wide divergence in these estimates results more from the different definitions of HANPP than from uncertainties in the data (ibid). The definition that Haberl et al. propose is: 'the difference between the NPP of the natural vegetation thought to exist in the absence of land use [. . . NPPpot . . .] and the fraction of NPP remaining in the ecosystem after harvest under current conditions [. . . NPPeco . . .]. That is, HANPP equals NPPpot minus NPPeco' (Haberl et al. 2014, p. 366).

Using this definition, which is somewhat different from Vitousek's, they estimate HANPP to be 24 percent for total terrestrial NPPpot in 2000. About 10 percent of the biomass produced annually in terrestrial ecosystems is consumed by humans. The remaining amount is lost through human alterations to the biosphere's productivity (Haberl et al. 2006). Haberl et al. (2014) provide estimates of how global HANPP as a percentage of total terrestrial NPPpot has increased: it was 13 percent in 1910, 18 percent in 1950 and 25 percent in 2005. These increases reflect changes in population density, food consumption, livestock husbandry, agricultural intensity and deforestation (Haberl et al. 2014, p. 375).

The relationship between economic growth and HANPP over time is illustrated in Figure 7.2, which shows that since 1910, global GDP grew much faster than global HANPP. This is an example of relative decoupling. Haberl et al. (2014) report that studies of specific countries such as Austria and the UK show examples of absolute decoupling for some periods of time. They attribute this to the conversion of some agricultural land to forests and an increase in the NPP of agricultural land from changes in farming practices. These have outweighed the growth of HANPPharv (harvested NPP) and the expansion of built-up land in these countries, but as Haberl et al. (2014) point out, the increases in NPP entailed considerable

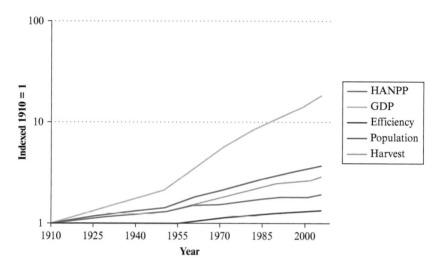

*Source:*    Haberl et al. (2014, p. 374).

*Figure 7.2    Global HANPP and GDP 1910–2005*

ecological costs from the increase in irrigation, the application of massive amounts of fertilizers and pesticides, and reductions in the diversity of agricultural landscapes with adverse impacts on soils, groundwater, and biodiversity.

In their examination of ecological embeddedness of the economy from 1700 to 2000, Haberl et al. (2006) conclude that:

> the efficiency increases in terms of a reduction in resource use per unit of GDP may be beneficial but are certainly not sufficient to result in a reversal of current trends . . . the developing countries will find it impossible to follow the trajectory the industrial core has followed in the last two centuries. (2006, p. 4903)

In a comment that anticipates some of the analysis in the next chapter, they say that 'efficiency increases are rather fuelling GDP growth than helping to reduce aggregate resource consumption' (2006, p. 4903).

## 7.3    THE ECOLOGICAL FOOTPRINT

Haberl et al. (2014) also describe a consumption-based version of HANPP which shows the HANPP resulting from the production chain of a product or of a regional or national economy which they term eHANPP. This version of HANPP is similar, though narrower in scope, to the ecological footprint introduced by Wackernagel and Rees (Wackernagel and Rees 1996). The ecological footprint is defined as 'the land (and water) area that would be required to support a defined human population and material standard of living indefinitely' (1996, p. 158). The ecological footprint includes all resource flows that require biologically productive land for their production or absorption of greenhouse gases. HANPP relates only to biomass use, except for the area used by infrastructure. The ecological footprint uses many weighting factors to aggregate different land uses into a common unit. HANPP is measured in terms of a single unit of the quantity of carbon/year, thus avoiding aggregation complications. By including an estimate of the land required to sequester all of the $CO_2$ released annually into the atmosphere from the combustion of fossil fuels and other sources, it is possible for the ecological footprint to exceed the biocapacity of the planet, something less readily detected by HANPP.

According to the estimates made by the Global Footprint Network, human uses of ecological resources surpassed the capacity of the Earth to support these uses sustainably in the early 1970s and by 2013 were exceeding this capacity by 70 percent and rising, as shown in Figure 7.3. By 2013, the biocapacity equivalent of 1.7 Earths was needed to provide the natural resources and services humanity consumed in that year (Global

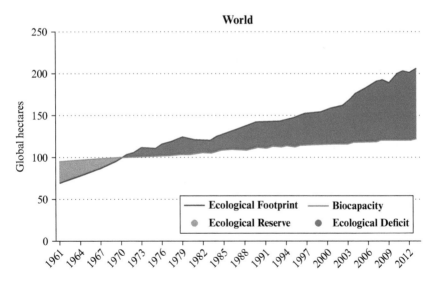

*Source:* Global Footprint Network 2017 National Footprint Accounts.

*Figure 7.3    World ecological footprint*

Footprint Network 2018). A global ecological footprint larger than the available ecologically productive area means that the Earth's capacity to support the human population with today's technologies and practices is being exceeded. This 'overshoot' can only be maintained temporarily while stocks of renewable and non-renewable natural resources are depleted and degraded, with consequences already evident for people and other species. This is illustrated by the Global Living Planet Index, which declined 58 percent between 1970 and 2012 (WWF 2016, p. 14). Vertebrate species populations on Earth are about 40 percent of what they were in 1970, which is astonishing and extremely troubling (WWF 2016, p. 12).

The ecological footprint has its critics. One criticism concerns the calculation of the ecological footprint attributed to fossil fuel consumption (Neumayer 2003). This component of the footprint is calculated by estimating the land area required to grow trees in sufficient numbers to sequester the carbon that is released when fossil fuels are burned. Neumayer argues that carbon sequestration is only one means of dealing with fossil fuels. If solar technologies were substituted for fossil fuels, the ecological footprint of the global economy would be greatly reduced. This is because the land area required to sequester carbon dioxide from fossil fuel combustion accounts for nearly 50 percent of the global footprint.

The inclusion of the land area required to sequester carbon is not a fundamental weakness of the ecological footprint, though whether the use of a land-based metric to measure implications of the excess emission of greenhouse gases is helpful when other more direct metrics are available is a moot point. The ecological footprint was designed to measure the impact of human activity as it is on the environment, not as it might be with different technologies. Applying the ecological footprint to new technologies can be useful for providing insight into the contribution that they could make in reducing the size of the overall ecological footprint of an economy. However, measurement of the ecological footprint is based on 'prevailing technology and resource management' (Kitzes et al. 2007). It would be misleading to estimate the ecological footprint of today's economy assuming tomorrow's technologies, except as an assessment of what might be possible in the future. In the period covered by Figure 7.3 the world was relying on natural processes to absorb the carbon dioxide released from fossil fuel combustion, and the capacity of these processes was being exceeded, as indicated by the increase in the concentration of carbon dioxide in the atmosphere. The world's ecological footprint will change if we reduce emissions of carbon dioxide or find ways to prevent it from reaching the atmosphere. Technology can help but it must actually do so before it affects this particular measure of the impact of our economies on the environment.

The aggregate nature of the ecological footprint is another point of criticism since very different activities are assessed in terms of area as a common unit of measurement, neglecting possibly critical differences. This feature of the ecological footprint is a strength and a weakness. Aggregation across very different categories of land use, from agricultural production to carbon sequestration, requires simplification, and important information can be lost in the process. In this respect, the ecological footprint is no different from GDP. Yet the ecological footprint is easier for most people to understand than GDP and it specifically addresses the environmental dimension of economic activity, which GDP ignores. The ecological footprint provides a valuable reminder of the extraordinary impacts of the human economy on the environment, wherever they may be felt, even if the metric is not perfect. And it can be calculated for global, national and regional economies as well as for individuals based on their specific levels and patterns of consumption. This flexibility is another advantage of the ecological footprint and one that has contributed to its popularity.[3]

Figure 7.4 shows the relationship between average GDP per capita and the average ecological footprint per capita in 2013 on an unweighted national basis. Visually it is apparent that, with exceptions, the countries with a higher GDP per capita also have a higher ecological footprint per

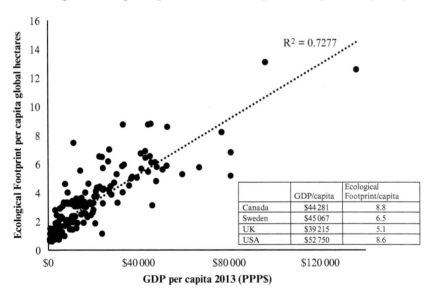

*Sources:* Based on data from World Bank (2016e), World Development Indicators; Global Footprint Network (2018), National Footprint Accounts.

*Figure 7.4    GDP per capita (PPP$) for countries and their per capita ecological footprint in 2013*

capita. The strength of this relationship is indicated by the high correlation coefficient of 0.73. The ecological footprint per capita of countries increases roughly 0.1 for every $1000 increase in per capita GDP though, as can be seen from the inset in Figure 7.4 showing data for Canada, Sweden, the UK and USA, this is only an approximate relationship. As Figure 7.4 shows, there is considerable variation of ecological footprints for countries with similar per capita GDPs (looking vertically) and even greater variations in per capita GDPs for countries with similar ecological footprints (looking horizontally). This suggests possibilities for reducing ecological footprints without reducing GDP per capita. But it also shows the difficulty of reconciling growth in GDP per capita with an absolute reduction in ecological footprints.

The well-known deficiencies in GDP as a measure of well-being (see Chapter 9) are partially remedied by the UN's Human Development Index, which is based on life expectancy at birth, education and income per capita. 'The HDI was created to emphasize that people and their capabilities should be the ultimate criteria for assessing the development of a country, not economic growth alone' (United Nations Development Programme 2015b). The more recent Inequality-adjusted IHDI (United Nations Development Programme 2015c) based on the HDI captures the losses in human development due to inequality in health, education and income. Figure 7.5 shows the relationship between the IHDI and the

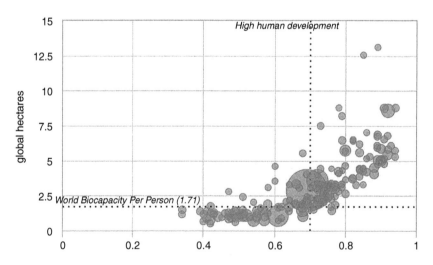

*Source:* GFN (2018).

*Figure 7.5   Human Development Index and the ecological footprint*

ecological footprint per capita based on the latest data available for 2013 for 176 countries. The circle is for each country scaled by population. The quadrant in the bottom right-hand corner of Figure 7.5 represents a combination of high and very high human development and a per capita ecological footprint no larger than the per capita biocapacity available on the planet. In 2013 only Sri Lanka and the Dominican Republic had an HDI value greater than 0.7 (high human development) and a per capita ecological footprint less than average world biocapacity of 1.71 global hectares per person. No country had an HDI exceeding 0.8 signifying 'very high' human development and a per capita ecological footprint less than 1.71 global hectares.

## 7.4  CONCLUSION

The purpose of this and the previous two chapters has been to show that we ought to take the biophysical limits to economic growth more seriously than we do. Limits are apparent in all the ways we rely on nature to support our economies: sources are becoming costly, financially and even more so, environmentally; sinks are overflowing; services are in decline, and all are interrelated. We are confronting these limits because of the growth agenda and we are not responding to them adequately. One thing is clear and that is that sources, sinks and services should be considered within the same framework and their connections to the economy should be examined together. HANPP and the ecological footprint provide useful metrics for integrating a variety of important considerations, and system dynamics provides an approach that captures the interrelated dynamics of economic and biophysical systems. The excessive pressures that the world's economies are placing on the biosphere are undeniable, calling for changes in the scale and pattern of humane economies. Economic growth as experienced in the rich countries is not an option for the 9 billion people expected to be living on the planet by mid-century. Growth should be concentrated where it can do the most good, that is, where it can raise the living standards of the poorest people on the planet, most of whom live in developing countries.

## NOTES

1.  Nordhaus critiqued Forrester's model not Meadows's because when he was writing he was unable to obtain a detailed account of Meadows's model. Details were subsequently published (Meadows 1974).

2. A UNEP study using a more recent global system dynamics model concluded that 'a green economy grows faster than a brown economy over time, while maintaining and restoring natural capital' (Bassi 2011, p.i). Several weaknesses in the analysis were exposed in Victor and Jackson (2012) including: (1) an inadequate $CO_2$ emissions reduction target; (2) assumed higher investment in the green economy scenario than in the brown economy scenario with no assessment of how the additional investment is to be financed; (3) unsatisfactory implicit assumptions about the distribution of global economic output between richer and poorer countries.

3. For criticism of the ecological footprint from a complex systems perspective see Giampietro and Saltelli (2014) and the detailed response by Goldfinger et al. (2014).

# 8.    Scale, composition and technology

> [C]ontinued growth greatly increases the severity of climate change. Indeed
> we find that climate change is a problem in large part 'caused' by exogenous
> population and productivity growth. Rapid reductions in growth make climate
> change a small problem; smaller reductions in growth imply climate change is a
> very serious problem indeed. (Kelly and Kolstad 2001)

In this chapter we analyze the impacts of humans on the environment in
terms of three components: the scale of economic activities; the composition of these activities in terms of whether they involve goods or services;
and the technologies employed. As we will see, by analyzing these three
components and their interactions, we will gain new insights into the possibilities for decoupling environmental impacts from economic growth, a
topic we first encountered in Chapter 2 and examined using historical data
in Chapters 5 and 6 on sources, sinks and services. Obviously, there are
huge and important differences between scale, composition and technology around the world and, to a lesser extent, within each country. We will
attend to some of these differences later in this chapter. For now we will
explain these components in a general way, and then introduce regional
differences when we look specifically at the problem of climate change.

## 8.1    SCALE

Many people concerned about the long-term availability of resources and the
environmental impacts of human economies focus on *scale*. They point to
the large and growing population, to increasing urbanization, to increasing
economic output. The world's population of 7.6 billion in 2018 is forecast to
rise to 9.8 billion by mid-century (United Nations 2017a, p. 1). It could be as
low as 9.4 billion or as high as 10.2 billion depending on what happens to the
fertility rate (that is, the average number of children born to a woman over
her lifetime) between now and then (2017a, p. 3). By 2100 the UN forecasts
that the world's population will be between 9.6 and 13.2 billion, with 11.2 billion considered most likely (2017a, p. 2). In 2016 54.5 percent of the world's
population was urbanized and 512 cities had more than 1 million inhabitants
(United Nations 2016a). The world's economic output in 2000 was 19 times

bigger than in 1900 (International Monetary Fund 2000). Hidden within these numbers is the massive scale of individual technologies. For example, in 2017 the Korean-built PPCL *Hong Kong* was the world's largest container ship with a capacity of 21 413 standard 20-foot containers (Marine Insight 2017).[1] The deepest mine in the world as of 2013 was the Mponeng gold mine in Johannesburg, South Africa with an operating depth range of 2.4–3.9 kilometers (Kable 2016), and the largest excavating machine, the Bagger 288, is 311 feet tall, 705 feet long and weighs 45 500 tons. In a day it can excavate enough coal to fill 2500 rail cars (Totaljobs 2017). The list could go on but the point is made. The increasing scale of human activity on Earth has changed the face of the planet, often to the detriment of people and other species. If the scale is increased still further with the same technologies, we will require proportionately more natural resources, we will produce proportionately more wastes, and we will occupy and transform proportionately more land. The outlook would be bleak indeed.

## 8.2   COMPOSITION

We will not simply expand the scale of our economic activities using the same technologies. If we change the *composition* of what we produce and consume, say by switching from goods to services, that alone could lessen impacts on the environment. Services such as banking and personal care typically require less energy and materials than most goods of equal monetary value. So, if the composition of GDP changes in favor of services and away from goods, GDP can rise with the same or even less impact on the environment. Changes in the composition of GDP help explain how the TMR (total material requirements) per capita in Germany, the Netherlands and the United States tended to converge and level off between 1975 and 1993 at about 75 to 85 metric tonnes per year while GDP per capita continued to grow (Adriaanse et al. 1997). But since the populations of these countries also continued to grow during this period, TMR increased, though more slowly than GDP. This is an example of relative but not absolute decoupling.

Another way in which the changes in the composition of a nation's GDP can affect the environment is through the substitution of imported goods for domestically made ones. If a rich nation replaces its own production of steel with imports made abroad, the environmental impacts of steel production will also be moved abroad. Changes like this in the composition of trade can give the appearance of growth being good for the environment, but only if seen from the perspective of the richer, importing country and only if transboundary environmental impacts are ignored (see Chapter 5).

## 8.3  TECHNOLOGY

Technology is another factor that can mitigate and prevent environmental impacts. New and improved technologies allow us to do more with less. Technology has allowed the average standard of living, as measured by GDP per capita, to increase in many countries while keeping ahead of impending shortages and solving some environmental problems. It can continue to do so, or so it is claimed by those who see a future of continuing population growth, economic growth, technical change and an improved natural environment. A well-known exponent of this view is the same Julian Simon who won the bet with Paul Ehrlich about mineral prices (see Chapter 5):

> The growth of population and of income creates actual and expected shortages, and hence leads to price rises. A price increase represents an opportunity that attracts profit-minded entrepreneurs to seek new ways to satisfy the shortages. Some fail, at cost to themselves. A few succeed, and the final result is that we end up better off than if the original shortage problems had never arisen. (Simon 1994, p. 29)

Simon makes a point of not saying we should deliberately create problems, though the logic of his argument might suggest otherwise. He claims that over the long term, increased scale (that is, more people with higher material incomes), combined with new and improved technologies, have made humanity much better off in the past two centuries and that this can continue into the future without limit. It is this projection into the future that we are calling into question in this book.

Closely linked to the kind of technological optimism that Simon espoused is the view that knowledge can increase exponentially or, what amounts to the same thing, knowledge accumulation has no limits. Knowledge can also be lost as it was when the Library of Alexandria was destroyed, or less dramatically when computer files are erased, or whenever, for any reason, the knowledge of one generation is not passed to the next. But let us allow that knowledge accumulation has no limits. This is not a statement about what that knowledge will consist of. If it became widely understood that economic growth as we have known it cannot be sustained, then that would constitute new knowledge. It is one thing to suggest that more will be learned. It is quite another to be confident about what will be learned and to assume that it will be embodied in ever more productive technologies.

Another view on technology and its continuing capacity to accommodate increasing human pressure on the environment is provided by Brander who, in his examination of the history of technology, reports three facts:

'i) Relatively little progress has been made in the energy sector over the past 50 years . . . ii) Progress in agriculture has slowed in recent years . . . iii) . . . If anything, human beings have lost ground since the 1970s in the battle against infectious disease' (Brander 2007, pp. 21–2). These facts are similar to the observations made by Gordon (2016) in his detailed account of US economic history and conclusion that the decline in the rate of the growth of the US economy is likely to continue for a long time. Brander identifies information technology and consumer electronics as the areas where technological improvements have been the greatest from about 1960 but suggests that for 'dealing with resource degradation problems, the potential contribution [of these technologies] seems modest and unlikely to have a major impact on ecological carrying capacity' (Brander 2007, p. 22).

## 8.4   IPAT

Scale, composition and technology in combination are the proximate determinants in an economy of what resources are required, what wastes will be generated, and how much land will be transformed. One way to investigate the relationships among scale, composition and technology is to start with the 'IPAT' equation (Chertow 2001; Ehrlich and Holdren 1971). We will first explain IPAT and some of its shortcomings, and then put it to work.

$$I = P \times A \times T \tag{8.1}$$

where:
$I$ = impact
$P$ = population
$A$ = affluence (GDP/population)
$T$ = technology (impact/GDP).

   In equation (8.1), $I$ can be any kind of environmental impact relating to sources, sinks and/or services and is measured as a flow, for example tonnes of carbon dioxide released per year, liters of contaminated water discharged into lakes and rivers per year, or hectares of land converted from forest to agriculture per year. $P$ and $A$ are both scale factors. Other things being equal, more population ($P$) and/or more affluence ($A$) means more environmental impact. Multiplying $P$ and $A$ gives GDP, the aggregate output of the economy. $T$ measured as impact per unit of GDP, is where technology comes in. Technology can have many different meanings (Franklin 1999). For our purposes technology means the extension of the human capacity to interact with nature: to use more or less materials and energy, to create more or less of different kinds of wastes, and to transform land in various ways and to varying extents. Technology encompasses what we produce and how, the kinds of goods and services that we consume and the transportation and information methods used in distribution. Usually the same technology operated at a larger scale will increase impact, but we can have economic growth without increasing impact if we also get a sufficient reduction in impact per unit of GDP from new and improved technologies. This is the hope and belief of the technological optimists (Lovins et al. 2007).

One of the criticisms of the IPAT equation is that it implies that the variables on the right-hand side (population, affluence and technology) are independent of one another when this is generally not the case. Population growth can affect affluence and vice versa. Affluence can affect technology and vice versa. While the basic arithmetic of the equation cannot be faulted, we should be careful how we use it. Because of the interconnectedness of population growth, economic growth and technological change, we may not have the option of simply changing just one of them to change impact ($I$). We are more likely to have to take a coordinated approach to two or all three (IPCC 2000). Another shortcoming of IPAT is that if it is used at too aggregated a level, it will fail to disclose important regional differences. Global application of IPAT will not reveal marked differences between developed and developing countries or between rich and poor regions within groups of countries or an individual country (IPCC 2000).

Any decoupling of economic growth from energy, materials and environmental impact will show up in changes in the value of $T$ (impact per dollar of GDP). $T$ can change if a different technology is used to produce the same level and composition of GDP – for example, if a more efficient production method is introduced to produce the same product. $T$ can also change if there is a change in the composition of GDP, without an increase or decrease in GDP. For instance, a greater proportion of services and a lower proportion of manufactured goods at the same level of GDP can reduce the value of $T$. So, although IPAT is sensitive to changes in the composition of GDP, it does not really distinguish between them and real changes in technology. Composition and technology both affect impact. In IPAT, their combined influence is expressed through their effects on the value of $T$, obscuring their individual contributions.

To look more closely at how changes in the composition of GDP alone can affect impacts on the environment, we have to sacrifice some of the simplicity of IPAT and add more detail. We do this in equation (8.2), which shows goods, services, imports and exports separately though the basic logic of IPAT is maintained:

$$I_T = [P \times D/P \times I_D] + [P \times S/P \times I_S] - M_I - X_I \qquad (8.2)$$

where:
$I_T$ = total impact
$I_D$ = impact per dollar of goods
$I_S$ = impact per dollar of services
$M_I$ = impact of producing and transporting imported goods and services
$X_I$ = impact of consuming and transporting exported goods and services
$P$ = population
$D$ = goods component of GDP
$S$ = services component of GDP.

Equation (8.2) is simply an expansion of equation (8.1). It distinguishes between goods, services, imports and exports, and the environmental impacts associated with each of them. The equation is essentially the same as IPAT except that goods and services are shown separately inside each set of square brackets and the impacts of importing ($M_I$) and exporting ($X_I$) goods and services that are primarily felt abroad are subtracted. (These subtractions are appropriate for understanding the impact of the economy on the domestic environment. They should not be made if interest is in global environmental impacts.) The impact of imports and exports of goods and services can also be decomposed using the same IPAT logic, but for our purposes it is unnecessary to show the detail.

Equation (8.2) allows us to distinguish between the effects on the total impact of changes in the composition of GDP (that is, the mix of goods and services, imports and exports – $D$, $S$, $X$ and $M$) and changes in technology (shown by changes in the impact or $I$ factors). Even with the added detail of equation (8.2), there are some rough and ready assumptions. Some of the environmental impacts of transporting internationally traded goods and services are incurred locally, such as from invasive species carried in ballast water disposed of in national waters. More significantly perhaps, many impacts start out locally, but since the environment does not respect national boundaries, may spread beyond national borders. Acid rain and greenhouse gases are obvious examples.

### 8.4.1 The Composition of GDP and Environmental Impact

We can now use equation (8.2) to examine the recent history of changes in scale, composition and technology and the magnitude of future changes required to reduce environmental impacts to acceptable levels. Assume for the moment an economy with no international trade and that the impact per dollar of services ($I_S$) is less than the impact per dollar of goods ($I_D$). If GDP remains the same but the share of services rises while the share of goods falls, the total environmental impact of the economy will decline without any change in technology. This would be an example of absolute decoupling of environmental impact from economic growth. Environmental impact can even decline if GDP is growing as long as the switch from goods to services is large enough to outweigh the overall increase in the scale of the economy. This is 'dematerialization' of the economy when services replace goods (Heiskanen and Jalas 2000).

In an economy closed to international trade, the substitution of services for goods applies equally to production and consumption. Now if we open the economy to international trade, the impact on the domestic environment can be reduced by exporting services and importing goods. The more immediate environmental impacts from producing goods will be displaced abroad, giving the appearance of decoupling. Of course, this is not a strategy that all countries can follow. It is short-sighted since many environmental impacts that appear local have regional and global consequences, and it is inequitable.

As an example of the impact of how international trade can affect the allocation of environmental impacts, consider Figure 8.1, which shows how the emissions of greenhouse gases (GHGs) embedded in consumption in various countries compare to the GHG emissions in those countries over the years 1995 to 2009. We can call these consumption-based and

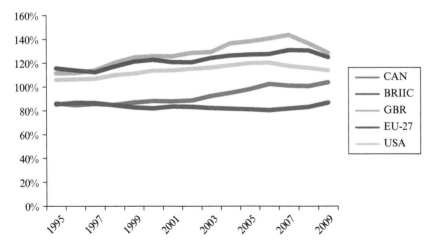

*Source:* Dolter and Victor (2016).

*Figure 8.1   Consumption-related GHG emissions as a percentage of production-related GHG emissions*

production-based emissions. In 2009 consumption-based GHG emissions in Great Britain were 30 percent higher than production-based emissions. This compares with the BRIIC countries where consumption-based GHG emissions were just over 80 percent of their production-based emissions. The deviations from 100 percent are entirely attributable to international trade with the BRIIC countries being net exporters of goods to Britain and other developed economies, whose economies relied more on the export of services. After 2006, even Canada with its strong resource base was responsible for greater GHG emissions from consumption than from production.

Figure 8.1 only considered one environmental impact, GHG emissions. (As noted earlier, for simplicity in this chapter we are referring to emissions as an environmental impact where in fact they are the cause of impacts.) It is an empirical question whether the environmental impact of a dollar of services is less than a dollar of goods. It can only be answered by a comprehensive assessment of the material and energy flows associated with the production and consumption of all goods and services produced, consumed and traded internationally by an economy. One approach that looks at the entire national economy is to use an environmentally extended input–output model. Victor (1972) was the first example of such a model applied to a national economy. More recent studies such as Dolter and Victor (2016) use multi-regional input−output models, which enable the different production processes in each country and trade among them to be more accurately taken into account.

The increasing availability of multi-regional input−output models, especially with environmental extensions, promises to deliver increasingly interesting detailed results as more researchers adopt their use. In the meantime, we can gain some appreciation of the different environmental impacts of goods and services by considering which economic sectors are classified under these two main headings. The goods-producing sectors of the economy are agriculture, forestry, fishing and hunting; mining and oil and gas extraction; utilities; construction; and manufacturing. Service sectors include: wholesale and retail trade; transportation and warehousing; information and cultural industries; finance and insurance, real estate and rental and leasing; professional, scientific and technical services; management of companies and enterprises; administrative and support, waste management and remediation services; educational; health care and social assistance; arts, entertainment and recreation; accommodation and food services; other services; and public administration (Statistics Canada 2016c). Services include some activities that have significant environmental impacts (for example, transportation and waste management), but overall the impact per dollar of services (*IS*) is less than the impact per dollar of goods (*ID*) given the nature of the goods-producing sectors.

So how has the mix of goods and services changed in advanced economies and what scope is there for further change? Table 8.1 shows the expenditure on services as a percentage of GDP in Canada, Sweden, the UK and the USA, in 1997 and 2016. In the mid-1990s expenditure on services in these countries was already two to three times greater than expenditure on goods, increasing still further in the twenty years that followed. This will be sobering news to those who think that economic growth could continue indefinitely if only economies were to switch from goods to services. The switch has largely happened in high-income countries and the prospects for further movement in this direction in terms of percentages of GDP are therefore quite limited.

The trend towards services in advanced economies is further illustrated in Figure 8.2, which shows the value added of industry, services, and agriculture as a percentage of GDP for high-income economies. Starting at

*Table 8.1    Percentage of GDP from expenditure on services*

|  | 1997 | 2016 |
|---|---|---|
| Canada | 65% | 71% |
| Sweden | 67% | 74% |
| UK | 72% | 80% |
| USA | 75% | 79% |

*Sources:*    Canada from Statistics Canada (2017h); Sweden, UK and USA from OECD (2017e).

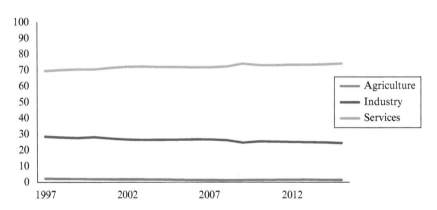

*Source:*    World Bank (2017b).

*Figure 8.2    Value added by sectors in high-income economies as a*
           *percentage of GDP*

below 60 percent in 1971 (not shown), rising steadily to 70 percent in 1997 and then to 75 percent in 2015, it is clear that the services sector already dominates the economies of the rich countries of the world.

Of course, while expenditures on goods as a percentage of GDP have been in decline in advanced economies, *total* real expenditures on goods have still been increasing since GDP has been growing: from 57 percent in Canada from 1997 to 2016 (Statistics Canada 2017h), 43 percent in Sweden, and 31 percent in the USA.[2] During the same period expenditure on goods in the European Union (28 countries) increased 22 percent, so the UK was an outlier in that expenditure on goods was virtually unchanged over the 20-year period (OECD 2017e). Because the environmental impacts relating to the production and disposal of goods rather than to services contributes disproportionately to the total impact of an economy, this increasing expenditure on goods – with the associated increase in material and energy flows even as economies move more towards services in proportional terms – is especially significant. The rapid growth in big box stores, the increase in housing space per person, and the proliferation of private storage facilities underline this continuing growth in the material possessions of those living in advanced economies (Center for Sustainable Systems, University of Michigan 2016; Sonne 2013; Storage World 2017; Moura et al. 2015).

We have seen that when we look at the composition of GDP in advanced economies, expenditures on services far exceed those on goods. However, when we look at the composition of their international trade, the situation is reversed, as shown in Table 8.2.

The percentage of exports represented by goods far exceeds that for services in Canada, Sweden and the USA. Only in the UK, where in 2016 goods represent only 55 percent of total exports, having declined from 72 percent in 1997, do services exceed 35 percent of exports in these countries. This could be due to the increasingly disproportionate contribution of financial services in the UK economy. Nonetheless, the dominance of

*Table 8.2   Goods as a percentage of exports and imports*

| Country | 1997 | 1997 | 2016 | 2016 |
|---|---|---|---|---|
| | Exports | Imports | Exports | Imports |
| Canada | 88% | 81% | 84% | 83% |
| Sweden | 83% | 75% | 68% | 69% |
| UK | 72% | 79% | 55% | 75% |
| USA | 73% | 84% | 65% | 81% |

*Source:*   OECD (2017e).

goods in the international trade of these countries remained strong. The relatively minor changes in the composition of their international trade are unlikely to have had much net impact on the domestic environment of the advanced economies since total exports and imports of goods increased at about the same pace and at much the same levels, other than in the UK. Paradoxically, it is the increasing shipment of goods (which is classified as a service), and the related increased fuel consumption that may have had the greatest impact on the environment.

Looking ahead, further changes in the composition of advanced economies or in the pattern of international trade will not do much to mitigate the impact of continuing economic growth on the environment. Services already dominate the composition of GDP in these economies so the possibility for reducing the environmental impact of economic growth through a sustained substitution of services for goods is largely non-existent. Economic growth has far outweighed changes in composition of GDP in the past and it can be expected to do so in a business-as-usual future. The main burden for reducing environmental impact in the face of continued economic growth must therefore fall on technology.

### 8.4.2   Changes in Technology and Environmental Impact

Differences in views about what technology has already contributed and what it might accomplish in the future separate the optimists from the pessimists. Engulfed as we are by a flood of new technologies based especially on miniaturization, computerization and the life sciences, it is understandable that many people think we can count on technology to see us through any future difficulties. They may be right. They may also be wrong. What if technological change proves unable to keep pace with the projected increase in scale? Precaution suggests that we should limit the increase in scale so that we do not have to count on technology alone bailing us out.

There are three good reasons for not relying too much on technology. First, new technologies can be a mixed blessing. They often solve one problem but create others. Examples abound: nuclear power stations generate electricity and radioactive waste. Jet planes transport people and goods around the world at unprecedented speed leaving greenhouse gases and noise pollution in their wake. Television entertains and informs us. It also promotes a high consumption lifestyle, glamorizes violence and deprives us of exercise. Computers and smart phones, with their increasing surveillance and targeted advertising, do much the same. Social media connects us to people however distant and isolates us from those around us. Monocultures and genetically modified organisms increase food and fiber production but reduce ecological resilience. And so on. It is hard to think of a technology that does not have a downside, often unanticipated. The faster we develop and implement new technologies, the more likely it is that we will have to deal with adverse effects. We will not be able to foresee them all. We are not that smart. But unwelcome surprises would be less likely if we took more time to think about and anticipate the consequences of new technologies and phased their introduction to allow more time to learn from experience. The aggressive pursuit of economic growth, or any one of its many surrogates – competitiveness, productivity, free trade and so on – stands in the way of a more thoughtful approach to new technologies throughout all stages of invention, design, development and diffusion. Yet, as IPAT reveals, the faster the rate of economic growth, other things equal, the faster must be the rate of technological improvement to compensate for the effects on the environment of scale.

We saw in Chapters 5 and 6 several areas where a rise in impacts cannot or should not be tolerated. It follows that we should be looking for ways to reduce requirements for resources and impacts on the environment. Can we strike a better balance between the rate of economic growth (a combination of GDP per person and population) and the rate at which new technologies are introduced? While there are many institutions in the public and private sectors promoting and contributing to growth, there is very limited institutional capacity to screen new technologies while they are under development, or after adoption and widespread use. Technology development and diffusion are driven primarily by expectations of profit. Profit is based on prices. We have already seen that prices are inadequate for conveying accurate and reliable information about resource scarcity and environmental impacts, so price-induced and profit-induced techno-logical change suffers as a result.

The second reason to be cautious about relying too much on technology to resolve problems arising from increasing scale is that some of these problems do not lend themselves to a technological solution. There are some aspects of nature, or differently stated, some services that nature provides, that human ingenuity cannot be expected to replicate or replace if they are lost or damaged. Regulation of the climate is one example. If our actions disturb the climate so that it 'flips' into another fairly stable but much less hospitable regime, it would be foolish to assume that we will develop a technology that could flip it back and do so in a timely manner (Schneider 2004). Less dramatic but still disturbing is the over-fishing of the cod stocks of the Grand Banks, believed for centuries to be inexhaust-ible. Yet 'in 1992 the cod fishery collapsed and 40,000 people lost their jobs including 10,000 fishermen. Today the cod stock, although showing signs of recovery, remains well below pre-collapse levels' (WWF Living Blue Planet Report 2015, p. 28).

The thousands of species that humans have driven to extinction are gone forever. Genetic information does not obey any law of conservation. Even if we preserve the genetic information of some species and scientists discover how to recreate members of extinct species, it would be very risky to re-introduce them into what could be very different habitats from the ones they evolved in. The ecological consequences are impossible to anticipate and unlikely to be favorable. Murphy's law that anything that can go wrong will go wrong is not just a joke. It's closely related to the law of unintended consequences: that any action has results that are not part of the actor's purpose. Let us not have blind faith in the ability of technology, now or in the future, to solve any and all problems that we create in the name of economic growth (Huesemann and Huesemann 2011).

The third reason why we should question how fast technological change will reduce environmental impacts is that even some of the greatest improvements in technology proceeded at quite a modest rate. A good example is the steam engine, which powered the first industrial revolution in Britain and then other countries from the mid-18th to the early 20th centuries. There were steam engines before James Watt designed his in 1769. Thomas Savery built a steam driven pump in 1698 based on a design by Denis Papin. The pump was used to remove water from mines to prevent flooding (Karwatka 2007). Thomas Newcomen improved Savery's design by incorporating a piston inside the cylinder in which the vacuum was formed. The first Newcomen steam engine for pumping water was installed at a coal mine in 1712. These steam driven pumps allowed deeper mines and greater access to Britain's rich deposits of coal and other minerals. That they were extremely inefficient did not matter very much as long as they were used at coal mines where plenty of fuel was available (Karwatka 2001). When Watt was repairing one of Newcomen's engines he realized that he could make it more efficient by using a separate condenser to cool the used steam. In 1781 Watt designed a steam engine that could deliver rotary power rather than the up and down motion required for pumping water. Now steam engines could be used in manufacturing and because of their improved efficiency, requiring less coal to produce a unit of useful energy, factories could be located close to their markets rather than to the coal mines. The most common applications for these new and improved steam engines were in textile production, and the textile industry became a catalyst of the industrial revolution in Britain (Dickenson 1935). Steam engines could also be used to power steam trains, and by the 1840s for the first time in history, people could move themselves and their freight faster than a horse could carry them (Smil 1994).

Throughout this period and beyond, many improvements were made in the design and construction of steam engines. In particular, they were made much more efficient. By 1910 the best steam engines were about 50 times more efficient than a Newcomen engine and about 12 times more efficient than a Watt engine (Smil 1994, Figure 5.3, p. 164). These were truly impressive gains but they did take a long time. Also, there is always a delay between the timing of a technological advance and its implementation. The average efficiency of steam engines at any time was always less than the best. A comparison of the gains in the efficiency of steam engines with the increase in installed capacity of steam engines in Britain shows that increases in scale outpaced improvements in efficiency by some 40 to 50 times (Crafts 2004). The increased use of coal to fuel the almost 2000-fold increase in steam power in Britain between 1760 and 1910 very likely caused a significant increase in environmental impacts as well.

Many of the most important technological advances in the 20th century involved electricity. While the pace of technological change quickened, the record of efficiency gains in the use of electricity in the 20th century is far less impressive than for steam in the 19th. Total end use of electricity in the USA increased over 630 times from an estimated 5700 GWh in 1902 to 3 606 500 GWh in 2000. The average secondary efficiency of this electricity use (that is, the conversion of electricity to useful work) increased from 51.4 percent in 1902 to 57.3 percent in 2000, having reached 55.4 percent as early as 1930 (Ayres et al. 2005). This very modest gain in average secondary efficiency of electricity hides some larger improvements in particular uses of energy. Motors used in elevators and lighting stand out as two uses where considerable gains in efficiency were made. Gains were made in other uses too that were well above the average. The reason why average efficiency for all uses of electricity increased so little is that the mix of uses also changed, with the least efficient uses, notably low temperature heat, increasing their share of total use. Ayres and colleagues correctly observe that using electricity to provide low temperature heat represents a promising opportunity for future gains (2005, p. 1131). Nonetheless the potential for further gains in many uses is quite limited, with efficiencies already at 70 percent or more.

Increases in scale can overwhelm increases in efficiency. This is the rebound effect that we encountered in Chapter 5. For example, homeowners might respond to an increased level of insulation by keeping their homes warmer in winter and cooler in summer. In doing so, they reduce the energy savings that they might have expected. A similar rebound effect is likely with the replacement of incandescent light bulbs by compact fluorescents or LEDs. These more efficient light bulbs reduce the energy costs of lighting and so people will keep the lights on longer. A more subtle effect is possible too. In winter in cold climates, the heat from electric lights reduces the requirement for heat from a furnace. By using more efficient light bulbs which produce less 'waste' heat, furnaces will run longer unless thermostat temperatures are lowered, which is unlikely. In this case energy savings at the end-use level are partially or fully negated by the greater use of energy required to run the furnaces. If the electricity used for lighting comes from hydroelectric or some other renewable source, and the furnace is fueled by oil or gas, then emissions of pollutants to the air would almost certainly increase. This is a rebound effect with a vengeance. Ayres (2005) has looked at the environmental implications of increasing technical efficiency and concludes that 'efficiency improvements have rarely, if ever, resulted in reduced aggregate energy (including materials) consumption'. Haberl et al. (2006) come to the same conclusion based on an analysis of data from 1700 to 2000: 'At least so far, efficiency increases are more than compensated by increases in consumption levels'.

Improvements in technology can reduce environmental impacts but too much reliance on technology without attending to scale will likely prove inadequate.

## 8.5   MAKING ROOM – THE CASE OF CARBON

Today there is talk of a 'carbon constrained world', referring to the need to reduce the release of carbon dioxide and other greenhouse gases to avoid catastrophic changes in the climate. Climate change is happening and further climate change is unavoidable, say most climatologists, because of the greenhouse gases already in the atmosphere (IPCC 2013). To avoid catastrophic climate change, releases of greenhouse gases must be greatly reduced by mid-century, if not before. This monumental task is sometimes given as just one more reason why economies, rich and poor, are said to need yet more economic growth. Without growth how will we pay for the costs of reducing emissions, for changing land use practices in forestry and agriculture, for redesigning urban form, for developing new technologies, and since all this will not be enough, for adapting to a changing climate? Surely we need economic growth more than ever?

If only it were that simple. If only economic growth would make all this and more possible. Some elementary analysis of our predicament suggests otherwise and shows why people in the rich countries should be prepared to manage without growth as the overarching economic policy objective. If changes in the composition of the economy and improvements in technology prove inadequate for dealing with climate change and other environmental threats, sooner rather than later people and nations will be compelled to manage without growth. They will be unprepared if we do not lay some of the groundwork.

Global emissions of greenhouse gases will have to decline by at least 60 percent over the next 50 years so that the concentration of these gases does not exceed a level so high as to threaten catastrophic climate change (IPCC 2014a). Others put the required level of reduction much higher (Monbiot and Matthew 2006, Chapter 1). What is required to meet even this target? Carbon dioxide accounts for about 65 percent of all anthropogenic greenhouse gases (US EPA 2017) and much comes from the production, transformation and use of energy (Netherlands Environmental Agency 2006; Olivier et al. 2016). We will focus on carbon dioxide from energy to show how rich countries could help make room for poorer ones by managing without growth.

As already mentioned, the world's population is forecast to increase by about 2.3 billion people between 2017 and 2060, by which time more than 9 billion people will have to be fed, housed, clothed, educated, transported and employed. This will be a major challenge in many respects, not least of which will be to do it in ways that reduce carbon dioxide emissions to the level required. Virtually all of the increase in population is forecast to occur in middle- and lower-income countries, as classified by the World Bank (2007). For carbon dioxide emissions, this is good news in that emissions of carbon dioxide per person in high-income countries are on average about three times higher than in middle-income countries and about 40 times higher than in low-income countries (World Bank 2016c, data for 2013).

If economic growth is based on a greater use of technologies widely in use today, it can only add to the problem. More people using today's technologies to produce and consume more goods and services will move us away from the carbon dioxide reduction target, not towards it. Increases in GDP with no change in technologies and no change in the mix of goods and services are bound to make a bad situation worse. It is precisely because growth in GDP is usually accompanied by a change in its composition (for example, services replacing goods) and in the efficiency with which energy and materials are produced and used, that the outlook is not necessarily so discouraging. The question is whether these types of changes can and will be sufficient to counteract increases in population and GDP.

One way to approach this question is with the help of a simple equation that relates carbon dioxide ($CO_2$) emissions to population, GDP and energy use:

$$CO_2 = \text{Population} \times \text{GDP/Population} \times \text{Energy/GDP} \times CO_2/\text{Energy} \quad (8.3)$$

Equation (8.3) is the Kaya equation (IPCC 2000). As with IPAT, equation (8.3) is true by definition. Its usefulness lies in highlighting how changes on the right-hand side contribute to changes on the left-hand side, which, in this case, is $CO_2$ emissions. $CO_2$ emissions depend upon the size of the population, the average per person standard of living as measured by GDP per person, energy per unit of GDP (a measure of energy intensity) and the $CO_2$ emitted per unit of energy. Changes in any of these variables will change $CO_2$ emissions. More people means more $CO_2$ if the values of the other variables remain the same. Higher GDP per capita raises $CO_2$ emissions, other things equal. Reductions in energy intensity (that is, lower energy per unit of GDP) and reductions in $CO_2$ per unit of energy both have a downward impact on $CO_2$ emissions.

Equation (8.3) has the same limitations as the IPAT equation (8.1). If applied at too high a level of aggregation it can hide important regional differences. Also, the values of the variables on the right-hand side are not necessarily independent of one another. Efforts to change the value of one of these variables might also have an effect on the others. Further, the right-hand variables (population, GDP per person, energy per unit of GDP, and $CO_2$ per unit of energy) are not necessarily the fundamental driving forces of $CO_2$ emissions. There are other sources of $CO_2$ such as cement production and deforestation in addition to energy that are not properly captured in the Kaya equation. More importantly, and something else entirely, namely the ideological and political commitment to growth, may be driving all the variables.

Bearing these caveats in mind, equation (8.3) 'can be used to organize discussion of the primary driving forces of $CO_2$ emissions' (IPCC 2000). We can ask the question: if population and/or GDP per person grow, how much must energy intensity and/or $CO_2$ per unit of energy decline to keep $CO_2$ emissions stable? How much more must they decline to reduce $CO_2$ emissions by a target amount over some time period, say 60 percent over 50 years or 80 percent over 35 years? We can answer these questions by looking at percentage changes on both sides of the equation. The sum of the percentage changes for each of the right-hand side variables gives a very good estimate of the percentage change in $CO_2$ emissions.[3]

When I addressed this question empirically in the first edition of this book, I looked at the percentage changes between 1992 and 2002 in the variables on the right-hand side of equation (8.3) – the independent variables – for two groups of economies as defined by the World Bank: (1) high-income economies (HIC) and (2) low- and middle-income economies (LMY) according to a threshold level of gross national income per capita (World Bank 2016a). I then projected these percentage changes 50 years into the future and compared the resulting $CO_2$ emissions from all economies against a target of a 60 percent reduction. The result was not encouraging. A simple extrapolation of the trends from the period 1992–2002 results in a 90 percent increase in annual emissions over 50 years. The World Bank data available in 2007 indicated that HIC and LMY economies were each responsible for about 50 percent of total $CO_2$ emissions in 2002 but if the trends of 1992–2002 were to continue for another 50 years, the emissions from HIC economies would far exceed those from LMY countries. This happens because the faster growth rates in population and GDP/capita in the LMY countries between 1992 and 2002 were more than compensated by the faster rates of reduction in energy/GDP and $CO_2$/energy.

The extrapolation of the 1992–2002 trends helped point the way in 2007 to the scope of changes required to reduce global $CO_2$ emissions by a substantial amount. As an illustration, a target of a 60 percent reduction over 50 years was used, which would now be considered too modest and insufficient for a 50 percent probability of not exceeding a 2 degree increase in average global temperature. This level of reduction is equivalent to an average annual *decline* in global $CO_2$ emissions of 1.8 percent per year. That said, the scope of changes were ambitious but plausible. They are summarized in Table 8.3.

The projected rate of increase in population in HIC and LMY economies shown in Table 8.3 was taken from the World Bank (2007) and it has not changed significantly since. The reductions in energy/GDP are ambitious but not unprecedented according to the data available in 2007, which gave these values for HIC economies in the 1972–82 period and the LMY economies in the 1992–2002 period. The values for reducing $CO_2$ /energy exceed what was experienced in the 1992–2002 decade and the two preceding decades, and would require a significant but not unrealistic transition from fossil fuel energy sources. And the rate of increase in GDP/capita for the LMY economies, as happened between 1992 and 2002 would bring a steady increase in incomes to billions of people if equitably distributed. What stands out in Table 8.3 is the zero value for increases in GDP/capita for the HIC economies. Combined with a zero rate of increase in population, this would mean zero growth in the GDP of these economies for a half century.

*Table 8.3    Meeting the 60% $CO_2$ emissions reduction target given trends of 1992–2002*

|  | Population | GDP/Capita | Energy/GDP | $CO_2$/Energy |
|---|---|---|---|---|
| HIC | 0.0% | 0.0% | −1.9% | −0.7% |
| LMY | 0.8% | 2.5% | −2.5% | −2.0% |

*Notes:*   HIC: high-income economies; LMY: low- and medium-income economies.

*Source:*   Victor (2008).

The contribution of managing without growth in advanced economies can be understood as one of reducing the scope of change required in the other variables in the Kaya equation, that is, the variables shown in Table 8.3. If the HIC economies are to reduce their $CO_2$ emissions by 60 percent over 50 years then any growth in GDP (with constant population) would have to be balanced by faster reductions in energy/GDP and/or $CO_2$/energy than shown in Table 8.3. Meeting the more ambitious targets of the Paris Climate Agreement: to hold 'the increase in the global average temperature to well below 2°C above pre-industrial levels and to pursue efforts to limit the temperature increase to 1.5°C above pre-industrial levels' will require much faster reductions in these variables.

The rates of change in the key variables shown in Table 8.3 were not meant as predictions of what is likely to happen. As long as the high-income economies maintain their commitment to continued economic growth and fail to reduce their energy and $CO_2$ intensities at an unprecedented rate this modest scenario will not be realized over the next 50 years or over any 50-year period no matter when it starts. If the high-income countries insist on pursuing increases in GDP of say 2 percent or even 3 percent per year despite the increased threat of catastrophic climate change, the required level of improvements in energy per dollar of GDP and $CO_2$ per unit of energy combined will have to rise well beyond the levels in Table 8.3 to meet a global target of 60 percent reduction in $CO_2$ emissions in 50 years. Continued economic growth in high-income countries will also increase the pressure on much poorer countries to use energy even more efficiently, to reduce $CO_2$ per unit of energy faster and even to reduce the rate at which their GDP rises even though it is these countries that would benefit the most from economic growth.

This was the situation as it appeared in 2007. Since then some things have changed that make the situation look much more bleak. Table 8.4 compares the values of the variables in the Kaya equation for 1992–2002 and 2002–13 for the world. The values for 1992–2002 are very similar to

*Table 8.4   Values for the Kaya equation – world*

|  | 1992–2002 | 2002–2013 |
|---|---|---|
| $CO_2$ emissions | 1.3% | 3.0% |
| Population | 1.4% | 1.2% |
| GDP/Population | 1.4% | 1.7% |
| Energy/GDP | −1.2% | −0.4% |
| $CO_2$/Energy | −0.3% | 0.4% |

*Source:*   Derived from World Bank (2016a).

those calculated previously from the World Bank (2007) despite revisions to the data, a reclassification of some economies from LMY to HIC based on their most recent performance and a change in the variable used to measure energy use.

Table 8.4 shows that global $CO_2$ emissions increased much faster after 2002 than before. Population increased more slowly but this was negated by the more rapid increase in GDP per capita. The biggest change came from the combined impact of the much slower reduction in energy per unit of GDP and the switch from a decline to an increase in $CO_2$ per unit of energy used in the economy. This occurred despite the increasing contribution of energy from renewable energy sources (IEA 2016a; 2016b; 2015) which was overwhelmed by the increasing use of fossil fuels in low- and middle-income economies, especially coal used in China and India for generating electricity (IEA 2016b; US EIA 2015). $CO_2$ emissions declined at an average annual rate of 0.2 percent in high-income economies between 2002 and 2013 but this was overwhelmed by the 5.8 percent rate of increase in the low- and middle-income economies. Hence a new picture emerges from more recent trends, one that shows that the bulk of reductions in $CO_2$ emissions will have to come from poorer countries if a substantial reduction in global emissions is to be achieved by mid-century. High-income economies can still play their part by resisting the temptation to pursue rapid economic growth and hence, other things equal, increasing their $CO_2$ emissions, because doing so simply places an even greater burden on others, less well off, to reduce theirs.

## 8.6   ECONOMIC GROWTH, $CO_2$ AND ENERGY

The closing sentence of the previous section connected higher rates of economic growth in high-income countries with increases in $CO_2$ emissions 'other things equal'. Some will argue that other things are not equal and that a higher rate of economic growth in high-income countries is necessary to realize the required reductions in energy intensity and $CO_2$ per unit of energy. By making the economy more efficient, we can have economic growth and make dramatic reductions in $CO_2$ emissions (OECD 2011a; 2011b; 2015d; Smart Prosperity 2016). Others take a different view (Ward et al. 2016). In contemplating the future, it is instructive to see what happened in the past.

To reduce total $CO_2$ emissions, a 1 percent increase in GDP has to yield more than a 1 percent decrease in $CO_2$ intensity ($CO_2$/GDP). Unless this condition is met, $CO_2$ emissions will still rise even if $CO_2$ intensity falls. Let us see what the data can tell us about this matter. What emerges may come as a surprise. Using data available from the World Bank Development Indicators from 1960 onwards, the relationship between changes in $CO_2$

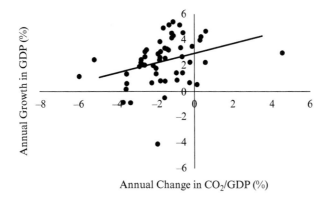

Source: World Bank Development Indicators (World Bank Group 2018).

*Figure 8.3    Annual change in CO₂ intensity and economic growth in high-income countries 1960–2014*

intensity and economic growth shows an *upward* trend, that is, the *faster* the rate of economic growth, the *slower* the reduction in $CO_2$ intensity, as shown in Figure 8.3. This relationship, though rather weak (a correlation coefficient of 0.34), is contrary to the expectation that *faster* rates of economic growth induce *faster* reductions in $CO_2$ intensity. If anything, the opposite relationship is indicated by the data: from 1961 to 2013, *larger* reductions in $CO_2$ intensity were associated with *slower*, not faster, rates of economic growth.

How can we explain this positive relationship between the rate of economic growth and $CO_2$ intensity? Although a few scientists were aware in the 1960s of the links between increases in global temperature and the concentration of atmospheric $CO_2$, the threat of climate change caused by $CO_2$ emissions was not widely appreciated and was not a concern. Therefore, there's no reason to expect a negative relationship between the rate of economic growth and the rate of reduction in $CO_2$ intensity, at least up to the early 1990s. With the negotiation of the United Nations Framework Convention on Climate Change in 1992 and the Kyoto Protocol in 1997 we might expect the data since 1992 to display a negative relationship between economic growth and $CO_2$ intensity. However, although the relationship weakened between 1992 and 2013, it still remained positive, with a correlation coefficient of 0.08.

In 2003–13, the most recent decade for which data are available and when international and national commitments for emissions reduction should have taken hold, the *positive* relationship between the rate of economic growth and *smaller* reductions in $CO_2$ intensity still did not disappear. In fact, it regained some strength, with the correlation coefficient rising to 0.12. The argument that faster growth is conducive to greater reductions in $CO_2$ intensity is not borne out by the data. Some might think that whether $CO_2$ intensity has gone up or down in relation to GDP in high-income economies does not mean very much because despite the international agreements and some notable national efforts, very little effort has yet been made to reduce $CO_2$ emissions. With the signing of the Paris Agreement in 2015 it is hoped this will change. Even so, the data suggest that *greater* decreases in $CO_2$ intensity do not require *faster* economic growth. The opposite is just as plausible.

People may not have concerned themselves much with $CO_2$ emissions in the years from 1961 to 2013 but no one would say the same for energy use. Companies, governments and individuals spend a lot of money on energy and they have a direct financial interest in economizing on its use. What are we to make, therefore, of the fact that exactly the same pattern of association just described between the rate of economic growth and reductions in $CO_2$ intensity also applies between the rate of economic growth and reductions in energy intensity? If higher rates of economic growth are so important for reducing energy intensity (energy use/GDP), and if investments in energy efficiency are easier to afford in times of rapid economic growth, we would expect to find the greatest reductions in energy intensity in those years when the economies of the high-income countries grew the fastest. Yet from 1972 to 2013 energy intensity decreased the *most* in years when economic growth was the *slowest* (with a correlation coefficient of 0.35). This relationship was strongest between 1972 and 1982 (correlation coefficient of 0.72) when OPEC increased the world price of crude oil, reducing the use of energy in high-income countries more than their growth rates. From 1992 when the UN Framework on Climate Change was signed to 2013, the same positive relationship, though weaker, was maintained just as it was with $CO_2$ intensity and economic growth (correlation coefficient of 0.12). Only in the most recent decade for which data are available, 2003–13, did the positive relationship disappear (correlation coefficient of 0.02).

So where does this leave us? Broadly speaking, in the decades up to 2013 *slower* rates of economic growth in high-income economies taken as a group were associated with *greater* reductions in $CO_2$ intensity and *greater* reductions in energy intensity. Conversely, *higher* rates of economic growth in these countries were associated with *smaller* reductions, even increases, in $CO_2$ and energy intensities. That being said, there was considerable variation within the group of high-income countries. In Canada for example, greater reductions in $CO_2$ intensity and energy intensity were weakly correlated with higher rates of economic growth from 1972 to 2002.

When a similar analysis is undertaken using data for various high-income countries as separate observations rather than grouping them all together, few statistically significant relationships, positive or negative, among rates of economic growth and reductions in $CO_2$ and energy intensity emerge.

So where does this leave us? The historical record shows that higher rates of economic growth are not required for reductions in $CO_2$ intensity and energy intensity. Nor do they automatically result in larger reductions in $CO_2$ intensity and energy intensity than slower rates of economic growth. Consequently, managing without growth should not be ruled out by the mistaken belief that growth in rich countries is needed to reduce humanity's impact on the environment. The evidence suggests otherwise.

## 8.7 THE COLORS OF GROWTH[4]

The idea of green growth is to have both economic growth and reduced environmental impact. It has become the objective of numerous governments and international organizations supported by think tanks across the political spectrum (OECD 2011a). Green growth can be understood in terms of the interaction of two variables: scale and intensity. Scale refers to the size of an economy, for example GDP, and intensity refers to the environmental impact per unit of output, for example $CO_2$ emissions/GDP. In the IPAT equation (8.1 above) population ($P$) multiplied by affluence ($A$) gives scale, and impact per unit of GDP ($T$) is intensity. In the Kaya equation (8.3 above) the same variables measure scale as in IPAT, but intensity is given by the multiplication of $CO_2$/energy and energy/GDP, which reduces to $CO_2$ per unit of GDP. Green growth requires the rate of reduction of impact per unit of GDP (intensity) to exceed the rate of increase in GDP (scale) so that environmental impact, which is determined by the multiplication of the two variables, declines over time.

We can extend this idea of green growth to other possible relationships between scale and intensity and so define other 'colors' of economic growth. If the rate of reduction in intensity is less than the rate of increase in GDP, then environmental impact increases. This can be described as 'brown' growth. 'Black' growth happens when both scale and intensity increase, as does impact. We can also identify three varieties of green degrowth. Scale declines in all of them but intensity behaves differently, as does impact. These six colors of growth are summarized in Table 8.5.

The colors of growth can also be represented in a single image, as shown in Figure 8.4, with scale and intensity combining to determine impact. Starting from the combination of scale and intensity given by the black dot, the red iso-impact line represents all combinations of scale which give

*Table 8.5    The colors of growth*

| Color of Growth | Scale | Intensity | Impact |
|---|---|---|---|
| Green growth | Rising | Falling faster than scale | Falling |
| Brown growth | Rising | Falling slower than scale | Rising |
| Black growth | Rising | Rising | Rising |
| Dark Green degrowth | Falling | Falling | Falling |
| Light Green degrowth | Falling | Rising slower than scale | Falling |
| Black degrowth | Falling | Rising faster than scale | Rising |

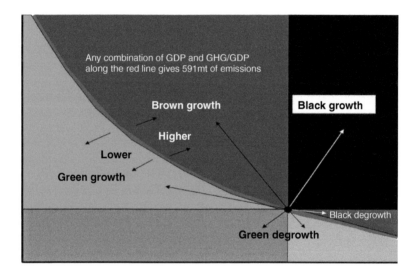

*Figure 8.4    Scale, intensity and the colors of economic growth*

the same impact. Points below this line represent combinations of scale
and intensity with a lower impact than those on the red line, and points
above it are combinations with a greater impact.

The arrows emanating from the black dot signify different growth paths.
Green growth is shown by the arrow heading northwest into the green
area labeled 'green growth' with intensity falling at a faster rate than the
increase in scale so that impact declines compared to its starting value.

Figure 8.4 can be used to describe the color of economic growth over
time in an economy. An example is shown in Figure 8.5, where greenhouse
gas emissions per unit of GDP are tracked against GDP in the United
States from 1990 to 2014 (1990 being the base year for the Kyoto Protocol).
In 1990 US GDP was $8955 billion (2009$) and the GHG intensity was
0.714 kt GHG/$m giving total GHG emissions of 6397 mt. Each small dot

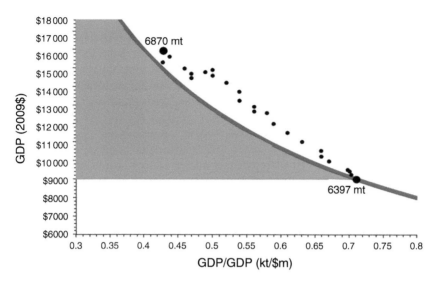

*Figure 8.5    Brown economic growth in the United States, 1990–2014*

in Figure 8.5 shows the GHG emissions resulting from the combination of scale and intensity in subsequent years after 1990, culminating in GHG emissions of 6870 mt in 2014 (shown by the larger dot). It is obvious from Figure 8.5 that in the years from 1990 to 2014 the USA experienced brown growth. Intensity declined but not fast enough to keep pace with the increase in scale. Total emissions of greenhouse gases increased by 7.4 percent, from 6397 mt to 6870 mt, even though intensity declined by 40 percent. This outcome illustrates the danger of policy objectives based on intensity reductions rather than total reductions in emissions, as has been characteristic of governments in the United States, Canada and other countries (Herzog et al. 2006), though with the commitments of Paris 2015 this should change.

## 8.8   CONCLUSION

In this chapter we have explored the potential for decoupling environmental impacts from economic growth. We have shown how this issue can be illuminated by looking at the interaction of the scale of an economy, measured by GDP, and intensity measured by the environmental impact per unit of GDP. We went deeper into the meaning and measurement of intensity in a discussion of the IPAT and Kaya equations. We considered the potential for changes in the composition of GDP from goods to services in advanced economies to reduce the environmental impacts of economic growth. Since services already account for about 70–80 percent of GDP in these economies, the potential for further shifts towards services is limited in terms of the role it can play in decoupling GDP from environmental impacts.

We also considered the contribution that technology has played in creating environmental impacts and what might be expected of technology in the future to mitigate and avoid them. Technology is the proverbial double-edged sword and we concluded that while it can and should play an important role in reducing the already excessive impacts of human economies on the environment, to rely on it to the exclusion of scale would not be smart.

When we looked at the trends in economic growth and $CO_2$ emissions from high-income and low- and medium-income economies we found they presented a much greater challenge than the same trends of a decade ago. If high-income economies choose to manage without growth to help and reduce their $CO_2$ emissions it will create some room and set a different example for low- and middle-income countries where the benefits of economic growth remain significant. However, it will not be enough. And if these rich countries resist this choice they will have to achieve even greater, year over year changes in intensity or expect the poorer countries to carry more of the burden. The challenge is greater than ever for poorer economies to avoid copying the example of the richer ones and to find alternative development paths that bring prosperity within the biophysical limits of the planet.

In later chapters we will consider policies for rich countries like Canada and the USA to influence the rate of population and economic growth, energy intensity and $CO_2$ emissions. The discussion will still be fairly general since the main concern is to present a case for rich countries to manage without growth. There will be plenty of work to flesh out the details of how best to do this if that is what they decide to do. Based on the argument and analysis in this chapter, just relying on more services and better technology to see us through does not look like a viable strategy. We must also address scale.

## NOTES

1. This is twice the capacity of the largest container ship when the first edition of this book was published.
2. USA from 1997 to 2015.
3. It is only an estimate because the arithmetic of multiplying percentage changes involves some small amounts that are omitted when the percentages are added together, but the result is close enough for our purposes.
4. This section is based on Victor (2010).

# 9.  Economic growth and happiness

> There is a paradox at the heart of our lives. Most people want more income and
> strive for it. Yet as Western societies have got richer, their people have become
> no happier . . . It is a fact proven by many pieces of scientific research. (Layard
> 2005b)

In Chapters 5, 6 and 7 we considered several biophysical limits to long-
term economic growth. In Chapter 8 we questioned the extent to which
changes in the composition of what we produce and consume and in
technology can be relied upon to overcome these limits. The outlook is
anything but rosy. What if the rich countries of the world have to make
room for the poor countries by deliberately slowing their rate of economic
growth? If the whole purpose of economic growth is to make people
happy, then does this mean that those who live in the rich countries are
doomed to a life of boredom and unhappiness? In this chapter we consider
the relationship between economic growth and human well-being and in
particular, the relationship between economic growth and happiness. We
will discover that higher incomes do make people happier but only up to a
point. After that, more money does not help very much. We will look at the
growing body of evidence on which this finding is based. A similar disconnect between economic growth and well-being is revealed by the Genuine
Progress Indicator, one of several attempts to develop an alternative metric
to GDP. And with the use of some elementary concepts, we will see how
a simple, two person, two product model can show how the pursuit of
status through consumption can be self-defeating and is best avoided. All
this is good news since it means that we can be happy without relying on
economic growth.

## 9.1   DOES GROWTH MAKE PEOPLE HAPPY?

The argument that economic growth does not necessarily make people
happier was famously stated by John Stuart Mill. When the industrial
revolution in the United Kingdom was barely 50 years old, Mill wrote:
'I am not charmed with the ideal of life held out by those who think that
the normal state of human beings is that of struggling to get on . . . nor

is there much satisfaction in contemplating the world with nothing left to the spontaneous activity of nature' (Mill 1848, Book IV, Chapter IV.6.5).

Following Mill, many writers, including some notable economists, have examined the link between economic growth and rising happiness or welfare.[1] Recently there has been a stream of quantitative analysis of the relationship between income and happiness triggered by Richard Easterlin's influential paper 'Does economic growth improve the human lot?' (1974). Richard Layard (2005b) provides a useful and provocative summary of this literature in *Happiness: Lessons from a New Science* and in the Annexes available over the Internet (Layard 2005a). Layard, a Professor of Economics at the London School of Economics and a member of the British House of Lords, is a thorough-going Benthamite utilitarian. He believes that the greatest happiness of all is the obvious aim for society and that it provides a sorely lacking overarching principle by which we should judge all our actions (Layard 2005b, Chapter 8). Layard draws on experimental results from modern brain physiology to support his case that happiness is indeed 'an objective feeling that can be properly compared between people' (Layard 2005b, pp. 17–20). By comparing variations in brain activity and self-reported feelings Layard concludes that 'there is no difference between what people think they feel and what they "really" feel', so happiness is measurable and comparable (2005b, p. 20). With a champion of Layard's stature, perhaps the measurement of happiness and interpersonal comparisons of utility will find their way back into mainstream economics.

Layard reports that real GDP per capita more than doubled in the USA in the half century following the end of World War II but the percentage of Americans who described themselves as 'very happy' hardly changed. The data on which this view is based are shown in Figure 9.1, which extends Layard's time series to 2014. Americans have been more successful decoupling GDP from happiness than in decoupling it from materials and energy.

Layard looks at cross-sectional data as well as time series. He reproduces Inglehart's graph of cross-sectional data of two variables: happiness (measured as the difference between (a) the percentage of the country's population that consider their lives very good or good and (b) the percentage that consider their lives fair or poor) and GDP per capita. Figure 9.2 is an updated version of Layard's graph. The happiness data taken from the World Values Survey Association (2015) are reported for the period 2010 to 2014 depending on the country, since the survey is not done for all countries annually. The GDP per capita data are for 2012. The happiness index is the difference between the percentage of people describing themselves 'taking all things together' as very happy or rather happy and

*Sources:*    US Bureau of Economic Analysis (2016); Smith (1979) (happiness data from the American Institute of Public Opinion for 1946–71); National Opinion Research Center (2007) (happiness data for 1972–2016). Based on the same method as used by Layard (2005b, p. 30).

*Figure 9.1    Income and happiness in the United States 1945–2014*

the percentage of those who describe themselves as not very happy or not at all happy (World Values Survey Association 2012).

Figure 9.2 shows virtually no relationship between income and happiness when compared across many countries. Some of the poorest countries, such as Kyrgyzstan and Rwanda, score as high or higher on the happiness measure than much richer countries such as Germany and Hong Kong. Interestingly, the threshold that appeared in earlier versions of this graph such as in Layard (2005b, p. 32) or Victor (2008, p. 127), where happiness rose until a GDP per capita of about $15 000 and then became unrelated to further increases, is not apparent in the more recent data.

Figures 9.1 and 9.2 display data from surveys of self-reported assessments of happiness. These assessments are not like measurements of height or weight. They are subjective and are not amenable to independent checking by a third party. How do we know if the term 'very happy' means the same thing to different people at the same time or to the same people at different times? To assume so is an example of interpersonal comparisons of utility, which have long been thought problematic especially

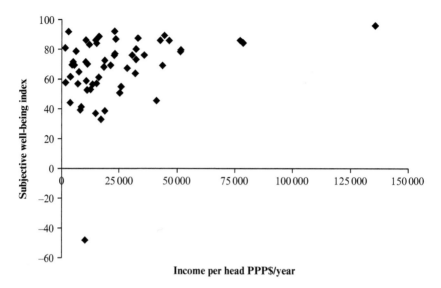

*Source:* Inglehart (1997) updated with data for 2010–2014 from the World Values Survey (World Values Survey Association 2015). Income is measured in 2012 PPP current international $ (World Bank Group 2016).

*Figure 9.2　Income and happiness: comparing countries*

by economists (Robbins 1932). Yet, notwithstanding Layard's confidence in measuring brain activity to measure happiness, happiness is essentially subjective and we must rely on people's own sense of happiness if we want to study it.

Accepting self-reported assessments of happiness as meaningful, we can look for an explanation of their lack of correlation with rising incomes within the framework of economics. Richard Easterlin, whose seminal article on whether economic growth enhances the human lot did so much to stimulate interest in this question, identified two factors that influence the impact of rising incomes on well-being. The first is 'hedonic adaptation', which is the process by which people adjust their aspirations as they become used to a higher material standard of living. If a person's happiness depends on the relationship between their aspirations and attainments, happiness will not rise with an increase in attainments if aspirations rise as well.

The second factor that Easterlin suggested is the extent to which one person's utility from a certain level of consumption depends on how much others have. If everyone's consumption rises with economic growth then no one is better off, because what matters to people is their relative rather than their absolute consumption. Ball and Chernova (2005) analyze data from the World Values Survey and conclude that 'quantitatively, changes in relative income have much larger effects on happiness than do changes in absolute income.' They place this finding in a larger context by also concluding that 'the effects of both absolute and relative income are small when compared to the effects of several non-pecuniary factors'. This conclusion is endorsed by Lane who, along with many others, is critical of the emphasis that capitalism places on material gains at the expense of closer social relationships (Lane 2000).

Easterlin has continued to lead research into the connections, or lack of them, between income and happiness. In his later work, he looks at how aspirations change over a person's life cycle as a result of rising income. Judgments about happiness made at any moment in time are based on a person's aspirations at that time. According to Easterlin, people think that a higher income will make them happier but overlook the rising aspirations that will accompany such an increase. He makes a distinction, uncommon in most economic theory, between 'decision utility' and 'experienced utility'. The former is what a person expects to get from a choice and the latter what they actually experience. Pigou, the founder of welfare economics, made the same distinction in 1920, but it has not received much attention in the literature (Pigou 1920[1952]). Because people do not anticipate the changes in their material aspirations that come with and can be caused by higher incomes, their experienced utility does not rise as expected (Easterlin 2001; 2003).

Binswanger (2006) attributes the disconnect between higher incomes and happiness to four 'treadmills': the positional treadmill (that is, the search for status), the hedonic treadmill (that is, aspirations rise with income), the multi-option treadmill (that is, frustration caused by the increasing range of choices) and the time-saving treadmill (that is, the effect of time-saving devices on making leisure time more intense rather than reducing time pressure). None of these ideas are new but their designation as treadmills nicely describes the mixed blessings of economic growth.

Another line of argument drawn from economics which might explain why economic growth does not necessarily increase well-being is that the environmental externalities and other adverse social effects of economic growth may be rising faster than personal incomes so that they outweigh the benefits of increased private consumption. This situation is accentuated if there is declining marginal utility of income and increasing marginal disutility from the externalities, as Daly argues in his assessment that the United States has moved into an era of 'uneconomic growth'; that is, economic growth where the costs of growth exceed the benefits (Daly 1996). According to this argument there is an increasing disparity between what matters to people and what is included in and excluded from GDP (see Chapter 1), and so further increases in GDP, unless carefully managed, will only make matters worse. Clearly, other factors besides GDP are at play in determining self-reported feelings of happiness.

### 9.1.1   World Happiness

In 2012 the first of a series of reports on world happiness was published. These reports are based on a detailed statistical analysis of responses to questions posed to people in many countries through the Gallup World Poll (2016), combined with data on social and economic conditions obtained from the World Bank and other sources (Helliwell et al. 2012; 2013; 2015; 2016; 2017). The reports also use data from the World Values Survey. The most recent of these World Happiness reports draws on responses from about 1000 people in each of more than 150 countries to the following question:

> Please imagine a ladder, with steps numbered from 0 at the bottom to 10 at the top. The top of the ladder represents the best possible life for you and the bottom of the ladder represents the worst possible life for you. On which step of the ladder would you say you personally feel you stand at this time? (Helliwell et al. 2017, p. 9)[2]

The authors of the reports attempt to explain differences in national responses to this question in terms of GDP per capita, social support, healthy life expectancy, social freedom, generosity and absence of corruption. Their findings are extremely interesting and are set out in detail in the various reports. They conclude that 'taken together, these six variables explain almost three-quarters of the variation in national annual average ladder scores among countries, using data from the years 2005 to 2016' (Helliwell et al. 2017, p. 15).

These results lend support to the view that GDP per capita used as the income measure remains an important contributor to people's happiness. When comparing this finding with the comments in the previous section about the lack of such a relationship especially at higher income levels, two considerations should be kept in mind. The first is the differences in the questions used to solicit people's assessment of their happiness. In Figures 9.1 and 9.2 the measure of happiness is based on responses to a question explicitly about happiness. People were asked to describe their happiness in terms of just four levels: very happy, rather happy, not very happy, not at all happy. Data used in the World Happiness reports from the Gallup World Poll are in response to a question asking people to evaluate their lives 'at this time' using an 11-point ladder or scale. The 11-step life evaluation scale allows for greater variation in responses than the 4-level happiness scale, which complicates comparison of the survey results. Also, differences in responses to questions about 'happiness' and questions about 'life evaluation', which may not be understood as the same as happiness by respondents, can be important. As Helliwell et al. note:

> Both types of comparison showed the effects of income on the happiness answers to be less significant than on satisfaction with life or the ladder . . . the finding that income has more purchase on life evaluations than on emotions seems to have general applicability, and stands as an established result. (Helliwell et al. 2016, p. 12)

The second consideration, somewhat more technical than the first, is that the measure of income per capita used in the statistical analysis of the World Happiness reports is the natural logarithm of GDP per capita rather than GDP per capita itself.[3] This approach automatically builds in a strong non-linear relation between GDP per capita and happiness (measured as life evaluation on the Cantril ladder). While the log of GDP per capita shows up as a significant determinant of the differences in the average life evaluation across 150+ countries in the World Happiness reports, the influence of GDP per capita in non-log form declines rapidly as GDP per capita increases. This is illustrated in Figure 9.3, which shows that at low levels of GDP per capita, increases in GDP per capita have a much larger impact on happiness than increases of similar size at higher levels of GDP per capita. For example, according to the equation presented in the World Happiness Report 2017 (Helliwell et al. 2017, p. 16) an increase of GDP

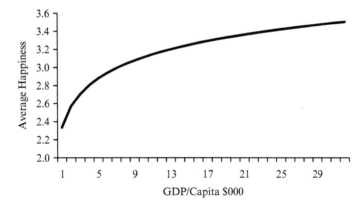

*Figure 9.3   The non-linear relationship between GDP/capita and happiness estimated by Helliwell et al. (2016, p. 16) holding other variables constant (GDP in 2011 PPP international dollars)*

per capita of 50 percent from $2000 to $3000 in a country raises average happiness by 14 percent. The same increase of $1000 in a country where the GDP per capita is $24 000 only raises average happiness by 1.4 percent, that is, a tenth as much, and by smaller and smaller amounts thereafter. This result provides strong support for the proposition that economic growth adds very little to the life evaluations of those already living at levels found in rich countries. The gains from growth in poorer countries are much more significant. So, in a world where economic growth is constrained by biophysical limits it makes sense for rich countries to manage without growth so as to leave room for growth in poorer economies.

## 9.2   THE GENUINE PROGRESS INDICATOR

The Genuine Progress Indicator (GPI) was developed to take account of the shortcomings of GDP as a measure of well-being and to get a better idea of whether real progress is being made as economies grow (Redefining Progress 2007). The GPI 'starts with the same accounting framework as the GDP, but then makes some crucial distinctions. It adds in the economic contributions of household and volunteer work, but subtracts factors such as crime, pollution, and family breakdown' (Redefining Progress 2007). It also includes an adjustment for income distribution so that if the gap between rich and poor decreases the GPI increases, and vice versa, whereas GDP is unaffected. Changes in leisure time also affect the GPI, as does the depletion of natural resources, but not GDP. All of these adjustments incorporated in the GPI suggest areas that could be the focus of policies designed to increase well-being rather than simply relying on increases in GDP.

Since both GDP and GPI are measured in money terms, they can be compared. The pattern of results for the United States shown in Figure 9.4 looks very similar to those obtained from the research on GDP and happiness. Figure 9.4 also has the same general pattern as that displayed by comparisons between GDP and biocapacity (Kubiszewski et al. 2013), further underlining the disconnect between economic growth and welfare. As shown in Figure 9.4, real GDP per capita in the USA grew fairly steadily, from about $12 000 in 1950 to about $35 000 in 2002 (all values in 2000 dollars). Over the same period real GPI per capita peaked in the 1970s when per capita GDP was about $20 000 and it has been essentially flat since then. Similar results based on more recent data have been reported for 16 other countries including Germany, Austria and the UK (Kubiszewski et al. 2013). Another striking finding by Kubiszewski et al. is that when the data are adjusted, somewhat ambitiously, to describe the whole world:

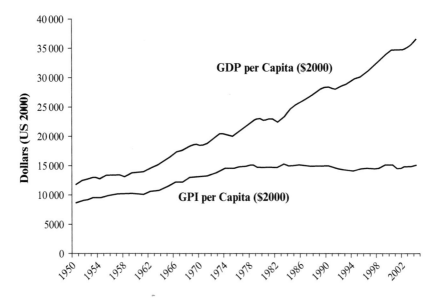

*Source:* Based on data from Redefining Progress (2007, Table 1).

*Figure 9.4 GDP and the Genuine Progress Indicator, United States 1950–2004*

this same pattern can be seen in the global estimate of GPI/capita. At the global level, the decrease begins to occur around 1978. This decrease has occurred while global GDP/capita has steadily increased – in some countries drastically, such as China and India. This shows that although GDP growth is increasing benefits, they are being outweighed by rising inequality of income and increases in costs ... We conclude that the ability of poor nations to increase their economic welfare may now be dependent upon rich countries abandoning their sole policy focus on GDP growth. This would provide the 'ecological space' for poor nations to experience a phase of welfare-increasing growth. (Kubiszewski et al. 2013, p. 66)

The contrast between the time path of GDP per capita and GPI per capita lends support to the proposition that economic growth has done little to improve people's welfare especially in rich countries over the past few decades. It follows that managing without growth in these countries might not involve a loss in welfare, or a reduction in happiness, at least not nearly as much as might be expected.

The findings obtained from comparison of the GPI and GDP are certainly interesting. However, the GPI does not overcome all the deficiencies of GDP as a measure of well-being and contains some of its own. Neumayer points out the arbitrariness and questionable theoretical basis for some of the adjustments made to derive the GPI (Neumayer 2003). He challenges the concept of defensive expenditures which are included in GDP but not GPI. Defensive expenditures are expenditures that people make 'to prevent an erosion in their quality of life or to compensate for misfortunes of various kinds' such as 'medical and repair bills from automobile accidents, commuting costs, and household expenditures on pollution control devices' (Redefining Progress 2007). Neumayer (2003) suggests that what counts as defensive expenditure is arbitrary. Yet if no adjustment is made and defensive expenditures increase in response to deteriorating conditions, the addition to GDP will give the wrong impression that people are becoming better off if GDP is misused as a measure of well-being as is so commonly the case. More urban sprawl brings more expenditure on commuting, accidents, and health care costs, all of which add to GDP but detract from welfare. Their exclusion from GPI may be somewhat arbitrary but it looks like an adjustment in the right direction.

Neumayer also questions the adjustment in the GPI for income distribution because 'the valuation of the distribution of income in a measure of welfare fails to command general agreement' (2003, p. 162). But as Neumayer acknowledges, not to make an adjustment to GDP if used as a welfare indicator is also arbitrary since it implicitly assumes that 'the marginal utility of income is constant and the same for rich and poor alike' (2003). There may be better ways to adjust for changes in the distribution of income than the one currently used in calculating the GPI, which uses changes in the distribution of income as measured by the Gini coefficient. Neumayer discusses alternatives but again it looks as though the adjustment made in the GPI, though not exact, is in the right direction.

Neumayer's third set of concerns about the GPI is the treatment of long-term environmental damage and resource depletion, both of which might be exaggerated using current methods. He questions the way in which the impacts of greenhouse gases are valued, charging that they are accumulated when they should only be counted in the year they are emitted. This is correct, if the damage estimates are in terms of their capitalized value (that is, a single amount of equal value to a stream of annual damages) rather than their annual value. Counting capitalized values more than once is a mistake. Counting annual values each year is not. Even so, Neumayer does allow the possibility that given the uncertainty and ignorance about the impacts of climate change, the estimated damages used in GPI calculations, even if incorrectly accumulated, may not be unreasonable. Neumayer also thinks that the costs of resource depletion, which are deducted from GDP in the calculation of GPI, are overstated and that more plausible assumptions about their replacement cost over time would reduce the difference between GDP and GPI.

Neumayer shows what happens to the comparison between GDP and GPI for the United States when some or all of the adjustments he criticizes are not made or are made in a manner he thinks is more defensible. He compares GDP and GPI but not on a per capita basis, though this would not affect the comparative trends. If the GPI is calculated without accumulation of carbon dioxide damage and no escalation in the cost of replacing depleted natural resources, the GPI plateaus around 1987 rather than in 1975 as in Figure 9.4. And if the adjustments for changes in the distribution of income are also omitted, the recalculated GPI continues rising to about 1998, the last year reported by Neumayer. So even without the adjustments that so concern Neumayer, GPI per capita in the US peaked before the end of the last century.

Neumayer reminds us of the dangers in making arbitrary assumptions when trying to modify GDP to make it a more reliable indicator of welfare. Perhaps it is taxing GDP too much to have it play this role, with or without appropriate adjustments. The inclusion of the personal consumption component of GDP in the GPI as a measure of welfare (making a small adjustment for how expenditures on consumer durables are counted and subtracting defensive expenditures) is itself questionable. It remains an open question as to whether the GPI and GPI per capita will prove a viable and acceptable substitute for GDP and GDP per capita for evaluating change. That two US states, Maryland and Vermont, have adopted the GPI as an official indicator shows there is some interest in finding alternative or complementary measures of progress in the USA, albeit at the sub-national level. Similar initiatives at national and international levels using approaches to measuring well-being other than the GPI have been introduced in the UK (Office for National Statistics 2016), Australia (Australian Bureau of Statistics 2015) and the OECD (OECD 2016b). Meanwhile independent researchers in academia, think tanks and NGOs around the world continue to push the frontiers of alternative measures of progress, with the ultimate goal of supplanting economic growth as measured by increases in GDP.

## 9.3 CONSUMPTION: USEFUL GOODS, STATUS GOODS AND PUBLIC GOODS

In 1899, American economist and sociologist Thorsten Veblen coined the term 'conspicuous consumption' (Veblen 1899). He was referring to items that people buy to indicate their social status rather than because they are useful. He referred to such people as members of the 'leisure class' and regarded them as parasitic, depending on the rest of society for their extravagant sustenance. Obviously, the more people who buy a particular good for the status it signifies, the less effective the good is for this purpose.

Fred Hirsch, a British economist and writer, building on predecessors like Veblen and Galbraith, explored the 'social limits to growth' (Hirsch 1976). Hirsch argued that as average consumption levels rise, 'the satisfaction that individuals derive from goods and services depends in increasing measure not only on their own consumption but on consumption by others as well' (1976, p. 2). He introduced the idea of 'positional goods', whose value to the owner depends on the extent to which other people do not have these goods. 'Positional goods . . . are goods such as cars, suburban housing, higher education, and country cottages, whose contribution to each person's welfare diminishes as others acquire them. Such goods are subject to "social congestion"' (Lintott 2005). Hirsch used this concept of a positional good to describe a wide range of crowding problems exemplified by road congestion and the despoliation of public spaces: any situation where those already enjoying an amenity or service find their enjoyment diminished as others join in.

According to Hirsch, the increasing presence of positional goods in modern economies explains why economic growth is ineffective in raising welfare. With positional goods, one person's gain is another's loss. When an increasing proportion of a society's consumption consists of positional goods, it reduces the capacity of economic growth to make people better off. In the extreme case, if all growth is in the provision of positional goods, growth is useless for advancing well-being.

Status is a key ingredient of many positional goods. A good bought for status conferred on its owner provides value only to those who have it when others are without. As soon as those without acquire the status good, it no longer indicates anything special about the owner, and those who can move on to something else, also of temporary value. Status goods can be contrasted with useful goods that are of value to the user regardless of whether other people have them.

A third category of goods that has been the focus of much attention by economists is 'public goods'. These are defined as goods and services that once made available to one person are available to everyone. The classic examples are light from a lighthouse and national defense, but environmental attributes such as clean air and peace and quiet also fit the standard definition of a public good. These are the kinds of environmental goods and services the supply of which has been diminished by growth, as recounted in Chapter 6. Public goods are also 'non-rival' in consumption, meaning that one person's enjoyment of a public good such as clean air does not reduce the amount available for others. If, as often happens, people cannot be denied access to public goods, then the market system cannot be relied upon to provide them in any significant quantity. No one can make a profit from providing something they cannot sell, like the light from a lighthouse or cleaner air, not because it is of no value, but because there is no means of imposing a price and excluding those who do not pay. In any case, why exclude anyone from a public good when their consumption of the good does not come at the expense of anyone else? It is well established that public goods should be provided and paid for collectively in society, usually through some form of taxation (Musgrave et al. 1987, Chapter 3).

So now we have three categories of goods: useful goods, status goods and public goods. These may be thought of as 'ideal' types though perhaps not ideal enough, since a study by Solnick and Hemenway (2005) showed that public goods can be positional as well. In what follows, we will only consider status from private goods. Many goods are desired for both use and status. A person may buy an expensive car partly for transportation and partly to indicate their wealth. Also, the same good may be assessed differently by different people. What may appear purely functional to one person may be desired by others for the status they believe comes with its ownership. However, within any society there is bound to be a measure of agreement about status symbols simply because something confers status on one person only if it is recognized as doing so by others.

## 9.4  STATUS, CONSUMPTION AND GROWTH

It is not difficult in general terms to theorize about what happens as people spend more and more of their rising incomes on goods and services for status rather than for use. Status obtained through conspicuous consumption is gained by one person at another's expense. In the language of welfare economics, a person's utility depends not only on what they themselves consume, but on what others consume as well. When a person buys a commodity exclusively to enhance their status, others suffer a loss in status unless they make a similar purchase, in which case no one is better off. In both cases buying for status can be a zero sum game in which one person's gain is completely balanced by the losses of others. Either no one gains, or one person's gain is another's loss.

Interdependent utility functions are inconsistent with the assumptions required for a competitive economy to be Pareto efficient and are implicitly or explicitly assumed away in most economic analysis. Roger Mason (1998), in his *Economics of Conspicuous Consumption*, surveyed the treatment of status as a motive for consumption in economics from Adam Smith to the mid-1990s. He concludes that there has been 'an almost total neglect of status consumption within economic theory and thought. As a consequence, a significant part of the economic activity of modern societies lacks any theoretical explanation, and the social, economic and policy implications remain largely unexplored' (Mason 1998). He might well have included the environmental implications as well. Mason attributes much of this neglect of status as a motivation for consumption to the difficulties first identified by Marshall of deriving a market demand curve by adding individual demand curves if the demand of any one individual depends on the quantity purchased by others.

As if rising to Mason's challenge, Brekke and Howarth published *Status, Growth and the Environment*, in which they explore the implications of interdependent utility functions and, in particular, the relationship between status, growth and the environment (Brekke and Howarth 2002). Mason describes several proposals for taxing luxury goods proposed by various authors. Brekke and Howarth develop the theoretical basis for such proposals in some detail and show how the tax system might be used to internalize status externalities to complement the more conventional proposals for taxes to internalize environmental externalities.

Brekke and Howarth (2002) examine Hirsch's conjecture that the share of income allocated to positional goods increases with economic growth and show that it depends on the assumed utility functions. They consider the case of a typical person buying a single composite commodity that provides both use value and status in some proportion. Their measure of status is the ratio of a person's consumption of the composite commodity and the average consumption level. In equilibrium, if everyone is the same they each consume the same average amount of the single consumption good.

Brekke and Howarth (2002) also assume that both use value and status value are subject to diminishing marginal utility. They then show that the desire for social status through consumption does not dominate as incomes rise. Brekke et al. (1998) obtain a similar result when two goods are included, one that is desired only for use and the other only for status, but different results are obtained depending on the degree of substitution between status and use.

## 9.5   KATIE AND ROBERTO GO SHOPPING

Mason is correct: the extension of the theory of demand to incorporate interdependent utility functions is difficult, yet something must be done because 'consuming for status has, in fact, become a defining element of the new consumer societies' (Mason 1998, p. vii). In this section, we describe HappyGrow, a simulation model of a simple two-person economy that shows what can happen when people buy commodities (goods and services) for use and for status.[4] The purpose of HappyGrow is to illustrate what happens to people's well-being when they spend an increasing proportion of their growing incomes on goods for the status they bring rather than for their usefulness. We will see that the more people concern themselves with status when they go shopping, the less we should expect economic growth to increase happiness.

The protagonists in our model are Katie and Roberto. Using HappyGrow, we see how they would allocate their growing incomes among two private goods and a public good based on assumptions of utility maximization. The two private goods are 'consumables' and 'durables'. The difference between them is the rate at which they depreciate. Depreciation is used here to include what is normally understood as consumption or use. The act of consumption reduces the capacity of a good to continue to provide service. This capacity can also decline if a good is simply neglected: food goes stale, equipment that is not maintained seizes up. We use depreciation here to cover the loss of service due to both use and neglect. Consumables depreciate rapidly and durables depreciate slowly. Katie and Roberto spend their incomes to replace or add to these depreciating stocks.

You can think of the two private goods as specific goods such as food (consumables) and cars (durables) or as aggregations of similar types of goods. Likewise, the single public good in HappyGrow can represent all public goods paid for out of income tax and enjoyed by both Katie and Roberto. Katie and Roberto can be two individuals or they can represent two different classes of people, rich and poor, distinguished by the initial stocks of the two private goods and/or different incomes. For simplicity, we treat them as two individuals.

Katie and Roberto value both private goods for their usefulness and for the status conferred by their possession though not necessarily to the same extent. They measure status by the percentage of the total consumption of each private good that they consume personally. In HappyGrow Katie and Roberto start out with stocks of consumables and durables from which they obtain utility.

Figure 9.5 shows the main components of HappyGrow and their connections. Economic growth raises people's incomes before tax. Katie and Roberto pay income tax, which is used to pay for the public good. They use all of their after-tax incomes to buy private goods from which only the buyer benefits, though where status is involved their enjoyment also depends on how much the other person owns of each good.

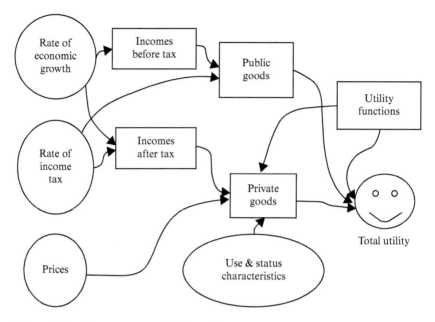

*Figure 9.5    The structure of HappyGrow*

There are no savings in HappyGrow. How Katie and Roberto spend their after-tax incomes depends on the prices of the goods, which are the same for both of them. It also depends on how they each assess the goods for their usefulness and status. In HappyGrow, these assessments can be different for each person as can the utility they derive from the usefulness and status of each good.

The total utility of each person is the sum of the utility they obtain from their ownership of each private good and the utility they obtain from the public good. The total utility from the economy as a whole is the sum of the utilities of the people in the economy. This addition of utilities requires an interpersonal comparison of the utility of different people. Many economists frown on such comparisons on the grounds that there is no scientific basis for making them. This does not seem to prevent them from saying that economic growth is beneficial even though it entails winners and losers. If we are to say anything overall about the relationship between economic growth, consumption and well-being within a utilitarian framework we must be prepared to compare utilities. 'The impossibility results of Arrow, ... Sen, ... Kemp and Ng, ... and Parks, ... show the impossibility of reasonable social decisions without interpersonal comparisons of cardinal utility' (Ng 1997). HappyGrow allows us to see how the relationship between GDP and total utility is affected by different mixes of the use and status characteristics for the two private goods as seen by each person. We can use HappyGrow to generate scenarios by varying the rate of economic growth, the rate of income tax, the rates of depreciation and the prices of consumables and durables. We can also see what happens when Katie and Roberto are not equally rich and when they derive different levels of utility from the same level of consumption from usefulness and status.

### 9.5.1 Consumption and Utility in HappyGrow

Both consumables and durables can be useful and can give status to their owners. We will assume that the value of consumables and durables to Katie and Roberto is simply the addition of the use and status value of each of them. Standard economics does not usually analyze goods in terms of their characteristics but it is useful for our purposes. Lancaster (1968) reformulated consumer theory in terms of characteristics, and Brekke and Howarth (2002) take a similar approach. We will also assume for now that Katie and Roberto assess and value the use and status characteristics of consumables and durables in the same way. Later we will see what happens when we change these assumptions.

To be more specific about the relationship between use and utility, Figure 9.6 shows the standard assumption that the marginal utility of

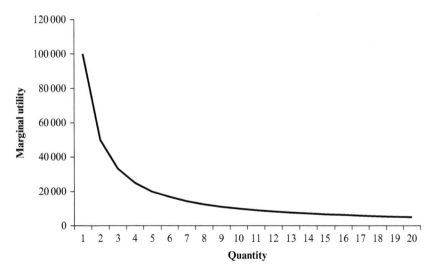

*Figure 9.6    Marginal utility from use*

a good declines when only the use characteristic is considered. (The equations behind Figures 9.6–9.8 are described in 9A, the Annex to this chapter.)

The units used to measure utility are arbitrary. You can think of them as 'utils' as the earlier economists did. Nowadays economists avoid measuring utility in any specific units and conduct their analysis using concepts of more or less utility (ordinal utility) rather than saying by how much utility rises or falls (cardinal utility). Or they avoid the language of utility altogether and conduct the analysis in terms of marginal rates of substitution. Many results are the same whichever approach is used. Diminishing marginal utility, or diminishing marginal rates of substitution, is commonly assumed in standard economics. It works well for most goods and services, especially those that are bought because of their usefulness. Food is a good example. If you are hungry, the more you consume at a single meal or over a week, the less you are likely to value a further serving.

The marginal utility of goods bought primarily or exclusively for status is another matter and is not well illustrated by Figure 9.6. Status comes from having something others lack, so it is the share of the good that a person has that matters most, not the absolute quantity. In addition, marginal utility from status is likely to *increase* as the share of consumption rises, at least over a significant range, after which it might decline. The rationale for this (which differs from the assumption made by Brekke and Howarth (2002)) is that ownership of a very small proportion of a good bought for status is not likely to yield much utility because it will likely go unnoticed. With increasing purchases, the incremental status may rise until a person, in a two-person world, has 50 percent or more of the good in question. Once parity has been obtained with the other person, the marginal utility from status may decline or it may continue rising for a while and then decline. Both of these options can be examined in HappyGrow. The default assumption in HappyGrow of increasing then decreasing marginal utility from status is illustrated in Figure 9.7.

In HappyGrow the marginal utility of each good in terms of use and status can be different for each person though the same general shapes of the relationships are as shown in Figures 9.6 and 9.7. The public good is assumed to provide diminishing marginal utility for each person, as shown in Figure 9.8. It does not fall to zero because unlike most private goods, which require additional time for more consumption, many public goods such as improvements in the environment can be consumed without being constrained by time.

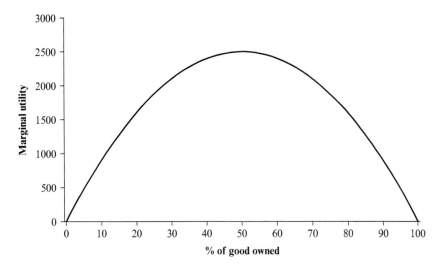

*Figure 9.7    Marginal utility from status*

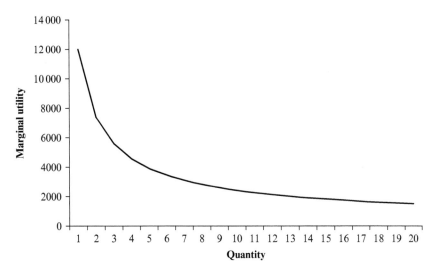

*Figure 9.8    Marginal utility of a public good*

## 9.5.2   Scenarios

Having set the stage we can now use HappyGrow to examine some
scenarios in which we explore the implications of a variety of assumptions
about consumption, status and well-being. All of the input values for the
following scenarios are shown in Table 9.1.

**Scenario 1: people are the same**
In this scenario Katie and Roberto have identical incomes and wealth.
They both view consumables as purely useful and durables as purely a
source of status, and they obtain the same utility from these characteristics. Consumables depreciate at a rate of 90 percent per year so they have to
be replenished frequently. The depreciation rate of durables is 10 percent
per year. The rate of economic growth is 2 percent per year and the rate of
income tax is zero so there is no public good available. The results of these
assumptions are shown in Figure 9.9.

The upper half of Figure 9.9 shows the stocks of consumables and durables owned by Katie and Roberto. At first, Katie and Roberto spend all
their income on consumables (only useful) but then switch almost entirely
to durables (only status) in about year 30, buying only enough consumables to replace those used (depreciated) that year. There is no expenditure
on the public good because in this scenario the rate of income tax is zero.

The lower half of Figure 9.9 shows that total income (GDP) rises
throughout but total utility reaches a maximum at about 30 years and
then levels off when Katie and Roberto switch their expenditures from
consumables to durables.[5] There are two reasons for this trend in total
utility. First, with declining marginal utility from use, as Katie and Roberto
buy more consumables which offer only useful qualities in this scenario,
the rate of increase in total utility declines even before they start buying
durables for status. This is easily seen in the lower half of Figure 9.9 for
total utility in the first few years of the scenario.

Katie and Roberto switch over to durables when they have bought so
many consumables that the marginal utility from consumables, which
started out above the marginal utility from durables, is less than the marginal utility from durables. Since the prices of consumables and durables
are the same in this scenario, Katie and Roberto switch to durables as
soon as the marginal utility from durables starts to exceed the marginal
utility from consumables. Sadly they both strive to increase their share of
durables which, by assumption, they value only for status, but their efforts
are futile. They start out with a 50 percent share of all the durables and no
matter how much their individual spending on durables rises, since they
are both behaving the same way their shares remain constant at 50 percent.

*Table 9.1 Input assumptions for HappyGrow scenario*

| | 1 | 2 | 3 | 4 | 5 |
| --- | --- | --- | --- | --- | --- |
| | The same | Rich and poor | Use and status | Public good | Mixed |
| Characteristics of goods (1 pure useful, 0 pure status) | | | | | |
| Katie | | | | | |
|   Consumables | 1 | 1 | 0.7 | 1 | 0.7 |
|   Durables | 0 | 0 | 0.3 | 0 | 0.3 |
| Roberto | | | | | |
|   Consumables | 1 | 1 | 0.7 | 1 | 0.7 |
|   Durables | 0 | 0 | 0.3 | 0 | 0.3 |
| Prices | | | | | |
|   Consumables | 1 | 1 | 1 | 1 | 1 |
|   Durables | 1 | 1 | 1 | 1 | 1 |
| Initial Income | | | | | |
|   Katie | 10 | 5 | 10 | 10 | 5 |
|   Roberto | 10 | 20 | 10 | 10 | 20 |
| Initial stock of Consumables | | | | | |
|   Katie | 6 | 2 | 6 | 6 | 2 |
|   Roberto | 6 | 6 | 6 | 6 | 6 |
| Initial stock of Durables | | | | | |
|   Katie | 2 | 1 | 2 | 2 | 1 |
|   Roberto | 2 | 2 | 2 | 2 | 2 |
| Initial stock of Public Good | | | | | |
|   Katie and Roberto | 0 | 0 | 0 | 0 | 0 |
| Happiness Constants (higher values more utility) | | | | | |
| Katie | | | | | |
|   Utility – use | 5000 | 5000 | 5000 | 5000 | 5000 |
|   Utility – status | 100 | 100 | 100 | 100 | 100 |
| Roberto | | | | | |
|   Utility – use | 5000 | 5000 | 5000 | 5000 | 5000 |
|   Utility – status | 100 | 100 | 100 | 100 | 100 |
| Economic growth (%/yr) | 2 | 2 | 2 | 2 | 2 |
| Rate of income tax (%) | 0 | 0 | 0 | 20 | 20 |
| Depreciation rate (%/yr) | | | | | |
|   Consumables | 90 | 90 | 90 | 90 | 90 |
|   Durables | 10 | 10 | 10 | 10 | 10 |
|   Public Good | 10 | 10 | 10 | 10 | 10 |

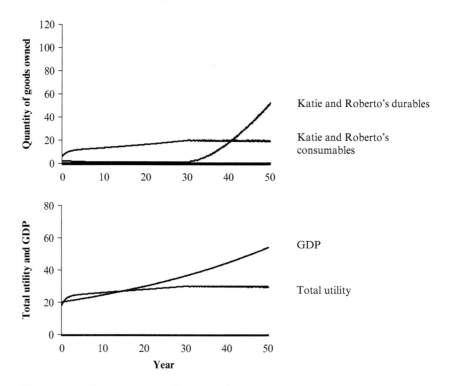

*Figure 9.9    Scenario 1: Katie and Roberto are the same*

Hence their utility remains unchanged even though their incomes grow another 50 percent from year 30 to year 50. This result is similar to the pattern displayed in Figure 9.1, where GDP per capita in the USA increased steadily from 1945 to 2014 but the percentage of very happy people stayed more or less constant. It is also similar to the pattern in Figure 9.4 comparing US GDP per capita with GPI per capita. This is not to suggest that the US experience was due only to the rise in the significance of status as a motivating factor driving consumer demand but it could well have been a contributing factor.

**Scenario 2: rich and poor**

What happens when one person (Katie) is poor and the other (Roberto) is rich? Let us assume that Katie's initial income is 5, Roberto's is 20, and that Katie starts out with two units of consumables and one unit of durables compared with six and two for Roberto. We still assume that they both value the characteristics in the same way and see the goods as providing these characteristics in the same way.

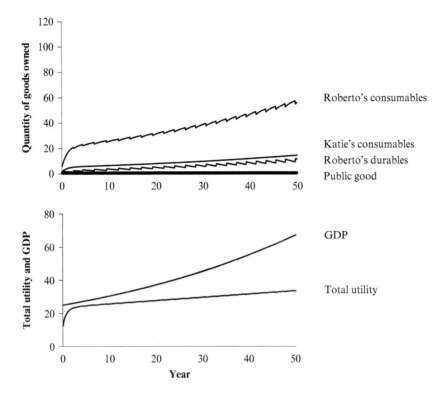

*Figure 9.10    Scenario 2: rich and poor*

Figure 9.10 shows that in this scenario Katie and Roberto start by spending all their money on consumables. After about three years, Roberto starts buying durables as well. The 'saw tooth' pattern in Figure 9.10 in Roberto's ownership of consumables and durables is due to their periodic replacement owing to depreciation. Katie sticks with consumables and spends nothing on durables, ever. She just cannot compete with Roberto on status.

In the lower part of Figure 9.10, we see that unlike the previous scenario, total utility rises throughout the 50 years, though far more slowly than total income, after Roberto starts buying durables. Interestingly most of this increase in total utility comes from Katie and Roberto's purchases of consumables. Roberto gains comparatively little from buying durables because he started out with 75 percent of all of the durables. Adding to this percentage hardly improves his utility from status. Once you own most or all of the status goods in a society, your utility from status cannot rise much by owning even more. There is a limit to satisfaction from status alone.

**Scenario 3: use and status**

People buy many goods for both use and status. We can examine the implications of such a mixture in HappyGrow. If Katie and Roberto view both goods as providing the same mix of use and status characteristics, rather than switching from spending only on one good entirely to the other (apart from replacement) they may continue to spend on both. This is shown in Figure 9.11, where both Katie and Roberto consider the utility of consumables to come 70 percent from the use characteristic and 30 percent from the status characteristic. They perceive durables in the opposite way, 30 percent from use and 70 percent from status.

In scenario 1 Katie and Roberto valued consumables exclusively for use and durables exclusively for status. They began by buying only consumables then, with economic growth, both switched to durables, spending only enough on consumables to replace those that were consumed or wore out.

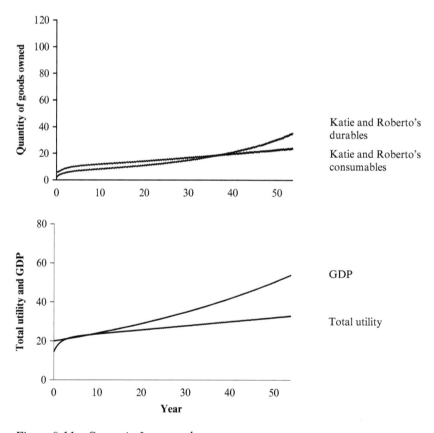

*Figure 9.11    Scenario 3: use and status*

In this third scenario, where the value of the two goods depends on both use and status, Katie and Roberto buy both goods all the time. They start out by buying more consumables, which are valued more for use than status. As their incomes rise, they gradually spend more on durables which have stronger status value. Total utility rises throughout, but again, much more slowly than total income.

**Scenario 4: public good**
In all the scenarios considered so far, the rate of income tax has been zero and there has been no provision of the public good. This scenario is identical to scenario 1, with the exception that the rate of income tax is set at 20 percent and the revenues are used to provide Katie and Roberto with the public good. The difference in the results is clear, as shown in Figure 9.12. When the public good is introduced, total utility rises faster and longer over the entire 50-year period and does not stop rising even when Katie and

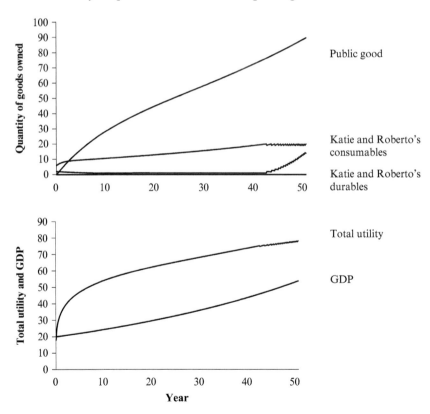

*Figure 9.12   Scenario 4: public good*

Roberto start to spend their rising incomes on durables after about 43 years in the pointless, zero sum pursuit of status. This result is largely due to the assumption that, while the marginal utility of the public good declines, it does not decline to zero as its quantity is increased. Hence an increase in availability can continue to yield positive marginal utility without limit.

**Scenario 5: mixed**
HappyGrow can be used to examine changes in many variables at one time. As an example, consider what happens when the Rich and Poor scenario (Roberto has higher initial income and stocks of both goods) is combined with the Use and Status scenario (both goods are valued for use and status) and the Public Good scenario (income tax at 20 percent).

Figure 9.13 shows that with this combination of features both Katie and Roberto buy both goods throughout the 50 years and total utility rises rap-

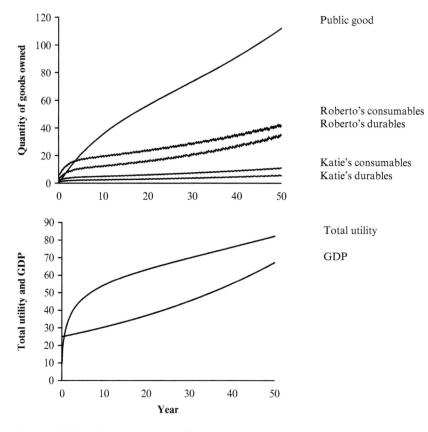

*Figure 9.13    Scenario 5: mixed*

idly at first and continues to rise with economic growth though not at such a high rate towards the end of the 50-year simulation. Additional mixed strategies that can be explored with HappyGrow can allow for differences in how Katie and Roberto perceive consumables and durables in terms of their status and use characteristics and in the levels of utility each of them obtains from the two products. Different prices, depreciation rates, growth rates and tax rates allow even more interesting possibilities.

Cooper et al. (2001) include the further dimension of research and development (R&D) in their model of growth and status. They show that as an economy grows, resources for R&D are increasingly devoted to generating innovations in status goods: 'The resulting long-run rate of utility growth is negative'.

### 9.5.3   HappyGrow and the Real World

Models like HappyGrow do not tell us anything about the real world directly because they are not based on real data. It is impossible to test output from HappyGrow against anything measurable. Only the pattern or shape of the results, not specific values or timing, means anything. Even so, HappyGrow can help us think about the world and better understand how it functions. It can also suggest new questions and it can remind us of things we have known all along or would have known if we had thought about them. Models like HappyGrow can surprise us when results emerge that do not make much sense at first, but which on further inspection ring true.

When it comes to relating what we learn from HappyGrow to the real world it is helpful to think of consumables, durables and the public good not as single commodities but as categories of goods with different mixes of use and status characteristics. The same can be said of Katie and Roberto. Think of them as representing whole groups of similar people.

So, what have we learned from the scenarios? In scenario 1, we saw that people can spend all their rising incomes chasing status in a race that no one wins. Does this sound familiar? There were only two types of goods in the model with different characteristics and, aside from gender, two identical people. In the real world, there are many different people and countless goods, with new ones being introduced all the time, often promoted to appeal to our desire for status. Sometimes this message is about belonging to a group; beer ads are notorious for this. Sometimes it is about setting ourselves apart from a group, such as in ads for 'prestige' cars. Long before we can acquire all these goods and achieve the status their consumption is supposed to bring, new goods that promise to enhance our status even more come on the market and the chase for status through more consumption continues apace.

Of course, we know that people are not all the same. Some are very rich and some are very poor and most are somewhere in between. Some value a good primarily for its value in use and only secondarily for status. Others look at the same good and value it for precisely the opposite reasons. In subsequent scenarios, we saw that assumptions chosen to represent these situations can affect how people spend their incomes and what they achieve through such expenditures. The rich do spend disproportionately more on goods that demonstrate their status in society, as in scenario 2. But who is their audience or reference group? If it is the poor, then there is a point beyond which it is hardly worth going. Consuming 20 times more than someone else is unlikely to add much to a person's status than consuming only 19 times more. But if rich people compare themselves against other rich people then we are back to the first scenario where essentially similar people compete through consumption in an ever-rising spiral of pointless expenditures. All expenditures become defensive.

If we were to differentiate between people in terms of the utility they derive from the same level of consumption we would see that it can have quite an impact on how people spend their incomes. Some people might use consumption to demonstrate status while others avoid this approach for no other reason than that their appreciation of the characteristics of the goods is different. Whether or not a person believes that consumption of the right goods really helps demonstrate their status in society is greatly influenced by their socialization during childhood and how it is reinforced in later life. If people understood that demonstrating status through consumption is self-defeating, it might help relieve the pressure on the environment caused by making, distributing, using and disposing of these goods as well as on the people themselves.

Another difference is in how people perceive the same good. Some look at a house and see a place to live. Others worry more about living at the right address. Some wear clothing with the manufacturer's logo prominently and proudly displayed. Others studiously avoid clothing that advertises its designer or maker. These sorts of differences can have interesting implications. If people attach status value to different goods, then the search for status through consumption is no longer so pointless. Everyone can consume a substantial share of the good that they think is important even if others do not share this view. We see this in different age groups and different ethnic groups where within the group there is consensus about which goods signify status, but between groups there are major differences. Young male teenagers fuss over their skateboards. Older male teenagers are more concerned about their cars, cell phones and social media connections. Women working in the financial districts of large cities feel the need to dress in a certain way. Elderly women in nursing homes worry more about who is sitting in which chair.

There are, however, limits to the extent to which people can disagree on the goods valued for status. Status is a social phenomenon, determined by and for groups. Anyone wishing to belong to such a group is obliged to adopt the consumption standards and habits of its members. So though everyone does not have to see all goods in the same way, as long as sufficient numbers broadly agree, ambitions to achieve status through competitive consumption will remain largely unfulfilled.

When we introduced the public good into the mix paid for by taxation we were able to turn a situation of rising incomes and stagnant utility into one of improved well-being for all. This is the lesson of scenario 4. In a society in which consumer goods are available in prodigious quantities, where many of these goods are purchased primarily for status, access to increasing amounts of public goods may be essential if economic growth is to yield significant benefits. Furthermore, with increasing congestion and deteriorating environments, protected urban spaces and natural environments become quintessential public goods of increasing value that should be provided in growing quantities in mature economies.

Finally, all the scenarios have in common the feature that total utility increases most rapidly in the early years when people are buying goods entirely or mostly for use. When the desire for status drives people's consumption, total utility can still rise but more slowly. This is consistent with the general notion of the diminishing marginal utility of income: people fulfill their most urgent needs first. It is also consistent with the data on GDP and happiness, though it remains a matter of conjecture as to how far an increasing search for status through consumption explains it.

## 9.6   CONCLUSION

There is more to happiness than income, much more. As Easterlin, Layard and others have reported, absolute income plays a very small role in explaining a person's happiness. Relative income is more important, but that is a zero sum game. By comparing subjective well-being data from many countries, Helliwell finds that 'measures of social capital, including especially the corollary measures of specific and general trust, have substantial effects on well-being beyond those flowing through economic channels' (Helliwell 2005). These considerations, which, as Helliwell explains, have implications for the workplace, communities and government, should play an important role in setting the institutional context of managing without growth.

The measurement of happiness has confounded economists ever since it was proposed by Bentham and the other early Utilitarians. Rather than pursue the impossible, economists gradually moved away from the quantification of happiness, first by reconstructing the theory of demand based on ordinal utility and then by avoiding interpersonal comparisons of utility. This allowed some normative statements to be made about specific changes in an economy but made it very difficult for economists to say anything about the relationship between economic growth and happiness. In *The Economics of Welfare* (1920[1952]), Pigou devoted several chapters to the 'national dividend' (that is, gross domestic product) and tried to establish the conditions under which an increase in GDP entailed an increase in welfare. Eighty-four years later, Just, Hueth and Schmitz, in an authoritative survey of welfare economics nearly 700 pages in length and subtitled 'A practical approach to project and policy evaluation', avoid this issue entirely (Just et al. 2004). They are not alone. Other surveys of the subject do the same (Johansson 1991; O'Connell 1982).

We have reached a point where welfare economics, which provides the formal normative framework and criteria in economics for assessing change, has nothing to say about economic growth. Instead economic growth is promoted and defended in terms of other macroeconomic, social and environmental objectives that it is purported to help achieve, such as full employment, eradication of poverty, and environmental protection. Its incomplete success in doing so is the subject of the next chapter.

## NOTES

1. 'Welfare' and 'well-being' are used synonymously in this chapter.
2. This imaginary ladder was first introduced by Cantril (1966) and is sometimes referred to as the Cantril ladder.
3. The natural logarithm of a number is the power to which $e$ would have to be raised to equal it.
4. The HappyGrow Model and details of its structure, assumptions and equations are available on www.pvictor.com.
5. Total utility is divided by 10000 in Figures 9.8 to 9.12 so that the same scale can be used for total utility and GDP. It is the relative shapes of the total utility and GDP curves that is of interest, not their absolute levels.

# ANNEX 9A

In this annex, we look at the equations used by Brekke and Howarth (2002) in their analysis of status and growth and the equations used in HappyGrow.

The typical person in Brekke and Howarth's model buys a single composite commodity that provides both use value and status value in some proportion (w). The typical person's social status depends on the ratio (s) of their consumption (c) and the average consumption level c. In equilibrium, if everyone is the same c = c and s = 1.

The assumed utility function is:

$$U = (1 - w)\ln c + w\ln s \qquad (9A.1)$$

where c is the consumption level and s is status.

The logarithmic function ensures that both the marginal utility of consumption c and status s decline. With rising incomes, the amount of consumption required to maintain a fixed level of status also rises, since c is increasing, which means that the status obtained from an incremental increase in consumption falls with economic growth.

HappyGrow allocates the after-tax incomes of Katie and Roberto between consumables and durables so that they maximize their individual utility. This is accomplished when their expenditures are such that the ratio of the prices of the products is equal to the ratio of their marginal utilities. The marginal utility of consumables and durables to Katie and Roberto is the sum of their marginal utilities from the use and status characteristics of each good. The marginal utility of each of these characteristics is a function of the amount that each of them owns. HappyGrow allows different prices of consumables and durables to be chosen, though it is the relative rather than absolute prices that determine how Katie and Roberto spend their incomes.

Figure 9.6 shows diminishing marginal utility for the use characteristic. It is a graph of an equation in which marginal utility is equal to a constant K divided by quantity x of the good:

$$MU^{use} = K/x \qquad (9A.2)$$

In HappyGrow we can make different assumptions about the marginal utility from the use of consumables and durables for Katie and Roberto by choosing different values for the constant K in equation (9A.2). Total utility from use is given by equation (9A.3).

$$TU^{use} = K \ln x \qquad (9A.3)$$

Figure 9.7 shows the assumption that the marginal utility of status rises then falls. It is a graph of equation (9A.4):

$$MU^{status} = ax - x^2 \qquad (9A.4)$$

where $x$ is the percentage of a good owned.

HappyGrow includes equation (9A.4) separately for Katie and Roberto. By selecting different values for $a$ in HappyGrow for Katie and Roberto the marginal utility of status can be different for each person. This option provides a means for examining the implications of differences in people's propensity to enjoy consumption.

The total utility from status is given by equation (9A.5):

$$TU = ax^2/2 - x^3/3 - F \qquad (9A.5)$$

where $F$ is a constant.

Figure 9.8 shows the marginal utility of the public good is assumed to provide diminishing marginal utility for each person. Unlike the declining marginal utility from use, which declines to zero upon saturation, the marginal utility from the public good is assumed to decline to a positive level. It is a graph of equation (9A.6):

$$MU^{public} = Dknk - 1 \qquad (9A.6)$$

where:
$n$ = quantity of the public good
$k < 1$
$D$ is a constant.

Total utility from the public good for an individual is given by equation (9A.7):

$$TU^{public} = Dnk \qquad (9A.7)$$

## NOTE

Total utility is divided by 10 000 in Figures 9.9 to 9.12 so that the same scale can be used for total utility and GDP. It is the relative shapes of the total utility and GDP curves that is of interest, not their absolute levels.

# 10. The disappointments of economic growth

Growth is widely thought to be the panacea for all major economic ills of the modern world ... poverty ... unemployment ... overpopulation ... environmental degradation. (Daly 2005)

For a long time, economic growth has been regarded as a remedy for so many problems. By increasing the amount of goods and services produced and sold in an economy, economic growth makes everything possible, or so it is claimed: reduces and removes poverty, generates full employment, provides more resources for government to spend on national defense, health care, education, infrastructure, social security, environmental protection, the arts, development aid and so on. And what makes growth so appealing is that it allows more to be spent on everything at the same time as the economic pie gets bigger and bigger. This is not to say that tradeoffs are eliminated. When growth in any year is insufficient to cover all the extra spending that people, corporations, NGOs and governments desire, some tradeoffs must be made, but without growth, tradeoffs cannot be avoided and are more acute.

Few would dispute the tremendous contribution that two centuries or more of economic growth have made to raise the standard of living of people in countries fortunate enough to have experienced it. Economic growth has made it possible for people to live longer, healthier lives at a level of comfort that even the wealthy in pre-industrial societies could scarcely imagine, let alone experience. Easterlin (1996) puts the case well, though Douthwaite (1999) is less impressed. But economic growth has its costs. These can be categorized as environmental costs and social costs. Environmental costs include the adverse effects of resource extraction, waste disposal, and the loss of habitat and species, which were discussed in Chapters 5, 6 and 7. Social costs include the breakdown of communities, alienation, crowding and crime. Some of these costs have been borne by those who have benefited from growth. Others have been borne by those who have benefited far less from growth. Sometimes the disparity between the gains and losses from economic growth is local and regional, as between people living in different parts of a city or different regions in the same country. The more egregious disparity is between entire countries, where economic growth in some has taken place at the cost of de-development and oppression in others. The impact of the European colonizers on the native populations of the Americas, the deliberate destruction of India's textile industry to serve British interests, and the reliance on slavery in the American cotton industry are just three examples of the dark side of economic growth (Frank 1966).

We cannot undo the sins of the past. The era of European colonization is over. Now we like to think that the countries of the world can determine their own paths into the future, tempered by the increasing mobility of capital and labor, which are supported and enforced through international trade agreements and institutions. Advocates of globalization insist that it will bring the benefits of economic growth to all (Krueger 2002). Others are far more critical of globalization, arguing that it is best understood as economic colonialism, where territory is captured through legal means through the use of capital and materials without taking land through occupation (Zekos 2015).

One of the arguments of this book is that the biophysical limits of the planet will prevent the kind of economic growth enjoyed by rich countries from being extended to all peoples of the world. Rich countries should make room for economic expansion in those countries where the need is greatest. This pill is very hard to swallow, especially for those who believe economic growth is the key to solving many, if not all, of society's ills (Friedman 2005). The main purpose of this chapter is to lay more of the groundwork for managing without growth by looking at how successful growth has been in the past few decades for generating full employment, eliminating poverty, reducing inequality and protecting the environment. As we shall see, it is a mixed record. Employment has seldom been full, poverty has not been eliminated, inequality has risen and the environment remains a major public concern – in some respects, more so than ever. Economic growth is certainly not sufficient for meeting more specific public policy objectives. In the next chapter, we will show that it is not necessary either. Other policies are required. The problem is that in the to and fro of debate about public policy, these other policies are not implemented consistently and diligently, on the grounds that they are bad for the economy, bad for competitiveness, bad for trade: that is, bad for growth.

Although the commitment to economic growth remains strong and widespread, there are signs of increasing recognition that growth has its problems. In the 1970s, the proposition that there are limits to growth was resisted mightily by most economists and though it generated some interest in government circles, the interest was short-lived (see Chapter 7). The ferocity of attack on limits to growth, and the abiding resistance to the idea that there are such limits, may be related to something deep in the human psyche (Becker 1973; Vargish 1980). Economic growth offers the promise of a better future and with the declining influence of religious narratives about the afterlife, in Western countries at least, that's a hard promise to give up. Nonetheless, there are clear signs that growth has proved disappointing. In a comparison of the USA with 19 other major economies in the OECD, Speth (2012) reports that 'the United States now ranks at or very near the bottom of important areas' (2012, p. 1). These include: the poverty rate, inequality of incomes, government spending on social programs for the disadvantaged as a percentage of GDP, the UN's indices of material well-being of children and gender inequality, social mobility, life expectancy, student performance in mathematics, Yale University's Environmental Performance Index, ratification of international agreements, and international development expenditure and humanitarian assistance as a percentage of GDP. Speth notes that the USA ranks at or near the top on rates of infant mortality, obesity, percentage of people without health care due to cost concerns, consumption of antidepressant drugs, high school dropout rate, homicide rate, imprisonment, ecological footprint per capita, military spending and arms sales.

This comparatively poor performance of the USA, which has the highest GDP in the world, reflecting its long period of high rates of growth, and one of the highest GDPs per capita, exemplifies the disappointments of economic growth. Many pundits attribute the election of Donald Trump as President of the United States in 2016 to these disappointments, in particular to the rise in income and wealth inequality.

Another indication of the disappointments of economic growth is the proliferation of different kinds of growth indicated by a panoply of adjectives: green growth (Bowen 2012); inclusive growth (World Economic Forum 2017a; Ianchovichina and Lundstrom 2009); sustainable growth (European Commission 2012; The Royal Swedish Academy of Sciences 2018); smart growth (US EPA 2017b); broad-based growth (Fields 1995); clean growth (Government of Canada 2017f); shared growth (Holmes and McGuinty 2015; PwC 2015); resilient growth, climate-friendly growth (OECD 2017c); and pro-poor growth (Kakwani et al. 2004; Wiggins and Higgins 2008; Melamed 2010). The fact that it has been found useful, necessary even, to qualify the type of growth that is being sought is a clear indication that economic growth as experienced and expected falls short in many key respects: it is not green, or inclusive, or sustainable, or smart, or broad-based, or clean, or shared, or resilient, or climate-friendly, or pro-poor. No wonder there is interest in finding an alternative path into the future.

## 10.1   ECONOMIC GROWTH AND FULL EMPLOYMENT

Economic growth was originally adopted as an objective of government policy for the purpose of ensuring full employment in the post-World War II era (see Chapter 1). At that time, William Beveridge, in his influential report to the British government, suggested that for Britain a rate of unemployment of 3 percent was full employment, defined as a situation when the number of people looking for work equaled the number of vacancies (Beveridge 1945). The OECD defines full employment some-what differently, without specifying a particular rate of unemployment at which the labor force is deemed fully employed. 'Full employment occurs when the economy is producing to its maximum sustainable capacity, using labor, technology, land, capital and other factors of production to their fullest potential' (OECD 2004). There is no longer an official definition of full employment in Canada and so there is no level of unemploy-ment that can be used as a benchmark for assessing the extent to which Canada has achieved full employment. The USA Congressional Budget Office avoids the term 'full employment' and instead defines the 'natural' rate of unemployment as 'the rate of unemployment arising from all sources except fluctuations in the overall demand for goods and services' (US Congressional Budget Office 2016). In the UK, Chancellor of the Exchequer (that is, Minister of Finance) George Osborne announced that the Conservative Party was committing itself to achieving full employ-ment, without defining it precisely. He repudiated his predecessor Norman Lamont who, in 1991, proclaimed that unemployment was a price worth paying to reduce inflation (Heyes 2014).

The idea that the objective of full employment should be tempered by considerations of controlling inflation led to the emergence of NAIRU, the 'non-accelerating inflation rate of unemployment', as an alternative policy objective. In the 1980s, NAIRU supplanted full employment as the employment objective of many OECD countries including Canada (Hazeldine 1992). NAIRU is not the same as full employment. As shown in Figure 10.1, OECD estimates for NAIRU for Canada, Sweden, UK and USA change over time and are two to three times greater than the 3 percent originally proposed by Beveridge.

In the absence of official definitions of full employment in percentage terms we can at least observe the lowest rates of unemployment that have been achieved following the commitment of the OECD in 1960 to promote economic growth and the highest employment (OECD 1960). These rates can serve as a measure of frictional unemployment and give us working measures of full employment for different economies, recognizing that

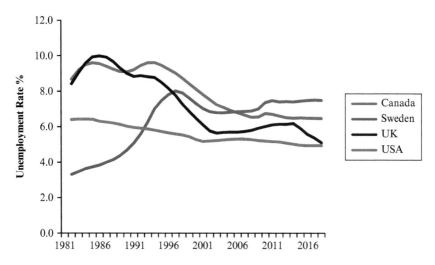

*Source:* OECD (2017a) dataset.

*Figure 10.1 Estimates of NAIRU 1981–2017*

over time frictional employment rates can also change as circumstances change. Most OECD member countries experienced their lowest rate of unemployment in the 1960s: for example Canada 3.3 percent (1966), Sweden 1.5 percent (1965), the UK 2.7 percent (1965) and the USA 3.5 percent (1968). It is to be expected that frictional unemployment would be higher in Canada and the USA because they are geographically much larger than Sweden and the UK. It is more difficult for a vacancy in one part of a large country to be filled by someone who may be living thousands of kilometers away. So, for our purposes, based on experience since 1960 when OECD countries formally adopted economic growth as their top economic policy objective, we will assume that full employment in Sweden means 2 percent unemployment, 3 percent in the UK and 4 percent in Canada and the USA. These values are just below the average rates of unemployment for the decade of the 1960s (OECD 1960). Any level of unemployment above these values represents the extent to which the economies have failed to generate full employment.

Figure 10.2 shows that rates of unemployment have fluctuated widely over the half century from 1960 to 2017, ranging, for example, between 1.5 and 11.7 percent annually in Sweden, 2.7 and 11.8 percent in the USA, 3.3 and 12.0 percent in Canada, and 3.5 and 9.7 percent in the UK. These fluctuations correspond to very large changes in the numbers of people looking for work but unable to find it. There were 32.5 million

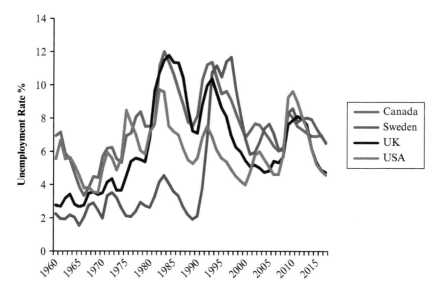

*Source:* OECD (2016e) dataset.

*Figure 10.2 Unemployment rate % 1960–2017*

unemployed in OECD economies in 2000 when unemployment rates were comparatively low, rising to 49 million in 2010 following the financial crisis of 2008/09 (OECD 2016e). There is a great deal of human frustration and tragedy hidden in these figures as people struggle to find work that these growth-based economies failed to provide.

Superimposed on these fluctuations of unemployment are other changes that make the situation even worse for the workers and their families unable to find employment. In times of high unemployment some people stop looking for work and so they are excluded from the unemployment statistics. This means that unemployment rates can understate the extent of unemployment, especially in hard times. For those who stay in the labor force there has been an increase in precarious or 'non-standard' employment. This is employment that is 'temporary and part-time wage work, own-account self-employment and other forms of employment that are not fully covered by labor laws and policies' (Cranford et al. 2003). Between 1995 and 2013, more than 50 percent of all jobs created in OECD countries were classified as 'non-standard' (OECD 2015a, p. 29). The causes of this increase in precarious employment include globalization, technological change and weaker labor unions – trends not unrelated to the push for economic growth.

Despite vigorous growth of these economies since the 1960s, unemployment remained well above frictional levels for most of the past half century
or more. Economic growth has not generated full employment largely
because of increases in the labor force and labor productivity that have
accompanied growth. The relationship between GDP, productivity, the
labor force and the rate of unemployment is shown in equation (10.1),
which states that economic output measured as GDP is simply the multiplication of average GDP per employed person and the number of people
employed:

$$GDP = P(1 - u)L \qquad (10.1)$$

where:
*GDP* is real Gross Domestic Product
*P* is productivity (real GDP per employed person)
*L* is the labor force (employed plus unemployed persons)
*u* is the unemployment rate (unemployed/labor force).

Table 10.1 summarizes the changes in the value of these variables between
1971 and 2016. Comparing 2016 with 1971 we see from Table 10.1 that
the number of unemployed people increased by 200 000 in Sweden,
850 000 in Canada, 640 000 in the UK, and nearly 3 million in the USA.
Unemployment rates also rose, except in the USA, where it was 17 percent
lower in 2016 than in 1971. Clearly, economic growth which was very
substantial in this 46-year period did not generate full employment because
both productivity and the labor force grew as well.

We can use equation (10.1) to consider how circumstances might have
been different. If the increases in productivity and the labor force had
been the same but the rate of growth of GDP had been lower, the rate of
unemployment would have been higher. This is just a matter of arithmetic
but it is the rationale for the argument that economic growth is required

*Table 10.1   Change in GDP and related variables 1971–2016*

|  | Canada | Sweden | UK | USA |
|---|---|---|---|---|
| Real GDP | 234% | 160% | 167% | 241% |
| Productivity | 50% | 106% | 107% | 78% |
| Labour Force | 125% | 31% | 30% | 90% |
| Unemployment Rate | 15% | 101% | 24% | −17% |
| Unemployed # | 852,176 | 217,869 | 642,512 | 2,903,844 |

*Source:*   OECD (2016a).

for full employment. A different counterfactual scenario is one with the
same growth in GDP and lower increases in productivity and/or the labor
force. In this case, the rate of unemployment would have been lower. This
possibility suggests that policies designed to increase productivity and the
labor force may raise the rate of unemployment unless they also raise the
rate of economic growth sufficiently to absorb new and displaced workers.
In view of the concerns discussed in Chapters 5, 6 and 7, raising the rate of
economic growth is not a feasible proposition over the long term, so these
kinds of policies will have to be rethought. We will make a start on that in
the next chapter.

One possible way out of the dilemma created by these opposing influences on employment is to consider the average number of hours worked
by an employed person. If more people worked fewer hours without affecting total working hours, it should be possible to have full employment
without relying so much on economic growth. Equation (10.2) shows how
this is possible:

$$GDP = aP_e(1 - u)L \tag{10.2}$$

where:
$a$ = the average hours worked per employed person
$P_e$ = productivity (real GDP per employee per hour).

The first two rows of data in Table 10.2 show the average number of hours
worked per employed person in 1971 and 2016 in the four countries. As
we have seen, this corresponded to rates of unemployment far in excess of
full employment. The third row of Table 10.2 shows the average number
of hours worked in 2016 that would have fully employed the labor force
in each country, given the increases in productivity per hour and the labor
force since 1971. Rows 4 and 5 show the actual percentage reduction in

*Table 10.2    Average hours employed and full employment*

|  | Canada | Sweden | UK | USA |
|---|---|---|---|---|
| Av hours worked 1971 | 1912 | 1698 | 1899 | 1890 |
| Av hours worked 2016 | 1703 | 1621 | 1676 | 1783 |
| Full Employment hrs | 1647 | 1544 | 1639 | 1765 |
| Actual Reduction | 10.9% | 4.5% | 11.7% | 5.7% |
| Reduction for FE | 13.8% | 9.1% | 13.7% | 6.6% |
| Additional Employment | 608,665 | 246,433 | 702,920 | 1,527,502 |

*Source:*   Based on data from OECD (2016d) and equation (10.2).

average hours worked and the percentage reduction that would have given full employment. The sixth row shows the additional number of jobs that would have been created had this happened. In Canada, for example, if the average number of hours worked had declined by 13.8 percent between 1971 and 2016 rather than 10.9 percent, then the unemployment rate in 2016 would have been 4 percent and not 6.9 percent, and over 600 000 people looking for work would have found it. The situation in the USA is especially striking because full employment in 2016 would have required an average work year of 1765 hours, which is considerably greater than the average work year in Sweden in 1971. In 2016 the average work year was already less than 1600 hours in Germany, the Netherlands, Norway, Denmark, France, Luxembourg, Belgium and Switzerland through a combination of a shorter work week and more vacation days. This suggests that the values for the average hours worked annually required for full employment in Canada, Sweden, the UK and the USA are not at all unrealistic.

The critical significance of the average time spent at work in influencing the rate of unemployment is made even clearer by looking at what would have happened had there been no decrease in the average hours worked between 1971 and 2016. For the same increases in GDP, productivity per hour and the labor force, the rate of unemployment would have been 17.3 percent in Canada, 10.9 percent in Sweden, 16.3 percent in the UK and 10.3 percent in the USA. These results show how sensitive the rate of unemployment is to the average length of the work year. By spreading work among a larger number of employees, the unemployment rate can be lowered significantly, providing productivity per hour is unaffected.

To conclude this section, economic growth has generated employment, if not full employment. This should not be a surprise. Governments initially adopted growth as a policy objective in order to achieve full employment. That it should have been less than successful is a disappointment, especially to all those who failed to find work and their dependents. Some were unemployed for relatively short periods and depending on the country and specific circumstances, they received a substantial level of income support while they searched for employment. Others were less fortunate. Table 10.3 shows the net replacement rate (NRR) in 2015 (that is, the proportion of net income in work that was maintained after job loss) for a one-earner couple, with two children aged 6 and 4, previously earning the average wage. The levels of income replacement during periods of unemployment were highest in Canada in the short term but higher in the UK for prolonged periods of unemployment. The USA offered the lowest level of income replacement, well below the average for all OECD countries.

Unemployment is a major cause of poverty. The partial replacement

*Table 10.3*   *NRR: the percentage of net income maintained after job loss*
               *in 2015: married couple with two children (includes applicable*
               *housing and social assistance benefits)*

|        | NRR – initial unemployment | NRR – in the 60th month of unemployment | NRR – 5-year average |
|--------|:--------------------------:|:---------------------------------------:|:--------------------:|
| Canada | 85 | 62 | 65 |
| Sweden | 61 | 61 | 61 |
| UK     | 71 | 71 | 71 |
| USA    | 49 | 34 | 35 |

*Source:*   OECD Indicators (2016c).

of net income provided in OECD countries, while appearing generous in many cases, may not be sufficient to prevent families becoming impoverished. As we shall see in the next section, fluctuations in the rate of unemployment are closely related to fluctuations in the number of people living in poverty, even with the various forms of income supplements provided. Economic growth has not provided full employment. It has done even less to eradicate poverty.

## 10.2   ECONOMIC GROWTH AND POVERTY

The definition and measurement of poverty is even more challenging than for full employment (Corak 2016). Most agree that poverty encompasses more than simply a lack of income, though that is certainly a major aspect. Poverty is also social, political and cultural. Moreover, it is considered to undermine human rights – economic (the right to work and have an adequate income), social (access to health care and education), political (freedom of thought, expression and association) and cultural (the right to maintain one's cultural identity and be involved in a community's cultural life) (UNESCO 2016).

Sometimes these non-economic aspects of poverty are summed up in the term 'social exclusion', when people are denied access to rights, opportunities and resources widely available to others in their society. Social exclusion is often related to a lack of income relative to others, but that need not be the case. There can be ways of ameliorating social exclusion independently of redistributing income, such as through publicly funded health care, education and libraries. Likewise, a more equal distribution of income does not guarantee a reduction in social exclusion if the exclusion is based on religious, racial or ethnic grounds.

Another reason for distinguishing between economic and non-economic aspects of poverty is that it provides a wider range of options for reducing poverty than relying on rising incomes alone. Decades, even centuries, of economic growth have not eliminated poverty, and there is no reason to think that further economic growth will get the job done.

We turn now specifically to the economic dimension of poverty. When considering a lack of income as a source of poverty, a distinction is often made between 'absolute' and 'relative' poverty. Absolute poverty is defined in terms of the satisfaction of basic material needs. This requires specification of these basic material needs, which is value laden, and the income required to meet them. It cannot be done entirely independently of comparison with others and data limitations can be challenging. Even the most ardent advocates of poverty as an absolute condition acknowledge that 'the quality and standards of each of the "needs" is relative to one's own society. Shelter, for example, is a basic need in all societies but the nature of that shelter will vary from nation to nation' (Sarlo 2013, p. 29).

One attempt to gauge changes in absolute poverty in several OECD countries compared the relative threshold in a base year (that is, half the median income in the mid-1990s) unchanged in real terms with incomes in later years. For 15 OECD countries having the requisite information it was concluded that 'even when relative income poverty is rising – most of the [15] OECD countries achieved significant reductions in absolute poverty between the mid-1990s and mid-2000s' (OECD 2008b, p. 130). In particular, using this approach to measure changes in 'absolute' poverty, by the mid-2000s it was reduced by about 60 percent in the UK, about 25 percent in Sweden and about 5 percent in the USA (OECD 2008b, p. 128, Figure 5.4). These are encouraging findings.

Sarlo takes a different approach to estimating the extent of absolute poverty in Canada. He defines 'basic needs poverty lines . . . intended to measure the number and proportion of Canadians who cannot afford the basic necessities of life, such as food, clothing, shelter, and other household essentials' (Sarlo 2006). Using his definition of poverty, with each component specified in some detail and with data from Statistics Canada, Sarlo estimated the Canadian poverty rate at intervals from 1969 to 2009. If we exclude the precipitous drop from 1969 to 1974, which Sarlo says 'may be a data issue as opposed to a real change in people's living standards' (Sarlo 2013, pp. 22–3), then between 1974 and 2009 the overall trend in the percentage of Canadian households living in poverty was downward, but not for children and persons: 'Indeed, it appears that the historical low for both person poverty and child poverty was in 1974' (ibid, p. 22).

An alternative approach to the definition and measurement of poverty uses 'relative' income. For example, in OECD publications, anyone whose after-tax income is less than half the median income in their country is considered poor (Förster and d'Ercole 2005). LIM (the 'low-income measure') is widely used in international comparisons of poverty, partly because it is easy to estimate from the available data. It is usually defined as 50 percent of the median household income in an economy with an adjustment based on household size. Eurostat, the European statistical agency, refers to its measure, which is like LIM, as an 'at risk of poverty' measure (Statistics Canada 2015b, p. 1). One implication of LIM as a poverty measure is that no matter how much incomes rise, if the distribution remains unchanged, there is no reduction in poverty. The same proportion of households would still have incomes less than 50 percent of the median. Seen this way, poverty is entirely a matter of income inequality rather than sufficiency. Yet it seems too extreme to exclude a relative component of poverty entirely. Poverty is not just a matter of physical need but one of social need and social inclusion as well. If a person lacks the resources required to participate in their society then they are poor, even if their basic physical needs are met (Canadian Council on Social Development 2001).

Figure 10.3 shows data for LIM after taxes and transfers for Canada, Sweden, the UK and the USA from the mid-1970s to 2015 (2014 for the USA).[1] The pattern of change differs considerably among the four countries. The US has consistently had a higher proportion of people

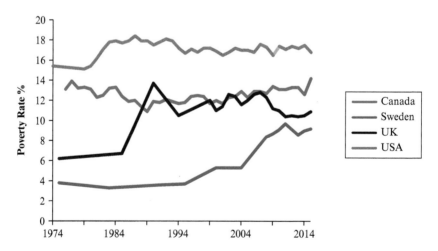

*Source:*   OECD (2016d) Dataset: Income Distribution and Poverty.

*Figure 10.3*   *Poverty rate after taxes and transfers (LIM) 1974–2015*

living with an income below LIM, around 17 percent over several decades. For much of the time, Sweden, with its higher taxation rate and more generous support programs, had the lowest proportion below LIM, close to 5 percent, though from 2004 onwards it began to converge to levels in the UK (9 percent) and Canada (13 percent).

Simply knowing the proportion of people in a country living in families with incomes below LIM does not reveal how far their income fell below the LIM or what has been happening to this gap over time. For each of the four countries considered here, the gap, with minor fluctuations, widened between the mid-1970s and the first years of this decade. As of 2013 the average gap in Sweden (that is, families with income below the Swedish LIM) fell short on average by 26 percent. In the UK it was 31 percent, Canada 32 percent and in the USA in 2014 it was 41 percent (OECD 2016d).

Figure 10.4 shows how the number of households with incomes after taxes and transfers using the LIM measure changed from the mid-1970s to 2015 in Canada, Sweden, the UK and the USA. The increase is most dramatic in the USA and Canada: from 71.2 million households in 1974 in the USA to 125.5 million households in 2015 and from 7.6 million households in 1976 in Canada to 14.2 million households in 2015. From 26.4 million in 1975, the UK experienced a modest decrease in the number

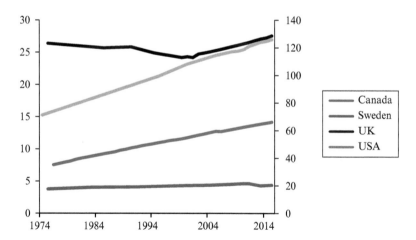

*Note:*   Data for the USA are on the right-hand axis.

*Source:*   OECD (2016d) Dataset: Income Distribution and Poverty.

*Figure 10.4    Millions of households below LIM (after taxes and transfers) 1974–2015*

of households with incomes below LIM until the turn of the century after which it increased to 27 million in 2015. In Sweden the number of households with incomes below LIM increased from 3.8 million in 1975 to 4.4 million in 2015.

These changes reflect a combination of increases in the number of households over the 40-year period and changes in the LIM-based poverty rate. LIM is closely related to the distribution of household incomes since it is based on household incomes relative to the median. Increases in inequality will show up as an increase in poverty as measured by LIM even if all households experience an increase in incomes but those with higher incomes gain the most. This comes back to the earlier discussion of whether poverty is best understood as relative or absolute. Undoubtedly, it has elements of both features, though there can be disagreement about the balance.

In addition to LIM some countries use other measures of low income. Canada for example uses two additional low-income measures 'to provide some indication of the extent, nature, and evolution of persons with low incomes who may be said to be at-risk of poverty' (Murphy et al. 2012, p. 6). These two measures are the low-income cut-off (LICO) and the Market Basket Measure (MBM). The LICO is an income threshold 'below which a family will likely devote a larger share of its income on the necessities of food, shelter and clothing than the average family' (Statistics Canada 2007). Statistics Canada describes a family in this situation as living in 'straitened circumstances' (2007, p. 7), but insists that LICOs are 'quite different from measures of poverty' (Fellegi 1997). However, Fellegi (1997), then Chief Statistician at Statistics Canada, also notes that 'some people and groups have been using the Statistics Canada low-income lines as a de facto definition of poverty. As long as that represents their own considered opinion of how poverty should be defined in Canada, we have no quarrel with them'.

The MBM 'reflects the cost of a basket of goods and services that are deemed essential to maintain physical health and to moderately participate in community activities' (Zhang 2010, p. 8). Since data on MBM have only been published in Canada from 2000 onwards and in any case have tracked LICO very closely, we will focus on LICO, for which a much longer time series is available.

As with LIM, LICO is a relative measure of low income because it compares the expenditures of families against the expenditures of the average family, allowing for differences in urban and rural locations, community and family size. Statistics Canada publishes 35 pre-tax and 35 post-tax LICOs to capture these differences (Statistics Canada 2007). The LICOs are 'rebased' periodically because over time Canadian families have spent a declining percentage of their incomes on food, clothing and shelter and the LICOs are calculated in relation to these percentages. The last rebasing was in 1992.[2]

LICO is also an absolute measure of low income in that it can be used to calculate the additional income required to bring families below the LICO up to the specified level. Unlike LIM, which uses a purely distributional measure of poverty, all families in a community could have incomes at or above LICO and none would be living in poverty under this definition.

In 1977 Canadian families with incomes less than LICO after tax and transfers fell short by an average 36.8 percent. The gap narrowed for a time, reaching 30.2 percent in 1989 but then widened again to 36.5 percent in 2012, declining only slightly in the two subsequent years (Statistics Canada 2016b). Not only did the low income gap of Canadians based on LICO fail to decline during forty years of economic growth, the number of Canadians living below the LICO lines after taxes and transfers increased from a low of 3.0 million in 1976 to 4.4 million in 1996, falling back to 3.0 million in 2014. In light of the increase in population over that period there is some good news. The percentage of Canadians with incomes below LICO which increased from 13 percent in 1976 to a high of 15.2 percent in 1996, declined to 8.8 percent in 2014, rising to 9.2 percent in 2015 (Statistics Canada 2016b).

In 1980, it would have required $11.4 billion in 2014 constant dollars to raise the incomes of all Canadians up to the LICO. By 2005, this number had risen to $16.0 billion. It rose to $17.6 billion in 2012 and 2013 and fell back to $16.1 billion in 2014.[3] One benefit of economic growth is that in 1980 the sum required to raise the after-tax incomes of all Canadians up to the LICO was 2.1 percent of all market incomes. In 2005, this percentage had fallen to 1.8 percent, having been as high as 2.9 percent in 1996 (Statistics Canada 2011) and in 2014 was at a low of 1.5 percent (Statistics Canada, personal communication). To put these amounts into perspective, in 2005 the combined surplus of Canada's federal, provincial, territorial and local governments was $20.9 billion (Statistics Canada 2009).[4] In other words, Canadian governments had the financial means to eliminate poverty in 2005 by redistributing more income to those at the lowest end of the income scale and still run an overall budget surplus. This situation prevailed until 2008 when the combined surplus of all Canadian governments peaked at $31.5 billion (Statistics Canada 2009) only to fall to $2.4 billion in 2009, largely as a result of the financial crisis but contributed to by the Conservative Government's reductions in tax rates (Department of Finance Canada 2008).

In sum, there were more Canadians with incomes less than the LICO after taxes and transfers in 2015 than there were in 1981 despite real

Canadian GDP having grown 125 percent and real per capita GDP 56 percent. While the percentage of Canadians with incomes below LICO declined, which is good, the absolute increase in their numbers is especially sobering since poverty is felt by people, not by percentages. Moreover, on average those with low post-tax incomes were even further below the LICO in 2014 than they were in 1980 in real terms. The gap has not closed, though the experience of sub-groups in the population has differed considerably. Economic growth has not solved the problem of poverty in Canada.[5] This conclusion is amply supported by Corak's (2016) commentary and critique of all of the standard statistical measures of poverty and his review of the Canadian data on low incomes over the past four decades.

> With inequality up, with no strong upward trend in middle incomes, with a good deal of volatility and uncertainty in job prospects and market outcomes, and with an unclear picture of the population living in poverty, we should exercise a certain caution in suggesting that the welfare of all Canadians has unambiguously improved over the past 40 years. (Corak 2016, p. 404)

## 10.3   ECONOMIC GROWTH AND INCOME INEQUALITY

In section 10.2 we considered the incomes of the poorest inhabitants of four advanced economies. This is certainly the aspect of the overall distribution of income that is most related to the question of poverty. However, it is worth looking at the distribution of income in its entirety to see how inequality has changed during recent decades of economic growth. This requires taking into account the whole spread of incomes rather than just those at the bottom of the distribution. One way to do this is to use the Gini coefficient, which is a measure of the inequality of income that varies from 0 (completely equal) to 1 (completely unequal). Figure 10.5 shows a clear upward trend in the Gini coefficient for incomes after taxes and transfers for all four countries. Inequality in the distribution of incomes is greatest in the USA throughout the period and lowest in Sweden. In all four countries, the distribution of incomes was considerably more unequal after forty years of economic growth. This means that the increases in income brought by economic growth over this extended period went disproportionately to those at the upper end of the income distribution.

One useful measure of the way in which those at the top of the income distribution have benefited disproportionately from economic growth is the 90/10 decile ratio, which is the ratio of the lowest income of the top 10 percent of income earners to the highest income of the lowest 10 percent

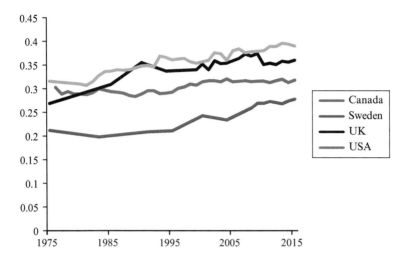

*Source:*  OECD (2018) Dataset: Income Distribution and Poverty.

*Figure 10.5    Gini coefficient of income inequality (after taxes and transfers) 1974–2015*

of income earners. This ratio increased in all four countries between the early 1970s and 2013/14, with Canada showing the lowest increase from 4.1 to 4.4, Sweden from 2.6 to 3.3 especially after 2004, the UK from 3.2 to 4.2 peaking at 4.6 in 1990, and the USA from 4.8 to 6.4.[6] The OECD's assessment of the trends of the past 25 years is especially sobering:

> Income inequality in OECD countries is at its highest level for the past half century. *The average income of the richest 10% of the population is about nine times that of the poorest 10%* across the OECD, up from seven times 25 years ago. Only in Turkey, Chile, and Mexico has inequality fallen, but in the latter two countries the incomes of the richest are still more than 25 times those of the poorest. The economic crisis has added urgency to the need to address inequality. Uncertainty and fears of social decline and exclusion have reached the *middle classes* in many societies. Arresting the trend of rising inequality has become a priority for policy makers in many countries. (OECD 2017b, emphasis in the original)

The increasing inequality in the distribution of income and wealth attracted significant attention in 2014 with the publication in English of Thomas Piketty's book *Capital in the Twenty-First Century* (Piketty 2014). Piketty set out to explain the historical pattern of income distribution in an economy through a few simple relationships between the rate of return to capital, the rate of economic growth, and the rate of savings. He concluded, based on a number of key assumptions, that slower rates of economic growth increase the share of national income accruing to the owners of capital at the expense of labor. One of Piketty's assumptions concerned the ease with which capital could be substituted for labor, which is both a technical issue and a matter of the relative power of the owners of capital and labor. If it is fairly easy to substitute capital for labor, then Piketty's result holds, assuming his other key assumptions about the determinants of the returns to capital and labor and the stability of the savings rate are also satisfied. But if the substitution of capital for labor is more difficult, then even with the other assumptions, at slower rates of economic growth the opposite happens: the share of national income going to capital declines (Jackson and Victor 2016).[7] This result is illustrated in Figure 10.6, which shows that the share of income going to capital rather than labor depends on whether the elasticity of substitution ($\sigma$) between capital and labor is greater or lower than 1. It increases over time when $\sigma$ exceeds 1 (5 in Figure 10.6), remains constant when $\sigma = 1$ and decreases when less than 1.[8] These results follow from the same economic model that Piketty used to generate

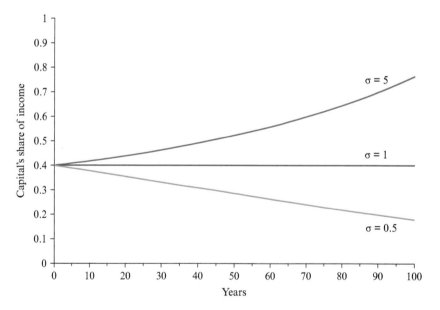

*Source:* Jackson and Victor (2016).

*Figure 10.6    Share of income going to capital depending on the elasticity of substitution between capital and labor*

his now well-known results. The only difference lies in the assumed values of the elasticity of substitution.

There are two distinct considerations when thinking about the ease with which capital will be substituted for labor in the future. One is that robotics and artificial intelligence will substitute for labor in an increasing range of occupations. The other is that aging populations will require more personal services such as nursing and home care, which are not well provided by machines. The pattern of employment will continue to evolve but with these conflicting forces in play, the implications for the distribution of income between labor and owners of capital remain unclear.

Whatever turns out to be the case, we know that the system of taxes and transfers in a country can have a marked effect on the difference between the distribution of incomes before and after taxes and transfers. Heisz and Murphy (2016) analyzed the impact of taxes and transfers on income distribution in Canada from 1976 to 2011. They found that:

> Total redistribution through taxes and transfers reached its highest point in 1994, following waves of increasing redistribution during the early 1980s and early 1990s. In 1994, taxes and transfers reduced income inequality by about one-third of its pre-tax-and-transfer level, as measured by the Gini coefficient. In the 2000s, government redistribution reduced market income inequality. (2016, p. 463)

Income inequality is not simply a matter of fairness. In their review of 168 analyses of the relationship between income inequality and health, Wilkinson and Pickett (2006) 'suggest that inequality is related to health insofar as it serves as a measure of the extent of the same processes of class differentiation and social distances in a society which are responsible for class difference in health'. They state that 'Not only are more unequal societies likely to have a bigger problem of low social status, but there is now substantial evidence to suggest that inequality is socially corrosive, leading to more violence, lower levels of trust, and lower social capital' (2006, p. 1778). Economic growth from 1980 onwards did little to help the poorest families, squeezed those with incomes in the middle range and gave the greatest income gains to those at the top end of the income scale. If governments had continued to compensate for the increasing inequality of pre-tax incomes with more generous redistributive measures in the tax-transfer system and limits on rent (income earned through ownership, not work), the outcome would have been different. But for the most part, they chose other priorities (Stiglitz 2016).

## 10.4 ECONOMIC GROWTH AND WEALTH INEQUALITY

'Just 8 men own same wealth as half the world'. This was the startling and disturbing headline in an Oxfam media release on 16 January 2017 (Hardoon 2017, p. 2). A year later, with new data available, Oxfam revised the number from 8 to 61, but the message remains the same: extreme wealth inequality prevails globally. And the situation is getting worse: '82% of all growth in global wealth in the last year went to the top 1%, while the bottom half of all humanity saw no increase at all' (Vásquez Pimentel et al. 2018, p. 10). Statistical information about wealth distribution is harder to find than for income distribution. No international standards exist for the collection of wealth data by national statistics agencies, though in 2013 the OECD issued guidelines for gathering data on household wealth (Murtin and d'Ercole 2015). The first results from a newly established OECD database on wealth distribution are now available, though the most recent year for the data is generally 2010. Figure 10.7 shows the wide range of household wealth ownership in OECD countries. The fact that the mean

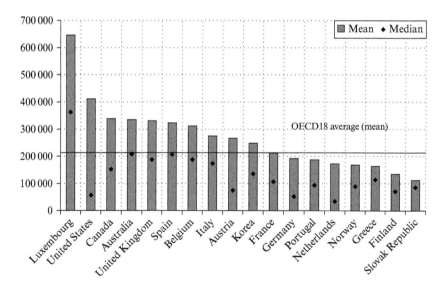

*Source:* OECD (2015c).

*Figure 10.7 Mean and median net wealth per household in selected OECD countries 2010 or latest available year, values in 2005 USD PPPs*

is so much greater than the median in the USA, Austria, Germany and the Netherlands in particular, indicates a high level of inequality in the distribution of wealth among households.

Wealth distribution is far more unequal in OECD countries than income distribution. The share of wealth of the top 1 percent is almost as large as the share of income of the top 10 percent (Murtin and d'Ercole 2015, p. 4). It is astonishing that in the USA the top 10 percent own more wealth than 75 percent of the country's population, compared with about 45 percent in the UK, and the trends are not promising. Thomas Piketty (2014) drew much needed attention of the economics profession, politicians, the media and the broader public to the rapidly rising increase in the unequal distribution of wealth, most notably in the USA. Figure 10.8 shows how the steady decline in the inequality of wealth distribution in the USA, the UK, France and South Africa started to reverse around 1980.

Several factors contributed to this increase in wealth inequality: more years spent in school before entering the labor market full-time and the greater debt load of students; gains in the stock market that primarily benefited wealthier families; accumulation of debt by poorer families because of easier access to credit to pay for consumption expenditures; increases in contributions to registered (tax sheltered) retirement savings

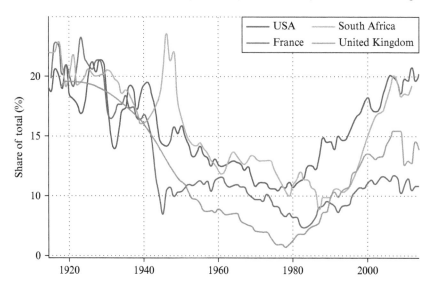

*Source:*   World Wealth & Income Database (2017).

*Figure 10.8    The share of net personal wealth owned by the top 1%, 1915–2015*

plans by families in the middle of the wealth distribution; and the growth of inheritances and gifts (Morissette et al. 2002, pp. 20, 21).

### 10.4.1   Wealth Distribution in Canada

In 2014 Canadians were asked two questions about the distribution of wealth in Canada (Broadbent Institute 2014). Breaking the population into the richest 20 percent, second, third and fourth richest 20 percent and the bottom 20 percent:

1.   What percent of Canada's wealth should each group control?
2.   What percent of Canada's wealth do you think each group controls?

The results, shown in Figure 10.9, are compared with what each group actually controls.

Two things are striking about Figure 10.9: (1) Canadians desire a substantially more equal distribution of wealth than they believe the distribution to be, and (2) the actual distribution of wealth in Canada is far more unequal than they believe it to be. They think that the wealthiest 20 percent of the population should control 30 percent of the total wealth and estimate that in fact they control 55 percent. The correct number is 67 percent. They think that the poorest 20 percent should control 12 percent of the total wealth, estimate that they control only 6 percent whereas the actual number is −0.1 percent (rounded to 0 percent in Figure 10.9). In other words, the poorest 20 percent of Canadians have liabilities that exceed their assets.[9]

As we discussed in the previous chapter, people's sense of well-being can be significantly affected by their relative position. So, although economic growth brought substantial increases in total wealth in Canada between 1999 and 2012, 66 percent of the increase in Canadian wealth went to the top 20 percent of Canadians and only 10 percent went to the bottom 50 percent (Macdonald 2014). Well-being of Canadians would have improved far more had the distribution of wealth become more rather than less equal over this period. Maroto (2016) shows that when you break down the poorest 20 percent you find that 'disparities have continued to grow for certain disadvantaged groups. Family households with adult immigrants, people with disabilities, and those with less education held less in net worth [after 13 years] even after accounting for differences in age, earnings, and inheritance.' (2016, p. 152). Morissette and colleagues (2002) concluded their analysis of the evolution of wealth distribution inequality in Canada between 1984 and 1999 with the still valid observation that there is a growing proportion of young couples with children who have zero or

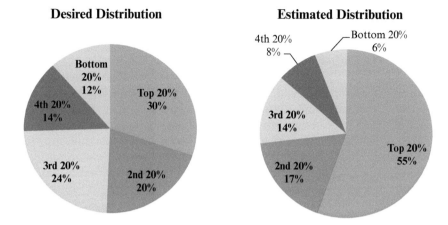

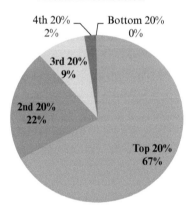

*Source:* Based on data from The Broadbent Institute (2014).

*Figure 10.9 Desired, estimated and actual distribution of wealth in Canada*

negative wealth and who may be vulnerable to economic shocks having no accumulated savings to fall back on (2002, p. 21).

As with the increasing inequality of income, the increasing inequality of wealth confirms the view that for quite some time, decades rather than years, the bulk of the increase in incomes and wealth has accrued to a small minority of the populations of rich countries (Stiglitz 2016). No wonder the progress in reducing poverty in these countries has been so disappointing. Should we not have expected more from so much economic growth?

## 10.5  ECONOMIC GROWTH AND THE ENVIRONMENT

### 10.5.1  The Environmental Kuznets Curve

Economists have examined the proposition that environmental damage follows a predictable relationship with economic growth, starting with an increase in damage in the early stages of industrialization, reaching a peak as the economy expands, and then declining with further economic growth (Grossman and Krueger 1995). This is known as the 'environmental Kuznets curve', named after Simon Kuznets, who proposed a similar relationship between economic growth measured as income per capita, and income inequality. The declining portion of the environmental Kuznets curve is attributed to several aspects of economic growth. One possibility is that as incomes rise people attach more importance to the environment, having met their more urgent needs. This may be reflected in a shift in consumption expenditures and in more stringent environmental regulations. Another possibility is that economic growth brings improved, more efficient technologies and a switch to producing services, shifting away from manufactured goods which should reduce environmental impacts.

The environmental Kuznets curve hypothesis has been the subject of much study and debate (Dinda 2004). While the environmental Kuznets curve may hold for obvious local environmental problems, such as urban air quality, it is far less robust and probably non-existent for global, less obvious problems, such as climate change and species extinction (Czech 2008). It does not seem to work for municipal waste generation, either. In a comprehensive view of the methodology and data used to estimate environmental Kuznets curves, Stern concludes that 'the statistical analysis on which the environmental Kuznets curve is based is not robust. There is little evidence for a common inverted U-shaped pathway that countries follow as their income rises' (Stern 2004, p. 1435).

The environmental Kuznets curve can be understood in terms of the concepts of scale and intensity that were discussed in detail in Chapter 8, as illustrated in Figure 10.10. In the right-hand quadrant of Figure 10.10 there is a set of iso-impact curves. The size of the environmental impact obtained by multiplying scale and intensity is equal along each curve. The further a curve is from the origin, the higher is the impact. Consider an economy that starts from point 'a' with an environmental impact of EI.[10] Over time, if the economy moves along path 'abc', GDP increases and intensity declines. Up to and including the move to point 'b', the rate of increase in GDP exceeds the rate of decrease in intensity and so environmental impact rises. This is brown growth. Environmental impact reaches

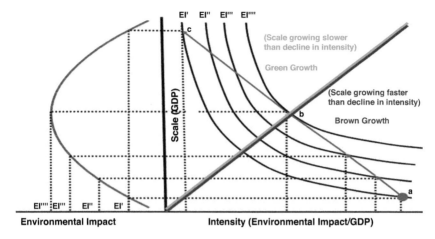

*Source:* Victor (2010).

*Figure 10.10 Scale, intensity and the environmental Kuznets curve*

EI'''' at point 'b' on a line that is 45 degrees from the origin (the angle follows from the fact that the iso-impact lines are rectangular hyperbolas). Beyond this point, the rate of reduction in intensity begins to exceed the rate of increase in GDP. This is green growth. GDP continues to rise but environmental impact declines so that at point 'c' it is back to level EI', the same as at point 'a', but with a much higher level of GDP. In the left-hand quadrant of Figure 10.10, this relationship between GDP and environmental impact is traced out and this is the environmental Kuznets curve. Hence, the environmental Kuznets curve can be understood as resulting from the combined effects of scale and intensity. The theory is sound. It's the lack of support from the data that's the problem.

## 10.5.2 The Environmental Record

The discussion of sources, sinks and services in Chapters 5 and 6 revealed less than satisfactory progress in reducing the impact of humans on the biosphere. In fact, most of the information we have before us, especially at the broader global level, is a reminder that we have been moving in the wrong direction for some time. This is the message of the planetary boundaries and the ecological footprint literature. There is an increasingly urgent need to reverse these trends. Whether this can be accomplished while economic growth remains the paramount economic policy of countries, whatever their situation, is the central question that this book tries to answer. The promise once offered by the environmental Kuznets curve provides little comfort. As with all green growth narratives, it requires that GDP growth outpace the decline in environmental impact per dollar of GDP for which there is little historical evidence at anything other than the local level.

This is the long run story, but what about more recent trends when environmental issues have been on the international agenda, and in particular, on the agenda of the OECD? Has economic growth in the world's richest countries resulted in a reduction in environmental impacts caused by the economies of these countries, though not necessarily all felt within their own borders? We saw in Chapter 5, Figure 5.4 that from 1990 to 2008 the material footprint of OECD countries increased in parallel with GDP. It stands to reason, and more importantly to the first and second laws of thermodynamics, that this steady increase in material extractions (including fossil fuels) is likely to have caused at least a proportional increase in environmental impacts given the limited capacity of sinks provided by the biosphere to absorb the resultant wastes.

To its considerable credit, the OECD does an impressive job of collating information about the environmental dimension of the economic activity of its members. Data for a number of the figures in this book have been obtained from this source. The OECD also publishes *Environment at a Glance*, a very useful compendium of environmental indicators (OECD 2015b). In Figure 10.11 we see that GDP and population for Canada, Sweden, the UK, the USA and the OECD as a whole increased substantially between 2000 and 2012, while emissions of GHGs, sulfur oxides (SOx) and nitrogen oxides (NOx) declined by even greater percentages. These are the only pollutants for which comparable time series data are included in OECD's overview publication. More data are available on the OECD website (OECD: http://stats.oecd.org).

The data in Figure 10.11 provides some examples of absolute decoupling. The OECD attributes these positive developments to 'the rise of the services sector and with it, the displacement of resource- and pollution-intensive production abroad, as well as to policy action and technical progress. The economic crisis also contributed to relieve some pressures on the environment' (OECD 2015b, p.5). We have already considered these factors in previous chapters. The transition to service-based economies in OECD countries is already far advanced such that services already exceed 70 percent of GDP, though if policy makers have their way it will be reversed.[11] The displacement of resource- and pollution-intensive production abroad may have improved conditions within the OECD (though not of course for climate change) but at the expense of others. There have indeed been important policy initiatives and considerable technical progress which,

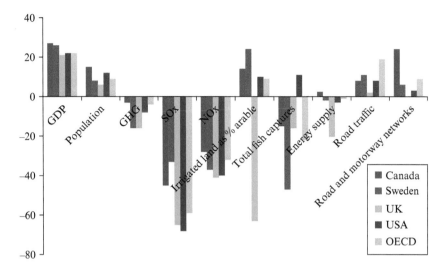

*Source:* Data from Environment at a Glance 2015 (OECD 2015b).

*Figure 10.11  Percentage change in GDP, population and several environmental indicators in OECD countries 2000–2012*

from an environmental perspective, is a mixed blessing. (See Chapter 8.) Significantly, the OECD's own assessment of its data is cautionary:

> Environment at a Glance also reveals where progress has slowed or is insufficient. There is substantial scope for strengthening air and climate policies, changing patterns of energy consumption, improving waste and materials management, preserving biodiversity and natural assets, and implementing more integrated policies ... Many positive developments still take place at the margin and policies often lack coherence, thus undermining efforts to reduce negative environmental impacts. (OECD 2015b, p. 5)

Further insight on the environmental performance of OECD countries can be obtained from the 'Commitment to Development Index', which compares the performance of OECD countries in relation to: aid, finance, technology, environment, trade, security and migration (Barder and Käppeli 2017). In 2016 Sweden was ranked the 4th best performer out of 27 OECD countries in terms of environment, the UK 11th, Canada 23rd and the USA 24th. These rankings have changed little since the CDI was first produced in 2003. In 2016 Slovakia was ranked 1st largely because of its high gasoline taxes and low GHG emissions. Canada and the USA, with low gasoline taxes and high GHG emissions, ranked among the lowest of the 27 countries despite other promising indicators such as the lowest import of tropical timbers in Canada. The USA's announced withdrawal from the Paris agreement on climate change is likely to push it even further down the rankings in future years.

The last year that Canada published a comprehensive State of the Environment Report was 1996 (Government of Canada 1996). These 700+ page reports were published at five-yearly intervals starting in 1986 and covered many aspects of Canada's environment. The reports provided a basis for determining where Canada's environment was improving and where it was deteriorating. Statistics Canada continues to publish the more modest, topic specific, annual series, *Human Activity and the Environment*. Other reports and data on specific environmental topics giving a picture of how Canada is faring in environmental terms are also produced by government agencies at the federal, provincial and municipal levels. A rich online database of indicators for air, water, wildlife and habitat, and socio-economic conditions is available from Environment and Climate Change Canada (2017) but the absence of a comprehensive, authoritative national state of the environment report for Canada invites different groups and individuals to select their own data and reach their own conclusions. Not surprisingly, there is no consensus. For example, the Fraser Institute, a business-friendly think tank, periodically publishes reports on Canada's environment that present a very positive picture (Brown et al. 2004; Sklenar and Holden 2007; McKitrick and Aliakbari 2017). Another business-friendly organization, the Conference Board of Canada (2016), takes a different view of Canada's environmental performance ranking Canada third-last among 15 peer countries. Similar low rankings were obtained for the comparative environmental performance of OECD countries in studies by Boyd (2003), the Sustainable Planning Research Group (2005) and Gunton and Calbrick (2010).

## 10.6  CONCLUSION

Taking Canada, Sweden, the UK and the USA as examples of advanced economies, economic growth since around 1980 has not eliminated unemployment or poverty. By some measures both have risen. At the same time the distributions of income and wealth have become significantly more unequal. Economic growth has not been a panacea for environmental problems. Some local conditions with respect to key air pollutants and water treatment have improved, globally many conditions have worsened; climate change, habitat destruction and loss of biodiversity being the most significant and troubling. Degradation of renewable resources and depletion of non-renewable resources continue apace, displacing increasing numbers of people often in distant lands. Growth is a clumsy way to meet important social, economic and environmental objectives, but it can provide the means.

Now we are facing a future where economic growth is not a long-term option for the world at large. Rich countries can keep pursuing economic growth but global biophysical constraints increasingly in evidence will make it harder for poorer countries to get their fair share of what the world can produce sustainably. Is there an alternative for a high-income country such as Canada? What are the implications of a substantial diversion of investment away from activities that degrade the environment to those that reduce the burden that economic activity imposes on the biosphere? Would the rate of economic growth increase because spending would rise, or would it decline as capital is diverted away from more profitable uses? Could Canada make a significant contribution to improving the global environment, leave more room for poor nations to raise their living standards and eliminate unemployment and poverty at home without relying on economic growth? Better still, could this be done while improving the quality of life for all? It is to these questions that we now turn.

## NOTES

1. The OECD revised the definition of income in 2012 so the values from 2012 on may not be directly comparable with those before 2012. However, examination of the data suggests that any differences are minor.
2. Corak (2016) points out that measuring poverty in relation to expenditure patterns from a quarter of a century ago is unsatisfactory. He argues that LICO should be updated or dropped.
3. Cansim Table 2020805 from which the 1980 data was originally obtained and converted to 2014$ using the Consumer Price Index has been deleted from the Statistics Canada website. The value for 2014 was provided on request by Statistics Canada.
4. This number includes $9.3 billion in net contributions to the Consolidated Canada Pension Plan and Quebec Pension Plan. In 2007 the combined government surplus was $28.6 billion including net contributions to the Consolidated Canada Pension Plan and Quebec Pension Plan of $10.1 billion (Statistics Canada Cansim Table 380-0001).
5. Analysts at the New Economics Foundation reach the same conclusion in their assessment of global economic growth and its impact on poverty. They show that 'between 1990 and 2001, for every $100 worth of growth in the world's per person income, just $0.60 found its target and contributed to reducing poverty below the $1-a-day line. As a result, to achieve a single dollar of poverty reduction, $166 of extra global production and consumption is needed with enormous environmental impacts which counter-productively hurt the poorest most' (Woodward and Simms 2006, p.i).
6. The OECD revised the definition of income in 2012 so the values from 2012 on may not be directly comparable with those before 2012. However, examination of the data suggests that any differences are minor.
7. By easy we mean the elasticity of substitution between capital and labor in a CES production function exceeds and by hard we mean it is less than 1. It is a measure of

the rate at which capital is substituted for labor in response to changes in their relative prices.

8. If competition prevails then the elasticity of substitution between two inputs in the production process is the percentage change in the ratio of two inputs to a percentage change in their prices.

9. Very similar results were obtained for the USA (Norton and Ariely 2011) for the desired and estimated distributions. But when it comes to the actual distribution of wealth, the USA is far more unequal than Canada, with 84 percent of US wealth controlled by the richest 20 percent of the population, and the poorest 40 percent having just 0.3 percent of total wealth.

10. In this analysis, environmental impact is caused by a flow rather than a stock. The significance of this difference is explained in Chapter 2.

11. President Trump's 2016 election promise to 'Make America Great Again' was all about attracting manufacturing back to the USA.

# 11. Managing without growth: exploring possibilities

## Co-authored with Tim Jackson[1]

---

> The real issue is whether it is possible to challenge the 'growth-at-any-cost model' and come up with an alternative that is environmentally benign, economically robust and politically feasible. (Larry Elliot 2008)

Many early critics of growth had no formal, explicit model of a modern economy. Sometimes they offered quantitative information to support and illustrate their arguments, but stopped short of employing formal models to elaborate their critiques. Meadows and colleagues (1972) did base their analysis of limits to growth on a quantitative model, but it used systems theory rather than a recognizable economic framework. As a result, it encountered vigorous disapproval from many conventional economists (see Chapter 7). The ideological nature of some of these criticisms is clear. The outright rejection of the Meadows' work by conventional economists not only led to considerable miscommunication, it also closed down important conversations about the limits to growth for decades. But rejecting formal economic models entirely is just as likely to lead to unproductive dialogue. This has been the case amongst some proponents of 'degrowth' who have argued not only that the pursuit of economic growth should be abandoned in favor of goals like social justice and ecological sustainability, but also that economics itself (and economic models in particular) should be regarded with suspicion (D'Alisa et al. 2015).

There are signs that this somewhat unproductive polarization of attitudes towards economic modeling is beginning to change. Hardt and O'Neill (2017) list 22 publications with ecological macroeconomic models, including some that are empirical. Our own recent work together has aimed to make a significant contribution to this emerging debate.[2] It is our belief that the development of coherent economic models, grounded firmly in empirical data, is an essential step in managing without growth. The aim of this chapter is to present just such a model and to use it to explore various potential scenarios under different assumptions about key macroeconomic, social and environmental variables. In the next section we present a brief overview of the LowGrow SFC model and discuss some of its theoretical and empirical foundations. Following that we describe two composite performance indicators that we use to measure the performance of the LowGrow SFC economy over time. We then present and discuss three key scenarios for the Canadian economy from 2017 to 2067. In the final section of the chapter we discuss the implications of our findings for the future of capitalism.

## 11.1   AN OVERVIEW OF LOWGROW SFC[3]

Our broad approach in LowGrow SFC is to bring together three primary spheres of modeling interest and explore the interactions among them. These spheres are: (1) the environmental and resource constraints on economic activity; (2) a full account of production, consumption, employment and public finances in the 'real economy' at the level of the nation state; (3) a comprehensive account of the financial economy, including the main interactions between financial agents. Interactions within and between these spheres of interest are modeled using a system dynamics framework. Our approach has some similarities to the World 3 model used by the Meadows (1972) in the sense that it uses a system dynamics framework to model non-linear relationships and feedback loops among stocks and flows. But there are also significant differences from that early work. Unlike the *Limits to Growth* work, LowGrow SFC conforms quite closely to standard economic frameworks. Indeed, our data are drawn directly from the Canadian national accounts and some of the behavioral relationships in the model are estimated econometrically on the basis of times-series data from the Canadian economy. At the same time, we depart from more conventional econometric approaches, not just by incorporating time-lags, feedbacks and expectations in the model, but also by allowing for some potentially radical variations on 'typical' macroeconomic policy.

The theoretical basis for our work draws heavily on the post-Keynesian macroeconomic approach of Godley and Lavoie (2012), which places a particular emphasis on a full and consistent account of the relationships between monetary stocks and flows within and between different financial sectors. In the aftermath of the 2008 financial crisis, so-called stock-flow consistent (SFC) modeling has gained a particular traction because of its ability to provide a comprehensive account of financial transactions in the economy and to map the impact of these on financial balance sheets – something that was conspicuously missing in the run-up to the crisis. The overall rationale of SFC macroeconomics is to account consistently for all monetary flows across all sectors of the economy. This rationale can be captured in three broad axioms: first, that each expenditure from a given sector is also the income to another sector; second, that each sector's financial asset corresponds to some financial liability for at least one other sector, with the sum of all assets and liabilities across all sectors equalling zero; and finally, that changes in stocks of financial assets are consistently related to flows within and between economic sectors. These simple understandings lead to a set of accounting principles with implications for actors across the economy which can be used to test the consistency of economic models and scenario simulations. LowGrow SFC is articulated in terms of six interrelated sectors: households, firms, banks, government, a central bank and the 'rest of the world' (or 'foreign' sector). It models a range of financial assets and liabilities, including: deposits, loans, mortgages, government bonds and firms' equities.

LowGrow SFC embodies a lot of theory but it is not a purely theoretical model. It has been calibrated using Canadian data from 2011, so that the initial values are calculated for the start of 2012 in Canada. The simulation results are reported for 2017 to 2067. Some of the behavioral relationships in the model are based on econometric estimations. For instance, household consumer spending is estimated from historical data using disposable income and household wealth as independent variables. Others reflect plausible assumptions informed by the relevant literature. For instance in looking at how firms finance their capital investment we make an assumption about the desired ratio between debt and equity based on empirical data. When using a model to describe alternative economic futures over half a century or more, statistical relationships estimated from data for the past two or three decades are not a very reliable guide. It is best therefore to think of the model as employing 'stylized facts' (Godley and Lavoie 2012) that are grounded in empirical data to paint a consistent and plausible picture about future possibilities. 'The main use of models is to elucidate basic principles, consider different future scenarios, and perhaps even make the system less stressed and unpredictable in the first place' (Orell 2017, p. 244).

Above all, LowGrow SFC is an ecological macroeconomic model. The application of SFC modeling to ecological macroeconomics is less well-developed, but several of the models reported in Hardt and O'Neill (2017) also draw on the post-Keynesian tradition. LowGrow SFC incorporates numerous features related to resource use, emissions and the environmental performance of the economy. For instance, a key focus of the model is on climate change and greenhouse gas emissions. Another important element in the model is the existence of a dedicated sub-model to describe the electricity sector.[4] This is critical to an assessment of environmental impact of economic activity, in particular to the level of greenhouse gas emissions in the economy. Critical to this environmental assessment (and indeed to the performance of the LowGrow SFC economy) is the question of investment. The investment decisions of today determine the energy and material flows required tomorrow. For example, investment in highways supports a very different transportation system than investment in train tracks and bike paths. Each has very different environmental consequences. Our approach to investment is therefore a central aspect of LowGrow SFC and worth elaborating in a little more detail. Broadly speaking, LowGrow SFC models firms' investment decisions through a capital–stock adjustment process. Firms have a target level of capital sufficient to meet an expected level of output. If at any time the actual capital–output ratio falls short of the target ratio then investment is undertaken to close that gap. The rate at which the gap is closed by new investment is determined by an adjustment factor that can either be assumed constant or made dependent on the rate of profit or the rate of economic growth.[5]

One of the most important elements in the model relates to investments undertaken to reduce environmental impact. A future in which economies reduce the burden placed on the biosphere will only come about if investment that reduces environmental impacts displaces investment that increases them. We distinguish between what we call 'brown' investment, which can broadly be characterized as investment that expands the productive capital stock in the conventional way, and 'green' investment, which has the specific goal of reducing the environmental impact of the economy. Some portion of brown investment will also have a tendency to reduce the environmental impact per unit of economic output. For this reason we incorporate a 'business-as-usual' improvement in the environmental performance of the economy in the model. Likewise, some proportion of green investment will contribute to the productive capacity of the economy, much as conventional investment does. We call this portion of green investment 'productive'. But some green investment can only be undertaken at a net cost or with a rate of return too low to be competitive with other investments. We refer to this latter type of green investment as 'non-productive', recognizing of course that 'productive' here is being used in a conventional economic sense. In a wider sense of the word, green investment plays a fundamental role in protecting the ability of our economies to produce anything at all. But the distinction between productive and non-productive investment is nonetheless a useful one in understanding the impact of green investment on the macroeconomy and on economic growth. Productive green investment contributes to the capital stock of the economy used in the production of goods and services that make up GDP. Non-productive investment clearly generates environmental benefits but it does not in itself contribute to the productive capital stock.

*Table 11.1    Four categories of green investment and their macroeconomic effects*

|  | Productive | Non-productive |
|---|---|---|
| Additional | Increases productive capital stock. Adds to aggregate demand. | No effect on productive capital stock. Adds to aggregate demand. |
| Non-additional | No effect on productive capital stock. No effect on aggregate demand. | Reduces productive capital stock. No effect on aggregate demand. |

We make a further distinction that is important for assessing the macroeconomic impact of green investment. It concerns what we call 'additionality'. Some green investment will be carried out in addition to the 'business-as-usual' investment expenditures of the sector undertaking them, for instance, as determined by the stock-adjustment calculation. Other 'non-additional' green investments will simply displace some of these conventional investments. Additional green investment adds to GDP since it increases expenditure on investment. Non-additional green investment does not increase GDP since it replaces other investment expenditures. Table 11.1 summarizes the four categories of green investment resulting from these distinctions: productive or non-productive; additional or non-additional. As the table shows, each combination of features has different macroeconomic effects. Additional, productive green investments add to the capital stock of the economy, increasing its capacity to produce goods and services. Assuming the economy is not already operating at full capacity, they also increase aggregate demand. In contrast, non-additional, non-productive green investments generate important environmental benefits. But they act to reduce the productive stock of the economy and have no effect on aggregate demand, because they simply substitute for productive investment.

This typology of green investment allows us to explore the implications of different allocations of investment expenditures in some detail. In the simulations described later in the chapter it is assumed that all green investment is non-additional, that is, that it displaces other intended investments. The reason for this is to avoid attributing to green investment expansionary effects that arise simply because an economy is not at full capacity. Under such circumstances, any increase in expenditures would have similar expansionary effects, there being nothing special in this respect about an investment being green. In the event that there is insufficient brown investment to allow all green investment in a scenario to be non-additional, the model makes up the difference with additional green investment expenditures.

The extent to which investment is geared towards productive or non-productive green investment will be highly influenced by government policy and by future technological developments. Our default assumption in the scenarios in this chapter is that 50 percent of total green investment will be non-productive. If it turns out to be lower than this, then the implications of green investment for economic growth will be less than indicated in the scenarios. If it turns out to be greater, then the opposite will be true. It seems likely that if the situation becomes more urgent as time passes, an increasing proportion of green investment will be non-productive. This is because it will emphasize measures designed to lessen adverse impacts on the environment which, though performing a useful service to protect an economy's productive capacity, do not increase it. Examples include seawalls built to protect coastlines from rising sea levels, and stronger buildings to withstand more violent storms. They protect productive capital, they do not add to it. All of these assumptions can be changed in the model to explore different scenarios.

In summary, LowGrow SFC is not simply a macroeconomic model in the conventional model nor an ecological model in the tradition of the Limits to Growth work. Rather it seeks explicitly to capture key environmental concerns and simulate policies to address them in the context of a recognizable macroeconomic framework. It is therefore quite precisely an ecological macroeconomic model in the sense called for by Jackson (2009) and others. An illustrative overview of the model is shown in Figure 11.1. For all the reasons set out in previous chapters, our interest here is in whether important policy objectives can be achieved in a modern economy without relying on economic growth. In particular, therefore, we are interested in whether we can have full employment, reduced inequality, healthy balance sheets and substantial reductions in greenhouse gas emissions and other environmental pressures, all in the context of much slower or even zero economic growth. If we find that such an arrangement is possible then we can dispense with the argument that economic growth is essential to social progress. Instead we can look seriously at managing without growth, starting in advanced economies, so that those in poorer nations who really do need economic growth stand a better chance of benefiting from it without compromising the biophysical limits of the planet.

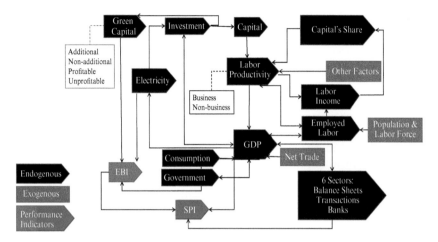

*Figure 11.1    Illustrative overview of LowGrow SFC*

## 11.2   PERFORMANCE INDICATORS

LowGrow SFC generates the values of many variables which can be used to assess the performance of the economy. In the scenarios described in the next section, several conventional indicators are reported, including: GDP, the rate of unemployment, greenhouse gas emissions, the ratio of government debt to GDP, and the ratio of household loans to net worth. Sometimes it is useful to combine several indicators into a single index to gain an overall assessment of system performance. As noted in previous chapters, GDP is all too often used as an indicator of well-being despite the inclusion of items that bear no relation to well-being, the exclusion of others that do, and the reliance on market prices to measure value. These inadequacies of GDP are well-known and yet its popularity remains strong. One of the reasons for this is that economists have developed an extensive understanding of GDP and what lies behind it. When GDP grows, and we have some understanding of the reasons for the growth, we can make forecasts of future growth and design policies to promote it.

   The fact that GDP emerges from a model of the economy is both a blessing and a curse. It is a blessing because it means that GDP is not just a passive metric that can be measured and monitored but about which nothing can be done. It is a curse because it only captures a part of what matters in society and by promoting its growth with such enthusiastic single-mindedness we can miss opportunities that have a more beneficial effect on well-being. Worse than that, as has been mentioned previously, we may be mortgaging the future by the destructive processes that underlie increases in GDP. To offset this danger, we have developed two additional composite indicators to describe the scenarios in LowGrow SFC: the Environmental Burden Index (EBI) and the Sustainable Prosperity Index (SPI). The EBI is designed to capture the environmental impacts of economic activity notably absent from GDP. The SPI is based on a combination of economic, environmental and social variables that provides a more comprehensive measure of how well or badly the economy is doing. Both of these indicators should be regarded as preliminary in that there are many ways in which they could be improved if more and better data were available. However, the EBI and SPI both share with GDP the redeeming feature that they emerge from a model of the system in whose performance we are interested and so can be used to measure the effect of measures designed to make the system work better.

### 11.2.1   The Environmental Burden Index (EBI)

Economic activity has a diverse range of impacts on the environment. Chapters 5 and 6 gave a general assessment of some of the key environmental trends and pressures that are exacerbated by economic growth, calling into question its long-term feasibility and desirability. In LowGrow SFC we make no attempt to capture these pressures in any detail. Rather we employ an environmental burden index (EBI) which, while comprehensive in scope, lacks specificity other than with respect to greenhouse gas emissions. The structure of the EBI, which has an initial value of 100, is shown in Figure 11.2. A '+' indicates that the two connected variables move in the same direction, and a '−' indicates that the two connected variables move in the opposite direction. For example, as total GHG emissions increase, so does the EBI. On the other hand, as green services increase, the EBI excluding GHG emissions declines.

In the top panel of Figure 11.2 three sources of GHG emissions are shown: from electricity generation, from road and rail transportation, and from all other sources. GDP is one of the main determinants of the level of emissions from each of these sources. Estimates of the first two come from the electricity sector sub-model. GHG emissions from other sources, and the costs of reducing them are adapted from Cline (2011).

Reductions in GHG emissions are often related to reductions in emissions of contaminants providing what are called 'co-benefits'. These are health and environmental benefits that come from reductions in GHG emissions when contaminants such as particulates are also reduced but are not the primary intent of the GHG reductions. There is a considerable body of literature on these co-benefits, pointing out that their size relative

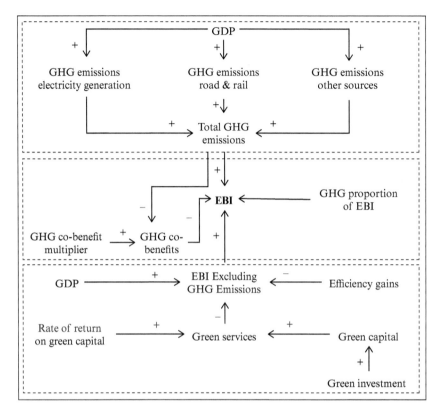

*Figure 11.2    The structure of the Environmental Burden Index*

to the climate change benefits from reduced GHG emissions depends very much on time, place and circumstances (UNECE 2016; Hamilton et al. 2017). In LowGrow SFC the default assumption is that co-benefits are equivalent to 20 percent of the benefits of reductions in GHG emissions.

All of the other non-GHG-related pressures on the environment are included in the bottom panel of Figure 11.2. These pressures are assumed to decline per unit of GDP through technological change giving improved efficiency. This introduces a degree of relative decoupling in the calculation of the EBI. The default assumption for these efficiency gains is based on Cline's projections of improvements in efficiency (2011, chapter 4). Another major contributor to the reduction in non-GHG-related environmental pressures is the 'green capital' that results from non-GHG-related green investment. Given the very heterogeneous nature of this capital, the kinds of services that it provides and the range of environmental pressures that it is designed to mitigate, there are no data on which a meaningful rate of return can be based. For example, stilts can be used to provide space between the ground and the first floor of buildings located by the coast to reduce flood damage from rising ocean levels. This extra investment may only yield benefits rarely, but when it does, the benefits can be very significant. Improved soil management might only change yields marginally at first, but by enabling a more sustainable capacity of the soil to support crop growth they provide a lasting supply of food well into the distant future. In the EBI, the default assumption is that the accumulated non-GHG green capital produces green services at a rate of 5 percent per year. This rate results in the effectiveness of investment in non-GHG green investment for reducing the EBI comparable with investment in GHG emissions reduction.

As shown in Figure 11.2, GHG emissions, co-benefits from reductions in these emissions, and the green services from non-GHG green capital all contribute to the EBI. Adding them together requires a set of weights. The default weight given to GHG emissions in the EBI is 25 percent. This is the weight given to 'climate and energy' in the Environmental Performance Index produced by Yale University (Hsu et al. 2016). Co-benefits from GHG emissions reduction effectively increase its weight in the EBI to 30 percent. The remaining 70 percent of the EBI is attributed to all the non-GHG-related environmental issues of concern that are reduced by services achieved by investing in green capital.

Yale's Environmental Performance Index is broad, detailed and well-documented, yet, as the authors acknowledge, it is not fully comprehensive because of a lack of globally comprehensive data. Areas where the data are incomplete include: freshwater quality, species loss, indoor air quality of residential and commercial buildings, toxic chemical exposures, municipal solid waste management, nuclear safety, wetlands loss, agricultural soil quality and degradation, recycling rates, and adaptation, vulnerability and resiliency to climate change (Hsu et al. 2016, p. 33). Some of these topics overlap with climate and energy, but nonetheless, if they were included in Yale's Environmental Performance Index, it is likely that the weight given to climate and energy would be reduced.

### 11.2.2   The Sustainable Prosperity Index (SPI)

In order to compare and assess scenarios generated by the model described in this chapter, we have developed one further index drawn from variables of interest in the model and combined into a Sustainable Prosperity Index (SPI). The SPI provides an overall assessment of the system's behavior. It also provides a means of assessing the results of any proposed policy intervention or system change that can be represented in the model. These are distinct virtues of SPI. Since GDP is also generated by LowGrow SFC, it is possible to compare GDP and SPI in any scenario.

Like all such composite indexes, the SPI has limitations. Its scope is restricted to the variables in LowGrow SFC and there is an inevitable arbitrariness to the weights used to add up these variables into a single number. Fortunately, these weights can be changed very easily to test the sensitivity of a comparison of scenarios to the chosen weights. Jones et al. (2016) recognize that 'quantified indicators for the implementation and measurement of social progress is a well-established policy tool', but that they can over-simplify and 'fail to do justice to objectives like sustainable prosperity'. They conclude that 'indicators can be a useful tool for constructing new understandings, holding powerful actors to account and enabling engagement with policy end goals' (Jones et al. 2016, p. 1). This is precisely in accord with our view of the SPI.

Our broad understanding of sustainable prosperity is that it consists in our ability to flourish as human beings on a finite planet.[6] The SPI aims to capture the breadth of such a definition through seven variables that reflect a range of economic, social and environmental factors. These variables are listed in Table 11.2 with a brief rationale for their inclusion in the composite indicator.

The default weights in the SPI that are used to add the variables in Table 11.2 into a single index are constants except for those applied to the unemployment rate, the ratio of unsecured household loans to incomes, the ratio of government debt to GDP and the EBI. The weights applied to these variables increase as their size rises, to reflect the observation that concern is low or non-existent at low levels but rises in a non-linear manner as they increase. The contrary is the case for the ratio assigned to GDP per capita since, following Helliwell et al. (2017), the logarithm of GDP per capita is used in the SPI with a constant weight (2017, Table 2.1). This has the effect of reducing the weight given to GDP per capita measured normally (see Chapter 9, Figure 9.3 in this volume).

The composition of the SPI is illustrated in Figure 11.3. Our broad aim in this chapter is to use the SPI as a diagnostic tool to explore the evolution of several different scenarios emerging from LowGrow SFC. We describe these scenarios (and the results of the model) in the following section.

## 11.3 SCENARIOS FOR THE CANADIAN ECONOMY

The former British Prime Minister, Margaret Thatcher, once insisted that 'there is no alternative' to the conventional economic model of economic

*Table 11.2   Variables in SPI*

| Variable | Relation to Sustainable Prosperity | Weight and Contribution to the SPI in 2017 |
|---|---|---|
| GDP per capita (ln) | The average amount of goods and services available in an economy contributes to people's assessment of their well-being. | Weight +.341 Contribution to SPI in 2017 +3.69 |
| Gini coefficient | Inequality in the distribution of incomes can cause social exclusion, unequal opportunities and a sense of unfairness. | Weight −1.75 Contribution to SPI in 2017 −.83 |
| Average hours worked | Shorter hours spent in paid work can give more time to people for social, cultural and political activities. | Weight −.0002 Contribution to SPI in 2017 −.34 |
| EBI | This index captures the environmental dimension of sustainable prosperity. | Weight (non-linear) Contribution to SPI in 2017 −.07 |
| Unemployment rate | The inability to find paid work is a major cause of poverty and stress. | Weight (non-linear) Contribution to SPI in 2017 −.07 |
| Government debt-to-GDP ratio | When government debt rises disproportionately to GDP, interest payment on the debt can limit a government's capacity to address other priorities. | Weight (non-linear) Contribution to SPI in 2017 −.03 |
| Household loans to value ratio | If household debt rises faster than household net worth the likelihood of personal bankruptcy increases, which, if on a large enough scale, threatens the viability of the financial system. | Weight (non-linear) Contribution to SPI in 2017 −.02 |

growth. One of the key findings from this book is that there are in fact many alternatives. In this section, we use the LowGrow SFC model to describe three potential scenarios for the Canadian economy. None of these scenarios is a prediction of the future. Rather they are intended to illustrate some of the possibilities facing Canada, to inform discussion and debate, and to suggest the kinds of choices available, not just to Canada but to other advanced economies, as we move further into the 21st century.

As noted earlier, there is a lot of empirical content in LowGrow SFC drawn from Canadian sources but it is best to regard the data in the model, the estimated or assumed relationships, and the values generated in the scenarios as 'stylized facts' that apply generally rather than as precise, accurate numbers at a given point in time. Furthermore, comparisons of scenarios are more reasonable than any individual scenario taken on its own in that differences between scenarios tend to reduce errors that are common to both. For this reason, in the results section below we present comparisons between the three scenarios based on the performance of the SPI and its components, including of course the behavior of GDP itself. First, however, we offer a brief description of each of the three scenarios.

### 11.3.1 An Overview of the Scenarios

Three distinct scenarios are summarized in Table 11.3. The scenarios presented here run over a period of 50 years from the beginning of 2017 until the beginning of 2067, the year in which Canada will mark the 200th anniversary of the establishment of the Canadian Federation. The first scenario, which we call the Base Case, is broadly a projection of current trends and relationships into the future.

This scenario assumes that the Canadian economy will perform on average over the period 2017 to 2067 in much the same way as it did in the preceding 25 years or so, with the rate of economic growth continuing to decline slowly. The Base Case scenario is therefore a benchmark against

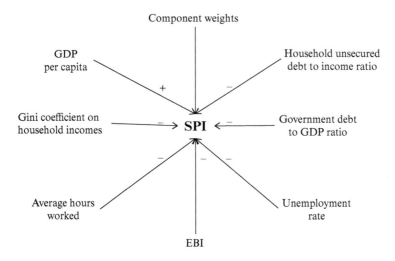

*Figure 11.3   Calculation of the SPI*

*Table 11.3   The scenarios*

| Scenario | Main Features |
|---|---|
| 1. Base case | Scenario 1<br>– continuation of current trends and relationships |
| 2. GHG reduction | Scenario 1 plus:<br>– carbon price on GHG emissions from electricity generation<br>– GHG abatement by non-electric industrial sources<br>– electrification of road and rail transport |
| 3. Sustainable prosperity | Scenario 2 plus:<br>– switch from brown to green investment<br>– increased transfer payments to reduce income inequality and reduce poverty<br>– lower rate of population growth<br>– reduced average hours worked |

which other scenarios can be compared. It is not in itself a prediction of what will happen in the absence of policy interventions. Some of the variables in the base case are based on projections from other sources. For instance, we use the Statistics Canada population projections to define population growth in the model,[7] and as described above, we have calibrated starting values for the financial stocks and flows and the greenhouse gas emissions (for example) based on Canadian data.

The Base Case scenario is a description of what would happen, broadly speaking, at the national level, if current trends continue through and beyond mid-century. It says nothing about the marked regional differences that would accompany such trends. LowGrow SFC is simply too highly aggregated to reveal anything quantitative at the sub-national level. However, we can be confident that, just as in the past, the economic fortunes of different parts of this vast country have moved in different, sometimes opposite, directions, so they will continue to do so in the future. Other than noting the importance of these regional differences, the focus in all that follows remains on national trends.

Our second scenario is called the GHG Reduction scenario. It simulates a comprehensive program of GHG emissions reduction consisting of a substantial carbon price on GHG emissions from the electric power sector, GHG emissions reduction investments in the other economic sectors, and the electrification of road and rail transport. A carbon price is a financial payment based on the quantity of greenhouse gas emissions.[8] The main means for imposing a carbon price is through a fee or tax, through emissions trading or a combination of the two (Canada's Ecofiscal Commission

2017b). Several Canadian Provinces have introduced carbon pricing schemes. For example, British Columbia has a carbon tax and Ontario and Quebec participate in a cap and trade emissions trading system.[9] There is no single carbon price in Canada, but in 2017 the Federal Government announced its intention to impose a floor price of $10 per tonne of GHG emissions, rising by $10 per year to $50 per tonne in 2022. This carbon price will be imposed by the Federal Government on Provinces that do not have at least an equivalent carbon price in place (Government of Canada 2017a). The federally established minimum is included in the base case for the electricity sector.

In the GHG Reduction scenario, the $10/year annual increase in the carbon price continues beyond 2022 for another 10 years, reaching a total of $300 per tonne on GHG emissions from the electric power sector. The effect of the carbon price is to increase the cost of generating electricity from fossil fuels and to increase the proportion of new generating capacity from renewable sources, leading to a reduction in GHG emissions. It also increases the price of electricity. Some of the additional costs of electricity to businesses are passed on to consumers, which tends to reduce households' demand for commodities in general. Increases in investment costs in the electricity sector stimulated by the carbon price (excluding the payment of the carbon price, which is a transfer between sectors) are treated as non-additional and non-productive investment (see Table 11.1 above). This scenario also includes substantial expenditures to reduce GHG emissions from the non-electricity sectors based on estimates of the costs adapted from Cline (2011).[10] These expenditures are considered non-additional and non-productive in this scenario.

The use of fossil fuels in road and rail transport accounts for about a quarter of Canada's total GHG emissions (Government of Canada 2017b). In the GHG Reduction scenario, the electrification of road and rail transport is assumed to proceed at 2 percent/year until 100 percent electrification is achieved. The transition will require more investment in the rail system (Fisher 2008) and in the installation of electric charging stations (Berman 2014). Electric vehicles are assumed to replace gasoline and diesel-powered vehicles as they are taken out of service at no additional cost. All of the investment associated with road and rail electrification is deemed to be non-additional and non-productive.

Our final scenario is the Sustainable Prosperity scenario, which includes all of the innovations included in the GHG Reduction scenario and, in addition, introduces further measures aimed at reducing a wider set of environmental impacts. It also includes policies aimed at achieving beneficial social outcomes. Specifically, starting in 2020 some of the depreciation of brown capital is invested in green capital. The percentage rises steadily over the next 20 years until a diversion rate of 20 percent is reached. Of this green investment, 50 percent is assumed to be productive, meaning that it continues to add to the capacity of the economy to produce goods and services that are included in GDP. The other 50 percent of this green investment is assumed to be non-productive, though of course it does generate significant (non-market) environmental benefits.

A second measure introduced in the Sustainable Prosperity scenario is a substantial increase in annual transfer payments to reduce the inequality of incomes. Starting in 2020 these additional transfer payments increase until they amount to $20 billion per year (in 2007$). They are distributed to each income category based on the proportion of people with pre-tax incomes greater than the average income in that category, using data from Statistics Canada (2017g). The greatest share of the increased transfers goes to people in the lowest income category of less than $5000 per year. Declining shares go to those in progressively higher income categories until those with incomes greater than $250 000 per year receive no additional transfers. The model calculates the change in the Gini coefficient of the distribution of pre-tax incomes over time from the additional transfer payments.[11]

Two further assumptions are changed in this third scenario. Specifically we assume a slower rate of population growth (the low projection in Statistics Canada 2017f stabilizing after 2063) and a decline in average hours worked.

### 11.3.2   Results of the Model

It is instructive to start our comparison by looking at the estimated GDP per capita over the period. Figure 11.4 shows this comparison for the three scenarios. There are some striking differences, particularly between the

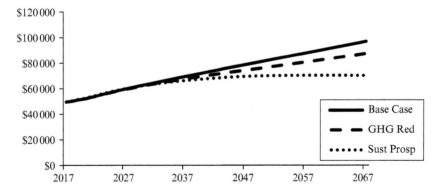

*Figure 11.4   GDP per capita in the LowGrow SFC scenarios*

Base Case and the Sustainable Prosperity scenario. Under the Base Case, per capita GDP increases from $50 000 in 2017 to $97 000 in 2067, with an average growth rate of 1.3 percent.[12] This is essentially a conventional, growth-based view of the future, in which the economy as a whole (taking into account population growth of around 44 percent) increases its magnitude 2.8 times by the year 2067.

The GHG Reduction scenario has a somewhat lower average growth rate in GDP per capita of 1.1 percent, with incomes in 2067 achieving a level of $87 000 per annum. It is worth remarking that the reduced rate of economic growth in this scenario is at the high end of the range of estimates of the impact on GDP from achieving significant reductions in greenhouse gas emissions, as cited in the literature (Ekins 2017). It also runs counter to the view that a green economy grows faster than a brown one (Bassi 2011; Victor and Jackson 2012). In LowGrow SFC, the reduction in economic growth comes about because of the diversion of investment away from the expansion of conventional 'brown' capital. Slower growth in brown capital means slower growth in labor productivity and hence a slower rate of growth in GDP. Other studies obtain an increase in the rate of economic growth from environmental expenditures seemingly because of the assumption that there is unused capacity in the economy and these expenditures increase aggregate demand.

The most marked difference, however, is between the Base Case and the Sustainable Prosperity scenarios. The latter illustrates what is essentially a stabilization of per capita income at a level above current income levels. Specifically, the GDP per capita in 2067 is $70 000, an average annual increase of only 0.7 percent over the period. More significantly, GDP and GDP per capita are essentially stable over the final twenty years of the scenario. This scenario thus illustrates a transition from a growth-based economy to an economy managing without growth. Unlike the simulations in the first edition of this book in which zero growth was imposed on the model, in LowGrow SFC, these very low rates of economic growth, and ultimately its cessation altogether, result from shorter work hours, the greatly reduced investment in brown capital and the consequential lower labor productivity. The impact on economic growth of this very different pattern of investment is similar to the output from the EETRAP model described in Chapter 5. There we saw what happens when renewable energy sources with a lower energy return on investment (EROI) replace non-renewable energy sources with higher EROI. The diversion and absorption of investment within the energy sector reduces economic growth just as it does here when looked at within the wider scope of LowGrow SFC.

Conventional wisdom would suggest that such a transition towards what is effectively a steady-state economy is impossible without causing

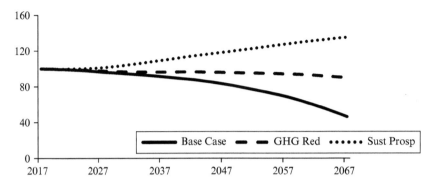

*Figure 11.5    SPI in the LowGrow SFC scenarios*

irreparable damage to prosperity and well-being in society. But Figure 11.5 suggests that this undesirable outcome is avoided in LowGrow SFC. In fact the composite SPI described in the previous section rises significantly in the Sustainable Prosperity scenario despite falling in both the other two scenarios. Starting from a base of 100 in 2017, the SPI falls precipitously by more than 50 percent in the Base Case. Even in the GHG Reduction scenario the SPI declines 10 percent. In the Sustainable Prosperity scenario, by contrast, the SPI increases 35 percent from 2017 to 2067.

To understand these differences, we must examine the component parts of the SPI (Table 11.2) in more detail. One of those components is the GDP per capita itself, which pushes the SPI upwards, the higher the level of GDP. This ought to help to maintain a high level of the SPI, so clearly there are other factors which offset this apparent advantage for the Base Case. Alongside GDP per capita lie a variety of other indicators, some environmental, some social, some financial in nature, each of which has some effect on the overall measure of the SPI. These components are sufficient to allow the Sustainable Prosperity scenario to perform much better over the long run. It is worth looking at each of them in turn.

### 11.3.3    Environmental Influences on the SPI

Principal amongst the factors which favor the Sustainable Prosperity over the Base Case in the SPI is the Environmental Burden Index (EBI), designed to include, amongst other things, the negative impact of greenhouse gas emissions. Figure 11.6 illustrates the changes in the indexed value of the EBI over time. Clearly, here is a partial explanation for the reversal of fortunes witnessed as we move from an indicator based on GDP towards a broader measure of sustainable prosperity such as the SPI. The

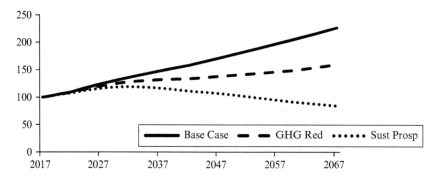

*Figure 11.6    EBI in the LowGrow SFC scenarios*

EBI for the Base Case more than doubles over the period of the scenario, as greenhouse gases continue to rise and little is done to offset other environmental impacts from the economy. Since a rising EBI depresses the SPI, there is a partial explanation here for the poor performance of the Base Case in Figure 11.5.

The EBI for the GHG Reduction scenario performs significantly better. The main reason for this is a significant decline in GHG emissions resulting from the combination of measures described in the previous section, alongside the somewhat lower rate of economic growth. Figure 11.4 shows that the GDP per capita still increases by 75 percent by 2067 for the GHG Reduction scenario while greenhouse gas emissions decline to 27 percent of their level in 2017.[13] This is a version of 'green growth', though growth here is slower (not faster as some would claim) than the Base Case. Disappointingly, the reduction in GHG emissions by 2067, while substantial, still falls far short of the Canadian government's 80 percent target reduction by 2050 from 2005 levels (Munson 2016) with a projected decline of only 45 percent. Even by 2067 the reduction in emissions falls short of the 80 percent target. Nonetheless, the reduction in GHG emissions suppresses the rise in the EBI and in doing so has a notably positive effect on the SPI (Figure 11.5). Certainly, the steep decline in SPI visible for the Base Case has been avoided. With a determined effort to reduce GHG emissions, the SPI declines much less than in the Base Case, most of the decline coming after 2050. Put another way, even though GDP per capita is projected to grow at an average 1.1 percent per year in the GHG Reduction scenario, well-being declines slowly but steadily as measured by the SPI.

By comparison, the Sustainable Prosperity scenario achieves a 60 percent reduction in GHG emissions by 2050, an 80 percent reduction target by 2060, and an 85 percent reduction by 2067. Alongside other green

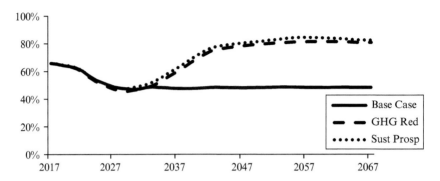

*Figure 11.7    Proportion of renewable electricity in the LowGrow SFC scenarios*

investment measures, the reduction in economic growth in this scenario facilitates a decline in the EBI to 84 percent by the end of the period, contributing significantly to the improved SPI score for this scenario.

Some of the decline in the EBI, in particular for the Sustainable Prosperity scenario, is also due to the deliberate policy of shifting the electricity sector towards renewable energy sources induced by the carbon price on greenhouse gas emissions. Figure 11.7 illustrates the proportion of electricity delivered through renewable energy over the lifetime of each scenario. There is a substantial difference between the Base Case and the other two scenarios. Despite the significant drop in the costs of renewable technologies in the past several years, especially solar photovoltaics and wind, they are still more expensive than non-renewable technologies, especially when storage costs are included. Even allowing for further reductions in these costs as more capacity is installed and the wind and solar technologies improve, their costs are projected to remain higher than non-renewable alternatives for some time.[14]

For these reasons, the proportion of electricity from renewable sources in the Base Case is projected to fall over the initial period and to remain below 50 percent of the total over the course of the run.[15] However, in the other two scenarios, the carbon price imposed on greenhouse gas emissions from the electricity sector has a decisive effect on the choice between non-renewable and renewable electricity generation. In the GHG Reduction scenario electricity from renewable sources rises to an 80 percent share in 2045 where it remains. At the same time, total electricity demand is greater than in the Base Case scenario because of the electrification of road and rail transportation. In the Sustainable Prosperity scenario, the proportion of renewables in the electricity rises even further. Interestingly, this is not because of any further measures introduced in the electricity sub-model, but flows instead from the reduced rate of economic growth and a lower requirement for additional generating capacity.

### 11.3.4  Social Influences on the SPI

Two specific social measures adopted in the Sustainable Prosperity scenario also contribute to the improved performance of this latter case over the other two scenarios. The first of these is the redistributive fiscal policy described in the previous section, in which transfer payments are progressively increased from 2020 and distributed preferentially to the lower income categories.[16]

These enhanced transfers have the effect (Figure 11.8) of achieving a significant reduction in the Gini coefficient in the Canadian economy on pre-tax incomes, which declines from 0.47 in 2017 to 0.21 in 2067. A lower Gini coefficient improves the performance of the SPI and this accounts for some of the advantage of the Sustainable Prosperity scenario over both the Base Case and the GHG Reduction scenario.

The second preferential social policy adopted in the Sustainable Prosperity scenario is the reduction in the annual average hours worked across the workforce. The average paid employee in Canada worked a little over 1700 hours in 2017. In the Base Case and GHG Reduction scenarios, this does not change significantly (Figure 11.9). Increases in labor productivity (the output per hour) are more or less offset by increases in output in

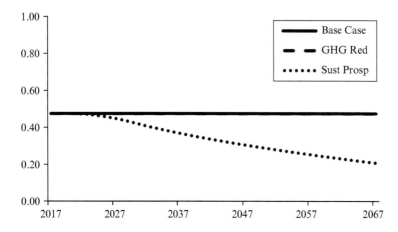

*Figure 11.8*   *Gini coefficient on pre-tax incomes in the LowGrow SFC scenarios*

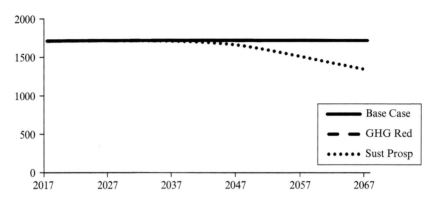

*Figure 11.9    Annual hours worked in the LowGrow SFC scenarios*

these two cases and the small fluctuations in the rate of unemployment in these scenarios have a minimal impact on average work hours.

In the Sustainable Prosperity case, however, the average hours worked in the economy fall to around 1340 hours per year by 2067, with an average annual rate of decline of 0.5 percent. The decline in hours worked is made possible by a combination of labor productivity growth and a stabilized level of output. It offers more opportunities for people to enjoy time with their families and friends, perhaps volunteering in the community or taking advantage of increased leisure, much as Keynes predicted in his famous (1930) essay on 'Economic possibilities for our grandchildren'. This reduction in the time spent in work is deemed to be a positive contribution to people's well-being and quality of life and contributes positively to the SPI, explaining some of its improved performance in the Sustainable Prosperity scenario.

Reduced working hours also play a significant role in preventing unemployment rising as output stabilizes. As discussed previously, a stabilization of output in the context of increasing labor productivity would tend to exacerbate unemployment, leading to perverse social outcomes. Figure 11.10 reveals that unemployment is very similar in all three scenarios.

### 11.3.5   Financial Influences on the SPI

The advantage of a stock-flow consistent model such as LowGrow SFC is its ability to articulate the financial positions of different sectors in a meaningful and consistent way. So, for example, the net lending positions[17] of each sector can be determined under any scenario, as can the long-term

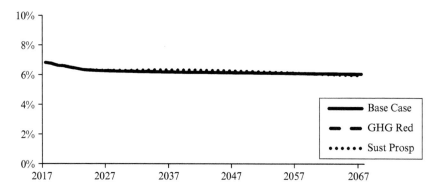

*Figure 11.10    Rate of unemployment in the LowGrow SFC scenarios*

impact of these positions on the financial worth of different sectors of the economy. The financial positions of the firms and banks sectors are obviously crucial to the long-term stability of the economy. In LowGrow SFC, stability in these sectors is achieved largely through financing and profit-sharing rules which aim to maintain relatively consistent net lending positions at or close to zero.[18] As we have mentioned, a consistently negative trade balance can also have a destabilizing effect on the long-term position of the Canadian economy, with respect to the rest of the world. In all three scenarios a zero trade balance is assumed after 2017, a year in which it was showing a small positive balance.

The financial position of the remaining sectors in the economy (households and government) are influenced by two things. First, the basic mechanism of stock-flow consistency ensures that the sum of all net lending across the economy (including the foreign sector) is equal to zero. For as long as banks, firms and the foreign sector maintain net lending positions close to zero, this means that any positive net lending position for government is offset by a corresponding negative net lending position for households (and vice versa). As a consequence, the state always has the ability to balance the net lending position of households: by increasing its deficit when household saving drops too far or reducing it when household net worth rises excessively. In the long term, the health of the economy depends on having both public sector debt and household debt lie within reasonable bounds. The final two components of the SPI aim to reflect this requirement.

Figure 11.11 shows the ratio of combined government debt to GDP across the three LowGrow SFC scenarios. In 2017, the public debt in Canada was around 55 percent of GDP, somewhat lower than in other

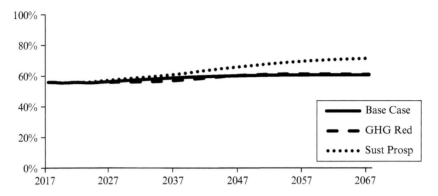

*Figure 11.11    Government debt-to-GDP ratio in the LowGrow SFC
            scenarios*

rich economies, partly because of the country's relative financial prudence
in the run up to the 2008 crisis. In the Base Case and GHG Reduction
scenarios, this value rises slightly to about 60 percent, indicating a relatively stable position in relation to Canada's public debt. In the Sustainable
Prosperity scenario, however, the debt-to-GDP ratio rises steadily, reaching 70 percent of the GDP by the end of the run. This is partly of course
because the GDP itself has stabilized at that point in time. The rise in
this indicator suppresses the SPI and raises a potential concern over the
long-term sustainability of the Canadian economy. Nonetheless, it is
worth pointing out that even at the end of the run, the debt-to-GDP ratio
remains at a level that has been far surpassed by many countries without
the collapse of their economies. As an example, Japan's debt-to-GDP ratio
has exceeded 200 percent since 2009, reaching 250 percent in 2016 (Trading
Economics 2018).

It is also interesting to note here that modern money theorists such as
Wray (2012) advise against the use of the debt-to-GDP measure as an
indicator of long-run resilience, on the grounds that in countries with sovereign monetary systems such as Canada, the UK and the USA, the state
does not have a budget constraint comparable to that of a household. The
argument is that government can always pay debts denominated in their
own currency (Wray and Nersisyan 2016). One approach to reducing the
debt-to-GDP ratio in the Sustainable Prosperity scenario would, accord-
ingly, be to allow the government to issue debt-free sovereign currency
and spend this directly into circulation. In fact, LowGrow SFC allows
for this possibility and when utilized it shows a dramatic reduction in the
debt-to-GDP ratio and a consequent boost in the SPI. For the purposes

of this chapter, however, we omit this possibility from our scenarios, leaving us with a rather conservative estimate of the SPI for the Sustainable Prosperity scenario.[19]

With government running a deficit, it follows from the stock-flow consistency of the model (and the financial behaviors of the other sectors) that the overall net lending position of the household sector is positive in all three scenarios, leading to a healthy (if stabilizing) position in terms of household net worth. This expectation is confirmed in the findings from LowGrow SFC (Jackson and Victor 2018). Even so, it remains possible that households' consumption decisions and portfolio preferences can lead them towards financial instability. For instance, it is still possible, even with positive net lending, for the ratio of households' loans to incomes to rise to a level where banks' confidence in their ability to repay those loans could fall. If the banks were then to impose a constraint on lending (as is possible in the model), it could have a destabilizing effect on household spending and potentially send the economy into a spiral of recession. This is why we have included households' loan-to-value ratio as a component of the SPI (Table 11.2) to measure the overall performance of the economy.

As Figure 11.12 reveals, there are minor increases in the ratio of household loans to incomes in all three scenarios, with the smallest being in the Sustainable Prosperity scenario.

In summary, the results discussed in this section suggest that the Sustainable Prosperity scenario remains a very realistic alternative to the conventional wisdom of continual exponential growth, outperforming the Base Case in several important ways over the next half a century. It is particularly satisfying to find that even the financial indicators of a low growth economy can, under the right conditions, remain relatively

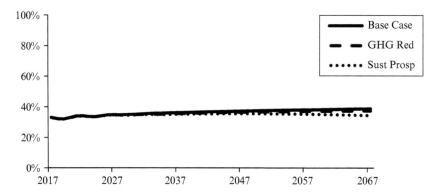

*Figure 11.12*   *Households' loan-to-value ratio in the LowGrow SFC scenarios*

sustainable. Investment portfolios have changed, productivity growth has declined, consumption demand has stabilized, but the economy is nonetheless still financially resilient, its social outcomes are improved and its environmental burden on the planet is dramatically reduced.

An interesting question arises at this point. Does the Sustainable Prosperity scenario still describe a viable form of capitalism? Or do the various policies and measures introduced to improve social and environmental outcomes and to maintain financial stability essentially mean that LowGrow SFC no longer describes a capitalist economy? It is to this question that we now turn.

## 11.4 CAPITALISM WITHOUT GROWTH?

Robert Solow, one of the most distinguished economists of the second half of the 20th century, and famous for his theory of economic growth (1956) has stated that:

> There is no reason at all why capitalism could not survive with slow or even no growth ... It is possible that the US and Europe will find that ... either continued growth will be too destructive to the environment and they are too dependent on scarce natural resources, or that they would rather use increasing productivity in the form of leisure. There is nothing in the system that says it cannot exist happily in a stationary state. (Solow 2008)

In this regard, Solow is at odds with those who insist that there is a 'growth imperative' in capitalism and that capitalism cannot survive without economic growth. If this latter view is correct, it would mean that economic growth is an inherent feature of the capitalist system, without which capitalism would collapse. It would suggest, in other words, managing without growth is not an option for capitalist economies.

Various writers have argued for a 'growth imperative' in capitalism (Foster 2015). For Marx, the growth imperative is the impulse of capitalists to accumulate capital through investment in the search for profit. He thought this process contained the seeds of its own destruction, arguing that over time the rate of profit would decline and workers would become impoverished. Significantly for the argument of this book, Marx also noted that capitalism ruins 'the lasting fertility of the soil' (Marx 1887[2003]), giving another reason for the eventual collapse of capitalism:

> All progress in capitalistic agriculture is a progress in the art, not only of robbing the laborer but of robbing the soil; all progress in increasing fertility of the soil for a given time is a progress towards ruining the lasting sources of

that fertility . . . Capitalist production, therefore, develops technology, and the combining together of various processes into a social whole, only by sapping the original sources of all wealth: soil and laborer. (Marx 1887[2003], p. 330)

Gordon and Rosenthal (2003) argue that capitalism's growth imperative resides in the need for growth to avoid widespread bankruptcy and collapse. A further argument is that capitalism's growth imperative lies in its debt-based money system. In such a system, which is prevalent in all capitalist countries today, most of the money in the economy is created when banks make interest-bearing loans. Growth, it is argued, is required to cover the interest payments on these loans (Binswanger 2009; 2015). Our own work has challenged this latter conclusion. Using a stock-flow consistent model (Jackson and Victor 2015a) we have shown that a relatively stable, quasi-stationary economy is entirely possible even in the presence of interest-bearing debt, provided that banks' profits are distributed to shareholders for recirculation in the economy and that governments are prepared to take a guiding role in the financial stability of the economy.

Ultimately though, what is at stake here is the question of whether a non-growing economy is in any sense still a capitalistic economy. Opinions in the literature differ widely. For example, Lawn (2011) argues for the viability of steady-state capitalism defining steady-state in terms of throughput rather than GDP but also stating that 'there is no doubt that real GDP would effectively cease to grow in a steady-state economy' (p. 4). Taking a different view, Richard Smith agrees that 'we need to . . . "downshift" to a simpler life, find meaning and self-realization in promoting the common good instead of accumulating stuff', but he considers ecological economists 'from Herman Daly to Tim Jackson' to offer 'unworkable, warm and fuzzy capitalist utopias, with no plausible means of escaping the iron cage of consumerism or the "growthmania" of the market' (Smith 2010).

In his most recent book Jackson (2017) follows Baumol (who follows Marx) 'in the assumption that capitalistic economies are those where ownership and control of the means of production lies in private hands' (2017, p. 222). However, Jackson observes that capitalism, in fact, allows for a 'wide spectrum of ownership' (2017, p. 223) including public ownership and various models of distributed ownership. He expects these other forms of ownership, with motives other than profit maximization, to become more prominent in a post-growth world. In such a world, Jackson notes that some investments may not generate sufficient financial returns to satisfy the private sector. Whether we call this a capitalist world or something else, he argues, ultimately matters less than whether it allows people to flourish on a finite planet.

Emphasizing changing patterns of ownership makes sense, not just because of the increasing role of unproductive investment necessary for reducing the burden economies place on the biosphere. Other changes are also happening that will require more widely distributed ownership. It is anticipated by some that automation, roboticization and artificial intelligence will displace labor faster than it can be re-employed even in a rapidly growing economy (Bruckner et al. 2017). In an economy that is managing without growth this threat becomes even more serious. A redistribution of income, as included in the Sustainable Prosperity scenario, would mitigate some of the worst effects of the contemplated rise in unemployment. But will that be enough? Will increasing numbers of people receiving income for little or no work feel they are worthy, productive, contributing members of society? Probably not. As ownership of capital becomes concentrated in fewer and fewer hands (Piketty 2014), a society with an economy which achieves little or no economic growth and in which increased productivity reduces employment will have to tackle the question of ownership. And depending on how it does this will determine whether such an economy will be capitalist or something else. This and related themes are taken up in detail by Alperovitz (2011) in *America beyond Capitalism*, who reports that already there are 'more than 48,000 co-ops operating in the United States – and that 120 million Americans are co-op members' (2011, p. 88). Change is underway.

According to Streeck (2016), 'the history of modern capitalism can be written as a succession of crises that capitalism survived only at the price of deep transformations of its economic and social institutions, saving it from bankruptcy in unforeseeable and often unintended ways' (2016, p. 4). He points to the sequence of 'global inflation in the 1970s, the explosion of public debt in the 1980s, and rapidly rising private indebtedness in the subsequent decade, resulting in the collapse of financial markets in 2008' (2016, p. 16). Streeck describes the period we are now in as a lasting '*interregnum* . . . a period of social entropy, or disorder (and precisely for this reason a period of uncertainty and indeterminacy)' (2016, p. 13).

One of the factors contributing to this *interregnum* is the 'tension . . . between the capitalist principle of infinite expansion and the finite supply of natural resources . . . no one seriously denies that the energy consumption patterns of rich capitalist societies cannot be extended to the rest of the world without destroying essential preconditions of human life', he remarks (2016, p. 62). Streeck (2016) describes 'a race between the advancing exhaustion of nature on the one hand and technological innovation on the other' and then asks 'what actors and institutions are to secure the collective good of a liveable environment in a world of competitive production and consumption?' (2016, pp. 62, 63). These observations and questions resonate with much of what is in this book.

We can learn something about the viability of capitalism in the absence of economic growth from the scenarios described in this chapter. We have already seen how the Sustainable Prosperity scenario offers the possibility of a relatively orderly transition from a growth-based economy to a quasi-stationary economy and at the same time provides for an improvement in overall performance as indicated by the SPI which captures environmental, social and financial indicators. The behavior of the financial indicators is of particular importance to the question of capitalism. Consistent net lending positions, a modest rise in the debt-to-GDP ratio and a relatively stable loan-to-value ratio for households all provide some indication of financial stability in the economy. They do not immediately suggest that capitalism is impossible in a low/no-growth environment. But we should at least explore some other indicators of the economy before reaching firm conclusions about this.

What about the rate of profit on capital or the shares of capital and labor in the national income? Do these also remain within broad historical bounds as defined by capitalism? Or do they suggest a completely different organizational form for the economy? A positive rate of profit on capital invested is a quintessential requirement for a functioning capitalist economy. Without an expectation of profit, there would be no investment and without investment there would (eventually) be no capital. Piketty (2014, Chapter 6) emphasizes the importance of the division of national income between capital and labor and alludes to the idea that they should remain within bounds for capitalism to survive. He observes that since 1770, capital's share of national income has fluctuated between 20 to just above 40 percent in the UK and since 1820 between about 15 and just above 40 percent in France. These ranges serve as useful benchmarks for assessing this aspect of capitalism in the scenarios. Marx's expectation that labor would become increasingly poorer under capitalism, leading to insurrection, has not yet materialized. Is it likely to materialize under any of the scenarios explored here?

In the first place, Figure 11.13 shows that the post-tax rate of profit from capital in the Base Case and GHG Reduction scenarios remain fairly stable over the 50-year projection and are very similar. The rate of profit in the GHG Reduction scenario rises above the value in the Base Case. This is because even though profits are reduced in the GHG Reduction scenario compared with the Base Case, the reduction is proportionately less than the reduction in capital so the rate of profit increases. More challenging is the decline in the Sustainable Prosperity scenario, where the post-tax rate of profit falls from 5.7 percent in 2017 to 4.6 percent towards the end of the period. While this is a significant reduction, and one that would be vigorously resisted by the owners of capital, it does not rule out the possibility of continuing returns from capital, well into the future.

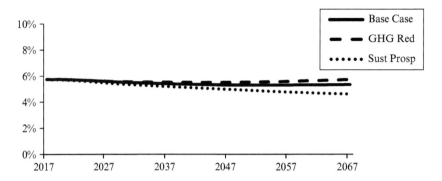

*Figure 11.13   Rate of profit in the LowGrow SFC scenarios*

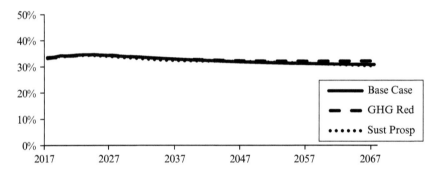

*Figure 11.14   Capital's share of national income in the LowGrow SFC scenarios*

The division of national income between capital and labor is illustrated in Figure 11.14. The share of income going to capital rises at first then declines somewhat in all three scenarios, with the lowest decline coming in the GHG Reduction scenario. Also, the share of income to capital remains within the historical norms associated with a capitalist economy in all three scenarios. It is the decline in absolute returns to capital (and labor) compared with the Base Case, rather than their respective shares, that could cause strong resistance to the Sustainable Prosperity scenario. The kinds of changes proposed in the Sustainable Prosperity scenario are as much social in nature as they are economic or financial, and they depend on political and public acceptability. It is certainly conceivable that changes of this kind would necessitate some decline in the power of those who own capital assets, particularly where this power is concentrated in a few very wealthy people. At the very least, it seems clear that the form of hyper-capitalistic society that characterizes the early 21st century would have to

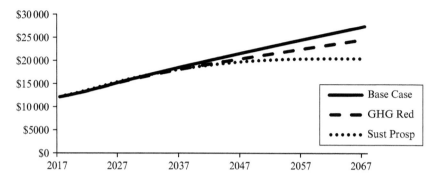

*Figure 11.15* *Government spending per capita in the LowGrow SFC scenarios*

change substantially. But none of this entirely excludes the possibility that some aspects of a capitalist economy would survive.

Finally, it is worth looking at government expenditure per capita to assess whether the range of services which people have come to expect from government can be sustained even in a low or non-growing economy. If per capita spending drops too low it could generate widespread disaffection with the system, undermining political stability. In fact, Figure 11.15 shows that government expenditure per person increases in all three scenarios but stabilizes in the last decade in the Sustainable Prosperity scenario at a level consistent with an ample provision of public services.

On the face of it, therefore, even the Sustainable Prosperity scenario remains broadly compatible with a capitalist economy. Yet this scenario offers environmental and social benefits which are clearly unavailable in the other two scenarios. In the long-run therefore, the 'less capitalistic' scenario could prove to be more resilient than the 'more capitalistic' ones. We certainly anticipate that environmental, social and indeed financial pressures will grow stronger over the next half century, particularly without appropriate policy responses. Changes in the organization of society are almost inevitable. Fifty years from now, people will look back and say either that capitalism proved resilient and evolved, or that capitalism, in any form in which we recognize it today, passed into history.

## 11.5 CONCLUSION

In this chapter we presented a simulation model of a national economy, broadly calibrated using Canadian data. We used the model to generate three very different stories about the future, covering the half century from 2017 to 2067: a Base Case in which current trends and relationships are projected into the future, a GHG Reduction scenario in which several measures are introduced specifically designed to reduce GHG emissions, and a Sustainable Prosperity scenario which includes additional measures to improve environmental, social and financial conditions across society. Only in this third scenario, with its much slower rate of economic growth, do we see an overall improvement in performance as indicated by the SPI, an index comprised of seven variables whose values are calculated in the simulation model. Recognizing that this exercise is at best exploratory, it is nonetheless reasonable to suggest that the chapter supports the following conclusions:

1.   The pursuit of economic growth at the expense of a deepening environmental crisis has a very high probability of catastrophe.
2.   Substantial reductions in GHG emissions can clearly be achieved without massive changes to the structure of society. But the impact on the rate of growth, while modest, is larger than others have suggested and at odds with those who see a 'green' economy as growing faster than a 'brown' one. Furthermore, this 'green growth' scenario falls well short of the Government of Canada's greenhouse gas target reduction of 80 percent by 2050.
3.   Sustainable prosperity is attainable but it will require a major reorientation of society's priorities towards improvements in social equity, economic security and environmental quality. These changes may well lead to a low or no-growth economy but they will also deliver a better quality of life. Managing without growth may not be entirely incompatible with capitalism; but it will look very different from the overfinancialized consumer capitalism of the early 21st century and may well be worthy of a different name altogether.

## NOTES

1.   The macroeconomic model that is featured in this chapter is a substantial redesign and updating of the original LowGrow model that was presented in the first edition of this book. Many of the improvements are the result of an ongoing collaboration between Professor Tim Jackson and me in the development of ecological macroeconomics. (See the several entries in the references to publications by Jackson and Victor and Victor and Jackson.) I am delighted that Tim agreed to co-author this chapter.
2.   Five of the models listed in Hardt and O'Neill (2017) and which are empirically based are by Jackson and/or Victor.
3.   This section provides a brief overview of the model. A more detailed description of LowGrow SFC is given in Jackson and Victor (2018) and the model itself can be

accessed at https://tinyurl.com/LowGrowSFC, www.pvictor.com, and at https://www.cusp.ac.uk/themes/s2/lowgrow-sfc/.

4. Various data sources were used to calibrate the electricity sector sub-model, the main ones being the US EIA 2016 and 2017, the IEA 2014 and Environment Canada 2014. These sources provided information on the capital costs, fixed and variable operating costs and GHG emissions for each technology.

5. For more information on the adjustment coefficient see Tutulmaz and Victor (2014).

6. See Jackson (2017) for a fuller discussion of this characterization. See also www.cusp.ac.uk.

7. Statistics Canada (2017f) provides three projections to the year 2063, each of which can be selected in LowGrow SFC. Population values for years after 2063 are extrapolated based on the trend in the data. In the Base Case, we use the central population projection in which the Canadian population is expected to rise from 36.7 million to 52 million in 2067.

8. Depending on the scope of the carbon pricing system, greenhouse gases in addition to carbon dioxide are converted to a $CO_2$ equivalent and the price is imposed on the total quantity.

9. The Progressive Conservative Government elected in Ontario in June 2018 announced its intention to cancel Ontario's cap and trade system for greenhouse gases and immediately introduced legislation to do so.

10. Data limitations prevented simulation of a carbon tax applied to these sectors.

11. The available data on income distribution does not permit the calculation to be based on households. Since some households have more than one income earner, the Gini coefficient for the distribution of pre-tax household income is different from (likely lower than) the pre-tax individual incomes.

12. Unless otherwise stated, values are in 2007$.

13. Canada's GHG emissions were 738 mts in 2005 and 722 mts in 2015 (Government of Canada 2017c).

14. See *supra* note 6 for data sources.

15. Electricity from renewable sources includes large-scale hydro with limited potential for expansion in Canada. The increasingly important contribution from solar and wind is apparent in later years.

16. In practice, a proportion of these transfers might take the form of housing, food and other programs rather than cash. Or the transfers could be in the form of a universal basic income. The income transfers in the simulation can be considered a proxy for these.

17. The net lending position of a sector refers to the amount of money the sector has over from its income once its consumption and investment spending is accounted for.

18. In the case of banks this is by construction zero and in the case of firms, net lending is maintained in a slight negative position, consistent both with the empirical data and the notion that net financial worth of firms, though typically negative, is more than offset by the value of physical assets (capital) in the economy. For more details see Jackson and Victor (2018).

19. For further details of this option and its impacts on the SPI see Jackson and Victor (2018).

# 12. Managing without growth: from simulations to reality

> What all this amounts to is a different sort of macroeconomic policy in an environmentally friendly world. The centrepiece will be a shortening of standard working hours backed up by public investment in environmental productivity improvements. (Booth 2004)

> [M]acroeconomic policies must be judged not on whether they promise growth, but on what kind of qualitative change. (Harris and Goodwin 2003)

The opening chapter of this book described the emergence of the idea of economic growth and its comparatively recent ascent as the near universal, overarching public policy objective of government, no matter how rich their economies. That the OECD would launch an initiative named 'Going for Growth' in 2005 (OECD 2005) shows how important 'vigorous sustainable economic growth' remains to the governments of its member countries. Each year since its inception the OECD has published a lengthy report recommending policies to member countries aimed at increasing their rate of economic growth and improving its characteristics in some respect. The 2017 report, for example, emphasizes 'inclusive' growth recognizing that growth since at least 2000 has been anything but inclusive. As Jonathan Porritt states, 'Of all the defining characteristics of post-World War II capitalism, the centrality of economic growth as the overarching policy objective is perhaps the most important' (Porritt 2005, p. 45). Is vigorous, sustainable economic growth feasible in OECD countries if it is also to be enjoyed by much poorer countries where the contribution of economic growth to well-being is so much greater and more obvious?

In Chapter 2 we described economies as open systems embedded in and dependent on the closed system of planet Earth. Material and energy flows between the economy and the environment are increasing while the capacity of the environment to accommodate them is not. If anything, it is shrinking. When economies were small in relation to the environment, these considerations were less obvious and were largely neglected by governments, corporations, individual citizens and most economists. In market economies, we rely on prices to convey accurate information about relative scarcity. Markets do this best, though often inadequately, for resources that are within the economy; resources conventionally categorized as land, labor and capital, and owned by someone or some organization that has the legal right and capacity to determine their use. It is this right which is traded in a market exchange of property. As explained in Chapters 3 and 4, prices contain little or no information about the increasing stresses and strains that the economy is placing on the environment. As the burden of economies on the environment has increased, prices have become less and less useful for conveying the information needed for fully informed decisions that affect how the economy interacts with the environment. Efforts to price nature are fraught with conceptual, methodological and empirical problems that render the results rhetorically useful but whose precise meaning is often unclear. Prices also fail in the matter of justice since they reflect any and all inequities in the distribution of income and wealth.

Chapters 5, 6 and 7 gave an overview of some of the most troubling environmental problems associated with economic growth. The energy–emissions trap was described, revealing the difficulty of transitioning from fossil fuels to renewable sources of energy while simultaneously generating sufficient net energy and keeping within a global carbon budget, without diverting so much capital to the energy sector that economic growth is seriously constrained. In Chapter 8 we looked at the size of the population, GDP per capita, the composition of GDP, and technology as the proximate determinants of impacts on the environment. Using climate change as an example, we considered the contribution that changes in each of these factors might make to reducing GHG emissions. We concluded the task was much greater than a decade ago because of the changes in the intervening years. We reiterated the argument of previous chapters that higher rates of economic growth necessitate faster reductions in GHG intensity to reach any emissions reduction target. We found that the requirement for very rapid reductions in GHG intensity can be mitigated by lower rates of economic growth. And as Chapter 9 suggested, people would be no less happy. We might even be happier if we spent less of our incomes on positional goods and concentrated more on what is really useful and beneficial.

Economic growth has brought many benefits to those countries that have experienced it the most. That is why it is so important for countries that have experienced the least growth to remedy the situation. Yet even where long-term growth has been achieved it has not been an unmitigated success. In Chapter 10, looking at Canada, Sweden, the UK and the USA since the 1970s, we saw that economic growth has not brought full employment, it has not eliminated poverty – in fact by some measures poverty has increased – income and wealth inequality have risen, and economic growth has not solved key environmental problems, the opposite in many important respects. Clearly economic growth is not sufficient for meeting any of these objectives. Is it necessary? That is the question that we sought to answer in Chapter 11 with the help of LowGrow SFC, a simulation model of the Canadian economy. What we found is that it is possible to develop scenarios over a 50-year time horizon for Canada in which full employment prevails, incomes are more evenly distributed, people enjoy more leisure, greenhouse gas emissions are drastically reduced as are other environmental burdens, and household and government debt is contained, all in the context of a cessation of economic growth.

To translate computer simulations into real action will require an ambitious, some might say impossible, redirection of public policy, which will not happen without dramatic changes in individual mindsets and societal values. It may require more than that. The dilemma for policy makers is that the scope of change required for managing without growth is so great that no democratically elected government could implement the requisite policies without the broad-based consent of the electorate. Even talking about them could make a politician unelectable. The upsurge of interest in the environment in the first two decades of the 21st century is encouraging but we have seen this sort of thing before. Anthony Downs named the phenomenon the issue-attention cycle in his prescient analysis in the 1970s (Downs 1972). Since then we have experienced the rise and fall of environmentalism following the Brundtland report (World Commission on Environment and Development 1987), which popularized the term, if not the practice, of sustainable development. We also saw the enthusiasm and government support for renewable energy and energy conservation, stimulated by the oil price increases in the 1970s and early 1980s, virtually disappear in the 1990s when oil prices declined, then return when oil prices rose again, until 2014 when another oil price surge peaked and fell. This time may be different though because renewable sources of energy have become more cost competitive as a result of technological improvements and government support (though, as we saw in Chapter 6, avoiding the energy–emissions trap while maintaining the rate of economic growth may be impossible). Then at the start of this century we witnessed a coalescing of concern over climate change which promises to be more enduring, but even so, action has fallen far short of commitments. The failure of most signatories to the Kyoto Protocol to meet their modest targets for 2008 to 2012 showed the limited ability of the nations of the world, including the richest who should be leading, to rise to even this one challenge. Some progress has been made since then through a continuing series of international conferences, but as noted in Chapter 6, even if countries meet their voluntary commitments to reduce GHG emissions collectively they will fall short of what's required for a 66 percent chance of not exceeding a temperature increase of 2°C. In 2017 the 'conference of the parties' held in Germany made some advances but with decidedly mixed results (Timperley 2017).

Coping with the transition from fossil fuels to reduced GHG emissions while maintaining the supply of net energy presents a problem of daunting magnitude, especially if we expect to maintain high rates of economic growth. In addition, we are facing the ongoing losses of ecosystem services underlined by the accelerating loss of habitat and disappearance of species on a scale meriting the designation of the sixth extinction. And we are in an era of increasing inequality and displacement of people seeking better lives. It is difficult to believe that these problems will be any easier to solve when the population of humans has increased by another 2 billion by mid-century and 3.5 billion by 2100.

Still, we should not give up: there are options, there are alternatives. People can be creative and ingenious, and can accomplish great things, especially when they cooperate. Chapter 11 pointed a way forward. Seen from a macro level, important economic, social and environmental objectives can be achieved in a country like Canada without relying on never ending economic growth. In this chapter we will examine some of the policy choices that would take us in this direction. The potential scope of such an examination is considerable, ranging across the full spectrum of policy areas for which governments have traditionally been responsible, and possibly some new ones as well. It could also include an examination of the changing roles and responsibilities of the private, cooperative and not-for-profit sectors and also of individual citizens. Then there is the question of jurisdiction. Some issues need to be addressed internationally, others nationally and sub-nationally and still others are essentially local issues.

Clearly the multiple dimensions of policies for managing without growth demand a much fuller treatment than can be offered in a single chapter (see Brown and Garver 2009; Speth 2012; Maxton and Randers 2016; Jackson 2017; and Von Weizsäcker and Wijkman 2018 for related discussions). What follows is not comprehensive, but the topics are not chosen arbitrarily. They follow from the argument and analysis of the previous chapters. Again, we will use Canada as an example but much of what is said relates to other advanced economies facing similar difficult challenges.

## 12.1   POPULATION

Increases in population may or may not be necessary for economic growth. However, if the population is growing, economic growth is essential if per capita GDP is not to decline. Ultimately managing without economic growth requires a stable population. Fortunately, this is the direction in which the populations of most rich countries are headed. Some were already there in 2010 when 'about 48 percent of the world population had an average total fertility of less than 2.1 per woman' (United Nations 2017b). This included most rich countries such as Canada, Sweden, the UK, Germany, Japan, Austria and Italy, as well as many more with lower incomes. In the period 2010–15 the average total fertility rate of high-income countries taken as a group was 1.69, having declined from 2.32 in the 1970–75 period (United Nations 2017b). Total fertility rates at or below replacement have to be maintained for some time before the natural increase in population stabilizes or declines, as it has in Japan.

At nearly 10 million square kilometers, Canada is the second largest country in the world, with a land area greater than the United States and Europe, though only 5 percent of Canada is arable. In 2017, the Canadian population was 36.7 million (Statistics Canada 2017a), making Canada at 3.5 people per square kilometer one of the least densely populated countries in the world: 6 times less than Sweden, 9 times less than the USA, and 75 times less than the UK (Index Mundi 2017). This does not mean that most Canadians live in low density settings. Canada is a highly urbanized country, with more than 80 percent of its inhabitants living in urban areas. Three metropolitan areas – Toronto, Montreal and Vancouver – provide homes to more than one-third of the entire population. Furthermore, two-thirds of Canadians live within 100 kilometers of the Canada–US border (Statistics Canada 2017b). So even though, statistically speaking Canada is a lightly populated country, the day-to-day experience of most Canadians is that of living in the kind of urban areas found in rich countries and regions everywhere.

The views of Canadian governments on population and policies related to population changed little between 2005 and 2013, as can be seen from Table 12.1. Canada does not have an explicit policy for the size and growth of its population although various Canadian governments have expressed views on population. In this respect, Canada is no different from most countries. Table 12.1 shows a change in the government's view of the rate of population growth from 'satisfactory' in 2005 to 'too low' in 2011, but there were no policies for intervention. Nonetheless, governments at all three levels do have policies that affect population, the most important of which is the Federal government's immigration policy. In 2016/2017, a fairly typical year, net international migration accounted for about two-thirds of the increase in Canada's population of 316 798 (Statistics Canada 2017c).

*Table 12.1    Canadian government views and policies on population*

| Population policy variable | View/policy 2005 | View/policy 2013 |
|---|---|---|
| **Population size and growth** | | |
| View on growth | Satisfactory | Too low[a] |
| Policy on growth | No intervention | No intervention |
| | | |
| **Population age structure** | | |
| Level of concern about: | | |
| Size of the working-age population | Major concern | Major concern[a] |
| Ageing of the population | Major concern | Major concern |
| Measures to address population ageing | – | Neither |
| | | |
| **Fertility and family planning** | | |
| View on fertility level | Too low | Too low[a] |
| Policy on fertility level | No intervention | No intervention |
| Government support | Indirect | Indirect |
| Adolescent fertility: | | |
| Level of concern | Major concern | Major concern |
| Policies and programmes | Yes | Yes |
| | | |
| **Health and mortality** | | |
| View on life expectancy at birth | Acceptable | Acceptable[a] |
| View on under-five mortality | Acceptable | Acceptable |
| View on maternal mortality | Acceptable | Unacceptable |
| Level of concern about overweight and obesity | – | Major concern |
| Level of concern about HIV/AIDS | Major concern | Major concern |
| Measures implemented to control HIV/AIDS | All five | All six |
| Grounds on which abortion is permitted | All seven | All seven |
| | | |
| **Spatial distribution & internal migration** | | |
| Views on spatial distribution | Minor change desired | Minor change desired |
| Policy on rural to urban migration | No intervention | Lower |
| Policies on internal migration | No intervention | No intervention[a] |
| | | |
| **International migration** | | |
| View on immigration | Too low | Satisfactory[a] |
| Policy on immigration | Raise | Maintain |
| Policy on permanent settlement | Raise | Maintain |
| Policy on temporary workers | Raise | Maintain[a] |
| Policy on highly skilled workers | Raise | Raise[a] |
| Policy on family reunification | Raise | Raise[a] |

*Table 12.1*   (continued)

| Population policy variable | View/policy 2005 | View/policy 2013 |
|---|---|---|
| Policy on integration of non-nationals | Yes | Yes |
| Policy on naturalization | – | Yes |
| Level of concern about irregular immigration | – | Minor concern[a] |
| View on emigration | Satisfactory | Satisfactory[a] |
| Policy on emigration | No intervention | No intervention |
| Policy to encourage return of citizens | No | No[a] |

*Note:*   [a] Not collected for the 2013 revision. Refers to 2011.

*Source:*   Based on UN Department of Economic and Social Affairs (2013).

### 12.1.1   Natural Increases

Statistics Canada has developed several population projections for Canada to 2063. Low, medium and high projections are shown in Figure 12.1.

These projections involve different assumptions about the rate of natural increases in the population (that is, differences in birth and death rates and life expectancy) and net migration. The main driver of population in Canada over the next half century's growth is expected to be migration, as it has been since the early 1990s. It is striking that the *spread* of values between the low to the high scenarios projected for 2063 of 23.5 million is the same as the *total* population of Canada in 1976 (Statistics Canada 2017c). This shows just how sensitive the population projections are to the assumptions on which they are based.

Natural increases in Canada's population are projected to become negative from 2030/31[1] in the low scenario, to fall to virtually zero around 2050 in the medium scenario (see Figure 12.2), and remain positive throughout in the high scenario.

### 12.1.2   Immigration

Canada was born out of British and French imperial ambitions. In 2016 only 4.8 percent of Canada's population identified with the Aboriginal peoples of Canada (Statistics Canada 2017d) who suffered enormous hardships because of the influx of Europeans to their land. In the first 60 years of the 20th century, 90 percent of immigrants to Canada came from

in thousands

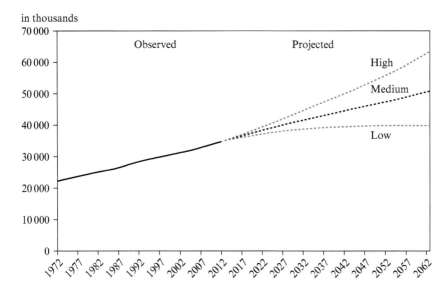

*Notes:*  Population, observed (1972–2013) and projected (2014–2063) according to the low-growth, medium-growth and high-growth scenarios, Canada.

*Source:*  Statistics Canada (2015a).

*Figure 12.1   Projections of the Canadian population, 2013–2063*

Europe. Of the 1.8 million immigrants who arrived in the 1990s nearly 60 percent came from Asia including the Middle East, and 20 percent from Europe. The rest came from the Caribbean, Central and South America (11 percent), Africa (8 percent) and the USA (3 percent) (Department of Foreign Affairs and International Trade 2003). This pattern continued in the first decades of this century, as shown in Figure 12.3. Between 1951 and 2016/17, immigration to Canada fluctuated between a high of 17 per 1000 Canadians in 1956 and a low of less than 4 per 1000 residents between 1983/84 and 1985/86. By 1992/93 immigration surpassed 200 000, peaking at 323 000 in 2015/16, a rate of 9 per 1000 (Statistics Canada 2017c; 2017d). In its various population projections Statistics Canada assumes that the immigration rate will vary from just over 5 per 1000 in the low scenario to well over 9 per 1000 in the high scenario. The future size of Canada's population is very much dependent on this assumption. By 2050 it could be as low as 39.8 million and declining or as high as 56.0 million and increasing, depending to a significant extent on immigration.[2]

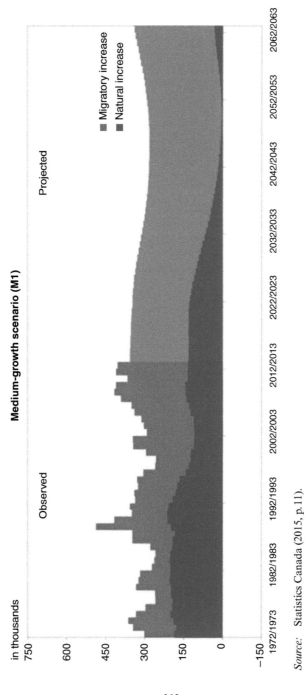

*Source:* Statistics Canada (2015, p. 11).

*Figure 12.2 Sources of Canada's population growth: medium*

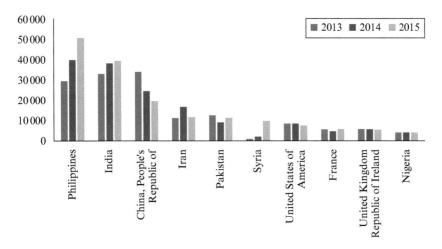

*Source:*   Government of Canada (2017e).

*Figure 12.3*   *Immigrants to Canada (permanent residents) by country,*
*2013–15*

### 12.1.3   Population and Immigration Policy in Canada

Immigration is not just a matter of assumption. It is also a matter of policy. Canada's immigration policy is its de facto population policy. While this seems obvious given the very major role that immigration plays and will continue to play in determining the size of Canada's population policy, it is not necessarily central to discussions of immigration policy in Canada (Beach et al. 2003). Immigration policy is a very sensitive issue that touches not only on matters of economic growth, but on individual human rights and freedoms and social justice. Human history is bound up with the large-scale movement of populations around the globe. Newcomers have been welcomed; at other times, they have been treated with suspicion, leading to resentment and resistance, sometimes with force. Often it is those entering new territories that do so with violence, as in the creation of empires from the Romans and before, to the Europeans and after.

Some populations have been moved against their will, the African slave trade being the most horrific example. The creation of reserves for Aboriginal peoples in North America and Australia and the displacement of entire communities in the name of development or progress when their land is required for other purposes have also brought extreme hardship. And now changing climate conditions are already affecting the most vulnerable populations. Environmental migrants are on the move and many more are expected (UNHCR 2015). Since Canadians generate one of the highest levels of GHG emissions per capita in the world and Canada being a large, prosperous country, do we have a moral obligation to admit vastly more immigrants than even the 450 000 per year that the Advisory Council on Economic Growth recommends (Advisory Council on Economic Growth 2016) – not for the sake of economic growth in Canada, but because of the reduced chances for development in poorer countries?

In the 2001 census almost 4 million people identified themselves as belonging to a visible minority, representing 13.4 percent of the population. By 2016 this had risen to 22.3 percent and is projected to continue to rise (CBC 2017). The changing pattern of Canada's population makes any discussion of immigration policy problematic because the motivation to engage in such a discussion may be suspect. There are certainly those who are not well disposed to the increasing diversity in the Canadian population but for most Canadians it is something to be celebrated. It is with the latter view in mind that this discussion of immigration policy as population policy proceeds.

Broadly speaking Canada's immigration policy has three main components: economic immigrants who will contribute to Canada's economic growth, family immigrants to unite family members, and refugee and humanitarian immigrants. In terms of numbers, the economic category is by far the largest, as can be seen in Table 12.2, which summarizes the Federal government's immigration targets for 2018 to 2020.

The first priority of the Government's immigration plan is clear: 'through increased immigration levels we will bring more people to Canada who can contribute to our economic growth' (Hussen 2017, p. 1). This is a position that hasn't changed in over one hundred years. 'Since the early 1890s, when Wilfrid Laurier implemented the most ambitious immigration expansion we have ever seen, we have always understood that immigration is essentially an economic policy' (Trudeau 2014, p. 262). Economic growth is mentioned ten times in the Government's immigration plan, sustainable development only once and then only in the title of

*Table 12.2   Canada's immigration levels plan*

| Immigration Category | 2018 | 2019 | 2020 |
| --- | --- | --- | --- |
| Economic | 177,500 | 191,600 | 195,800 |
| Family | 86,000 | 88,500 | 91,000 |
| Refugees and Humanitarian | 46,500 | 49,900 | 53,200 |
| Total | 310,000 | 330,000 | 340,000 |

*Source:*   Government of Canada (2017d).

another document. 'Through increased immigration levels we will bring more people to Canada who can contribute to our economic growth' (Hussen 2017, p. 3). In pursuit of economic growth 'Canadian businesses need access to talented workers from around the world' (Hussen 2017, p. 1).

What about economic growth in the countries from which the immigrants to Canada come? Is that not important too? Is it not more important? Many of the people that Canada wishes to attract in the economic category are highly educated, good at language, flexible and have skills that can be transferred between various types of employment. Yet these are the same qualities that are of benefit to the country of origin of an increasing proportion of Canada's immigrants.

Canada's efforts to increase the supply of skilled labor by attracting workers from abroad, including many from developing countries, have not gone unnoticed. UNCTAD comments that Canada and Australia have 'substantially liberalized their immigration regimes since 2000 with regard to skilled workers from abroad' (United Nations Conference on Trade and Development 2007, fn 3, p. 158). The UNCTAD report contrasts the views of the migration 'optimists' and 'realists' who disagree about the impact on developing countries of migration to developed countries. The optimists note the positive impacts of remittances to low- and middle-income countries estimated by the World Bank at US$167 billion in 2005 (2007, p. 142) rising to US$450 billion in 2017 (World Bank 2017a, p. v), overlooking perhaps whether this really contributes to development. They also point to positive impacts on human capital in the home countries following an increase in opportunities for those remaining. Other possible benefits include technology and knowledge transfer and diaspora links (UNCTAD 2007, p. 141).

The 'realists' question these benefits, especially for the least developed countries where remittances are lowest and where there is no necessary stimulus for those who stay behind to fill the gaps left by the emigrants. From the realists' point of view, the data are not encouraging. Skilled out-migration from developing countries increased from 12 to 20 million in the 1990s and as many as 30 to 50 percent of people trained in science and technology in developing countries live in developed countries (UNCTAD 2007, pp. 144, 145). It is estimated that by 2004, one million tertiary educated people from the least developed countries had emigrated. Some 15 percent of all those educated to an advanced level in these countries were living in rich countries (2007, p. 148).

Whether remittances spur economic growth in the countries that receive them is in dispute. 'Although many observers hope or expect remittances to promote economic growth, research in this area consistently fails to find a strong connection between the two . . . there is no example of a country

for which remittances have clearly driven its economic development'
(Fullencamp 2015). Fullencamp gives several reasons for these findings.
Remittances are often used to buy land or existing homes which drive up
their prices but do not contribute to GDP. People who receive remittances
have less incentive to work. Remittances can create a danger of dependence. None of this means that remittances do not help large numbers of
people to meet basic needs, but it raises the question of whether the recipi-
ent countries would be further ahead if their skilled emigrants had stayed
home. 'Excessive brain drain can hurt developing countries and LDCs [less
developed countries] in particular' (UNCTAD 2007, p. 153).

In normal times, the relocation of individuals and families is regulated
by the immigration policies and practices of nation states acting alone or
together as in the European Union. Rich countries such as Canada attract
immigrants seeking better lives but not all are admitted. They have to meet
certain criteria. As we have seen, Canada targets immigrants considered
economically useful to the Canadian economy. We have already seen
that some of the countries from which immigrants to Canada come may
suffer from their departure, so while immigration from these countries
may increase economic growth in Canada it can have a negative effect in
countries where the case for growth is stronger.

What about the interests of the immigrants themselves? Should these
not be paramount in any consideration of immigration policy? Presumably
anyone who migrates of their own choice believes they will benefit. Why
should Canada or any country for that matter restrict the free movement
of people? Capital is increasingly mobile, its owners seeking to increase
their profits by moving it from one country to another as they see fit.
Barriers to prevent the movement of capital have been reduced; shouldn't
the same be true of barriers to migration? This is a major ethical question
for which there is no easy answer. In practical terms, it comes down to a
question of power and self-interest. Rich countries seek to protect their
wealth by selectively limiting immigration and use whatever means they
have to do so. Writing about Europe, but with relevance to Canada, Paul
Demeney (2003) says, 'Pressures of an aging population notwithstanding,
official immigration policy is exclusionary: it aims at reducing the annual
flow, save for special categories of skilled workers'. What could be a
situation of sharply conflicting interests may be less of a problem given
Canada's particular circumstances. In Statistics Canada's low projection,
the Canadian population rate of growth slows steadily and the population
virtually levels off at 40 million by 2050. Immigration remains significant
at just over 200 000 per year, while emigration is at about 73 000 per year.
At this level of immigration Canada could still welcome the 132 500 immigrants per year in the family and refugee/humanitarian categories as in

the Federal government's immigration levels plan for 2018 (Table 12.2). It would still require 67 500 economic immigrants to maintain a stable population. In other words, with the low population projection Canada can continue to fulfill its policy objectives for family unification and refugees and it would still require substantial numbers of economic immigrants. At the same time, a reduction of economic immigrants would help reduce the brain drain from developing countries.

The same logic holds with the medium and high population projections, but the numbers are bigger, and the population is projected to keep growing during 2062/63. In the medium scenario, immigration starts at 260 000 in 2013/14 and reaches 392 000 in 2062/63. In the high scenario, the numbers are 265 000 immigrants in 2013/14, rising to 590 000 in 2062/63. In both these cases, Canadian GDP will have to continue increasing beyond mid-century just to prevent a decline in per capita GDP.

The conventional view is that immigration is needed for economic growth in countries where the natural rate of increase is declining. This logic can be reversed. Immigration makes economic growth essential just to prevent a decline in GDP. Managing without economic growth implies a stable population. This is a goal that Canada can achieve through an immigration policy that still caters to humanitarian interests and, in comparison with current (2017) policy, contributes to prosperity and development where the need is greatest. However, to admit large numbers of environmental refugees without an increase in Canada's GDP would involve a decline in GDP per capita. This is not a prospect that most Canadians would welcome, but it may be one that is hard to avoid, even with economic growth, unless the deteriorating environmental trends are reversed and soon.

## 12.2   ENVIRONMENT

Once we understand economies as open systems dependent on the environment in which they are embedded, we begin to appreciate that environmental policy, defined broadly to include natural resources and environmental protection, is qualitatively different from other policy dimensions. This is not generally understood by governments that regard environmental departments as junior to departments of finance or industry or trade. Nor is it adequately recognized when governments require that resource or environmental protection policies be subjected to conventional benefit–cost analyses before they are implemented. To do so assumes that the prices used to value the benefits and costs, perhaps with some shadow-pricing to fix the most obvious errors, contain all the necessary information required for this purpose. As we saw in Chapter 3, this assumption does not hold for many reasons. One of the most important is that market prices do not capture information about the optimal scale of an economy in relation to the environment. Hence, it makes little sense to use them in analyses, at least without severe qualification, which are intended to inform decisions on the material and energy flows between economy and environment, especially when these flows affect the scale of the economy.[3]

Another consideration that makes environmental policy special is that it is where we confront the fact that humans are only one of millions of species that live on the planet and that, because of the power we wield, we have a moral obligation to consider their interests. Conventional approaches to managing natural resources and agriculture typically regard nature as an object solely for human use and benefit. Environmentalism, which has been a major factor in the development of environmental policy, brings a different perspective, one which also recognizes the existence of subjects other than humans that have interests too. Indicators such as the ecological footprint, the human appropriation of net primary production (HANPP) and the Living Planet Index show that humans are increasingly crowding out other species (see Chapter 6). This bad situation is likely to get a lot worse as and when the population of humans, with a rising material standard of living, increases to nearly 10 billion by 2050. Managing without growth in rich countries may not be an adequate response to this bleak outlook for other species but it would help.

According to Daly and Farley (2011) there are decisions to be made about the scale of an economy, the distribution of wealth and income, and efficiency with which resources are used. They argue that decisions on scale should come first, then distribution and finally efficiency. Once scale has been decided and limits on throughput are in place, market prices will adjust to reflect the prevailing distribution of wealth and income and the relative scarcity of the material and energy inflows and outflows. Following this line of reasoning, let us see what guidance we can get on scale.

### 12.2.1 Daly's Three Principles of Environmental Management

Daly (1990) has proposed three principles on which to base limits on the throughput of an economy so that it does not become too large in relation to the environment:

1. renewable resources should be harvested at rates that do not exceed regeneration rates;

2.  the rate of depletion of non-renewable resources should not exceed the rate of creation of renewable substitutes; and
3.  waste emissions rates should not exceed the natural assimilative capacities of ecosystems into which they are emitted.

We would add a fourth principle: that the destruction of habitat on land and water should be reversed to the point that the rate of loss of species is reduced to the pre-industrial level. Daly also recommends that 'man-made' capital should be kept intact and that we should emphasize technologies that increase resource productivity, measured as the amount of value extracted per unit of resource, rather than technologies for increasing the resource throughput itself (1990, pp. 4, 5).

Daly and Farley argue that throughput can be controlled most effectively by limiting depletion directly and relying on the law of conservation of matter–energy to yield beneficial outcomes for pollution (Daly and Farley 2011, p. 420). If less goes into the economy, less will come out. However, the environmental and health impacts of materials and energy disposed of into the environment depend on the quality, quantity, timing and location of the discharges, and these aspects cannot be addressed simply by focusing on the input flows. Controls at both ends of throughput are required to prevent unwanted environmental impacts.

Another problem with placing so much emphasis on throughput is that it overlooks the enormous differences among the environmental impacts of the different constituents of throughput. For example, variations in the toxicity, persistence and bioaccumulative potential of different chemicals can vary by many orders of magnitude. Likewise, the extraction of the same quantity of a particular resource can have vastly different environmental consequences depending on the location and technology employed. Aggregating all material flows into a single measure of throughput, presumably by a common measure such as mass, conceals a great deal of crucial information needed for making policy (Weisz et al. 2006).

In this book we have used GDP as the measure of the size of an economy and have understood growth to mean growth in GDP. We investigated the relationship between growth and throughput in Chapter 5 and found that despite increases in efficiency, an absolute decoupling of GDP and throughput has yet to manifest itself. By focusing on growth in GDP rather than growth in throughput, we are not rejecting Daly and Farley's view that limits should be placed on throughput. Rather we are working with the conventional measure of economic growth, growth in real GDP, to see if we can achieve important welfare-enhancing objectives without relying on growth in its most widely understood sense. This is important for defusing the argument that growth in GDP is *necessary* for the achievement of these objectives and therefore should take priority. If throughput becomes limited as a matter of policy, GDP might still grow, though not as fast as it would without such limits. If we can manage without growth in GDP or GDP per capita, then it will be that much easier with some growth, providing appropriate limits on throughput are met. In any case, lacking comprehensive data on throughput we are obliged to conduct quantitative analysis about economic growth using GDP, at least until better data become available.

### 12.2.2    Policies for Limiting Throughput: Limits, Taxes and Trading

It would be quite misleading to suggest that Canada has adopted the Daly and Farley position that throughput should be controlled by setting and enforcing quantitative limits. Yet there is a modest but discernible trend towards quantitative limits in Canadian resource and environmental policy that could provide the foundation for a more comprehensive approach. Examples include Canada's compliance with the Montreal Protocol limiting the production and release of ozone-depleting substances, fishing bans and quotas to protect what is left of the East and West coast fisheries, the provisions of the Canada–US Agreement on the Great Lakes requiring the virtual elimination of toxic substances, the prohibition of bulk water exports from the Great Lakes, the establishment of a green belt around the Greater Toronto Area to contain urban sprawl, and the establishment of a comprehensive system of national and provincial parks. These are the kinds of limits on throughput and land use that are required to protect the environment from excessive use.

Far too many environmental regulations, standards and guidelines are written in terms of emission rates expressed as kilograms per unit of output or as concentrations in mg/liter or some similar measure. Regulations, standards and guidelines written this way do not prevent total emissions from rising even if the letter of the law is followed. Whenever a regulated activity increases, say because of increased production, emissions are allowed to rise. Or if a new source is established in a jurisdiction with these kinds of regulations, total emissions from all sources will rise unless there is a mechanism to reduce emissions from existing sources.[4]

Perhaps the most egregious example of this type of approach to protecting the environment is intensity targets for greenhouse gases. Instead of limiting total emissions of greenhouse gases, intensity targets expressed as $CO_2$ equivalents per unit of production allow emissions to rise with production. This is their purpose, so that economic growth is not constrained by a need to respect biophysical limits. Unless intensity declines faster than production grows, total emissions are bound to increase. Such an increase can be prevented if intensity targets are combined with limits on total emissions, but then the intensity targets become redundant. Clearly intensity targets are not intended to limit total emissions.

Canada has been slow to use prices to limit emissions of pollutants, either by imposing emissions charges or setting up tradable emission systems, even though John Dales, one of the originators of emissions trading, was Canadian (Dales 1968). The provincial and federal governments have preferred to use more traditional command and control measures and, especially in the few years following the mid-1990s, have sought compliance on a voluntary basis. Although Canada still enjoys a good reputation for environmental management, the record is increasingly being called into question (Boyd 2003; Wendling et al. 2018).

The desire to limit total emissions of greenhouse gases and some other common air pollutants has generated a great deal of interest in emissions trading.[5] Of the various systems, cap and trade offers the most direct control on total emissions of one or more pollutants. Under this kind of emissions trading system the regulatory agency sets a limit or cap on total emissions from the sources included in the trading area. Allowances for specific quantities of emissions are distributed to the sources (usually companies but others such as municipalities can be included) so that total emissions from all sources in the trading system do not exceed the cap. The allowances may be given away free or increasingly commonly some or all of them are sold at auction. Sources can trade these allowances if they wish. Those that can reduce their emissions relatively cheaply are able to sell their excess allowances to other sources for which emissions reduction is more costly. Trades can be direct, source to source, or indirect through brokers such as on the Chicago Climate Exchange. In all cases, total emissions are still limited by the cap but emissions reduction takes place where it is least costly.

This is the sort of emissions trading scheme that was introduced in the USA to control emissions of acid rain precursors in the Clean Air Act of 1990 and in the European Union for greenhouse gases in 2005. There is no national cap and trade system in Canada. Some forms of emissions trading exist at the provincial level. Since the mid-1990s, Ontario has had an emissions trading system which sets caps for emissions of nitrogen oxides and sulfur dioxide for several industrial sectors. It allows sources not included under the caps to create emission reduction credits by reducing their own emissions and selling the credits to the sources covered by the caps (Ontario Ministry of the Environment 2006). In 2014 Quebec joined California in a cap and trade system for GHG emissions and Ontario joined in 2017 (WCI Inc. 2017), but has since decided to leave.

Most environmental regulations do not allow trading. They may require some sort of performance standard and some even specify particular technologies that must be employed. This is referred to as command and control. The same is true for resource use as well where management rules are governed by regulation. Under emissions trading and its resource equivalent in which, for example, fish catch allowances or water use allowances can be traded, government sets the quantity and the market determines the price. An alternative approach which also brings market incentives to bear on emissions reduction and resource conservation is for governments to impose a price or tax directly on unwanted emissions or resource use and to let the various actors determine the quantities they emit or resources they extract. If total emissions or extraction rates are too high, the price can be raised until those responsible find it in their financial interest to avoid the charge by reducing emissions or reducing extraction.

LowGrow SFC includes a price on greenhouse gas emissions from electricity generation. We saw in Chapter 11 that by setting it at a rate rising to $300 per tonne of $CO_2$ equivalent, Canadian GHG emissions would be reduced considerably. Revenues can be offset in LowGrow SFC by reductions in the rates of personal income and corporations' profits tax so that total government revenues are unaffected by the tax on greenhouse gases.[6] This revenue neutrality is often included as a feature of a greenhouse gas tax by its proponents. Another option is to use some of the revenues to support the development of new technologies and to promote other beneficial changes. Rigidly earmarking revenues from an emissions tax to pay for specific programs is not a good idea since the revenues from the tax may be too much or too little for the designated purpose. If the former, funds will be wasted, and if the latter, worthwhile programs will be underfunded. For this reason, it is generally better for governments to determine their revenue and expenditure priorities separately.

Another risk is that an emissions tax may come to be seen as an important revenue source and its primary function as an environmental policy instrument could be compromised. The tax rate that meets a revenue target may be quite different from the rate required to reduce emissions to a desired level. If revenue becomes the main objective of an emissions tax, it may be set at a low rate for fear of discouraging emissions and losing revenues. This is one of the reasons why revenue neutrality is an attractive feature of emissions taxes when the main purpose is to meet an environmental policy objective. In 2008 the government of British Columbia introduced a revenue-neutral carbon tax.

An emissions trading system that yielded a similar price for greenhouse gas emissions from the same sources would have much the same effect as an emissions tax except for one very important difference. If allowances are given away based on historical emission levels, which is not uncommon, those who receive them can then make trades if they wish. No revenues accrue to government through this process. Government only receives revenues if allowances are auctioned. If they are all auctioned a greenhouse gas trading system and an emissions tax would be symmetric. With emissions trading the total quantity of emissions is set by government and a price is established by auction and by trading. In the other, the government sets the price and the quantity of emissions depends on how the sources respond.

It is easy to see why emissions trading has found more favor than emissions taxes especially among corporations responsible for large quantities of greenhouse gas emissions. As long as they receive the bulk of their allowances free, they are financially better off than if they had to pay a charge or a tax on all their emissions. But is this better public policy? It has the advantage that the total emissions from all sources covered by the trading scheme is known and controlled directly though the cap is subject to political pressures, so this environmental advantage may be more ephemeral than it seems. [7] The cap can also be compromised when 'offsets' created by others and which can be hard to verify are sold to the sources in lieu of their own emissions reduction. Over time total allowances can be ratcheted down although there will be resistance from sources if the price of allowances becomes too high. With a tax, the price of emissions is known but the total quantity of emissions, which depends on responses to the tax by the sources, can only be estimated. Should it fall short of the target reduction the rate of the carbon tax will have to be raised and there will be resistance to that as well.

One practical point in favor of an emissions tax rather than emissions trading is that governments have plenty of experience with tax systems. They have tax collection agencies in place and well-established policing and enforcement procedures with which the courts are familiar. Emissions trading requires the establishment of new institutional structures for making a market where none previously existed. This is proving more complicated than anticipated by many proponents of emissions trading. Issues that must all be resolved in the design of a cap and trade scheme include whether unused allowances can be banked for future use, whether they can be sold if a company goes bankrupt, and whether those not covered by a cap can create and sell offsets to those who are and what would count as an offset. In his review of eight emissions trading programs Sovacool (2011) finds many examples of compromises in program design, high transaction costs, significant price volatility, and environmental degradation. The proliferation of emissions trading lawyers and brokers is a testament to the complexities that have emerged in practice with emissions trading systems.

Another advantage of emission charges or taxes is that they can be imposed on more diverse and smaller sources than are usually covered in emissions trading systems, the so-called 'large emitters'. If there are insufficient large emitters for a reasonably competitive market in allowances, the gains from trading will be reduced. This could be a problem for a country like Canada unless it participated in an international trading scheme. An emissions trading scheme can work for greenhouse gases since the environmental impact of a tonne of $CO_2$ equivalent is essentially the same regardless of location. However, for most emissions of concern impacts can differ markedly depending on local demographic and meteorological conditions which make emissions trading less suitable and more complicated. Even with greenhouse gases there are advantages to a 'harmonized price-type' measure that avoids problematic negotiations about baselines and treats early joiners and late joiners the same (Nordhaus 2006).

An emissions tax can be imposed on sources of all types as long as they measure and report their emissions, which they have to do under most regulatory systems anyway. In the case of greenhouse gas emissions from energy use, such as from individual vehicles, an emissions tax can be charged at the pump, whereas emissions trading is clearly infeasible at that level. It has to be implemented upstream, on refiners, for example, making the refineries responsible for the emissions from their product and not just from their own activities, which is not a bad idea, but one that the companies might resist. In the end, what really matters for managing without growth is that quantitative targets on resource inputs, waste outputs and habitat loss be established based on Daly's principles. The decision about the best policy instrument for implementing these limits, while it is important and should be done well, is secondary.

## 12.3   POVERTY AND INEQUALITY

In Chapter 10 we discussed poverty, emphasizing the income dimension but also recognizing that there is more to poverty than just income. Poverty includes interrelated factors such as social exclusion, illiteracy, a lack of power and self-esteem, homelessness and poor health. It is experienced disproportionately by some groups more than others. 'People living with disabilities, single parents, elderly individuals, youth, and racialized communities are more susceptible' to poverty (Canada Without Poverty 2017). Poverty is not an absolute. It depends on time and place and is closely related to inequality in each of its several dimensions.

While poverty is more than a lack of income, a lack of income is certainly a key aspect of poverty and a good place to start. In 2014 the lack of income was a $16 billion problem in Canada (see Chapter 10). This is the sum that would have been required to bring all Canadians with post-tax incomes below the LICO poverty line up to that level: 1.5 percent of all market incomes in that year. With a GDP surpassing $2 trillion in 2018, elimination of this level of income deficiency is within the country's means.

Burstein notes that the terms 'poverty' and 'social exclusion' are increasingly linked. He believes that the shift in terminology 'reflects an ideological shift that sees poverty as largely imposed, a function of institutional arrangements, global forces, and powerlessness' (Burstein 2005, p. 1). This broader conceptualization of poverty comes through in the taxonomy of anti-poverty measures developed by Burstein from a review of policies and policy discussions in Canada and the European Union. Drawing from mainstream policies, fringe policies that are well known but in limited use, and experimental policies only at the demonstration stage, Burstein's taxonomy in Box 12.1 shows the richness of the policies available and required to combat poverty and social exclusion.

According to Burstein the taxonomy in Box 12.1 is incomplete and he gives no indication of the cost of the various measures. However, a multi-billion dollar budget comparable with the LICO poverty gap in 2014, if well spent, would go a long way to eradicating poverty and dramatically reducing social exclusion in Canada. The simulations described in the previous chapter used the tax and transfer system to redistribute up to $20 billion per year with the greatest share going to those in the lowest income categories. This is an approximate way of representing a complex and well-coordinated anti-poverty and social inclusion program that is more than just income redistribution. Yet as Burstein observes, 'No matter what clever new policies are devised, income supports will continue to play a crucial role in alleviating deprivation and poverty. Research shows that transfers produce sizeable reductions in long-term poverty among all five at-risk groups' (2005, p. 12).

Lack of income and income inequality are only part of the story. The distribution of wealth is considerably more unequal than the distribution of income (see Chapter 10). In Canada, property is taxed at the municipal level and estates are taxed upon death. Michalos (1988) makes the case for a progressive annual wealth tax levied on net wealth 'comprehensively defined as what is left over when total debts are subtracted from total assets' (p. 112). He argues that the redistribution of wealth 'should be regarded as a fundamental feature of any national socio-economic development plan' (p. 105). Such a tax would be applied only to the top quintile of families at an average rate of 2 or 3 percent, with higher rates, up to 5 percent, paid by the wealthiest. Evans (2013) makes the useful distinction among taxation on holdings of wealth (for example property tax), taxation on the transfer of wealth (for example inheritance and gift taxes), and taxation on the appreciation of wealth (that is, capital gains tax). He reports that most developed countries have some form of capital gains tax, but

## BOX 12.1  MEASURES TO COMBAT SOCIAL EXCLUSION AND POVERTY

1. Macro-stabilization and framework measures
   - macro-fiscal policies and monetary policy, tax benefits and credits, asset policies, pensions etc.;
   - universal child-care benefits;
   - promoting social cohesion and solidarity for example through citizenship education; and
   - framework legislation establishing rights and freedoms.
2. Protective measures aimed at maintaining a safety net
   - targeted transfers, social assistance, employment insurance, social housing, in-kind support, means-tested income supplements, etc.; and
   - rights-based remedies (to enable claims by individuals and by non-governmental agents acting on their behalf).
3. Measures to promote work incentives and to support labor market entry and participation
   - provision of information and active counseling;
   - education, skills training, literacy and numeracy training, language training, orientation and settlement, information technology training etc.; and
   - work incentives, including work income supplementation, and asset-based policies.
4. Measures aimed at creating/expanding/maintaining economic opportunity
   - job creation, employer job subsidy measures;
   - support for self-employment; and
   - promoting the social economy.
5. Area-based measures targeting local economics and neighborhood quality
   - community social and economic development, community development corporations, neighborhood renewal, rural sustainability, safe communities etc.;
   - local support for culture, sports and recreation; and
   - improvement of social capital.
6. Measures to reform and open up institutions
   - promoting better access to public and private services and programs (including access to health services, educational services, training facilities, financial institutions, and so on); and
   - adaptations focusing on where services are located, transportation, cultural training for staff, availability of translators, outreach, etc.
7. Measures promoting quality of life, well-being and personal development
   - investments in health, including measures to address drug issues, teen pregnancy, and mental health; and
   - investments in quality of housing and education.
8. Measures aimed at enhancing receptivity by the community at large
   - anti-discrimination measures, etc.; and
   - promoting solidarity, including citizenship education, cross-cultural sensitivity, education, etc.

*Source:* Based on Burstein (2005), pp. 13, 14.

taxes on wealth holdings have declined in recent decades remaining only in France, Norway and Switzerland. Wealth transfer taxes are more common though even these are in decline. It is understandable that wealthy people do not want their wealth to be subject to taxation. But since wealth confers great advantages on those who have it, often at the expense of those who do not, its distribution should not be permitted to become as extremely unequal as it has. Inherited wealth in particular is the least justifiable since the beneficiaries did nothing to create it.

In Chapter 10 we commented on the close relationship between low incomes and unemployment. Others have observed the same relationship (Picot and Myles 2004). Single mothers in particular face poverty because of low employment rates and low working hours rather than low hourly earnings (Burstein 2005, p. 7). This fact highlights a dilemma for managing without growth because other things equal, an expansion of employment adds to total output. There is a way to expand employment without increasing output and that is to reduce the average time that each person spends at work and to spread the same amount of work, income and leisure across a larger number of people. This can be through a shorter work week, more vacation time, time off for parental duties, more part-time work, fewer years spent in the work force or a combination of all these. We turn to how this might be achieved in the next section.

## 12.4   REDUCED WORK TIME

Industrialized countries have experienced a dramatic reduction in the length of the working week: a reduction of 41 percent between 1870 and 2000 with reductions weighted by population and 47 percent based on the unweighted average of decreases in each of 15 countries (Ueberfeldt 2006). Ueberfeldt found that the decline in average hours was driven mainly by a decline in the length of the working week (2006, p. 2). In a similar analysis of the data from 1870 to 1992 Bosch observes that in five industrialized countries (USA, Germany, Japan, France and the UK) working time declined between 36 percent and 50 percent, hourly productivity rose between 919 percent and 4352 percent, and GDP increased between 502 percent and 2632 percent (Bosch 2000). During this long stretch of history, the quest for shorter hours has sometimes been of great concern to organized labor. At other times, it has been ignored or resisted. Recently there has been a resurgence of interest in the labor movement in shorter working hours (De Spiegelaere and Piasma 2017). No one would deny that a substantial decline in the average working time of around 3000 hours per year, typical of the 1870s, has been in the interests of the employees (Huberman and Minns 2007, Table 3). It was coupled with a much greater increase in real hourly earnings so that material living standards and leisure have risen together. These have been the fruits of economic growth.

The decline in hours worked slowed down after the mid-1970s in many countries and average hours worked leveled off in the 1990s (Lee 2004), resuming a gentle decline to 2016 (OECD 2017d, p. 209). The average hours worked per person in employment in the OECD declined from 1842 hours in 2000 to 1764 hours in 2016, somewhat above the Canadian values of 1779 hours in 2000 and 1703 hours in 2016. This does not mean that people are content with the hours they work especially when they are unsure from day to day and week to week how many hours they can count on (Gleason and Lambert 2014). Many in part-time work would like to work longer hours; others would like shorter hours. On balance, the latter outweighs the former in industrialized countries especially among those 35 and older. Lee defines excess hours worked as the difference between a person's current working hours and the hours they desire to work. He comments that this subjective measure of excess hours corresponds quite closely to a threshold of 50 hours per week which can be measured more objectively (2004, p. 41). Using hours worked in excess of 50 hours per week (49 in the USA and Japan) as the definition of excess hours, Lee reports the percentage of employees in 18 industrial countries who worked excess hours in 1987 and 2000. There is considerable variation among the countries, ranging from 1.4 percent of employees in the Netherlands to 28.1 percent in Japan who worked excess hours in 2000. In 16 of the 18 countries these percentages increased from 1987 (2004, p. 42).

People in rich countries can continue to strive for economic growth despite the strong evidence that continual long-term economic growth is not an option from which all can benefit. Or we can try a different tack. We can place less emphasis on work, production and consumption, especially those of us who have them in excess, share what we do have with the less advantaged, and get more out of life by having more time to ourselves. One of the ways of doing this is to further reduce the average hours of employment for the bulk of the working population and increase the employment opportunities for the unemployed and underemployed.

The arithmetic of reducing the rate of unemployment by reducing the average hours each employed person works is compelling. To take a simple example, if the rate of unemployment is 10 percent, the same amount of work could be done if the 90 percent of people in work reduced their average hours by a tenth and the unemployed made up the difference by working at the new lower average number of hours and at the average productivity per hour. Hourly pay could remain the same. Achieving such gains in employment in the real world is another matter but in a review of studies of the employment effects of working time reductions Bosch finds that most show a gain of '25–70 per cent of the arithmetically possible effect' (Bosch 2000, p. 180).

European countries have been more proactive than Canada and the USA in reducing working time as an instrument of employment policy. Bosch examined the European experience, and the six conditions he identified as particularly important for the success or failure of this policy are summarized in Box 12.2. He points out that general political conditions must be suitable for a policy of reducing working time to reduce unemployment. There must be acceptance from employees, trade unions and employers, and support of the state.

---

### BOX 12.2   POLICIES FOR REDUCING THE WORKING WEEK

1. Wage compensation – 'if working time reductions and pay increases are negotiated as a total package, then the compensatory increase for the working time reduction can be offset by lower pay rises' (Bosch 2000, p. 182). This could become more difficult with no or low growth.
2. Changes in work organization – 'larger reductions in working time generally have to be accompanied by changes in work organization' (ibid. p. 183), otherwise firms will rely on overtime and the employment effects will not materialize.
3. Shortages of skilled labor – 'an active training policy is an indispensable supplement to working-time policy' (ibid. p. 183) to ensure that there are people with the necessary skills to pick up the slack when skilled workers reduce their hours.
4. Fixed cost per employee – such as benefits paid on a per-employee basis rather than an hourly basis, are an obstacle to reducing working hours because it is costly to employers. Canada shares with most Western European countries the practice of financing statutory social programs through contributions that are usually a proportion of earnings or through taxation, minimizing this fixed cost problem.
5. The evolution of earnings – 'the decreasing rate of real wage rises in most industrialized countries has reduced the scope for implementing cuts in working time and wage increases simultaneously' (ibid. p. 184). This would be a serious obstacle unless there is widespread support for seeking prosperity without growth though it can be mitigated by a more equal distribution of income: 'one fundamental precondition for the working time policy pursued in Germany and Denmark, for example, was a stable and relatively equal earning distribution' (ibid. p. 185).
6. The standardization of working hours – any reduction in standard working hours must strongly influence actual hours worked. If it merely generates more overtime for those already with jobs it will fail to increase employment. Work reorganization will be required to allow more flexibility in hours worked.

*Source:*   Summarized from Bosch (2000).

Looking at working time policy in the future, Bosch concludes that 'shorter working hours are an indicator of prosperity' (2000, p. 192). They have been in the past, though more recently we have seen the emergence of a sector of the labor force that is 'overemployed'. This refers to people working long hours and 'failing to achieve a desired balance in their lives between paid work, family life, personal, and civic time' (Figart and Golden 2000). The overemployed are usually men with higher levels of education holding management positions. Simultaneously there are people who are underemployed and poorly paid, who are more often than not women. These circumstances contribute to and accentuate the rising income inequality that was documented in Chapter 10.

Layard in his work on economics and happiness concludes 'that people over-estimate the extra happiness they will get from extra possessions' because of 'habituation'. 'The required correction is towards lower work effort and thus lower consumption' (Layard 2006). This means that a shorter working week would not only contribute to reducing unemployment but could also increase the general level of happiness for employees who find themselves better off working fewer hours, for less income and consuming at lower levels.

Recognizing the contribution that reduced and more flexible working hours can make to people's well-being and to an environmentally sustainable economy, Pullinger (2014) recommends 'a green life course approach to the design of work time reduction policies' (p. 16). The life course approach 'focuses particularly on the individual rights to flexibly reduce working time at different periods of the working life, often with associated reductions in income' (p. 12). Based on his review of how this approach is used in Belgium and the Netherlands, Pullinger suggests that it could be extended to meet environmental objectives as well as objectives relating to personal freedom which lies at the heart of the life course approach to work time reduction. Pullinger's views are supported by the empirical analysis of data for 29 high-income OECD countries for 1970–2007 by Knight et al. (2013). They conclude that 'working time is significantly associated with environmental pressures and thus may be an attractive target for policies promoting environmental sustainability' (p. 698).

## 12.5   INVESTMENT

The issues we have considered so far in this chapter – population and immigration, environment, poverty and inequality and reduced working time – are well-practiced areas of public policy. Most if not all countries have measures in place to protect the environment, screen and limit immigrants, alleviate poverty and regulate hours worked. Managing without growth will likely require more determined efforts in all these areas but the general direction is not that different from where we are already heading. The same cannot be said of the next set of issues: investment, productivity, technology, trade and consumption. In these areas managing without growth requires something quite new.

Investment, productivity and technology are highly interrelated. Investment in new infrastructure, buildings and equipment is usually intended to raise productivity, improve service and, in the private sector, increase profits. Even when the main purpose of the investment is to replace old and worn out capital, the opportunity will usually be taken to improve productivity by installing new, more efficient technology. We are used to thinking of investment, productivity and technology in the context of economic growth. They are major contributors to it. What would be their role in an economy not geared to growth? To manage without growth, the pattern of investment should reflect and support the changing direction in how people lead their lives: more leisure and recreation, more time with family, friends and community, more public goods, reduced pressure on the environment, and fewer private, status goods.

In the simulation of the GHG emissions reduction scenario and to a much greater extent in the sustainable prosperity growth scenarios in Chapter 11, unproductive green investment displaced productive conventional brown investment. This reduced the build-up of productive capital and dampened the increase in labor productivity which slowed the rate of economic growth. At the same time, the SPI (sustainable prosperity index) fell precipitously in the business-as-usual scenario, declined somewhat in the GHG reduction scenario, and rose significantly in the sustainable prosperity scenario.

The policies that would bring about these gains include a price on carbon, which we have already discussed. Many jurisdictions have a mechanism in place for pricing carbon but the prevailing prices fall far short of what the model simulations suggest will be needed for an 80 percent or more reduction in GHG emissions by mid-century: something in the region of $250–$300 per tonne. The carbon price in LowGrow SFC is only applied to GHG emissions from the electricity sector because of data availability. In practice, a carbon price is and should be applied more broadly, though for various reasons some exceptions should be expected. A broader application of a carbon price would help bring about the GHG emission reductions from other sources that are included in the simulations.

If strict limits on throughput and land use conversion are imposed by a combination of quantitative restrictions, tax and cap and trade measures as discussed under environment policy, there will be an impact on investment through an effect on prices. Investments in assets that use large amounts of natural resources or contribute large quantities of emissions to the environment will become unattractive. Investments in assets that conserve throughput will become more attractive.

The tax system can be used to supplement the limits on throughput if further action to reduce and redirect net investment is required. Three taxes that have been used in Canada and that have been criticized for discouraging investment could be used deliberately for this purpose: the corporate income tax, the capital gains tax and the capital tax. The first two of these are well known. The capital tax may be less familiar. It is a tax assessed on corporations based on the amount of capital they employ, and until 2006, when it was abolished, it was levied by the Federal Government. Using a two sector model of endogenous economic growth, Devereux and Love (1994) show that a capital tax discourages investment in produced assets and encourages investment in human capital. In a world committed to economic growth this can be a disadvantage, which is why capital taxes were phased out in Canada (Deloitte 2006, p. 2). When managing without growth we may find it useful to employ a capital tax precisely because it favors investment in people over capital.

The same may be said of taxes on capital gains and on corporate profits in so far as they discourage new investment. The tax system will have to be configured so that where investment takes place, say in the energy and transportation sectors, beneficial and less damaging technologies are preferred. There should be higher taxes on investments that increase throughput to reinforce taxes on throughput itself if they are insufficient to adequately constrain the material and energy used in the economy.

In an economy managing without growth, maintenance of the capital stock is just as important as in a growth-based economy, possibly more so. Seeking growth, public and private sector organizations can be tempted to postpone maintenance of the capital stock. The problem of deferred maintenance arises when non-essential repairs are not carried out and produced assets are allowed to deteriorate. It is a short-term cost saving measure but it can increase risks to the public and to workers. If having been built to last in the first place, we gave priority to the maintenance and repair of existing assets through preferential tax treatment of these expenditures, we would reduce the problem of deferred maintenance. We would also benefit more from improvements in throughput efficiency during repair and replacement if we designed the tax system to favor them.

The defining characteristic of the sustainable prosperity scenario in Chapter 11 is the diversion of a substantial proportion of the depreciation of brown capital to investment in green capital. To the extent that the investment in green capital is productive (that is, profitable if undertaken by the private sector and, if by the public sector meets the usual public investment criteria) then the diversion of investment from brown to green presents no significant policy issues. A combination of information campaigns, minor tax breaks and, in the public sector, policy directives, should be sufficient.

To promote green investment, several countries, including Canada, have introduced 'green' bonds. 'Green bonds are fixed-income financial instruments for raising capital to fund green projects, assets, or business activities with an environmental benefit' (Balducci and De Halleux 2016, p.3). In 2016 green bonds worth nearly US$42 billion were available on the market globally (Balducci and De Halleux 2016, p.2), yielding returns of 2–3 percent annually. Of this total, Canada accounted for CAN$2.9 billion (Heaps and Rubin 2016, p.1). In addition to green bonds there are 'climate-aligned' bonds which 'support projects that are aligned with climate mitigation or adaptation objectives, but are not necessarily labelled as such by the issuer' (Climate Bonds Initiative 2016). The universe of climate-aligned bonds was about five times the size of total green bonds in 2016. In Canada, the bulk of climate-aligned bonds were issued to finance hydroelectric projects, with transportation projects (mostly rail freight) making up most of the rest (Climate Bonds Initiative 2016).

Green bonds and climate-aligned bonds are useful primarily for financing productive green investments since they differ very little from conventional bonds. They appeal to investors seeking normal returns while supporting environmental objectives and they also enhance the reputation of the issuer (Climate Bonds Initiative 2016). Non-productive green investment is a different matter. By its nature, it does not generate financial returns that match market returns and may yield no financial returns at all. Investments that produce only environmental benefits (see Table 11.1 for examples) will require a greater reliance on public policy to oblige the private sector to undertake them – such as mandating pollution control equipment, and direct expenditure by government possibly financed by interest-free sovereign money.[8]

## 12.6   PRODUCTIVITY

Historically, investment in new capital has been the most important means for raising productivity of all inputs in production, especially labor. This relationship between the capital:labor ratio and labor productivity is a key feature of LowGrow SFC. Increases in productivity that reduce throughput per unit of output are welcome but only if they do not also increase total throughput as well. Increases in total throughput have often followed increases in efficiency as a result of unit cost reductions so this is something that really does need attention. Constraints on throughput should be supported by gains in productivity, not compromised by them. In the scenarios in Chapter 11, increases in labor productivity raise GDP for any level of inputs of labor and produced assets. These increases in GDP (and associated environmental impacts) could be avoided by reducing net investment or by increasing the rate of unemployment, which would not be desirable. Conversely, lower rates of increase in productivity can be conducive to more employment since with lower productivity more labor is required for any level of GDP.

Increases in the productivity of capital and labor do not have to be realized only as increases in output. They can instead allow people to work shorter hours and have more time to themselves. This has been the experience of industrialized countries at least as far back as 1870, though, as we have noted, the process slowed in many countries in recent years. When managing without growth, we would take most if not all of the gains in productivity as increased leisure to reduce the rate of unemployment and the burden on the environment.

Given all the reasons for weaning ourselves off the economic growth treadmill, we have to take an approach to productivity that economizes on the most significant among our scarce resources: the material, energy and services from the environment. Limits on throughput will help stimulate price changes throughout the economy that will favor reduced flows per unit of GDP. Another policy that would contribute to a redirection of productivity would be to educate and train more people to better appreciate the environmental consequences of all we do. This should include engineers, industrial designers, architects and planners whose decisions can be most effective in redirecting productivity in this way. And it should include economists. It should also include those engaged in more fundamental scientific work. Green chemistry (Anastas and Warner 1998) and biomimicry (Benyus 1997) are two examples of how the study and practice of science can contribute to the redirection of productivity so that it helps reduce the burden that our economy places on the environment.

## 12.7  TECHNOLOGY

In contemporary society, there is a tendency to equate increases in productivity with the adoption of new technology. The general idea is that new technologies allow us to produce more and different outputs, with fewer and different inputs. The different outputs may not be better than the old ones and the inputs may be more environmentally damaging, so we should be wary of claims that new technologies raise productivity. They may do so but only in terms of priced inputs and outputs, however misinforming the prices happen to be (see Chapter 3). If their external effects are large, unanticipated and unregulated, new technologies may not be better at achieving the goals that people really value.

If we follow Daly's advice and place stricter limits on throughput this will have a salutary effect on technology and productivity, but it may not be enough. We should look again at using 'technology assessment' in a more comprehensive manner to anticipate and prevent problems generated by new technologies. In 1972 the US Congress passed the Technology Assessment Act and created the Office of Technology Assessment (OTA) with a mandate to provide 'neutral, competent assessments about the probable beneficial and harmful effects of new technologies' (Bimber 1996). The OTA undertook 'in-depth studies of policy problems, which it would publish in comprehensive reports. These studies would provide expert judgement and "assessment" of questions posed by [Congressional] committees' (1996, p. 29).

The specific functions of the OTA under the law were to:

1. identify existing or probable impacts of technology or technological programs;
2. where possible, ascertain cause-and-effect relationships;
3. identify alternative technological methods for implementing specific programs;
4. identify alternative programs for achieving requisite goals; make estimates and comparisons of the impacts of alternative methods and programs;
5. present findings of completed analyses to the appropriate legislative authorities;
6. identify areas where additional research or data collection is required to provide adequate support for the assessments and estimates described in paragraph (1) through (5) of this subsection; and
7. undertake such additional associated activities as the appropriate authorities . . . may direct. (Vig and Paschen 2000)

In following its mandate, no one specific methodology was used and the OTA examined a wide array of subjects (US Congress, Office of Technology Assessment 1996). The Office influenced policy-making in two ways: rhetorically and analytically. Although OTA reports were often used to justify prior positions and to convince others, until it was closed in 1995 the OTA did contribute to rational debate about technology (Bimber 1996, p. 35).

Some European countries and the European Parliament have also employed formal procedures for technology assessment, modeled in part after the OTA (Vig and Paschen 2000, p. 5). In most cases, technology assessment has been designed to assist parliament. Two countries, the

Netherlands and Denmark, are an exception. There technology assessment is used to 'encourage public debate on the interaction between technology, people and society . . . Stimulating public debate and supporting political opinion forming' (Petermann 2000).

There is no central agency like the OTA in Canada although many government departments do their own technology assessments in-house. Of particular note is the Canadian Infrastructure Technology Assessment Centre (CITAC) under the National Research Council and the Canadian Agency for Drugs and Technologies in Health, which is accountable to Canada's Conference of Deputy Ministers of Health through a 13-member Board of Directors. Canada and the provinces also have extensive experience with environmental assessment, which has some of the characteristics of technology assessment.

We can draw on all this experience with technology assessment to design a system to help ensure that before new technologies are introduced or become widespread, they are scrutinized to assess their intended consequences and to anticipate and prevent unwanted effects as well. Obviously, it is impossible to anticipate all these consequences, good or bad, for any new technology. Yet in the absence of such a system, we will continue to be the victims as well as the beneficiaries of technological change that is driven primarily by the desire for profit and growth without paying adequate attention to the adverse personal, community, societal and environmental ramifications except in hindsight.

## 12.8   INTERNATIONAL TRADE

The gains from international trade, in particular from free trade, are an issue on which most economists seem to agree. At the same time, there is considerable opposition to free trade among large segments of the public. Coughlin (2002) summarizes the major theoretical findings on which the economic case for free trade has been built and contrasts their positive implications with the large negative components of US public opinion. He first explains Ricardo's principle of comparative advantage in which gains from international trade come from the specialization of each trading country in the activities at which it is comparatively, not necessarily absolutely, best (defined in terms of output per unit of a single scarce input). Then he describes the Heckscher–Ohlin theory, which explains that when countries use multiple inputs such as capital and labor, mutual gains from international trade arise when countries specialize in producing and exporting commodities that utilize the scarce resource which they have in relative abundance.

Coughlin fails to recognize that these foundational analyses on which economists base support for free trade assume that the scarce resources in each country are immobile across international borders. This is an argument made by Daly that has not been adequately met by mainstream economists (see the exchange of views by Daly (1993) and Bhagwati (1993) in *Scientific American*). In a world of increasingly mobile capital and to a lesser extent labor, the assumption that each trading country has a fixed quantity of capital and labor is not a sound basis on which to analyze the gains from trade. We should at least include the environmental impacts of transporting vast quantities of raw materials, semi-finished goods and finished products around the world. Also, we should be more sensitive to the concerns expressed by opponents of free trade, recounted by Coughlin: losses in employment especially among low skilled, low-income employees; possible exploitation of poor workers in developing countries; and harm to the environment (Coughlin 2002, pp. 12, 13). Nor should the charge be dismissed lightly that provisions in international trade agreements trump the will of the electorate (Bronckers 1999; Shaffer and Brenner 2004).

We live at a time when trade barriers have been systematically reduced globally through the World Trade Organization and regionally in the case of Canada, through the North American Free Trade Agreement. These institutional arrangements have been designed to promote increased international trade and, though it is sometimes less obvious, to reduce barriers to capital mobility. A country that moves away from the growth agenda will have to look again at these treaties. Export-led growth is something that all countries seem to want but globally net exports must be zero. It is impossible for one country to run a trade surplus without at least one other running a deficit. Countries that stand to gain the most from increasing exports should be allowed to do so and countries such as Canada should moderate their efforts to export more than they import. Changes in this direction might very well require a renegotiation of trade arrangements especially if the main objective shifts away from economic growth to sustainable prosperity.

## 12.9   CONSUMPTION

In Chapter 9 we discussed the literature which is challenging the widely held belief that higher incomes and the greater levels of consumption they permit make people happier. We saw that people can spend increasing amounts of money seeking status in competition with others who have similar intentions. The result is that everyone consumes more but no one is better off. They may even be worse off because the effort to earn more money and the increased time spent shopping and consuming comes at the expense of using that time in other ways. And yet we do it. Ours is a high consumption society, one in which we are exposed to hundreds, if not thousands of messages each day imploring us to consume. Now, information gleaned from our online activity is used to target ads at us to induce us to spend, and spending is becoming increasingly easier through home delivery services such as Amazon.

In a society seeking to manage without growth consumption would take on a different character. We would buy fewer private, positional goods and buy more goods that are truly useful. We would consume more services requiring less throughput and, on average, we would reduce our consumption expenditures. We might also ourselves produce more of what we consume. Collective consumption of public goods might increase, which, being non-rival, bring benefits to many at the same time. Advertising would provide information rather than encourage a 'lifestyle' geared to ever-increasing consumption. It would also be less intrusive. Ironically companies that thrive on the production and sale of goods and services that are exclusionary (that is, if you don't pay you don't get), continually seek advertising modes and opportunities from which people find it difficult or impossible to exclude themselves. It can even erode democracy (Couldry and Turow 2014). Subjecting people to advertising, whether or not they want it or like it, may be good for economic growth but it does not promote well-being.

Consumption is one area where people can take action as individuals to effect change in the economy and society. We have seen this in boycotts of South African goods, which helped bring down apartheid, and in campaigns against companies criticized for their environmental or employment practices. More positively, purchases of fair trade coffee and organically and locally grown food have helped stimulate the production of these products. Changes in our personal behavior are worthwhile and we can make them without having to secure the agreement of others. Changed behavior becomes much more powerful, however, if we act as a group, and the tax system can help. One possibility is the introduction of differential taxes on goods and services that favor those that are more durable, more useful and less harmful to the environment and health. We could also include a tax 'targeted on particular status goods' to deal with status good externalities (Brekke and Howarth 2002, p. 107). Layard makes a similar proposal, noting that people's happiness depends on their relative income as much if not more than their absolute income. He proposes a tax on income to account for 'the external disbenefit which comes from the rise in average income, which adversely affects the happiness of all . . . people' (Layard 2006, p. C27).

As with many of the policies discussed in this chapter, policy changes of this sort will not be driven solely from the top. They must be wanted and demanded by the public because they see a better future for themselves, their children and the children of others, if we turn away from the pursuit of unconstrained economic growth. Even this may be insufficient to change the trajectory of a modern economy in which power, influence and wealth are concentrated in a few hands, and where, especially in the case of Canada, many of those hands lie outside national borders.

## 12.10 CONCLUSION

Managing without growth will not appeal to those who believe any or all of the following: economic growth is good for its own sake, economic growth is necessary for achieving other objectives, economic growth is essential for avoiding economic and societal hardship. In this book we have shown that economic growth is an unduly narrow interpretation of the meaning of progress. We have also shown that important economic and social objectives can, in principle, be met in a rich country without relying on economic growth. Furthermore, there is mounting evidence that higher incomes and increased consumption beyond levels far surpassed in rich countries do not increase happiness.

As powerful as these arguments are for rich countries to manage without growth there is one that is even more compelling. The world's economies are encountering biophysical limits that are showing up in many ways, already disastrous for species such as the Pinta Island Tortoise, the Eastern Cougar, the Pyrenean Ibex, the Formosa Clouded Leopard, the Vietnamese Rhinoceros, the Christmas Island Pipistrelle, the Chinese Paddlefish, the Alaotra Grebe, the Long Jaw Tristramella, the Yangtze River Dolphin, the Black-Faced Honeycreeper, the Golden Toad, the Western Black Rhinoceros, and the Heredia Robber Frog, all believed to have become extinct between 2000 and 2015 (Hinckley 2015). The Sixth Extinction website which maintains a database on extinct species and sub-species, lists 878 species and 173 subspecies of all kinds that have recently become globally extinct, and the number is rising (Maas 2018). The combination of climate change, habitat destruction and resulting loss of biodiversity is taking a toll that is too much to bear.

In his inquiry into how civilization can be renewed in the face of accumulating global threats, Thomas Homer-Dixon wrote: 'in countries that are already very rich, we especially need to figure out if there are feasible alternatives to our hidebound commitment to economic growth, because it is becoming increasingly clear that endless material growth is incompatible with the long-term viability of Earth's environment' (2006, p. 292). To do this we have to transcend the evolutionary advantages that focusing on the local and short term gave our ancestors. This served them well when they lived and died in the same location and any one year was much like the last. But it won't do for us. We have to take the long view and think and act in terms of one planet. We need institutions that are smarter and better informed than each of us alone, yet with few exceptions, the ones we have are not rising to the challenge. Politicians are often too fixated on the next election and powerful corporations strive too hard to maximize short-term profits. This must change. Perhaps it will through the Internet connecting people around the world who are inspired by images from space reminding us that we are all passengers on a precious, isolated planet, circling the sun. We have prodigious amounts of data and computing capacity with which to analyze it, giving us an unprecedented window into threats and possibilities now and in the future. As we saw in Chapter 11, there are indeed feasible alternatives to business as usual. Getting to them will be beyond us unless we change how we think about our economy, society and environment, and undertake some close reflection on what is important to ourselves and others, including other species. We must develop a readiness to rethink and transform much of what we have come to take for granted, especially economic growth. If we can do that then we may indeed find a way forward that is slower by design, not disaster.

## NOTES

1. For much of its annual population statistics, Statistics Canada uses the period 1 July to 30 June.
2. The other variables that affect these projections are fertility, life expectancy and emigration but the differences in their values in the population projections are proportionately much less than for immigration (Statistics Canada 2015a, p. 11).
3. Spash (2007) makes similar points in his trenchant critique of the Stern Review on climate change.
4. Canada does not have an equivalent to the 'non-attainment' designation for regions in the USA that fail to meet the US Environmental Protection Agency's ambient standards. States can require existing sources in these regions to reduce their emissions so that emissions from a new source do not prevent progress towards attainment of the standards.
5. Interest in using economic instruments for environmental protection has been stimulated by the Ecofiscal Commission since it was established in 2014 (Canada's Ecofiscal Commission 2017a).
6. Commonly called a carbon tax, other less contentious terms are sometimes used to designate a price on emissions such as charge or fee.
7. Cancelled in 2018 by the Progressive Conservative Government elected in Ontario in June 2018.
8. www.sovereignmoney.eu.

# References

Adriaanse, A., S. Bringezu, A. Hammond, Y. Moriguchi, E. Rodenburg, D. Rogich and H. Shütz (1997), *Resource Flows: The Material Basis of Industrial Economies*, Washington, DC: World Resources Institute.

Advisory Council on Economic Growth (2016), *The Path to Prosperity: Resetting Canada's Growth Trajectory, Executive Summary*, accessed 2 December 2016 at https://www.budget.gc.ca/aceg-ccce/pdf/summary-resume-eng.pdf.

ALBA-TCP (2010), 'Nature has no price', Declaration of the Ministerial Committee for the Defense of Nature of ALBA-TCP, accessed 17 March 2017 at https://pwccc.wordpress.com/2010/11/05/declaration-alba-tcp-nature-has-no-price/.

Allen, R.C. and G. Rosenbluth (1992), *False Promises: The Failure of Conservative Economics*, Vancouver, BC: New Star Books.

Alley, W.M. and R. Alley (2014), 'The growing problem of stranded used nuclear fuel', *Environmental Science and Technology*, **48**, 2091–6.

Alperovitz, G. (2011), *America beyond Capitalism*, 2nd edn, Takoma Park, MD: Democracy Collaborative Press.

Alternative Fluorocarbons Environmental Acceptability Study (2006), 'Contribution of greenhouse gases to climate forcing relative to CO2', accessed 27 September 2007 at http://www.afeas.org/greenhouse_gases.html.

Altieri, M.A. (2009), 'The ecological impacts of large-scale agrofuel monoculture production systems in the Americas', *Bulletin of Science, Technology & Society*, **29**(3), 236–44.

Anastas, P.T. and J.C. Warner (1998), *Green Chemistry: Theory and Practice*, Oxford, UK and New York, USA: Oxford University Press.

Andersen, M.S. (2006), 'An introductory note on the environmental economics of the circular economy', *Sustainability Science*, **2**(1), 133–40.

Andersen, S.O., D. Brack and J. Depledge (2014), 'A global response to HFCs through fair and effective ozone and climate policies', Institute for Governance and Sustainable Development, accessed November 2016 at http://www.igsd.org/wp-content/uploads/2014/10/HFCsOzoneClimateAndersenBrackDepledge-1.pdf.

Arndt, H.W. (1978), *The Rise and Fall of Economic Growth*, Sydney: Longman Cheshire.

Arrhenius, S. (1896), 'On the influence of carbonic acid in the air upon the temperature of the ground', *Philosophical Magazine and Journal of Science*, **41**(5), 237–76.

Australia Bureau of Statistics (2015), 'Framework for Australian social statistics', accessed 16 November 2016 at http://www.abs.gov.au/ausstats/abs@.nsf/Lookup/4160.0.55.001main+features4Jun+2015.

Ayres, R.U. (1989), 'Industrial metabolism', in J. Ausubel and H. Sladovich (eds), *Technology and Environment*, Washington, DC: National Academy Press.

Ayres, R.U. (2005), 'Resources, scarcity, technology, and growth', in R.D. Simpson, M.A. Toman and R.U. Ayres (eds), *Scarcity and Growth Revisited*, Washington, DC: Resources for the Future, pp. 142–54.

Ayres, R.U. and A.V. Kneese (1969), 'Production, consumption and externalities', *The American Economic Review*, **59**(3), 282–97.

Ayres, R.U., L.W. Ayres and V. Pokrovsky (2005), 'On the efficiency of US electricity usage since 1900', *Energy*, **30**, 1128–54.

Babe, R.E. (2002), 'The "information economy", economics and ecology', in R. Mansell, R. Samarajiva and A. Mahan (eds), *Networking Knowledge for Information Societies: Institutions & Interventions*, Delft: Delft University Press, pp. 254–9.

Baccini, A., W. Walker, M. Farina, R. Houghton, L. Carvalho and D. Sulla-Menashe (2017), 'Tropical forests are a net carbon source based on aboveground measurements of gain and loss', *Science*, 28 September.

Bader, H-P. (2015), 'Saudi ministry says higher oil output driven by demand', CNBC, accessed May 2016 at http://www.cnbc.com/2015/06/09/saudi-ministry-says-higher-oil-output-driven-by-demand.html.

Bak, P. (1996), *How Nature Works: The Science of Self-Organized Criticality*, New York: Copernicus.

Balasubramaniam, A. and N. Voulvoulis (2005), 'The appropriateness of multicriteria analysis in environmental decision-making problems', *Environmental Technology*, **26**, 951–62.

Balch, O. (2013), 'Buen vivir: The social philosophy inspiring movements in South America', accessed December 2016 at https://www.theguardian.com/sustainable-business/blog/buen-vivir-philosophy-south-america-eduardo-gudynas.

Balducci, A. and A. de Halleux (2016), 'Sustainable development bonds', European Impact Investing, Luxembourg, accessed 8 December 2017 at http://www.innpact.com/_dbfiles/lacentrale_files/200/290/ada-sustainable-development-bonds-a4-final.pdf.

Baldwin, J.R., W. Gu, R. Macdonald and B. Yan (2014), 'Productivity:

What is it? How is it measured? What has Canada's performance been over the period 1961 to 2012?', *The Canadian Productivity Review*, **38**(2013), Statistics Canada 15-206-X accessed 1 November 2017 at http://www.statcan.gc.ca/pub/15-206-x/15-206-x2014038-eng.htm.

Balke, N.S., S.P.A. Brown and M.K. Yücel (2008), 'An international perspective on oil price shocks and US economic activity', Federal Reserve Bank of Dallas: Globalization and Monetary Policy Institute Working Paper No. 20.

Ball, R. and K. Chernova (2005), 'Absolute income, relative income, and happiness', *Social Science Research Network* (May), accessed 27 September 2007 at https://papers.ssrn.com/sol3/papers.cfm?abstract_id=724501.

Barder, O. and A. Käppeli (2017), '2016 commitment to development rankings: How all countries can do more to protect global progress', The Center for Global Development, accessed 24 August 2017 at https://www.cgdev.org/publication/commitment-development-index-2016.

Barnett, H.J. and C. Morse (1963), *Scarcity and Growth: The Economics of Natural Resource Availability*, Baltimore, MD: Johns Hopkins University Press.

Barney, G.O. and US Council on Environmental Quality (1980), *The Global 2000 Report to the President*, Washington, DC: Penguin.

Barnosky, A.D., E.A. Hadly, J. Bascompte, E.L. Berlow, J.H. Brown, M. Fortelius and W. Getz (2012), 'Approaching a state shift in Earth's biosphere', *Nature*, **486**, 52–8.

Barton, D.N. (2013), 'Payments for ecosystem services: Costa Rica's recipe', *International Institute for Environment and Development*, accessed 24 September 2016 at http://www.iied.org/payments-for-ecosystem-services-costa-rica-s-recipe.

Bassi, A. (2011), *UNEP GER Modeling Work. Technical Background Material, V.4*, Arlington, VA: Millennium Institute.

Bauermann, H. and H.M. Ross (1910), 'Coal', *Encyclopaedia Britannica*, 11th edn, New York: The Encyclopaedia Britannica Company, pp. 575–93.

Baumol, W.J. (1977), *Economic Theory and Operations Analysis*, 4th edn, Upper Saddle River, NJ: Prentice Hall.

Beach, C.M., A.G. Green and J.G. Reitz (eds) (2003), *Canadian Immigration Policy for the 21st Century*, Kingston: John Deutsch Institute for the Study of Economic Policy.

Becker, E. (1973), *The Denial of Death*, New York: The Free Press.

Beckerman, W. (1971), 'Why we need economic growth', *Lloyds Bank Review*, **102**, 1–15.

Beckerman, W. (1974), *In Defence of Economic Growth*, London: Jonathan Cape.

Beckerman, W. (1995), *Small Is Stupid: Blowing the Whistle on the Greens*, London: Duckworth.

Beckerman, W. (2003), *A Poverty of Reason: Sustainable Development and Economic Growth*, Oakland, CA: Independent Institute.

Benyus, J.M. (1997), *Biomimicry: Innovation Inspired by Nature*, New York: HarperCollins.

Berkes, F. (1993), 'Application of ecological economics to development: The institutional dimension', remarks at the 1992 Canadian International Development Agency conference on 'Ecological Economics: Emergence of a New Development Paradigm', Ottawa, 7–10 November.

Berman, B. (2014), 'The ultimate guide to electric car charging networks', *Plugin Cars.com*, accessed 28 November 2017 at http://www.plugincars. com/ultimate-guide-electric-car-charging-networks-126530.html.

Beveridge, W.H.B. (1945), *Full Employment in a Free Society*, London: Allen & Unwin.

Bhagwati, J. (1993), 'The case for free trade', *Scientific American*, **269**(5), 42–8.

Bimber, B.A. (1996), *The Politics of Expertise in Congress: The Rise and Fall of the Office of Technology Assessment*, Albany, NY: State University of New York Press.

Binswanger, M. (2006), 'Why does income growth fail to make us happier? Searching for the treadmills behind the paradox of happiness', *The Journal of Socio-Economics*, **35**, 366–81.

Binswanger, M. (2009), 'Is there a growth imperative in capitalist economies? A circular flow perspective', *Journal of Post Keynesian Economics*, **31**, 707–27.

Binswanger, M. (2015), 'The growth imperative revisited: A rejoinder to Gilányi and Johnson', *Journal of Post Keynesian Economics*, **37**(4), 648–60.

Blackett, P.M.S., E. Bullard and S.K. Runcorn (eds) (1965), 'A symposium on continental drift, held in 28 October 1965', *Philosophical Transactions of the Royal Society A*, **258**, 323.

Blackwell, R. (2015), 'Review panel okays Lake Huron site as potential nuclear-waste dump', *The Globe and Mail*, accessed 6 November 2016 at http://www.theglobeandmail.com/report-on-business/lake-huron-sh ores-near-ontarios-bruce-plant-to-act-as-nuclear-waste-site/article2430 0773/.

Bleys, B. (2012), 'Beyond GDP: Classifying alternative measures for progress', *Social Indicators Research*, **109**(3), 355–76.

Blomqvist, L., T. Nordhaus and M. Shellenberger (2012), 'The planetary boundaries hypothesis: A review of the evidence', accessed 5 September 2016 at http://thebreakthrough.org/archive/planetary_bound aries_a_mislead.

Bloomberg News (2010), 'China overtakes Japan as world's second-biggest economy', *Bloomberg L.P.*, accessed March 2016 at https://www.bloomberg.com/news/2010-08-16/china-economy-passes-japan-s-in-second-quarter-capping-three-decade-rise.html/.

Boarini, R., A. Johansson and M.M. d'Ecole (2006), 'Alternative measures of well-being', *OECD Social, Employment and Migration Working Papers* No. 33, accessed March 2016 at http://www.oecd.org/social/soc/36165332.pdf.

Booth, D.E. (2004), *Hooked on Growth: Economic Addictions and the Environment*, Lanham, MD: Rowman & Littlefield.

Bosch, G. (2000), 'Working time reductions, employment consequences and lessons from Europe', in L. Golden and D.M. Figart (eds), *Working Time, International Trends, Theory and Policy Perspectives*, London, UK and New York, USA: Routledge, pp. 177–211.

Boulding, K.E. (1966), 'Economics of the coming spaceship earth', in H. Jarrett (ed.), *Environmental Quality in a Growing Economy: Essays from the Sixth RFF Forum*, Baltimore, MD: Johns Hopkins University Press, pp. 3–14.

Bowen, A. (2012), '"Green" growth: What does it mean?', *Environmental Scientist*, December, pp. 6–11.

Bowley, A.L. (1942), *Studies in the National Income, 1924–1938*, Cambridge: Cambridge University Press.

Boyd, D. (2003), *Unnatural Law*, Vancouver, BC: UBC Press.

Boyd, J. (2006), 'Nonmarket benefits of nature: What should be counted in green GDP?', *Ecological Economics*, **61**(4), 716–23.

Boyd, J. and S. Banzhaf (2007), 'What are ecosystem services? The need for standardized environmental accounting units', *Ecological Economics*, **63**(2–3), 616–26.

Brander, J.A. (2007), 'Viewpoint: Sustainability: Malthus revisited?', *Canadian Journal of Economics*, **40**(1), 1–38.

Breitburg, D., L. Levin, A. Oschlies, M. Grégoire, F. Chavez, D. Conley, V. Garçon et al. (2018), 'Declining oxygen in the global ocean and coastal waters', *Science*, **359**(6371), 1–11.

Brekke, K.A. and R.B. Howarth (2002), *Status, Growth and the Environment: Goods as Symbols in Applied Welfare Economics*, Cheltenham, UK and Northampton, MA, USA: Edward Elgar Publishing.

Brekke, K.A., R.B. Howarth and K. Nyborg (1998), *Are there Social Limits to Growth?*, Discussion Paper No. 239, Kongsvinger: Statistics Norway.

Broadbent Institute (2014), *The Wealth Gap. Perceptions and Misconceptions in Canada*, Broadbent Institute, accessed 20 August 2017 at http://www.broadbentinstitute.ca/the_wealth_gap.

Bronckers, M.C.E.J. (1999), 'Better rules for a new millennium: A warning against undemocratic developments in the WTO', *Journal of International Economic Law*, **2**(4), 547–66.

Brown, J., L. Fredericksen, K. Green and S. Hansen (2004), *Environmental Indicators*, 6th edn, Vancouver, BC: Fraser Institute.

Brown, L.B. (2006), 'Exploding US grain demand for automotive fuel threatens world food security and political stability', accessed 2 September 2007 at http://www.earth-policy.org/Updates/2006/Update60.htm.

Brown, P.G. and G. Garver (2009), *Right Relationship: Building a Whole Earth Economy*, San Francisco, CA: Berrett-Koehler Publishers.

Bruckner, M., M. Lafleur and I. Pitterle (2017), 'Frontier issues: The impact of the technological revolution on labour markets and income distribution', Department of Economic & Social Affairs, UN, accessed 24 December 2017 at https://www.un.org/development/desa/dpad/wp-content/uploads/sites/45/publication/2017_Aug_Frontier-Issues-1.pdf.

Bryan, I. (2015), *Are We Running Out? The Sustainability of the World's Resources*, Sustainability Press.

Bryson, B. (2003), *A Short History of Nearly Everything*, 1st edn, New York: Broadway Books.

Buhl, J. (2014), 'Revisiting rebound effects from material resource use: Indications for Germany considering social heterogeneity', *Resources*, **3**(1), 106–22.

Buiatti, M., P. Christou and G. Pastore (2013), 'The application of GMOs in agriculture and in food production for a better nutrition: Two different scientific points of view', *Genes and Nutrition*, **8**, 255–70.

Burns, D.A., J. Aherne, D.A. Gay and C.M.B. Lehmann (2016), 'Acid rain and its environmental effects: Recent scientific advances', *Atmospheric Environment*, **146**, 1–4.

Burstein, M. (2005), 'Combating the social exclusion of at-risk groups', No. PH4-30/2005E-PDF, Policy Research Initiative, accessed 27 September 2007 at policyresearch.gc.ca/doclib/Pri-Burstein-e.pdf.

Butler, C., K.A. Parkhill and N.F. Pidgeon (2011), 'Nuclear power after Japan: The social dimensions', *Environment: Science and Policy for Sustainable Development*, **53**(6), 3–14.

Butler, R. (2016), 'Calculating deforestation figures for the Amazon', accessed 24 September 2016 at http://rainforests.mongabay.com/amazon/deforestation_calculations.html.

Caldecott, B., G. Dericks and J. Mitchell (2015), 'Stranded assets and subcritical coal: The risk to companies and investors', Smith School of Enterprise and the Environment, accessed December 2016 at http://www.smithschool.ox.ac.uk/research-programmes/stranded-assets/SAP%20Report%20Printed%20Subcritical%20Coal%20Final%20mid-res.pdf.

Campbell, C.J. (2005), *Oil Crisis*, Brentwood: Multi-Science Publishing Company.

Canada without Poverty (2017), 'Just the facts', accessed 3 December 2017 at http://www.cwp-csp.ca/poverty/just-the-facts/.

Canada's Ecofiscal Commission (2017a), 'What is ecofiscal?', accessed 2 December 2017 at https://ecofiscal.ca/what-is-ecofiscal/.

Canada's Ecofiscal Commission (2017b), 'Carbon pricing', accessed 13 November 2017 at https://ecofiscal.ca/carbon-pricing/.

Canadian Association of Petroleum Producers (2006), 'Canadian Association of Petroleum Producers', accessed 9 June 2007 at http://www.capp.ca/default.asp?V_DOC_ID=689.

Canadian Council on Social Development (CCSD) (2001), 'Defining and redefining poverty: A CCSD perspective', accessed February 2017 at http://www.ccsd.ca/index.php/policy-initiatives/policy-statements-briefs-submissions/112-defining-and-re-defining-poverty-a-ccsd-perspective.

Canadian Index of Wellbeing (2016), *How Are Canadians Really Doing? The 2016 CIW National Report*, Waterloo, ON: Canadian Index of Wellbeing and University of Waterloo, accessed 30 November 2017 at https://uwaterloo.ca/canadian-index-wellbeing/sites/ca.canadian-index-wellbeing/files/uploads/files/c011676-nationalreport-ciw_final-s_0.pdf.

Canadian Nuclear Safety Commission (2016), 'Low- and intermediate-level radioactive waste', Government of Canada: Canadian Nuclear Safety Commission, accessed 19 September 2016 at http://nuclearsafety.gc.ca/en g/waste/low-and-intermediate-waste/index.cfm#Intermediate-level.

Cantril, H. (1966), *The Pattern of Human Concerns*, New Brunswick, NJ: Rutgers University Press.

Carson, C.S. (1975), 'The history of the United States National Income and Product Accounts: The development of an analytical tool', *Review of Income and Wealth*, **21**(2), 153–81.

Carson, R. (1962), *Silent Spring*, Boston, MA: Houghton Mifflin.

CBC (2016), 'Imperial Oil unmoved by renewable energy', CBC News, 29 April, accessed 24 June 2016 at http://www.cbc.ca/news/business/impe rial-oil-renewable-energy-alberta-1.3559824.

CBC (2017), '21.9% of Canadians are immigrants, the highest share in 85 years: StatsCan', accessed 2 December 2017 at http://www.cbc.ca/news/politics/census-2016-immigration-1.4368970.

CBC News (2015), 'Nuclear waste: 5 things to know about the Lake Huron bunker project', accessed 5 November 2016 at http://www.cbc.ca/news/canada/nuclear-waste-5-things-to-know-about-the-lake-huron-bunker-project-1.3065407.

Center for Global Development (2015), 'Developing countries are responsible for 63 percent of current carbon emissions', accessed 7 October 2016 at http://www.cgdev.org/media/developing-countries-are-responsible-63 -percent-current-carbon-emissions.

Center for Sustainable Systems, University of Michigan (2016), 'US environmental footprint factsheet', Publication No. CSS08-08, accessed 3 August 2017 at http://css.umich.edu/sites/default/files/U.S._Environme ntal_Footprint_Factsheet_CSS08-08_0.pdf.

Chang, J-H. and P. Huynh (2016), 'ASEAN in transformation: The future of jobs at risk of automation', *Bureau for Employers' Activities*, Working Paper No. 9, Geneva: International Labour Office.

Chang, J-H., G. Rynhart and P. Huynh (2016), 'ASEAN in transformation: How technology is changing jobs and enterprises', *Bureau for Employers' Activities*, Working Paper No. 10, Geneva: International Labour Office.

Chertow, M.R. (2001), 'The IPAT equation and its variants', *Journal of Industrial Ecology*, **4**(4), 13–29.

Ciais, P., C. Sabine, G. Bala, L. Bopp, V. Brovkin, J. Canadell, A. Chhabra et al. (2013), 'Carbon and other biogeochemical cycles', Supplementary Material, IPCC Fifth Assessment Report.

Clack, C., S. Qvist, J. Apt, M. Bazilian, A. Brandt, K. Caldeira, S. Davis et al. (2017), 'Evaluation of a proposal for reliable low-cost grid power with 100% wind, water, and solar', *Proceedings of the National Academy of Sciences*, **114**(26), 6722–7, accessed 1 October 2017 at http://www.pnas. org/content/114/26/6722.full.pdf.

Clarke, T. and M. Boersma (2016), 'Sustainable finance?: A critical analysis of the regulation, policies, strategies, implementation and reporting on sustainability in international finance', UNEP *Inquiry Working Paper* No. 16/03, Geneva: International Environment House.

Climate Bonds Initiative and Sustainable Prosperity Institute (2016), 'Bonds and climate change: The state of the market, Canada edition', Climate Bonds Initiative and the Smart Prosperity Institute, October, accessed 8 December 2017 at https://www.climatebonds.net/files/files/ CB-HSBC-2016-Canada-Final-01A-1.pdf.

Cline, W. (2011), *Carbon Abatement Costs and Climate Change Finance*, Chapter 4, Washington, DC: The Peterson Institute for International Economics.

Cohen, D. (2016), 'Study links geography to obesity rates', *Yale News*, accessed 13 August 2017 at http://yaledailynews.com/blog/2016/12/06/st udy-links-geography-to-obesity-rates/.

Commission on Growth and Development (2008), *The Growth Report: Strategies for Sustained Growth and Inclusive Development*, Washington, DC: The International Bank for Reconstruction and Development and The World Bank.

Commoner, B. (1971), *The Closing Circle: Nature, Man, and Technology*, 1st edn, New York: Alfred A. Knopf.

Conference Board of Canada (2016), 'How Canada performs', accessed 23 August 2017 at http://www.conferenceboard.ca/hcp/provincial/enviro nment.aspx.

Cooper, B., C. García-Peñalosa and P. Funk (2001), 'Status effects and negative utility growth', *Economic Journal*, **111**(July), 642–65.

Corak, M. (2016), 'Inequality is the root of social evil, or maybe not? Two stories about inequality and public policy', *Canadian Public Policy*, **42**(4), 367–414.

Costanza, R., R. d'Arge, R. de Groot, S. Farber, M. Grasso, B. Hannon, K. Limburg et al. (1997), 'The value of the world's ecosystem services and natural capital', *Nature*, **387**, 253–60.

Costanza, R., M. Hart, S. Posner and J. Talberth (2009), 'Beyond GDP: The need for new measures of progress', *Pardee Paper* No. 4, Boston, MA: Pardee Center for the Study of the Longer-Range Future.

Costanza, R., R. de Groot, P. Sutton, S. van der Ploeg, S.J. Anderson, I. Kubiszewski, S. Farber and R.K. Turner (2014), 'Changes in the global value of ecosystem services', *Global Environmental Change*, **26**, 152–8.

Costanza, R., R. de Groot, L. Braat, I. Kubiszewski, L. Fioramonti, P. Sutton, S. Farber and M. Grasso (2017), 'Twenty years of ecosystem services: How far have we come and how far do we still have to go?', *Ecosystem Services*, **28**, 1–16.

Coughlin, C.C. (2002), 'The controversy over free trade: The gap between economists and the general public', *Review*, January, pp. 1–22.

Couldry, N. and J. Turow (2014), 'Advertising, big data and the clearance of the public realm: Marketers' new approaches to the content subsidy', *International Journal of Communication*, **8**, 1710–26.

Coulomb, R., S. Dietz, M. Godunova and T.B. Nielsen (2015), 'Critical minerals today and in 2030: An analysis for OECD countries', Environment Working Paper No. 91, ESRC Centre for Climate Change Economics and Policy, Grantham Research Institute on Climate Change and the Environment, accessed June 2016 at www.oecd.org/environment/work ingpapers.htm.

Crafts, N. (2004), 'Steam as a general purpose technology: A growth accounting perspective', *The Economic Journal*, **114**, 338–51.

Cranford, C.J., L.F. Vosko and N. Zukewich (2003), 'Precarious employment in the Canadian labour market: A statistical portrait', *Just Labour*, **3**(Fall), 6–22.

Critchlow, A. (2015), 'Saudi Arabia increases oil output to crush US shale frackers', accessed May 2016 at http://www.telegraph.co.uk/finance/

newsbysector/energy/11372058/Saudi-Arabia-increases-oil-output-to-cr
ush-US-shale-frackers.html.

Crutzen, P.J. and W. Steffen (2003), 'How long have we been in the
Anthropocene era? An editorial comment', *Climate Change*, **61**, 251–7.

Czech, B. (2008), 'Prospects for reconciling the conflict between economic
growth and biodiversity conservation with technological progress',
*Conservation Biology*, **22**(6), 1389–98.

Czech, B. (2013), *Supply Shock*, Gabriola Island, BC: New Society Publishers.

D'Alisa, G., F. Demaria and G. Kallis (2014), *Degrowth: A Vocabulary for
a New Era*, New York: Routledge.

Dales, J.H. (1968), *Pollution, Property and Prices*, Toronto, ON: University
of Toronto Press.

Daly, H.E. (1977), *Steady-State Economics*, San Francisco, CA: W.H.
Freeman and Co.

Daly, H.E. (1990), 'Toward some operational principles of sustainable
development', *Ecological Economics*, **2**(1), 1–6.

Daly, H.E. (1993), 'The perils of free trade', *Scientific American*, **269**(5),
50–55.

Daly, H.E. (1996), *Beyond Growth: The Economics of Sustainable
Development*, Boston, MA: Beacon Press.

Daly, H.E. (2005), 'Economics in a full world', *Scientific American*, **293**(3),
100–107.

Daly, H.E. (2014), *Uneconomic Growth to a Steady-State Economy*,
Cheltenham, UK and Northampton, MA, USA: Edward Elgar Publishing.

Daly, H.E. and J.C. Farley (2004), *Ecological Economics: Principles and
Applications*, 1st edn, Washington, DC: Island Press.

Daly, H.E. and J.C. Farley (2011), *Ecological Economics: Principles and
Applications*, 2nd edn, Washington, DC: Island Press.

Dawe, N.K. and R.L. Ryan (2003), 'The faulty three-legged-stool model of
sustainable development', *Conservation Biology*, **17**, 1458–60.

Deffeyes, K.S. (2005), *Beyond Oil: The View from Hubbert's Peak*, New
York: Hill and Wang.

Deloitte (2006), *Quick Tax Facts 2005*, accessed 15 August 2007 at http://
www.deloitte.com/dtt/cda/doc/content/ca_tax_QTF%202005%28 5%29.
pdf.

Delucchi, M.A. and M.Z. Jacobson (2011), 'Providing all global energy
with wind, water, and solar power, Part II: Reliability, system and transmission costs, and policies', *Energy Policy*, **39**(3), 1170–90.

Demeney, P. (2003), 'Population policy dilemmas in Europe at the dawn of
the twenty-first century', *Population and Development Review*, **29**(1), 1–28.

Deming, D. (2000), 'Oil: Are we running out?', remarks at the Second
Wallace E. Pratt Memorial Conference, San Diego, 12–15 January,

accessed 27 September 2007 at http://www.oilcrisis.com/deming/ aapg_oil.pdf.

Department of Finance Canada (2007), *Glossary*, accessed 18 August 2007 at http://www.fin.gc.ca.

Department of Finance Canada (2008), 'Archived: Overview (2007 Economic Statement)', accessed 26 February 2017 at http://www.fin.gc.ca/ec2007/pamph/pam-eng.asp.

Department of Foreign Affairs and International Trade (2003), *Canada Bulletin*, accessed 10 September 2007 at http://www.dfait-maeci.gc.ca.

De Spiegelaere, S. and A. Piasma (2017), *The Why and How of Working Time Reduction*, Brussels: The European Trade Union Institute.

Devereux, M.B. and D.R.F. Love (1994), 'The effects of factor taxation in a two-sector model of endogenous growth', *Canadian Journal of Economics*, **27**(3), 509–36.

Diamond, J.M. (2005), *Collapse: How Societies Choose to Fail or Succeed*, New York: Viking.

Dickenson, H.W. (1935), *James Watt: Craftsman and Engineer*, Cambridge: Cambridge University Press.

Dinda, S. (2004), 'Environmental Kuznets Curve hypothesis: A survey', *Ecological Economics*, **49**(4), 431–55.

Dolter, B. and P.A. Victor (2016), 'Casting a long shadow: Demand-based accounting of Canada's greenhouse gas emissions responsibility', *Ecological Economics*, **127**, 156–64.

Domar, E. (1946), 'Capital expansion, rate of growth, and employment', *Econometrica*, **14**(2), 137–47.

Doucet, I. (2012), 'Canada, the surprise "pariah" of the Kyoto Protocol', *The Guardian*, 26 November, accessed 2 December 2017 at https://www.theguardian.com/world/2012/nov/26/canada-kyoto.

Douthwaite, R. (1999), *The Growth Illusion: How Economic Growth has Enriched the Few, Impoverished the Many and Endangered the Planet*, Gabriola Island, BC: New Society Publishers.

Downs, A. (1972), 'Up and down with ecology: The issue–attention cycle', *Public Interest*, **28**(Summer), 38–50.

Drucker, P.F. (1969), *The Age of Discontinuity: Guidelines to our Changing Society*, New York: Harper & Row.

Dubos, R.J. (1965), *Man Adapting*, New Haven, CT: Yale University Press.

Dunckley, V.L. (2014), 'Grey matters: Too much screen time damages brain', *Psychology Today*, accessed 24 July 2017 at https://www.psychologytoday.com/blog/mental-wealth/201402/gray-matters-too-much-screen-time-damages-the-brain.

Dunkerley, J. (2006), 'Lessons from the past thirty years', *Energy Policy*, **34**, 503–507.

Easterlin, R. (1974), 'Does economic growth improve the human lot?', in D.P. Reder and M.W. Reder (eds), *Nations and Households in Economic Growth: Essays in Honor of Moses Abramovitz*, New York: Academic Press, pp. 89–125.

Easterlin, R. (1996), *Growth Triumphant: The Twenty-First Century in Historical Perspective*, Ann Arbor, MI: University of Michigan Press.

Easterlin, R. (2001), 'Income and happiness: Towards a unified theory', *Economic Journal*, **111**(July), 465–84.

Easterlin, R. (2003), 'Explaining happiness', *Proceedings of the National Academy of Sciences of the United States of America*, **100**(19), 11176–83.

Eckstein, O. (1961), *Water-Resource Development: The Economics of Project Evaluation*, Cambridge, MA: Harvard University Press.

Ehrlich, P.R. (1968), *The Population Bomb*, New York: Ballantine Books.

Ehrlich, P.R. (1981), 'An economist in wonderland', *Social Science Quarterly*, **62**(March), 44–9.

Ehrlich, P.R. and J.P. Holdren (1971), 'Impact of population growth science', *Science*, **171**(3977), 1212–17.

Eisner, R. (1994), *The Misunderstood Economy: What Counts and How to Count it*, Boston, MA: Harvard Business School Press.

Ekins, P. (2017), 'Ecological modernisation and green growth: Prospects and potential', in P.A. Victor and B. Dolter (eds), *Handbook on Growth and Sustainability*, Cheltenham, UK and Northampton, MA, USA: Edward Elgar Publishing.

Ekins, P. and R. de Groot (2003), 'Identifying critical natural capital', *Ecological Economics*, **44**(2–3), 159–63.

Eleven National Organizations (2006), 'Tracking Europe's natural resource consumption', accessed 16 November 2017 at https://wupperinst.org/uploads/tx_wupperinst/consensus_statement.pdf.

Elgie, S., M. Brownlee, S.J. O'Neill and M. Marcano (2016), 'Pricing works: How pricing of municipal infrastructure can lead to healthier and more efficient cities', *Metcalf Foundation Green Prosperity Papers*, July.

Elkington, J. (1998), *Cannibals with Forks: The Triple Bottom Line of the 21st Century Business*, Gabriola Island, NC: New Society Publishers.

Ellerman, D.A. and B.K. Buchner (2007), 'The European Union Emissions Trading Scheme: Origins, allocation, and early results', *Review of Environmental Economics and Policy*, **1**(1), 66–87.

Ellerman, D. and J-P. Montero (1998), 'The declining trend in sulphur dioxide emissions: Implications for allowance prices', *Journal of Environmental Economics and Management*, **36**(1), 26–45.

Elliot, L. (2008), 'Can a dose of recession solve climate change?', *The Guardian Weekly*, 25 August.

Ellis, E.C. (2011), 'Anthropogenic transformation of the terrestrial biosphere', *Philosophical Transactions of the Royal Society A*, **369**, 1010–35.

Engel, S., S. Pagiola and S. Wunder (2008), 'Designing payments for environmental services in theory and practice: An overview of the issues', *Ecological Economics*, **65**, 663–74.

Environment Canada (1997), *Global Benefits and Costs of the Montreal Protocol on Substances that Deplete the Ozone Layer*, Ottawa: Government of Canada.

Environment Canada (2014), *Canada's Emission Trends*, Tables A.5 and A.6, accessed 21 November 2018 at https://www.canada.ca/en/environ ment-climate-change/services/climate-change/publications/emission-trends-2014/annex-2.html.

Environment and Climate Change Canada (2013), 'Planning for a sustainable future: A federal sustainable development strategy for Canada 2013–2016', accessed January 2017 at https://www.ec.gc.ca/dd-sd/default .asp?lang=En&n=892FBDA6-1.

Environment and Climate Change Canada (2016), 'Achieving a sustainable future: A federal sustainable development strategy for Canada 2016–2019', accessed December 2016 at http://www.fsds-sfdd.ca/downloads/3130%20 -%20Federal%20Sustainable%20Development%20Strategy%202016-201 9_.pdf.

Environment and Climate Change Canada (2017), *Environmental Indicators*, Government of Canada, available at https://www.canada. ca/en/environment-climate-change/services/environmental-indicators. html.

Eriksen, M., L.C.M. Lebreton, H.S. Carson, M. Thiel, C.J. Moore, J.C. Borerro, F. Galgani et al. (2014), 'Plastic pollution in the world's oceans: More than 5 trillion plastic pieces weighing over 250,000 tons afloat at sea', *PLoS ONE*, **9**(12), 1–15, accessed 3 October 2017 at http:// journals.plos.org/plosone/article/file?id=10.1371/journal.pone.0111913& type=printable.

ESRB Advisory Scientific Committee (2016), 'Too late, too sudden: Transition to a low-carbon economy and systemic risk', Reports of the Advisory Scientific Committee, accessed 12 October 2017 at https://www. esrb.europa.eu/pub/pdf/asc/Reports_ASC_6_1602.pdf.

Estrada, A., P. Garber, A. Rylands, C. Roos, E. Fernandez-Duque, A. di Fiore, K. Nekaris et al. (2017), 'Impending extinction crisis of the world's primates: Why primates matter', *Science Advances*, **3**(1), 1–16.

Esty, D., M. Levy, T. Snebotnjak, A. de Sherbinin, C. Kim and B. Anderson (2006), *Pilot 2006 Environmental Performance Index*, New Haven, CT: Yale Center for Environmental Law and Policy.

European Commission (2010), 'Critical raw materials for the EU: Report of the ad-hoc working group on defining critical raw materials', Brussels: DG Enterprise and Industry.

European Commission (2012), 'Sustainable growth: For a resource efficient, greener and more competitive economy', accessed 26 February 2017 at http://ec.europa.eu/europe2020/europe-2020-in-a-nutshell/priorities/sustainable-growth/index_en.htm.

European Commission (2014), 'Report on critical raw materials for the EU: Report of the ad-hoc working group on defining critical raw materials', Brussels: DG Enterprise and Industry.

Evans, C. (2013), 'Wealth taxes: Problems and practices around the world', Centre on Household Assets and Savings Management, Briefing Paper, accessed 8 January 2018 at https://www.birmingham.ac.uk/Documents/college-social-sciences/social-policy/CHASM/briefing-papers/2013/wealth-taxes-problems-and-practices-around-the-world.pdf.

Ewing, B.R., T.R. Hawkins, T.O. Wiedmann, A. Galli, A.E. Ercin, J. Weinzettel and K. Steen-Olsen (2012), 'Integrating ecological and water footprint accounting in a multi-regional input-output framework', *Ecological Indicators*, **23**, 1–8.

Fallis, G. (2007), *Multiversities, Ideas and Democracy*, Toronto, ON: University of Toronto Press.

FAO (2015), *Global Forest Resources Assessment 2015: How are the World's Forests Changing?*, 2nd edn, Rome: Food and Agriculture Organization of the United Nations.

FAO (2016a), *State of the World's Forests, Forests and Agriculture: Land-Use Challenges and Opportunities*, Rome: Food and Agriculture Organization of the United Nations.

FAO (2016b), *The State of World Fisheries and Aquaculture 2016 (SOFIA): Contributing to Food Security and Nutrition for All*, Rome: Food and Agriculture Organization of the United Nations.

FAO (2016c), *In Brief. The State of Food and Agriculture*, Rome: Food and Agriculture Organization of the United Nations, accessed 13 August 2017 at http://www.fao.org/3/a-i6132e.pdf.

FAO (2017), *The State of Food Security and Nutrition in the World, Building for Peace and Food Security*, Food and Agriculture Organization of the United Nations, accessed 16 November 2017 at http://www.fao.org/3/a-I7695e.pdf.

Farley, J. (2008), 'The role of prices in conserving critical natural capital', *Conservation Biology*, **22**(6), 1399–408.

Farley, J. (2012), 'Ecosystem services: The economics debate', *Ecosystem Services*, **1**, 40–49.

Fellegi, I.P. (1997), 'On poverty and low income', Statistics Canada,

No. 13F0027XIE, accessed 20 July 2007 at http://www.statcan.gc.ca/pub/13f0027x/4053039-eng.htm.

Fields, G.S. (1995), 'Income distribution in developing economies: Conceptual, data, and policy issues in broad-based growth', *Cornell University ILR School: DigitalCommons@ILR*, accessed 26 February 2017 at http://digitalcommons.ilr.cornell.edu/articles/981/.

Figart, D.M. and L. Golden (2000), 'Introduction and overview, understanding working time around the world', in L. Golden and D.M. Figart (eds), *Working Time: International Trends, Theory and Policy Perspectives*, Abingdon, UK and New York, USA: Routledge, pp. 1–17.

Finance Canada (2017), *Glossary of Frequently-Used Terms*, accessed 26 July 2017 at http://www.collectionscanada.gc.ca/eppp-archive/100/201/301/plan_budgetaire/2000/html/glossaire/gloss-s_e.html#sus-dev.

Fischer-Kowalski, M. and C. Amann (2001), 'Beyond IPAT and Kuznets Curves: Globalization as a vital factor in analysing the environmental impact of socio-economic metabolism', *Population and Environment*, **23**(1), 7–47.

Fischer-Kowalski, M. and W. Hüttler (1999), 'Society's metabolism: The intellectual history of materials flow analysis, Part II, 1970–1998', *Journal of Industrial Ecology*, **2**(4), 107–136.

Fisher, D.R. and W.R. Freudenberg (2001), 'Ecological modernization and its critics: Assessing the past and looking toward the future', *Society and Natural Resources*, **14**, 701–9.

Fisher, G.T. (2008), 'Powering freight railways for the environment and profit electrification: Why and how', paper delivered at *Transport Canada On Board for a Cleaner Environment*: 2008 Rail Conference, 6–7 May.

Fletcher, D. (2010), 'The 50 worst inventions: CFCs', *Time Inc.*, accessed September 2016 at http://content.time.com/time/specials/packages/article/0,28804,1991915_1991909_1991757,00.html.

Fletcher, R. and J. Breitling (2012), 'Market mechanism or subsidy in disguise? Governing payment for environmental services in Costa Rica', *Geoforum*, **43**, 402–11.

Fleurbaey, M. (2009), 'Beyond GDP: The quest for a measure of social welfare', *Journal of Economic Literature*, **47**(4), 1029–75.

Forrester, J.W. (1969), *Urban Dynamics*, Cambridge, MA: MIT Press.

Forrester, J.W. (1971a), 'Counterintuitive behaviour of social systems', *Technology Review*, January, accessed 23 July 2007 at http://www.exponentialimprovement.com/cms/uploads/UrbanDynMfg 03.PDF.

Forrester, J.W. (1971b), *World Dynamics*, Cambridge: Wright-Allen Press.

Förster, M. and M.M. d'Ercole (2005), 'Income distribution and poverty in OECD countries in the second half of the 1990s', *OECD Social, Employment and Migration Working Paper No. 22*, accessed 20 August 2007 at http://search.oecd.org/els/soc/34483698.pdf.

Foster, J.B. (2015), 'Marxism and ecology: Common fronts of a great transition', *Great Transition Initiative*, accessed 16 January 2018 at reattransition.org/images/GTI_publications/Foster-Marxism-and-Ecology.pdf.

Frank, A.G. (1966), *The Development of Under Development*, Boston, MA: New England Free Press.

Franklin, U.M. (1990), *The Real World of Technology*, 1st edn, Toronto, ON: House of Anansi Press.

Franklin, U.M. (1999), *The Real World of Technology*, 2nd edn, Toronto, ON: House of Anansi Press.

Freedman, A. (2013), 'The last time $CO_2$ was this high, humans didn't exist', *Climate Central*, accessed March 2016 at http://www.climatecentral.org/news/the-last-time-co2-was-this-high-humans-didnt-exist-15938.

Friedman, B.M. (2005), *The Moral Consequences of Economic Growth*, 1st edn, New York: Alfred A. Knopf.

Friends of the Earth International (2015), 'Financialization of nature: Creating a new definition of nature', accessed August 2016 at http://www.foei.org/wp-content/uploads/2015/10/Financialization-of-Nature-brochure-English.pdf.

Fullencamp, C. (2015), 'Do remittances drive economic growth?', *World Economic Forum*, accessed 2 December 2017 at https://www.weforum.org/agenda/2015/02/do-remittances-drive-economic-growth/.

Fullerton, J. (2013), 'Financial overshoot: From stranded assets to a regenerative economy', Capital Institute, accessed 28 December 2017 at http://capitalinstitute.org/wp-content/uploads/2014/09/FINANCIAL-OVERSHOOTread.pdf.

Futurearth (2017), *Global Carbon Budget 2017*, 13 November, PowerPoint Version 1.0 accessed 18 November 2017 at http://www.globalcarbonproject.org/carbonbudget/17/files/GCP_CarbonBudget_2017.pdf.

Galbraith, J.K. (1958), *The Affluent Society*, Boston, MA: Houghton Mifflin.

Gallup World Poll (2016), http://www.gallup.com/services/170945/world-poll.aspx.

Gareau, B.J. (2010), 'A critical review of the successful CFC phase-out versus the delayed methyl bromide phase-out in the Montreal Protocol', *International Environmental Agreements: Politics, Law and Economics*, **10**, 209–31.

Georgescu-Roegen, N. (1971), *The Entropy Law and the Economic Process*, Cambridge, MA: Harvard University Press.

Georgescu-Roegen, N. (1975), 'Energy and economic myths', *Southern Economic Journal*, **41**(3), 347–81.

Gerland, P., A.E. Rafterty, H. Sevcikova, N. Li, D. Gu, T. Spoorenberg, L. Alkema et al. (2014), 'World population stabilization unlikely this century', *Science*, **346**(6206), 234–37.

Giampietro, M. and A. Saltelli (2014), 'Footprints to nowhere', *Ecological Indicators*, **46**, 610–21.

Giampietro, M., K. Mayumi and S.G.F. Bukkens (2002), 'Multiple-scale integrated assessment of societal metabolism: An analytical tool to study development and sustainability', *Environment, Development and Sustainability*, **3**, 275–307.

Giampietro, M., A.H. Sorman and G. Gamboa (2010), 'Using the MuSIASEM approach to study metabolic patterns of modern societies', in F. Barbir and S. Ulgiati (eds), *Energy Options Impact on Regional Security*, Dordrecht: Springer Netherlands.

Giovanni, E. (2008), *Understanding Economics Statistics: An OECD Perspective*, Statistics Directorate, Paris: OECD.

Giunta, C.J. (2006), 'Thomas Midgley, Jr., and the invention of chloro-fluorocarbon refrigerants: It ain't necessarily so', *Bulletin for the History of Chemistry*, **31**(2), 66–74.

Gleason, C. and S. Lambert (2014), 'Uncertainty by the hour', *Future of Work Project*, Open Society Foundations, accessed 3 December 2017 at http://static.opensocietyfoundations.org/misc/future-of-work/just-in-time-workforce-technologies-and-low-wage-workers.pdf.

Global Footprint Network (2013), *Global Footprint Accounts*, 2012 edn, Working Paper, accessed 17 November 2017 at http://www.footprintnetwork.org/content/images/article_uploads/National_Footprint_Accounts_2012_Edition_Report.pdf.

Global Footprint Network (2018), *Ecological Footprint Explorer*, accessed 15 February 2018 at http://data.footprintnetwork.org/#/. © Global Footprint Network 2017, National Footprint Accounts, 2017 edn. Licensed and provided solely for informational purposes. Contact Global Footprint Network at footprintnetwork.org to obtain more information.

Godley, W. and M. Lavoie (2012), *Monetary Economics*, 2nd edn, Basingstoke: Palgrave Macmillan.

Goldewijk, K.K., A. Beusen, G. van Drecht and M. de Vos (2011), 'The HYDE 3.1 spatially explicit database of human-induced global land-use change over the past 12,000 years', *Global Ecology and Biogeography*, **20**, 73–86.

Goldfinger, S., W. Wackernagel, A. Galli, E. Lazarus and D. Lin (2014), 'Footprint facts and fallacies: A response to Giampietro and Saltelli (2014) "Footprints to Nowhere"', *Ecological Indicators*, **46**, 622–32.

Gordon, M.J. and J.S. Rosenthal (2003), 'Capitalism's growth imperative', *Cambridge Journal of Economics*, **27**, 25–48.

Gordon, R.J. (2016), *The Rise and Fall of American Growth: The US Standard of Living since the Civil War*, Princeton, NJ: Princeton University Press.

Government of Canada (1996), *The State of Canada's Environment – 1996*, Ottawa: Government of Canada.

Government of Canada (2007a), 'Economic concepts, economic growth', accessed 10 July 2007 at http://www.canadianeconomy.gc. ca.ezproxy. library.yorku.ca/English/economy/economic_growth.html.

Government of Canada (2007b), 'Economic concepts, full employment', accessed 21 August 2007 at http://canadianeconomy.gc.ca/english/econo my/fullemployment.html.

Government of Canada (2017a), 'Pricing carbon pollution in Canada: how it will work: Backgrounder', Environment and Climate Change Canada, accessed 12 November 2017 at https://www.canada.ca/en/environment-climate-change/news/2017/05/pricing_carbon_pollutionincanadahowitw illwork.html.

Government of Canada (2017b), 'Greenhouse gas emissions by Canadian economic sector', accessed 13 November 2017 at https://www.canada.ca/ en/environment-climate-change/services/environmental-indicators/gree nhouse-gas-emissions/canadian-economic-sector.html.

Government of Canada (2017c), 'Greenhouse gas emissions', accessed 6 January 2018 at https://www.ec.gc.ca/indicateurs-indicators/default.asp? lang=en&n=FBF8455E-1.

Government of Canada (2017d), *Notice: Supplementary Information 2018–2020 Immigration Levels Plan*, 1 November 2017, accessed 2 December 2017 at https://www.canada.ca/en/immigration-refugees-citizenship/ news/notices/supplementary-immigration-levels-2018.html.

Government of Canada (2017e), *Facts & Figures 2015: Immigration Overview – Permanent Residents – Annual IRCC Updates*, accessed 2 December 2017 at http://open.canada.ca/data/en/dataset/2fbb56bd-eae7-4582-af7d-a197d185fc93.

Government of Canada (2017f), 'The Pan-Canadian Framework on Clean Growth and Climate Change: Canada's plan to address climate change and grow the economy', *Government of Canada* Catalogue No. En4-294/2016E-PDF, accessed 6 January 2018 at https://www.canada.ca/content/dam/ themes/environment/documents/weather1/20161209-1-en.pdf.

Graedel, T.E., E.M. Harper, N.T. Nassar and B.K. Reck (2015), 'On the material basis of modern society', *Proceedings of the National Academy of Sciences of the United States of America*, **112**(20), 6295–300.

Graedel, T.E., R. Barr, C. Chandler, T. Chase, J. Choi, L. Christofferson, E. Friedlander et al. (2012), 'Methodology of metal criticality determination', *Environmental Science and Technology*, **46**(2), 1063–70.

Green, T.L. (2012), 'Introductory economics textbooks: What do they teach about sustainability?', *International Journal of Pluralism and Economics Education*, **4**, 189–223.

Gross, B. (1987), 'Towards global action', *The Annals of the American Academy of Political and Social Science*, **492**(1), 182–94.

Grossman, G.M. and A.B. Krueger (1995), 'Economic growth and the environment', *The Quarterly Journal of Economics*, **110**(2), 353–77.

Gunderson, L.H. and C.S. Holling (eds) (2002), *Panarchy: Understanding Transformations in Human and Natural Systems*, Washington, DC: Island Press.

Gunton, T. and K.S. Calbrick (2010), 'Canada's environmental performance', paper prepared for the David Suzuki Foundation, accessed 20 August 2017 at http://www.davidsuzuki.org/publications/downlo ads/2010/OECD_Report_Final.pdf.

Haberl, H., K-H. Erb and F. Krausmann (2014), 'Human Appropriation of Net Primary Production: Patterns, trends, and planetary boundaries', *Annual Review of Environment and Resources*, **39**, 363–91.

Haberl, H., F. Krausmann and S. Gingrich (2006), 'Ecological embeddedness of the economy: A sociological perspective on humanity's economic activities 1700–2000', *Economic and Political Weekly*, **41**(47), 4896–904.

Hadhazy, A. (2015), 'Life might thrive a dozen miles beneath the earth's surface', *Astrobiology Magazine*, accessed 19 September 2016 at http:// www.astrobio.net/extreme-life/life-might-thrive-dozen-miles-beneath-ear ths-surface/.

Hall, C.A.S., J.G. Lambert and S.B. Balogh (2014), 'EROI of different fuels and the implications for society', *Energy Policy*, **64**, 141–52.

Hallmann, C.A., M. Sorg, E. Jongejans, H. Siepel, N. Hofland, H. Schwan, W. Stenmas et al. (2017), 'More than 75 percent decline over 27 years in total flying insect biomass in protected areas', *PLoS ONE*, **12**(10), accessed 18 January 2018 at http://journals.plos.org/plosone/article?id=10.1371/ journal.pone.0185809.

Halpern, B.S., S. Walbridge, K.A. Selkoe, C.V. Kappel, F. Micheli et al. (2008), 'A global map of human impact on marine ecosystems', *Science*, **319**, 948–52.

Halsall, P. (n.d.), 'Modern history sourcebook: Tables illustrating the spread of industrialization', Fordham University, accessed 31 July 2017 at https://sourcebooks.fordham.edu/mod/indrevtabs1.asp.

Hamilton, J.D. (2009), 'Causes and consequences of the oil shock of 2007–08', accessed 21 November 2018 at http://econweb.ucsd.edu/~jhamilton/ Hamilton_oil_shock_08.pdf.

Hamilton, K. (2000), 'Genuine saving as a sustainability indicator',

Environment Department, Environmental Economics Series Paper No. 77, Washington, DC: The World Bank.

Hamilton, K., M. Brahmbhatt and J. Liu (2017), 'Multiple benefits from climate change mitigation: Assessing the evidence', Policy Report, Grantham Research Institute on Climate Change and the Environment, accessed 10 January 2018 at http://www.lse.ac.uk/GranthamInstitute/wp-content/uploads/2017/11/Multiple-benefits-from-climate-action_Hamilton-et-al-1.pdf.

Hanley, N. and E.B. Barbier (2009), *Pricing Nature: Cost–benefit Analysis and Environmental Policy*, Cheltenham, UK and Northampton, MA, USA: Edward Elgar Publishing.

Harde, H. (2017), 'Scrutinizing the carbon cycle and $CO_2$ residence time in the atmosphere', *Global and Planetary Change*, **152**, 19–26.

Hardoon, D. (2017), 'An economy for the 99%', Oxfam Briefing Paper, January, Oxfam International, accessed 23 January 2018 at https://www.oxfam.org/sites/www.oxfam.org/files/file_attachments/bp-economy-for-99-percent-160117-en.pdf.

Hardt, L. and D.W. O'Neill (2017), 'Ecological macroeconomic models: Assessing current developments', *Ecological Economics*, **134**, 198–211.

Harris, J.M. and N.R. Goodwin (2003), *New Thinking in Macroeconomics: Social, Institutional, and Environmental Perspectives*, Cheltenham, UK and Northampton, MA, USA: Edward Elgar Publishing.

Harrod, R. (1939), 'An essay in dynamic theory', *The Economic Journal*, **49**(193), 14–33.

Hazeldine, T. (1992), 'A new direction for macroeconomic policy', in R.C. Allen and G. Rosenbluth (eds), *False Promises: The Failure of Conservative Economics*, Vancouver, BC: New Star Books, pp. 77–100.

Health Canada (2005), *Canada Health Act Overview*, accessed 26 August 2007 at http://www.hc-sc.gc.ca.ezproxy.library.yorku.ca/hcs-sss/medi-assur/overview-apercu/index_e.html.

Heaps, T. and M. Rubin (2016), 'Sizing the potential green bond market in Canada', *Corporate Knights*, accessed 8 December 2017 at http://www.corporateknights.com/wp-content/uploads/2017/04/GreenbondsPotential_Canada.pdf.

Heinberg, R. (2006), *The Oil Depletion Protocol: A Plan to Avert Oil Wars, Terrorism and Economic Collapse*, Gabriola Island, BC: New Society Publishers.

Heinberg, R. (2007), *Peak Everything*, Gabriola Island, BC: New Society Publishers.

Heinberg, R. (2011), *The End of Growth: Adapting to Our New Economic Reality*, Gabriola Island, BC: New Society Publishers.

Heiskanen, E. and M. Jalas (2000), 'Dematerialization through services:

A review and evaluation of the debate', The Finnish Environment 436, Ministry of the Environment, accessed 4 February 2017 at https://helda. helsinki.fi/bitstream/handle/10138/40558/FE_436.pdf?sequence=1.

Heisz, A. and B. Murphy (2016), 'The role of taxes and transfers in reducing income inequality', in D.A. Green, W.C. Riddell and F. St-Hilaire (eds), *Income Inequality: The Canadian Story Volume V*, Kingston, ON: McGill-Queen's University Press.

Helliwell, J. (2005), 'Well being, social capital and public policy: What's new?', paper presented at the special session on well-being at the Annual General Meetings of the Royal Economic Society, Nottingham, accessed 21 March 2017 at http://www.nber.org/papers/w11807.pdf.

Helliwell, J., R. Layard and J. Sachs (eds) (2013), *World Happiness Report 2013*, New York: UN Sustainable Development Solutions Network.

Helliwell, J., R. Layard and J. Sachs (eds) (2015), *World Happiness Report 2015*, New York: Sustainable Development Solutions Network.

Helliwell, J., R. Layard and J. Sachs (eds) (2016), *World Happiness Report 2016, Update (Vol. 1)*, New York: Sustainable Development Solutions Network.

Helliwell, J., R. Layard and J. Sachs (eds) (2017), *World Happiness Report 2017*, New York: Sustainable Development Solutions Network, accessed 3 August 2017 at http://worldhappiness.report/wp-content/uploads/ sites/2/2017/03/HR17.pdf.

Herzog, T., K.A. Baumert and J. Pershing (2006), *Target: Intensity. An Analysis of Greenhouse Gas Intensity Targets*, Washington, DC: World Resources Institute.

Hessing, M., M. Howlett and T. Summerville (2005), *Canadian Natural Resources and Environmental Policy: Political Economy and Public Policy*, 2nd edn, Vancouver, BC: UBC Press.

Heyes, J. (2014), 'Towards full employment in the UK?', *Sheffield Political Economy Research Institute*, accessed 19 November 2016 at http://speri. dept.shef.ac.uk/2014/05/13/full-employment-uk/.

Hilbeck, A., R. Binimelis, N. Defarge, R. Steinbrecher, A. Székács, F. Wickson, M. Antoniou et al. (2011), 'No scientific consensus on GMO safety', *Environmental Sciences Europe*, 27(4), 1–6.

Hinckley, S. (2015), '14 animals declared extinct in the 21st century', *The Christian Science Monitor*, 22 October.

Hirsch, F. (1976), *Social Limits to Growth*, Cambridge, MA: Harvard University Press.

Hirsch, R.L. (2007), 'Peaking of world oil production: Recent forecasts', DOE/nNETL-2007/1263, *National Energy Technology Laboratory*, accessed at http://www.peakoil.nl/wp-content/uploads/2008/08/peaking_ world_oil_production_recent_forecasts.pdf.

Hirsch, R.L., R. Bezdek and R. Wendling (2005), 'Peaking of world oil production: Impacts, mitigation, & risk management', accessed June 2016 at https://www.netl.doe.gov/energy-analyses/pubs/Oil_Peaking_N ETL.pdf.

Hitly, L.M., E.K. Seifert and R. Treibert (2005), *Information Systems for Sustainable Development*, Hershey, PA: Idea Group Publishing.

Hodgson, G.M. (2014), 'What is capital? Economists and sociologists have changed its meaning: Should it be changed back?', *Cambridge Journal of Economics*, **38**, 1063–86.

Hoggan, J. (2009), *Climate Cover-Up: The Crusade to Deny Global Warming*, Vancouver, BC: Greystone Books.

Holmes, A. and L. McGuinty (2015), 'Harnessing the power of the sharing economy: Next steps for Ontario', *Ontario Chamber of Commerce*, accessed 26 February 2017 at http://www.occ.ca/wp-content/uploads/2013/05/Harnessing-the-Power-of-the-Sharing-Economy.pdf.

Homer-Dixon, T.F. (2006), *The Upside of Down: Catastrophe, Creativity and the Renewal of Civilization*, Toronto, BC: A.A. Knopf Canada.

Hook, J., N. Bendavid and S. Power (2011), 'GOP wins deep cuts in environment spending', accessed December 2016 at http://www.wsj.com/articles/SB10001424052748703385404576258550820756980.

Hooker, C.A., R. van Hulst, R. Macdonald and P.A. Victor (1981), *Energy and the Quality of Life: Understanding Energy Policy*, Toronto, BC: University of Toronto Press.

Hotelling, H. (1931), 'The economics of exhaustible resources', *Journal of Political Economy*, **39**(2), 137–75.

Howard, E. (2015), 'Defra hit by largest budget cuts of any UK government department, analysis shows', accessed December 2016 at https://www.theguardian.com/environment/2015/nov/11/defra-hit-by-largest-budget-cuts-of-any-uk-government-department-analysis-shows.

Hsu, A. et al. (2016), 'Environmental Performance Index: Global Metrics for the Environment', New Haven, CT: Yale University.

Hubbert, M.K. (1956), 'Nuclear energy and the fossil fuels', Publication No. 95, Houston, TX: Shell Development Company, accessed 21 November 2018 at http://www.hubbertpeak.com/hubbert/1956/1956.pdf.

Huberman, M. and C. Minns (2007), 'The times they are not changin': Days and hours of work in Old and New Worlds, 1870–2000', *Explorations in Economic History*, **44**, 538–67.

Huesemann, M. and J. Huesemann (2011), *Techno-Fix: Why Technology Won't Save Us or the Environment*, Gabriola Island, BC: New Society Publishers.

Hussen, A. (2017), *Immigration, Refugees and Citizenship Canada:*

*Departmental Plan 2017–2018*, Minister of Immigration, Refugees and Citizenship, Immigration, Refugees and Citizenship Canada, accessed 2 December 2017 at http://www.cic.gc.ca/english/pdf/pub/dp-pm-2017-2018-eng.pdf.

Hussy, C., E. Klaassen, J. Koornneef and F. Wigand (2014), *International Comparison of Fossil Power Efficiency and CO₂ Intensity – Update 2014*, Utrecht: Ecofys.

Ianchovichina, E. and S. Lundstrom (2009), 'What is inclusive growth?', *World Bank Economic Policy and Debt Department (PRMED)*, accessed 26 February 2017 at http://siteresources.worldbank.org/INTDEBTDEPT/Resources/468980-1218567884549/WhatIsInclusiveGrowth20081230.pdf.

IGBP (2015), 'Great acceleration', accessed 31 March 2018 at http://www.igbp.net/globalchange/greatacceleration.4.1b8ae20512db692f2a680001630.html.

IISD (2016), *Comprehensive Wealth in Canada: Measuring What Matters in the Long Run*, The Institute for International Development, accessed 31 July 2017 at https://www.iisd.org/sites/default/files/publications/comprehensive-wealth-full-report-web.pdf.

Index Mundi (2017), 'Population density', accessed 23 November 2017 at https://www.indexmundi.com/g/r.aspx?v=21000.

Inglehart, R. (1997), *Modernization and Postmodernization: Cultural, Economic, and Political Change in 43 Societies*, Princeton, NJ: Princeton University Press.

International Energy Agency (IEA) (2012), *World Energy Outlook 2012*, Paris: IEA.

International Energy Agency (IEA) (2014), *Statistics Electricity Information*, Paris: IEA.

International Energy Agency (IEA) (2015), *2014 Annual Report*, Paris: IEA.

International Energy Agency (IEA) (2016a), 'Key world energy trends – excerpt from: *World Energy Balances 2016*', accessed 2 December 2016 at https://www.iea.org/publications/freepublications/publication/KeyWorldEnergyTrends.pdf.

International Energy Agency (IEA) (2016b), 'Tracking clean energy progress 2016: Energy technology perspectives 2016 excerpt, IEA input to the clean energy ministerial', Paris: IEA.

International Energy Agency (IEA) (2016c), 'Decoupling of global emissions and economic growth confirmed', accessed May 2016 at https://www.iea.org/newsroom/news/2016/march/decoupling-of-global-emissions-and-economic-growth-confirmed.html.

International Energy Agency (IEA) (2016d), '20 years of carbon capture and storage', Paris, accessed 12 October 2017 at https://www.iea.org/

publications/freepublications/publication/20YearsofCarbonCaptureand
Storage_WEB.pdf.

International Monetary Fund (IMF) (2000), *World Economic Outlook*,
Washington, DC: International Monetary Fund.

International Monetary Fund (IMF) (2016), 'World Economic Outlook
Database, April 2016', accessed 3 January 2017 at https://www.imf.org/
external/pubs/ft/weo/2016/01/weodata/weorept.aspx?pr.x=49&pr.y=3&
sy=2014&ey=2021&scsm=1&ssd=1&sort=country&ds=.&br=1&c=00
1&s=NGDP_RPCH&grp=1&a=1.

International Union for the Conservation of Nature and Natural Resources
(IUCN) (2007), *2007 Red List of Threatened Species*, accessed 21
September 2007 at http://www.iucn.org/themes/ssc/redlist2006/threaten
ed_species_facts.htm.

IPCC (1995), *IPCC Second Assessment, Climate Change 1995*, Geneva:
IPCC, accessed 27 September 2007 at https://www.ipcc.ch/pdf/climate-
changes-1995/ipcc-2nd-assessment/2nd-assessment-en.pdf.

IPCC (2000), *IPCC Special Report on Emissions Scenarios: Scenario
Driving Forces*, Cambridge: Cambridge University Press.

IPCC (2001), *Climate Change 2001: The Scientific Basis*, New York:
Cambridge University Press.

IPCC (2007), *Climate Change 2007: The Physical Science Basis*, Cambridge,
UK and New York, USA: Cambridge University Press, accessed 20 July
2007 at https://www.ipcc.ch/publications_and_data/publications_ipcc_
fourth_assessment_report_wg1_report_the_physical_science_basis.htm.

IPCC (2013), *Climate Change 2013: The Physical Science Basis.
Contribution of Working Group I to the Fifth Assessment Report of the
Intergovernmental Panel on Climate Change* (T.F. Stocker, D. Qin, G-K.
Plattner, M. Tignor, S.K. Allen, J. Boschung, A. Nauels et al. (eds)),
Cambridge, UK and New York, USA: Cambridge University Press.

IPCC (2014a), *Climate Change 2014: Mitigation of Climate Change*,
Contribution of Working Group III to the Fifth Assessment Report
of the Intergovernmental Panel on Climate Change (O. Edenhofer,
R. Pichs-Madruga, Y. Sokona, E. Farahani, S. Kadner, K. Seyboth,
A. Adler et al. (eds)), Cambridge, UK and New York, USA: Cambridge
University Press.

IPCC (2014b), *Climate Change 2014: Synthesis Report*, Contribution of
Working Groups I, II, and III to the Fifth Assessment Report of the
Intergovernmental Panel on Climate Change (core writing team R.K.
Pachauri and L.A. Meyer (eds)), Geneva: IPCC.

IPCC (2016), 'Press release: IPCC agrees special reports, AR6 workplan',
accessed 5 September 2016 at https://www.ipcc.ch/news_and_events/
pdf/press/160414_pr_p43.pdf.

Jackson, T. (2009), *Prosperity without Growth: Economics for a Finite Plane*t, 1st edn, London, UK and Sterling, VA: Earthscan.

Jackson, T. (2017), *Prosperity without Growth*, 2nd edn, London and New York: Routledge.

Jackson, T. and P. Victor (2011), 'Productivity and work in the "green economy": Some theoretical reflections and empirical tests', *Environmental Innovation and Societal Transitions*, **1**(1), 101–8.

Jackson, T. and P.A. Victor (2015a), 'Does credit create a "growth imperative"? A quasi-stationary economy with interest-bearing debt', *Ecological Economics*, **120,** 32–48.

Jackson, T. and P.A. Victor (2015b), 'Towards a stock-flow consistent ecological macroeconomics: An overview of the FALSTAFF framework with some illustrative results', CIGI Inquiry Working Paper 15/01, accessed 21 November 2018 at http://unepinquiry.org/wp-con tent/uploads/2015/04/Towards_a_Stock-Flow_Consistent_Ecological_ Macroeconomics.pdf.

Jackson, T. and P.A. Victor (2016), 'Does slow growth lead to rising inequality? Some theoretical reflections and numerical simulations', *Ecological Economics*, **121**, 206–19.

Jackson, T. and P.A. Victor (2018), 'LowGrow SFC: A stock-flow-consistent ecological macroeconomic model for Canada', CUSP Working Paper No 16, accessed 5 October 2017 at https://www.cusp. ac.uk/themes/aetw/wp16/ and www.pvictor.com.

Jackson, T. and R. Webster (2016), 'Limits Revisited: A review of the limits to growth debate, APPG on limits to growth', accessed 5 October 2017 at http://limits2growth.org.uk/publication/limits-revisited/.

Jacobson, M.Z. and M.A. Delucchi (2017), 'Line-by-line response', submitted to *Proceedings of the National Academy of Sciences of the United States of America*, accessed 1 October 2017 at http://web.stanford.edu/group/ efmh/jacobson/Articles/I/CombiningRenew/Line-by-line-Clack.pdf.

Jambeck, J.R., R. Geyer, C. Wilcox, T.R. Siegler, M. Perryman, A. Andrady, R. Narayan et al. (2015), 'Plastic waste inputs from land into the ocean', *Science*, 13 February, pp. 768–71.

Jeffrey, M., H. Wheatley and S. Abdallah (2016), 'Happy planet index 2016', *New Economics Foundation*, accessed August 2016 at http:// happyplanetindex.org/resources/.

Jevons, W.S. (1865), *The Coal Question: An Inquiry Concerning the Progress of the Nation, and the Probable Exhaustion of our Coal-Mines* (A.W. Flux (ed.)), New York: A.M. Kelley.

Johansson, P. (1991), *An Introduction to Modern Welfare Economics*, Cambridge, UK and New York, USA: Cambridge University Press.

Johnson, D.G. (2000), 'Population, food, and knowledge', *American Economic Review*, **90**(1), 1–14.

Joint Science Academies (2005), *Joint Science Academies' Statement: Global Response to Climate Change*, London: The Royal Society, accessed at http://sites.nationalacademies.org/cs/groups/international site/documents/webpage/international_080877.pdf.

Jones, A., S. Mair, J. Ward, A. Druckman, F. Lyon, I. Christie and S. Hafner (2016), 'Indicators for sustainable prosperity? Challenges and potential for indicator use in political processes', CUSP Working Paper No. 3, October, accessed 7 November 2017 at https://www.cusp.ac.uk/pub/wp3/.

Jones, C.I. and D. Vollrath (2013), *Introduction to Economic Growth*, 3rd edn, New York: W.W. Norton & Company.

Jorgensen, A.K. and B. Clark (2012), 'Are the economy and environment decoupling? A comparative international study, 1960–2005', *American Journal of Sociology*, **118**(1), 1–44.

Just, R.E., D.L. Hueth and A. Schmitz (2004), *The Welfare Economics of Public Policy: A Practical Approach to Project and Policy Evaluation*, Cheltenham, UK and Northampton, MA, USA: Edward Elgar Publishing.

Kable (2016), 'The top ten deepest mines in the world', mining-technology.com, accessed 9 November 2016 at http://www.mining-technology.com/features/feature-top-ten-deepest-mines-world-south-africa/.

Kakwani, N., S. Khandker and H.H. Son (2004), 'Pro-poor growth: Concepts and measurements with country case studies', *International Poverty Centre UNDP* Working Paper No. 1, accessed 26 February 2017 at http://www.ipc-undp.org/pub/IPCWorkingPaper1.pdf.

Karwatka, D. (2001), 'Thomas Newcomen, inventor of the steam engine', *Tech Directions*, **60**(78), 99–111.

Karwatka, D. (2007), 'Thomas Savery and his steam-operated water pump', *Tech Directions*, **66**(78), 100.

Keating, M. (1997), *Canada and the State of the Planet: The Social, Economic, and Environmental Trends that Are Shaping Our Lives*, Toronto, ON: Oxford University Press.

Kelly, D. and C.D. Kolstad (2001), 'Malthus and climate change: Betting on a stable population', *Journal of Environmental Economics and Management*, **41**, 135–61.

Kennedy, R. (1968), Remarks at the University of Kansas, 8 March, accessed 15 November 2017 at https://www.jfklibrary.org/Research/Research-Aids/Ready-Reference/RFK-Speeches/Remarks-of-Robert-F-Kennedy-at-the-University-of-Kansas-March-18-1968.aspx.

Keynes, J.M. (1923), *A Tract on Monetary Reform*, London: Macmillan & Co.

Keynes, J.M. (1930), 'Economic possibilities for our grandchildren', in

J.M. Keynes (1963), *Essays in Persuasion*, New York: W.W. Norton & Company.

Keynes, J.M. (1935), *The General Theory of Employment, Interest and Money*, New York: Harcourt Brace.

Kim, K.H., Z.H. Shon, H.T. Nguyen and E.C. Jeon (2011), 'A review of major chlorofluorocarbons and their halocarbon alternatives in the air', *Atmospheric Environment*, **45**, 1369–82.

Kitzes, J., A. Peller, S. Goldfinger and M. Wackernagel (2007), 'Current methods for calculating national ecological footprint accounts', *Science for Environment & Sustainable Society*, **4**(1), 1–9.

Klee, R.J. and T.E. Graedel (2004), 'Elemental cycles: A status report on human or natural dominance', *Annual Review of Environment and Resources*, **29**, 69–107.

Knight, K.W., E.A. Rosa and J.B. Schor (2013), 'Could working less reduce pressures on the environment? A cross-national panel analysis of OECD countries, 1970–2007', *Global Environmental Change*, **23**, 691–700.

Kogan, L.A. (2004), '"Enlightened" environmentalism or disguised protectionism: Assessing the impact of EU precaution-based standards on developing countries', accessed October 2016 at https://www.wto.org/english/forums_e/ngo_e/posp47_nftc_enlightened_e.pdf.

Kolbert, E. (2015), *The Sixth Extinction: An Unnatural History*, New York: Picador, Henry Holt and Company.

Kollar, L. and S. Mayer (2015), 'IAEA event features deep geological disposal of high level waste and spent nuclear fuel', International Atomic Energy Agency, accessed 1 August 2017 at https://www.iaea.org/newscenter/news/iaea-event-features-deep-geological-disposal-high-level-waste-and-spent-nuclear-fuel.

Korten, D. (1996), *Sustainable Development: Conventional Versus Emergent Alternative Wisdom*, accessed 20 July 2007 at http://dieoff.org/page86.htm.

Krausmann, F., S. Gingrich, N. Eisenmenger, K.H. Erb, H. Haberl and M. Fischer-Kowalski (2009), 'Growth in global materials use, GDP and population during the 20th century', *Ecological Economics*, **68**(10), 2696–705. Update of the global material extraction series 2017, available at https://www.aau.at/soziale-oekologie/data-download/.

Krueger, A.O. (2002), 'Supporting globalization', Remarks at the 2002 Eisenhower National Security Conference on 'National Security for the 21st Century: Anticipating Challenges, Seizing Opportunities, Building Capacities', Washington, DC, 26 September, accessed 10 October 2007 at http://www.imf.org/external/np/speeches/2002/092602a.htm.

Kubiszewski, I., R. Costanza, S. Anderson and P. Sutton (2017), 'The future value of ecosystem services: Global scenarios and national implications', *Ecosystem Services*, **26**, 289–301.

Kubiszewski, I., R. Costanza, C. Franco, P. Lawn, J. Talberth, T. Jackson and C. Aylmer (2013), 'Beyond GDP: Measuring and achieving global genuine progress', *Ecological Economics*, **93**, 57–68.

Kunstler, J.H. (2005), *The Long Emergency: Surviving the Converging Catastrophes of the Twenty-First Century*, London: Atlantic.

Kurek, J., J.L. Kirk, D.C.G. Muir, X. Wang, M.S. Evans and J.P. Smol (2012), 'Legacy of a half a century of Athabasca oil sands development recorded by lake ecosystems', *Proceedings of the National Academy of Sciences of the United States of America*, **110**(5), 1761–6.

Kuznets, S. (1934), *National Income, 1929–1932*, Senate document no. 124, 73rd Congress, 2nd session.

Lancaster, K. (1968), *Mathematical Economics*, New York: Macmillan.

Lane, R.E. (2000), *The Loss of Happiness in Market Democracies*, New Haven, CT: Yale University Press.

Latouche, S. (2009), *Farewell to Growth*, Cambridge, UK and Malden, MA, USA: Polity Press.

Lawn, P. (2003), 'A theoretical foundation to support the Index of Sustainable Economic Welfare (ISEW), Genuine Progress Indicator (GPI), and other related indexes', *Ecological Economics*, **44**, 105–18.

Lawn, P. (2011), 'Is steady-state capitalism viable? A review of the issues and an answer in the affirmative', *Annals of the New York Academy of Sciences*, **1219**, 1–25.

Layard, R. (2005a), 'Annexes to "Happiness"', accessed 21 August 2007 at http://cep.lse.ac.uk/layard/annex.pdf.

Layard, R. (2005b), *Happiness: Lessons from a New Science*, London: Allen Lane.

Layard, R. (2006), 'Happiness and public policy: A challenge to the profession', *Economic Journal*, **116**(March), C24–C33.

Lead Group Inc. (2011a), 'Chronology of leaded gasoline/leaded petrol history', Summer Hill, NSW: The Lead Group Incorporated.

Lead Group Inc. (2011b), 'Who will end the leaded petrol death trade?', The LEAD Group Incorporated, *Lead Action News*, **11**(4), 1–21.

Leahy, S. (2014), 'Canada is now the world's leading "deforestation nation"', *Rabble.ca*, accessed 8 November 2017 at http://rabble.ca/columnists/2014/10/canada-now-worlds-leading-deforestation-nation.

Lee, F.S. (2008), 'Heterodox economics', in Steven N. Durlauf and Lawrence E. Blume (eds), *The New Palgrave Dictionary of Economics*, 2nd edn, Palgrave Macmillan, accessed 21 November 2017 at http://www.dictionaryofecono mics.com/article?id=pde2008_H000175>doi:10.1057/9780230226203.0727.

Lee, M. (2008), *EU Regulations of GMOs: Law and Decision Making for a New Technology*, Cheltenham, UK and Northampton, MA, USA: Edward Elgar Publishing.

Lee, S. (2004), 'Working-hour gaps', in J.C. Messenger (ed.), *Working Time and Workers' Preferences in Industrialized Countries*, London, UK and New York, USA: Routledge, pp. 29–59.

Levin, K. and C.F. Tompkins (2014), 'Visualizing the global carbon budget', Washington, DC: World Resources Institute, accessed June 2016 at http://www.wri.org/blog/2014/03/visualizing-global-carbon-budget.

Liberal Party of Canada (2015), *Real Change: A New Plan for a Strong Middle Class*, Federal Liberal Agency of Canada, accessed 15 November 2017 at https://www.liberal.ca/wp-content/uploads/2015/10/New-plan-for-a-strong-middle-class.pdf.

Ligeti, E. (1996), *Ontario Regulation 482/95 and the Environmental Bill of Rights*, Toronto, ON: Commissioner of the Environment for Ontario.

Lintott, J. (2005), 'Evaluating the "Hirsch hypothesis": A comment', *Ecological Economics*, **52**(1), 1–3.

Lipsey, R.G. and K. Lancaster (1956/1957), 'The general theory of second best', *Review of Economic Studies*, **24**(1), 11–32.

Liverman, D. (2004), 'Who governs, at what scale and at what price? Geography, environmental governance, and the commodification of nature', *Annals of the Association of American Geographers*, **94**(4), 734–8.

Locatelli, B., V. Rojas and Z. Salinas (2008), 'Impacts of payments for environmental services on local development in northern Costa Rica: A fuzzy multi-criteria analysis', *Forest Policy and Economics*, **10**, 275–85.

Lomborg, B. (2001), *The Skeptical Environmentalist: Measuring the Real State of the World*, Cambridge, UK and New York, USA: Cambridge University Press.

Lovins, A., L.H. Lovins and P. Hawken (2007), 'A road map for natural capitalism', *Harvard Business Review*, July–August, pp. 172–83.

Lubchenco, J. (1998), 'Entering the century of the environment: A new social contract for science', *Science*, **279**(5350), 491–7.

Lynch, M. (1998), 'Crying wolf: Warnings about oil supply', accessed 20 July 2007 at http://sepwww.stanford.edu/sep/jon/world-oil.dir/lynch/worldoil.html.

Maas, P.H.J. (2018), The Sixth Extinction website, accessed 5 January 2018 at http://www.petermaas.nl/extinct-archive/lists/globally.htm.

Macdonald, D. (2014), *Outrageous Fortune: Documenting Canada's Wealth Gap*, Centre for Policy Alternatives, accessed 21 August 2017 at https://www.policyalternatives.ca/outrageous-fortune.

McKinsey & Company (2010), 'Impact of the financial crisis on carbon economics, Version 2.1 of the Global Greenhouse Gas Abatement Cost Curve', Exhibit 6, p. 8, accessed 4 November 2017 at https://www.mckinsey.com/business-functions/sustainability-and-res

ource-productivity/our-insights/impact-of-the-financial-crisis-on-carb on-economics-version-21.

McKitrick, R. and E. Aliakbari (2017), *Canada's Air Quality since 1970: An Environmental Success Story*, The Fraser Institute, accessed 23 August 2017 at https://www.fraserinstitute.org/sites/default/files/canadas-air-qu ality-since-1970-an-environmental-success-story.pdf.

MacNeill, J. (2006), 'The forgotten imperative of sustainable development', *Environmental Policy and Law*, **16**(3–4).

Magee, C.L. and T.C. Devezas (2017), 'A simple extension of dematerialization theory: Incorporation of technical progress and the rebound effect', *Technological Forecasting and Social Change*, **117**, 196–205.

Malthus, T.R. (1798), *An Essay on the Principle of Population, as it Affects the Future of Improvement of Society*, London: J. Johnson.

Marine Insight (2017), '10 world's biggest container ships in 2017', accessed 17 November 2017 at https://www.marineinsight.com/know-more/10-worlds-biggest-container-ships-2017/.

Maroto, M. (2016), 'Fifteen years of wealth disparities in Canada: New trends or simply the status quo', *Canadian Public Policy*, **42**(2), 152–67.

Marshall, A. (1920), *Principles of Economics*, 8th edn, London: Macmillan and Co.

Marx, K. (1887[2003]), *Capital: A Critique of Political Economy*, reprinted in London: Lawrence & Wisehart.

Mason, R.S. (1998), *The Economics of Conspicuous Consumption: Theory and Thought since 1700*, Cheltenham, UK and Lyme, NH, USA: Edward Elgar Publishing.

Matulis, B.S. (2013), 'The narrowing gap between vision and execution: Neoliberalization of PES in Costa Rica', *Geoforum*, **44**, 253–60.

Maxton, G. and J. Randers (2016), *Reinventing Prosperity: Managing Economic Growth to Reduce Unemployment, Inequality, and Climate Change*, Vancouver, BC: Greystone Books.

Mazzanti, M. and R. Zoboli (2008), 'Waste generation, waste disposal and policy effectiveness: Evidence on decoupling from the European Union', *Resources, Conservation and Recycling*, **52**(10), 1221–34.

Meadows, D.H., D.L. Meadows and J. Randers (1992), *Beyond the Limits: Confronting Global Collapse, Envisioning a Sustainable Future*, Toronto, ON: McClelland & Stewart.

Meadows, D.H., D.L. Meadows and J. Randers (2004), *Limits to Growth: The 30-Year Update*, White River Junction, VT: Chelsea Green Publishing Company.

Meadows, D.H., D.L. Meadows, J. Randers and W.W. Behrens III (1972), *The Limits to Growth*, London: Earth Island Limited.

Meadows, D.L. (1974), *The Dynamics of Growth in a Finite World*, Cambridge: Wright-Allen Press.

Mearns, E. (2014), 'Global oil and other liquid fuels production update', *Oilprice.com*, accessed 22 June 2016 at http://oilprice.com/Energy/Crude-Oil/Global-Oil-and-Other-Liquid-Fuels-Production-Update.html.

Mearns, E. (2016), 'ERoEI for beginners', *Energy Matters blog*, accessed 24 June 2016 at http://euanmearns.com/eroei-for-beginners/.

Meier, G.M. (2005), *Biography of a Subject: An Evolution of Development Economics*, New York: Oxford University Press.

Melamed, C. (2010), 'Introducing pro-poor growth', *Joint Steering Committee on Pro-Poor Growth*, Briefing Note no. 1, accessed 26 February 2017 at https://www.oecd.org/dac/povertyreduction/47466424.pdf.

Meyfroidt, P. and E.F. Lambin (2011), 'Global forest transition: Prospects for an end to deforestation', *Annual Review of Environment and Resources*, **36**, 343–71.

Michalos, A.C. (1988), 'A case for a progressive annual net wealth tax', *Public Affairs Quarterly*, **2**(April), 105–40.

Mill, J.S. (1848), *Principles of Political Economy: With Some of Their Applications to Social Philosophy*, London: J.W. Parker.

Millennium Ecosystem Assessment (MEA) (2005a), *Ecosystems and Human Well-being: Synthesis*, Washington, DC: Island Press.

Millennium Ecosystem Assessment (MEA) (2005b), 'Living beyond our means: Natural assets and human well-being', accessed 16 October 2007 at http://www.millenniumassessment.org/documents/document.429.aspx. pdf.

Miller, G.A. (2006), *WordNet*, accessed 16 October 2007 at http://wordnet. princeton.edu/.

Miller, G.T. (2004), *Living in the Environment: Principles, Connections, and Solutions*, 13th edn, Pacific Grove, CA: Brooks/Cole-Thompson Learning.

Miller, G. (2007), *Doing Less with Less: How Shortfalls in Budget, Staffing and In-House Expertise Are Hampering the Effectiveness of MOE and MNR*, Toronto, ON: Office of the Environmental Commissioner of Ontario.

Miller, R.E. and P.D. Blair (2009), *Input–Output Analysis: Foundations and Extensions*, Cambridge: Cambridge University Press.

Miller, R.G. and S.R. Sorrell (2014), 'The future of oil supply', *Philosophical Transactions of the Royal Society A*, **372**.

Mishan, E.J. (1967), *The Costs of Economic Growth*, New York: F.A. Praeger.

Mitchell, D.J. (2011), 'Real-world cases prove: Spending restraint works', *CATO Institute*, accessed December 2016 at https://www.cato.org/publi cations/commentary/realworld-cases-prove-spending-restraint-works.

Mitchell, D.J. (2014), 'Sweden, spending restraint, and the benefits of obeying fiscal policy's golden rule', *CATO Institute*, accessed December 2016 at https://www.cato.org/blog/sweden-spending-restraint-benefits-obeying-fiscal-policys-golden-rule.

Mohanraj, M., S. Jayaraj and C. Muraleedharan (2009), 'Environment friendly alternatives to halogenated refrigerants: A review', *International Journal of Greenhouse Gas Control*, **3**, 108–19.

Mol, A.P.J. (2000), 'The environmental movement in an era of ecological modernization', *GeoForum*, **31**, 45–56.

Molina, M.J. and F.S. Rowland (1974), 'Stratospheric sink for chlorofluoromethanes: Chlorine, atom-catalysed destruction of ozone', *Nature*, **249**(June), 810–12.

Monbiot, G. and P. Matthew (2006), *Heat: How to Stop the Planet from Burning*, Toronto, ON: Doubleday Canada.

Moncur, M. (2007), 'The quotations page', accessed 25 August 2007 at www.quotationspage.com/quote/862.html.

Montanari, S. (2017), 'Plastic garbage patch bigger than Mexico found in Pacific', *National Geographic*, 25 July, accessed 13 August 2017 at http://news.nationalgeographic.com/2017/07/ocean-plastic-patch-south-pacific-spd/.

Mooney, C. and B. Dennis (2018), 'The world has just over a decade to get climate change under control, U.N. scientists say', *The Washington Post*, 7 October, accessed 7 October 2018 at https://www.washingtonpost.com/energy-environment/2018/10/08/world-has-only-years-get-climate-change-under-control-un-scientists-say/?utm_term=.f80c4138ff8e.

Morissette, R., X. Zhang and M. Drolet (2002), 'The evolution of wealth inequality in Canada, 1984–1999', Statistics Canada, No. 187, accessed 16 October 2007 at http://publications.gc.ca/Collection/Statcan/11F0019MIE/11F0019MIE2002187.pdf.

Morneau, W.F. (2016), 'Growing the middle class', accessed December 2016 at http://www.budget.gc.ca/2016/docs/plan/budget2016-en.pdf.

Motesharrei, S., J. Rivas, E. Kalnay, G.R. Asrar, A.J. Busalacchi, R.F. Calahan, M.A. Kane et al. (2016), 'Modeling sustainability: Population, inequality, consumption, and bidirectional coupling of the Earth and Human Systems', *National Science Review*, **3**(4), 470–94, accessed 5 October 2017 at https://academic.oup.com/nsr/article/3/4/470/2669331/Modeling-sustainability-population-inequality#.

Moura, M.C.P., S.J. Smith and D.B. Belzer (2015), '120 years of US residential housing stock and floor space', *PLoS ONE*, **10**(8), 1–18, accessed 3 August 2017 at http://journals.plos.org/plosone/article/file?id=10.1371/journal.pone.0134135&type=printable.

Muller, N.Z. and R. Mendelsohn (2009), 'Efficient pollution regulation: Getting the prices right', *American Economic Review*, **99**(5), 1714–39.

Muller, N.Z., R. Mendelsohn and W. Nordhaus (2011), 'Environmental accounting for pollution in the United States economy', *The American Economic Review*, **101**(5), 1649–75.

Munda, G. (2004), 'Social multi-criteria evaluation: Methodological foundations and operational consequences', *European Journal of Operational Research*, **158,** 662–77.

Munson, J. (2016), 'Canada sets 2050 emissions target as Trump presidency approaches', *iPolitics*, 17 November, accessed 6 January 2018 at https://ipolitics.ca/2016/11/17/canada-sets-2050-emissions-target-as-trump-presidency-approaches/.

Murphy, B., X. Zhang and C. Dionne (2012), 'Low income in Canada: A multi-line and multi-index perspective', *Income Research Paper Series Statistics Canada*, Catalogue No. 75F00002M – No. 001, accessed 5 December 2016 at http://publications.gc.ca/collections/collection_2012/statcan/75f0002m/75f0002m2012001-eng.pdf.

Murphy, D.J. (2013), 'The implications of the declining energy return on investment of oil production', *Philosophical Transactions of the Royal Society A: Mathematical, Physical and Engineering Sciences*, **372**(2006), 20130126.

Murray, B.C. and N. Rivers (2015), 'British Columbia's revenue-neutral carbon tax: A review of the latest "grand experiment" in environmental policy', *Nicholas Institute Working Paper 15-04*, Durham, NC: Duke University.

Murtin, F. and M.M. d'Ercole (2015), 'Household wealth inequality across OECD countries: New evidence', *OECD Statistics Brief*, June, No. 21.

Musgrave, R.A., P.B. Musgrave and R.M. Bird (1987), *Public Finance in Theory and Practice*, 1st Canadian edn, Toronto, ON: McGraw-Hill Ryerson.

Nadal, A. (2016), 'The natural capital metaphor and economic theory', *Real-World Economics Review*, **74**, 64–84, accessed August 2016 at http://www.paecon.net/PAEReview/issue74/Nadal74.pdf.

NASA (2017), 'Short-lived greenhouse gases cause centuries of sea-level rise', *Global Climate Change*, accessed 4 October 2017 at https://climate.nasa.gov/news/2533/short-lived-greenhouse-gases-cause-centuries-of-sea-level-rise/.

National Energy Board (2016), 'Canada's energy future 2016: Energy supply and demand projections to 2040', accessed June 2016 at https://www.neb-one.gc.ca/nrg/ntgrtd/ftr/2016/2016nrgftr-eng.pdf.

National Ocean and Atmospheric Administration (2016), 'South Pole is the last place on Earth to pass a global warming milestone', accessed April 2017 at http://research.noaa.gov/News/NewsArchive/LatestNews/TabId/684/ArtMID/1768/ArticleID/11760/South-Pole-is-the-last-place-on-Earth-to-pass-a-global-warming-milestone.aspx.

National Opinion Research Centre (2007), 'General social surveys: General happiness', accessed 26 August 2007 at https://gssdataexplorer.norc.org/variables/434/vshow.

National Science Board (2012), *Diminishing Funding and Rising Expectations: Trends and Challenges for Public Research Universities, A Companion to Science and Engineering Indicators 2012*, Arlington, VA: National Science Foundation.

Natural Capital Committee (2013), 'The state of natural capital: Towards a framework for measurement and valuation', accessed December 2016 at https://www.cbd.int/financial/values/uk-stateof-naturalcapital.pdf.

Natural Capital Finance Alliance (2012), 'The natural capital declaration', accessed 29 September 2017 at http://www.naturalcapitalfinancealliance.org/the-declaration/.

Netherlands Environmental Agency (2006), 'Global greenhouse gas emissions increased 75% since 1970', accessed 16 August 2007 at http://www.mnp.nl/en/dossiers/Climatechange/TrendGHGemissions1990-2004.html.

Neumayer, E. (2003), *Weak Versus Strong Sustainability*, Cheltenham, UK and Northampton, MA, USA: Edward Elgar Publishing.

Ng, Y. (1997), 'A case for happiness, cardinalism, and interpersonal comparability', *Economic Journal*, **107**, 1848–58.

Nickell, S., L. Nunziata and W. Ochel (2005), 'Unemployment in the OECD since the 1960s: What do we know?', *Economic Journal*, **115**(500), 1–27.

Nordhaus, W.D. (1973), 'World dynamics: Measurement without data', *Economic Journal*, **83**(332), 1156–83.

Nordhaus, W.D. (1992a), 'Lethal model 2: The limits to growth revisited', *Brookings Papers on Economic Activity*, **1992**(2), 1–59.

Nordhaus, W.D. (1992b), 'Lethal model 2: Alternative mechanisms to control global warming', *American Economic Review*, **96**(2), 31–4.

Nordhaus, W.D. (2006), 'After Kyoto: Alternative mechanisms to control global warming', *American Economic Review*, **96**(2), 31–4.

Norgaard, R.B. (1990), 'Economic indicators of resource scarcity: A critical essay', *Journal of Environmental Economics and Management*, **19**(1), 19–25.

Norgaard, R.B. (2002), 'Optimists, pessimists, and science', *BioScience*, **52**(3), 287–92.

Norton, M.I. and D. Ariely (2011), 'Building a better America: One wealth quintile at a time', *Perspectives on Psychological Science*, **6**(1), 9–12.

Nuclear Waste Management Organization (2005), *Choosing a Way Forward*, Toronto: Nuclear Waste Management Organization, accessed 24 August 2007 at https://www.nwmo.ca/~/media/Site/Files/PDFs/2015/11/04/17/39/2680_nwmo_final_study_nov_2005.ashx.

Nuclear Waste Management Organization (2017), 'Why a deep geological repository?', accessed 19 September 2016 at https://www.nwmo.ca/en/A-Safe-Approach/Safety-Protecting-People-and-the-Environment/Why-a-Deep-Geological-Repository.

O'Brien, E. (2007), 'Countries where leaded petrol is possibly still sold for road use as at 22nd February 2007', accessed 19 August 2007 at https://www.lead.org.au/fs/fst27-20070222.html.

O'Connell, J.F. (1982), *Welfare Economic Theory*, Boston, MA: Auburn House.

OECD (1960), *Convention on the Organisation for Economic Co-operation and Development*, Paris: OECD Publishing, accessed 18 August 2007 at http://www.oecd.org/general/conventionontheorganisationforeconomicco-operationanddevelopment.htm.

OECD (1999), 'Energy: The next fifty years', accessed January 2017 at http://www.oecd.org/futures/17738498.pdf.

OECD (2001), 'Glossary of statistical terms: Gross Domestic Product (GDP)', accessed January 2017 at https://stats.oecd.org/glossary/detail.asp?ID=1163.

OECD (2004), 'Glossary of statistical terms', accessed 21 August 2007 at http://stats.oecd.org/glossary/detail.asp?ID=6266.

OECD (2005), *Economic Policy Reforms: Going for Growth*, Paris: OECD Publishing.

OECD (2008a), 'Measuring material flows and resource productivity: Synthesis report', accessed March 2016 at https://www.oecd.org/env/indicators-modelling-outlooks/MFA-Synthesis.pdf.

OECD (2008b), 'Growing unequal? Income distribution and poverty in OECD countries', accessed December 2016 at http://www.oecd.org/els/soc/growingunequalincomedistributionandpovertyinoecdcountries.htm.

OECD (2011a), 'Towards green growth: A summary for policy makers: May 2011', accessed June 2016 at http://www.oecd.org/greengrowth/48012345.pdf.

OECD (2011b), 'Towards green growth: Monitoring progress, OECD indicators', accessed December 2016 at http://www.oecd.org/greengrowth/48224574.pdf.

OECD (2014), 'Report on the OECD Framework for Inclusive Growth', accessed May 2016 at https://www.oecd.org/mcm/IG_MCM_ENG.pdf.

OECD (2015a), *In It Together: Why Less Inequality Benefits All*, Paris: OECD Publishing.

OECD (2015b), *Environment at a Glance 2015*, Paris: OECD Publishing.

OECD (2015c), 'Household wealth inequality across OECD countries: New OECD evidence', *OECD Statistics Brief*, June 2015, No. 21, available at https://www.oecd.org/std/household-wealth-inequality-across-OECD-countries-OECDSB21.pdf.

OECD (2015d), 'Towards green growth? Tracking progress', *OECD Green Growth Studies*, accessed May 2016 at http://www.oecd-ilibrary.org/environ ment/towards-green-growth_9789264234437-en;jsessionid=2bk6o7ifelqw 0.x-oecd-live-03.

OECD (2016a), 'Economic Outlook No. 99 – June 2016', accessed 9 December 2016 at https://stats.oecd.org/Index.aspx?DataSetCode=EO 99_INTERNET.

OECD (2016b), 'Measuring well-being and progress: Well-being research', accessed 16 November 2016 at https://www.oecd.org/statistics/measu ring-well-being-and-progress.htm.

OECD (2016c), 'Tax and benefit systems: OECD indicators', accessed February 2017 at http://www.oecd.org/social/benefits-and-wages.htm.

OECD (2016d), 'Income distribution and poverty database', accessed 4 August 2017 at http://stats.oecd.org/Index.aspx?DataSetCode=ANHRS.

OECD (2016e), *OECD.Stat* Unemployment Rate, accessed 20 November 2016 at https://stats.oecd.org.

OECD (2017a), 'NAIRU', accessed 22 November 2017 at http://stats.oecd. org.

OECD (2017b), 'Inequality', accessed 13 August 2017 at http://www.oecd. org/social/inequality.htm.

OECD (2017c), *Investing in Climate, Investing in Growth*, Paris: OECD Publishing, accessed 20 January 2018 at http://www.oecd.org/env/invest ing-in-climate-investing-in-growth-9789264273528-en.htm.

OECD (2017d), *OECD Employment Outlook 2017*, Paris: OECD Publishing.

OECD (2017e), 'OECD.Stat 1. Gross domestic product (GDP)', accessed 3 August 2017 at https://stats.oecd.org/index.aspx?queryid=60702.

OECD (2018), 'Income distribution and poverty database', accessed 15 June 2018 at http://stats.oecd.org/Index.aspx?DataSetCode=ANHRS.

Office for National Statistics (2016), 'Measuring national wellbeing: Life in the UK: 2016', accessed 23 March 2016 at http://www.ons.gov.uk/peopl epopulationandcommunity/wellbeing/articles/measuringnationalwellbein g/2016.

Olivier, J.G.J., G. Janssens-Maenhout, M. Muntean and J.A.H.W. Peters (2016), *Trends in Global $CO_2$ Emissions: 2016 Report*, Publication No. 2315, The Hague: PBL Netherlands Environmental Agency.

Onda, K., J. Lobuglio and J. Bartram (2012), 'Global access to safe water: Accounting for water quality and the resulting impact on MDG progress', *International Journal of Environmental Research and Public Health*, **9**, 880–94.

Ontario Ministry of the Environment (2006), *Emissions Trading*, accessed 9 July 2007 at http://www.ene.gov.on.ca.ezproxy.library.yorku.ca/program s/4346e02.htm.

Orrell, D. (2017), *Economyths. 11 Ways Economics Gets It Wrong*, London: Icon Books Ltd.

Osborn, T. and T. Kleinen (2008), '7: The thermohaline circulation', accessed 3 October 2016 at http://www.cru.uea.ac.uk/documents/421974/1295957/Info+sheet+%237.pdf/320eba6e-d384-497d-b4fc-2d2c187f805e.

Ostrom, E. (1990), *Governing the Commons: The Evolution of Institutions for Collective Action*, Cambridge: Cambridge University Press.

Ostrom, E. (2008), 'The challenge of common-pool resources', *Environment: Science and Policy for Sustainable Development*, **50**(4), 8–21.

Oxfam (2017), 'Just 8 men own same wealth as half the world', accessed 15 August 2017 at https://www.oxfam.org/en/pressroom/pressreleases/2017-01-16/just-8-men-own-same-wealth-half-world.

Pagiola, S. (2008), 'Payments for environmental services in Costa Rica', *Ecological Economics*, **65**, 712–24.

Parks, S. and J. Gowdy (2013), 'What have economists learned about valuing nature? A review essay', *Ecosystem Services*, **3**, e1–e10.

Parrish, D.D., H.B. Singh, L. Molina and S. Madronich (2011), 'Air quality progress in North American megacities: A review', *Atmospheric Environment*, **45**, 7015–25.

Pascual, U., R. Muradian, L. Brander, E. Gómez-Baggethun, B. Martin-Lopez, M. Verma, M. Christie et al. (2010), 'The economics of valuing ecosystem services and biodiversity', in P. Kumar (ed.), *The Economics of Ecosystems and Biodiversity: Ecological and Economic Foundations*, London: Earthscan.

Pavone, V., J. Goven and R. Guarino (2011), 'From risk assessment to in-context trajectory evaluation: GMOs and their social implications', *Environmental Sciences Europe*, **23**(3), 1–13.

PBL Netherlands Environmental Assessment Agency (2007), 'Press Release: Chinese $CO_2$ emissions in perspective', accessed March 2016 at http://www.pbl.nl/en/news/pressreleases/2007/20070622ChineseCO2emissionsinperspective.

Pearce, D., B. Groom, C. Hepburn and P. Koundouri (2003), 'Valuing the future: Recent advances in social discounting', *World Economics*, **4**(2), 121–41.

Pearsall, J. and B. Timble (eds) (1996), *The Oxford English Reference Dictionary*, 2nd edn, Oxford: Oxford University Press.

Pembina Institute (2007), *Cleaning the Air about Nuclear Power, Report Summary*, accessed June 2007 at https://www.pembina.org/reports/ClearingThAir_Summary_final.pdf.

Peres, S. and M. Gorbachev (2000), *Water: The Crisis of the 21st Century*, accessed 8 July 2007 at http://www.gci.ch/en/programs/confprevention/wfp/press/nobel.htm.

Petermann, T. (2000), 'Technology assessment units in the European parliamentary systems', in N.J. Vig and H. Paschen (eds), *Parliaments and Technology: The Development of Technology Assessment in Europe*, New York: State University of New York Press, pp. 37–65.

Petty, W. (1691), *Verbatim Sapienti*, accessed 15 November 2017 at https://en.wikisource.org/wiki/Verbum_Sapienti_(1899).

Pezzey, J. (1992), *Sustainable Development Concepts: An Economic Analysis*, Washington, DC: World Bank.

Pichette, L. (2004), 'Are wealth effects important for Canada?', *Bank of Canada Review*, Spring, pp. 29–35.

Picot, G. and J. Myles (2004), 'Income inequality and low income in Canada', *Horizons*, December, Government of Canada, Ottawa, accessed at http://policyresearch.gc.ca.ezproxy.library.yorku.ca/page.asp?pogcnm=V7N2_ART_03.

Pigou, A.C. (1920[1952]), *The Economics of Welfare*, 4th edn, London: Macmillan and Co.

Piketty, T. (2014), *Capital in the Twenty-First Century*, Cambridge, MA: Harvard University Press.

Pimental, D., M. Herz, M. Glickstein, M. Zimmerman, R. Allen, K. Becker, J. Evans et al. (2002), 'Renewable energy: Current and potential issues', *BioScience*, **52**(12), 1111–20.

Polanyi, K. (1944), *The Great Transformation*, Boston, MA: Beacon Press.

Pollard, S. (1971), *The Idea of Progress: History and Society*, Harmondsworth: Penguin Books.

Pope Francis (2015), *Laudato Si': On Care for Our Common Home* [Encyclical], accessed 10 August 2017 at http://w2.vatican.va/content/francesco/en/encyclicals/documents/papa-francesco_20150524_enciclica-laudato-si.html.

Population Reference Bureau (2016), 'Data finder: Canada', accessed June 2016 at http://www.prb.org/DataFinder/Geography/Data.aspx?loc=311.

Porras, I., D.N. Barton, M. Miranda and A. Chacón-Cascante (2013), *Learning from 20 years of Payments for Ecosystem Services in Costa Rica*, London: International Institute for Environment and Development, accessed 1 August 2017 at www.iied.org/pubs.

Porritt, J. (2005), *Capitalism as if the World Matters*, London: Earthscan.

Potapov, P., M. Hansen, L. Laestadius, S. Turuvabova, A. Yaroshenko, C. Thies, W. Smith et al. (2017), 'The last frontiers of wilderness: Tracking loss of intact forest landscapes from 2000 to 2013', *Science Advance*, **3**, 1–13.

PricewaterhouseCoopers LLP (PwC) (2015), 'Consumer intelligence series: The sharing economy', accessed 26 February 2017 at https://www.pwc.

com/us/en/technology/publications/assets/pwc-consumer-intelligence-series-the-sharing-economy.pdf.

Puko, T. and G. Kantchev (2016), 'Oil prices tumble below $30 a barrel', *The Wall Street Journal*, accessed March 2016 at https://www.wsj.com/articles/oil-prices-fall-below-30-a-barrel-1452853918.

Pullinger, M. (2014), 'Working time reduction policy in a sustainable economy: Criteria and options for its design', *Ecological Economics*, **103**, 11–19.

Radzicki, M.J. (1997), *Introduction to System Dynamics*, Washington, DC: United States Department of Energy, accessed 16 October 2007 at http://www.systemdynamics.org/DL-IntroSysDyn/inside.htm.

Randers, J. (2012), *2052: A Global Forecast for the Next Forty Years*, White River Junction, VT: Chelsea Green Publishing.

Raworth, K. (2012), 'A safe and just space for humanity: Can we live without the doughnut?', Oxfam Discussion Paper, February, accessed 5 September 2016 at https://pdfs.semanticscholar.org/458c/d1325da288d260340826bd84af36bf450f99.pdf.

Raworth, K. (2017), *Doughnut Economics: Seven Ways to Think Like a 21st Century Economist*, London: Random House Business Books.

Redefining Progress (2007), *Genuine Progress Indicator*, accessed 11 April 2007 at http://rprogress.org/sustainability_indicators/genuine_progress_indicator.htm.

Rees, W.E. (2006), 'Why conventional economic logic won't protect biodiversity', in D.M. Lavigne (ed.), *Gaining Ground: In Pursuit of Ecological Sustainability*, International Fund for Animal Welfare, Guelph, Canada and the University of Limerick, Limerick, Ireland, pp. 207–26.

Rees, W.E. (2017), 'What, me worry? Humans are blind to imminent environmental collapse: Accelerating biodiversity loss may turn out to be the sleeper issue of the century', *The Tyee.ca*, accessed 16 November 2017 at https://www.thetyee.ca/Opinion/2017/11/16/humans-blind-imminent-environmental-collapse/.

Reich, P.B., D. Tilman, F. Isbell, K. Mueller, S.E. Hobbie, D.F.B. Flynn and N. Eisenhauer (2012), 'Impacts of biodiversity loss escalate through time as redundancy fades', *Science*, **336**, 589–92.

Ripple, W.J., C. Wolf, T.M. Newsome, M. Galetti, M. Alamgir, E. Crist, M.I. Mahmoud et al. (2017), 'World scientists' warning to humanity: A second notice', *BioScience*, **67**(12), 1026–8, accessed 13 November 2017 at https://academic.oup.com/bioscience/article/doi/10.1093/biosci/bix125/4605229.

Roach, J. (2004), 'Source of half earth's oxygen gets little credit', *National Geographic*, accessed 3 October 2016 at http://news.nationalgeographic.com/news/2004/06/0607_040607_phytoplankton.html.

Robbins, L.C. (1932), *An Essay on the Nature and Significance of Economic Science*, London: Macmillan & Co.

Rockström, J. (2017), 'A fundamental misrepresentation of the planetary boundaries framework', Stockholm Resilience Centre, accessed 18 January 2018 at file:///Users/petervictor/Desktop/A%20fundamental%20misrepre sentation%20of%20the%20Planetary%20Boundaries%20framework%20 -%20Stockholm%20Resilience%20Centre.webarchive.

Rockström, J., W.L. Steffen, K. Noone, Å. Persson, F.S. Chapin III, E.F. Lambin, T.M. Lenton, M. Scheffer et al. (2009a), 'Planetary boundaries: Exploring the safe operating space for humanity', *Ecology and Society*, **14**(2), 32.

Rockström, J., W. Steffen, K. Noone, Å. Persson, F.S. Chapin III, E.F. Lambin, T.M. Lenton, M. Scheffer et al. (2009b), 'A safe operating space for humanity', *Nature*, **461**, 472–5.

Roper, L.D. (2017), 'Fossil fuels-energy return on energy invested', accessed 9 August 2017 at http://www.roperld.com/science/minerals/EROEIFossil Fuels.htm.

Rosen, C. (2000), *World Resources 2000–2001: People and Ecosystems: The Fraying Web of Life*, Washington, DC: World Resources Institute.

Rostow, W.W. (1960), *The Stages of Economic Growth: A Non-Communist Manifesto*, Cambridge: Cambridge University Press.

Rowe, J.W. (2009), 'Nuclear power in a carbon-constrained world', *Daedalus*, **138**(4), 81–90.

Royal Society (2007), *The Royal Society*, accessed 25 August 2007 at www.royalsoc.ac.uk.

Running, S.W. (2012), 'Measurable planetary boundary for the biosphere', *Science*, **337**, 1458–9.

Russell, B. (1918), *Proposed Roads to Freedom, Socialism, Anarchism and Syndicalism*, New York: Cornwall Press.

Samuelson, P. and W. Nordhaus (2009), *Economics 19e*, New York: McGraw-Hill Education.

Sánchez-Azofeifa, G.A., A. Pfaff, J.A. Robalino and J.P. Boomhower (2007), 'Costa Rica's payment for environmental services program: Intention, implementation, and impact', *Conservation Biology*, **21**(5), 1165–73.

Sandel, M.J. (2012), *What Money Can't Buy*, New York: Farrar, Straus and Giroux.

Sarlo, C. (2006), 'Poverty in Canada: 2006 update', *Fraser Alert*, accessed 16 October 2007 at https://www.fraserinstitute.org/sites/default/files/PovertyinCanada2006.pdf.

Sarlo, C. (2013), 'Poverty: Where do we draw the line?', accessed December

2016 at https://www.fraserinstitute.org/sites/default/files/Poverty-where-do-we-draw-the-line.pdf.

Sawe, B. (2017), 'Countries that still use leaded gasoline', Worldatlas, accessed 1 August 2017 at http://www.worldatlas.com/articles/countries-that-still-use-leaded-gasoline.html.

Schaffartzik, A., A. Mayer, S. Gingrich, N. Eisenmenger, C. Loy and F. Krausmann (2014), 'The global metabolic transition: Regional patterns and trends of global material flows, 1950–2010', *Ecological Economics*, **26**(May), 87–97.

Scheer, H. (2007), *Energy Autonomy: The Economic, Social and Technological Case for Renewable Energy*, London, UK and Sterling, USA: Earthscan.

Schmalensee, R., P.L. Joskow, A.D. Ellerman, J.P. Montero and E.M. Bailey (1998), 'An interim evaluation of sulfur dioxide emissions trading', *Journal of Economic Perspectives*, **12**(3), 53–68.

Schmelzer, M. (2016), *The Hegemony of Growth: The OECD and the Making of the Economic Growth Paradigm*, Cambridge: Cambridge University Press.

Schneider, S.H. (2004), 'Abrupt non-linear climate change, irreversibility and surprise', *Global Environmental Change*, **14**(3), 245–58.

Schor, J. (2010), *Plenitude: The New Economics of True Wealth*, Harmondsworth: Penguin Press.

Schumacher, E.F. (1973), *Small Is Beautiful: Economics as if People Mattered*, New York: Harper & Row.

Schumpeter, J.A. (1950), *Capitalism, Socialism, and Democracy*, 3rd edn, New York: Harper.

Schwanitz, V.J. (2013), 'Evaluating integrated assessment models of global climate change', *Environmental Modelling and Software*, **50**, 120–31.

Sen, A.K. (2001), *Development as Freedom*, Oxford, UK and New York, USA: Oxford University Press.

Sers, M. and P.A. Victor (2018), 'The macroeconomics of the energy-emissions trap', *Ecological Economics*, **151**, 10–21.

Shaffer, E.R. and J.E. Brenner (2004), 'International trade agreements: Hazards to health?', *International Journal of Health Services*, **34**(3), 467–81.

Simmons, M.R. (2005), *Twilight in the Desert: The Coming Saudi Oil Shock and the World Economy*, Hoboken, NJ: John Wiley.

Simon, J. (1994), 'More people, greater wealth, more resources, healthier environment', *Economic Affairs*, **14**(3), 22–9.

Simon, J. (1998), *Curriculum Vitae*, accessed 18 August 2007 at http://www.juliansimon.com/vita.html#education.

Simpson, E. (2015), 'What comes from the crypt', *Political Science*

*Publications*, Paper No. 112, accessed January 2017 at http://ir.lib.uwo. ca/politicalsciencepub/112.

Simpson, E. (2016), 'A precautionary tale', *Political Science Publications*, Paper No. 120, accessed January 2017 at http://ir.lib.uwo.ca/politicalsc iencepub/120.

Simpson, R.D., M.A. Toman and R.U. Ayres (2005), *Scarcity and Growth Revisited: Natural Resources and the Environment in the New Millennium*, Washington, DC: Resources for the Future.

Sjostrom, M. and G. Ostblom (2010), 'Decoupling waste generation from economic growth: A CGE analysis of the Swedish case', *Ecological Economics*, **69**(7), 1545–52.

Sklenar, J. and H. Holden (2007), 'Is Canada really an environmental laggard?', *Hamilton Spectator*, accessed 25 February 2017 at https:// www.fraserinstitute.org/article/canada-really-environmental-laggard.

Smakhtin, V., C. Revenga and P. Döll (2004), 'A pilot global assessment of environmental water requirements and scarcity', *Water International*, **29**(3), 307–17.

Smart Prosperity (2016), 'New thinking: Canada's roadmap to smart prosperity – executive summary', Ottawa: Smart Prosperity.

Smil, V. (1994), *Energy in World History*, Boulder, CO: Westview Press.

Smil, V. (2003a), *Energy at the Crossroads: Global Perspectives and Uncertainties*, Cambridge, MA: MIT Press.

Smil, V. (2003b), *The Earth's Biosphere: Evolution, Dynamics, and Change*, Cambridge, MA: MIT Press.

Smil, V. (2014), *Making the Modern World: Materials and Dematerialization*, Chichester: John Wiley & Sons.

Smil, V. (2016), *Energy Transitions: Global and National Perspectives*, 2nd edn, Santa Barbara, CA: Praeger.

Smith, A. (1776), *An Inquiry into the Nature and Causes of the Wealth of Nations*, London: W. Strahan and T. Cadell.

Smith, B. (2006), *Insurmountable Risks: The Dangers of Using Nuclear Power to Combat Global Climate Change: Summary*, Takoma Park, MD: IEER Press, accessed 24 August 2007 at http://www.ieer.org/reports/ insurmountablerisks/summary.pdf.

Smith, R. (2010), 'Beyond growth or beyond capitalism?', *Truthout*, 15 January, accessed 12 December 2017 at http://www.truth-out.org/news/ item/21215-beyond-growth-or-beyond-capitalism.

Smith, R. (2016), 'Natural capital measurement at Statistics Canada: Current status and untapped potential', *Sustainable Prosperity* and *Midsummer Analytics*, accessed December 2016 at http://nkp.smartprosperity.ca/sites/ default/files/publications/files/Natural%20Capital%20Measurement.pdf.

Smith, T.W. (1979), 'Happiness: Time trends, seasonal variations, intersurvey differences, and other mysteries', *Social Psychology Quarterly*, **42**(15), 18–30.

Smith, V.K. and John Krutilla (1979), *Scarcity and Growth Reconsidered*, Baltimore, MD: Johns Hopkins University Press.

Snowdon, K. (2015), 'Canada's universities: Cost pressures, business models and financial sustainability', *Canadian Association of University Business Officers (CAUBO)*, accessed August 2017 at https://www.caubo.ca/knowledge-centre/surveysreports/canadas-universities-cost-pressures-business-models-financial-sustainability/.

Solnick, S. and D. Hemenway (2005), 'Are positional concerns stronger in some domains than in others?', *American Economic Review*, **95**(2), 147–51.

Solow, R.M. (1956), 'A contribution to the theory of economic growth', *Quarterly Journal of Economics*, **70**(1), 65–94.

Solow, R.M. (2008), Quoted in 'The specter of a no-growth world' by Steven Stoll, *Harper's Magazine*, March.

Sonne, R.C. (2013), 'Self storage economics', *Appraisal Journal*, Summer, Chicago, IL: Appraisal Institute.

Sorrell, S. (2007), 'The rebound effect: An assessment of the evidence for economy-wide energy savings from improved energy efficiency', report produced by the Sussex Energy Group for the Technology and Policy Assessment function of the UK Energy Research Centre.

Sovacool, B.K. (2011), 'The policy challenges of tradable credits: A critical review', *Energy Policy*, **39**(2), 575–85.

Sovacool, B.K. (2016), 'How long will it take? Conceptualizing the temporal dynamics of energy transitions', *Energy Research & Social Science*, **13**, 202–15.

Spash, C.L. (2007), 'The economics of climate change impacts à la Stern: Novel and nuanced or rhetorically restricted?', *Ecological Economics*, **63**, 706–13.

Speer, S. and J. Emes (2014), 'Post-stimulus spending trends in Canada', *Fraser Research Bulletin*, accessed December 2016 at https://www.fraserinstitute.org/sites/default/files/post-stimulus-spending-trends-in-canada.pdf.

Speth, J.G. (2012), *America the Possible: Manifesto for a New Economy*, New Haven, CT and London, UK: Yale University Press.

Stander, L. and L. Theodore (2011), 'Environmental implications of nanotechnology: An update', *International Journal of Environmental Research and Public Health*, **8**(2), 470–79.

Statistics Canada (2007), 'Income in Canada 2005', *Statistics Canada* Catalogue No. 75-202-XIE, accessed 16 July 2007 at http://publications.

gc.ca/collections/collection_2007/statcan/75-202-X/75-202-XIE2005000.
pdf.
Statistics Canada (2009), 'Table 385-0001 Consolidated federal, provincial,
territorial and local government revenue and expenditures', accessed
November 2016 at http://www5.statcan.gc.ca/cansim/a26?lang=eng&retr
Lang=eng&id=3850001&&pattern=&stByVal=1&p1=1&p2=37&tabMo
de=dataTable&csid=.
Statistics Canada (2011), 'Table 202-0805: Low income gap, by economic
family type, 2008 constant dollars', deleted by Statistics Canada on 13
June 2011.
Statistics Canada (2015a), *Population Projections for Canada (2013–2063),
Province and Territories (2013 to 2038)*, by the National Population
Projections team N. Bohnert, J. Chagnon, P. Dion, Catalogue no. 91-520-
X, accessed 24 November 2017 at http://www.statcan.gc.ca/pub/91-520-
x/91-520-x2014001-eng.pdf.
Statistics Canada (2015b), 'Low income lines, 2013–2014: Update', *Income
Statistics Division*, Catalogue No. 75F0002M – No. 2, accessed 24
November 2016 at http://www.statcan.gc.ca/pub/75f0002m/75f0002m2
015002-eng.pdf.
Statistics Canada (2016a), 'Stock and consumption of fixed non-residential
capital', accessed December 2016 at http://www23.statcan.gc.ca/imdb/
p2SV.pl?Function=getSurvey&SDDS=2820.
Statistics Canada (2016b), 'Table 206-0041: Low income statistics by age,
sex and economic family type, Canada, provinces and selected census
metropolitan areas (CMAs)', accessed 29 November 2016 at http://www5
.statcan.gc.ca/cansim/a26?lang=eng&id=2060041.
Statistics Canada (2016c), 'Variant of NAICS 2012: Goods and services producing industries', accessed 4 February 2017 at http://www23.
statcan.gc.ca/imdb/p3VD.pl?Function=getVD&TVD=138253.
Statistics Canada (2016d), 'Table 378-0119: Financial flow accounts, quarterly (dollars)', CANSIM (database), accessed March 2016 at http://
www5.statcan.gc.ca/cansim/a26?lang=eng&id=3780119.
Statistics Canada (2017a), 'CANSIM table 051-0001', accessed 23
November 2017 at http://www5.statcan.gc.ca/cansim/a26?id=510001.
Statistics Canada (2017b), 'Population size and growth in Canada: Key
results from the 2016 Census', accessed 24 November 2017 at https://
www.statcan.gc.ca/daily-quotidien/170208/dq170208a-eng.htm.
Statistics Canada (2017c), 'CANSIM table 051-0004', accessed 24
November 2017 at http://www5.statcan.gc.ca/cansim/a26?lang=eng&ret
rLang=eng&id=0510004&&pattern=&stByVal=1&p1=1&p2=-1&tabM
ode=dataTable&csid=.
Statistics Canada (2017d), 'CANSIM table 051-0005', accessed 24

November 2017 at http://www5.statcan.gc.ca/cansim/a26?lang=eng&ret
rLang=eng&id=0510005&&pattern=&stByVal=1&p1=1&p2=-1&tabM
ode=dataTable&csid=.

Statistics Canada (2017e), 'CANSIM table 380-0064', accessed 28
March 2017 at https://www150.statcan.gc.ca/t1/tbl1/en/tv.action?pid=
3610010401.

Statistics Canada (2017f), 'CANSIM table 052-0005', accessed 7 January 2017
at https://www150.statcan.gc.ca/t1/tbl1/en/tv.action?pid=1710005701.

Statistics Canada (2017g), 'CANSIM table 111-0008', accessed 30
September 2017 at https://www150.statcan.gc.ca/t1/tbl1/en/tv.action?
pid=1110000801.

Statistics Canada (2017h), 'Table 379-0031: Gross Domestic Product
(GDP) at basic prices, by North American Industry Classification
System (NAICS), annual (dollars × 1,000,000)', CANSIM (database),
accessed 21 November 2018 at https://www150.statcan.gc.ca/t1/tbl1/en/
tv.action?pid=3610043401.

Steffen, W., W. Broadgate, L. Deutsch, O. Gaffney and C. Ludwig (2015b),
'The trajectory of the Anthropocene: The Great Acceleration', *The
Anthropocene Review*, **2**(1), 81–98.

Steffen, W., K. Richardson, J. Rockström, S.E. Cornell, I. Fetzer, E.M.
Bennett, R. Biggs et al. (2015a), 'Planetary boundaries: Guiding human
development on a changing planet', *Science*, **347**(6223), 1259855-1-10.

Stern, D.I. (2004), 'The rise and fall of the Environmental Kuznets Curve',
*World Development*, **32**(8), 1419–39.

Stern, N. (2006), '2A.1 Ethical frameworks for climate change', in *Stern
Review on the Economics of Climate Change*, H.M. Treasury, accessed 30
July 2017 at http://webarchive.nationalarchives.gov.uk/20080910155332/
http://www.hm-treasury.gov.uk/independent_reviews/stern_review_eco
nomics_climate_change/stern_review_report.cfm.

Stern, N.H., S. Peters, V. Bakhshi, A. Bowen, C. Cameron, S. Catovsky,
D. Crane et al. (2006), *Stern Review: The Economics of Climate Change*
(Vol. 30), Cambridge: Cambridge University Press.

Stiglitz, J. (2016), *Rewriting the Rules of the American Economy: An
Agenda for Growth and Shared Prosperity*, New York, USA and London,
UK: W.W. Norton & Company.

Stiglitz, J.E., A. Sen and J-P. Fitoussi (2009), 'Report by the Commission
on the Measurement of Economic Performance and Social Progress',
Paris: Commission on the Measurement of Economic Performance and
Social Progress.

Storage World (2017), 'Worldwide self storage industry: Fact sheet',
accessed 3 August 2017 at https://www.storageworld.ie/worldwide-self-
storage-industry-fact-sheet/.

Streeck, W. (2016), *How Will Capitalism End?* New York: Verso Books.

Study of Critical Environmental Problems (SCEP) (1970), *Man's Impact on the Global Environment: Assessment and Recommendations for Action*, Cambridge, MA: MIT Press.

Sullivan, S. (2012), 'Banking nature? The spectacular financialisation of environmental conservation', *Antipode*, **45**(1), 198–217.

Summers, L.H. (2016), 'The age of secular stagnation: What it is and what to do about it', *Foreign Affairs*, March/April, accessed 24 July 2017 at https://www.foreignaffairs.com/articles/united-states/2016-02-15/age-secular-stagnation.

Sustainable Planning Research Group (2005), 'The maple leaf in the OECD: Comparing progress towards sustainability', Vancouver, BC: David Suzuki Foundation, accessed 29 August 2007 at http://www.davidsuzuki.org/publications/downloads/2005/OECD-English2-FINAL.pdf.

Sustainable Prosperity (2016), 'New thinking: Canada's roadmap to smart prosperity', February, accessed 16 November 2017 at http://institute.smartprosperity.ca/sites/default/files/newthinking.pdf.

Taebi, B. (2011), 'The morally desirable option for nuclear power production', *Philosophy and Technology*, **24**, 169–92.

Tainter, J.A. (1988), *The Collapse of Complex Societies*, Cambridge, UK and New York, USA: Cambridge University Press.

Talberth, J., C. Cobb and N. Slattery (2007), 'The Genuine Progress Indicators 2006: A tool for sustainable development', Oakland, CA: Redefining Progress.

Tanabe, N. (2013), 'Transboundary air pollution from China: Possibilities for cooperation with Japan', *Ecology Webinar Series*, accessed 1 August 2017 at http://www.ecology.com/2013/11/22/transboundary-air-pollution-china/.

Temple, S. (2011), 'Forestation and its discontents: The invention of an uncertain landscape in Southwestern France, 1850–present', *Environment and History*, **17**, 13–34.

Teräväinen, T., M. Lehtonen and M. Martiskainen (2011), 'Climate change, energy security, and risk-debating nuclear new build in Finland, France and the UK', *Energy Policy*, **39**, 3434–42.

*The Economist* (2016), 'The trouble with growth', 30 April, accessed 25 September 2017 at https://www.economist.com/news/briefing/21697845-gross-domestic-product-gdp-increasingly-poor-measure-prosperity-it-not-even.

The Royal Swedish Academy of Sciences (2018), Press release: 'The Prize in Economic Sciences 2018', accessed 8 October 2018 at https://www.nobelprize.org/prizes/economics/2018/press-release/.

Tickell, C. (2003), *Water: The Big Issue for the 21st Century*, accessed 7 September 2007 at http://www.crispintickell.com/page30.html.

Tietenberg, T. and L. Lewis (2014), *Environmental & Natural Resource Economics*, 10th edn, Abingdon: Taylor and Francis Group.

Timmerman, P. (2017), 'Growth, development and learning to live in a finite world', in P.A. Victor and B. Dolter (eds), *Handbook on Growth and Sustainability*, Cheltenham, UK and Northampton, MA, USA: Edward Elgar Publishing, pp. 17–37.

Timperley, J. (2017), 'COP 23: Key outcomes agreed at the UN climate talks in Bonn', *CarbonBrief*, 19 November, accessed 23 November 2017 at https://www.carbonbrief.org/cop23-key-outcomes-agreed-un-climate-talks-bonn.

Tollerson, J. (2017), 'World carbon emissions set to spike by 2% in 2017', *Nature*, 13 November, **551**(7680), accessed 18 November 2017 at file:///Users/petervictor/Desktop/World's%20carbon%20emissions%20set%20to%20spike%20by%202%25%20in%202017%20:%20Nature%20News%20&%20Comment.webarchive.

*Totaljobs* (2017), 'Magnificent machines: The Bagger 288 Bucket Excavator', accessed 26 November 2018 at https://www.totaljobs.com/careers-advice/tj-knows-it/magnificent-machines-bagger-288-bucket-excavator.

Trading Economics (2018), 'Japan government debt to GDP', accessed 15 January 2018 at https://tradingeconomics.com/japan/government-debt-to-gdp.

Trainer, T. (2014), 'Some inconvenient theses', *Energy Policy*, **64**, 168–74.

Transition Network (2016), 'How to start', accessed April 2016 at https://transitionnetwork.org/do-transition/starting-transition/how-to-start/.

Tripati, A.K., C.D. Roberts and R.A. Eagle (2009), 'Coupling of CO2 and ice sheet stability over major climate transitions of the last 20 million years', *Science*, **326**(5958), 1394–7.

Trottier Energy Futures Project (2016), 'Canada's challenge & opportunity: Transformations for major reductions in GHG emissions', Montreal, QC: Trottier Energy Futures Project, accessed June 2016 at http://iet.polymtl.ca/en/tefp/.

Trudeau, J. (2012), 'In conversation: Justin Trudeau', interviewed by J. Geddes, *Maclean's*, 27 February, accessed 13 December 2016 at http://www.macleans.ca/politics/ottawa/what-would-push-him-to-the-separatist-side-and-why-hes-his-mothers-not-his-fathers-son/.

Trudeau, J. (2014), *Common Ground*, Toronto: HarperCollins.

Turner, G. (2008), 'A comparison of the limits to growth with thirty years of reality', *CSIRO Working Paper Series 2008-09*, Canberra: CSIRO Sustainable Ecosystems.

Turner, G. (2014), 'Is global collapse imminent? An updated comparison of *Limits to Growth* with historical data', Research Paper No. 4, August, Melbourne Sustainable Society Institute.

Tutulmaz, O. and P.A. Victor (2014), 'Labour oriented stock adjustment model estimations of total investment for Canadian industries', *International Proceedings of Economics Development and Research* (3rd International Conference on Economics Marketing and Management: ICEMM, Toronto), vol. 69, pp. 68–74.

Tverberg, G. (2016), 'An updated version of the "peak oil" story', *Our Finite World*, accessed January 2017 at https://ourfiniteworld.com/2016/08/08/an-updated-version-of-the-peak-oil-story/.

Ueberfeldt, A. and Bank of Canada (2006), *Working Time Over the 20th Century*, Ottawa: Bank of Canada.

UK Government (2005), 'Securing the future: The UK Government sustainable development strategy', Presented to Parliament by the Secretary of State for Environment, Food and Rural Affairs by Command of Her Majesty, March, accessed 26 July 2017 at https://sustainabledevelopment.un.org/content/documents/1408uk.pdf.

UK National Ecosystem Assessment Follow-on (2014), 'The UK national ecosystem assessment follow-on: Synthesis of the key findings', UNECE (2016), 'No. 2 Brief: The co-benefits of climate change mitigation', January, Information Service United Nations Economic Commission for Europe, accessed 6 November 2016 at http://www.unece.org/fileadmin/DAM/Sustainable_Development_No._2__Final__Draft_OK_2.pdf.

UNEP-WCMC, LWEC, UK, accessed 3 October 2017 at http://uknea.unep-wcmc.org/Resources/tabid/82/Default.aspx.

UNFCCC (2015), 'Synthesis report on the aggregate effect of the intended nationally determined contributions', *United Nations Framework Convention on Climate Change*, Conference of the Parties Twenty-First Session, accessed September 2016 at http://unfccc.int/resource/docs/2015/cop21/eng/07.pdf.

UNFCCC (2016), 'Aggregate effect of the intended nationally determined contributions: An update', *United Nations Framework Convention on Climate Change*, Conference of the Parties Twenty-Second Session, accessed 9 September 2016 at https://mitigationpartnership.net/sites/default/files/aggregate_effect_of_the_intended_nationally_determined_contributions_an_update.pdf.

Union of Concerned Scientists (n.d.), 'Environmental impacts of renewable energy', accessed 1 October 2017 at http://www.ucsusa.org/clean-energy/renewable-energy/environmental-impacts.

United Nations (1992), 'United Nations Framework Convention on Climate Change', accessed 6 September 2016 at http://unfccc.int/files/essential_background/background_publications_htmlpdf/application/pdf/conveng.pdf.

United Nations (2015a), 'Transforming our world: The 2030 agenda for sustainable development', accessed May 2016 at https://sustainabledevelopment.un.org/post2015/transformingourworld/publication.

United Nations (2015b), *The Millennium Development Goals Report 2015*, New York: United Nations, accessed 30 September 2017 at http://www.un.org/millenniumgoals/2015_MDG_Report/pdf/MDG%202015%20rev%20(July%201).pdf.

United Nations (2015c), 'Sustainable development knowledge platform: First global meeting of the 10FYP', accessed 26 July 2017 at https://sustainabledevelopment.un.org/index.php?page=view&type=13&nr=1612&menu=1634.

United Nations (2016a), *The World's Cities in 2016: Data Booklet* (ST/ESA/SER.A/392), Department of Economic and Social Affairs, Population Division, accessed 17 November 2017 at http://www.un.org/en/development/desa/population/publications/pdf/urbanization/the_worlds_cities_in_2016_data_booklet.pdf.

United Nations (2016b), *The First Global Integrated Marine Assessment: World Ocean Assessment I*, accessed 3 October 2016 at http://www.un.org/depts/los/global_reporting/WOA_RegProcess.htm.

United Nations (2017a), *World Population Prospects: The 2017 Revision, Key Findings and Advance Tables*, Department of Economic and Social Affairs, Population Division Working Paper No. ESA/P/WP.241, accessed 17 November 2017 at https://esa.un.org/unpd/wpp/Publications/Files/WPP2017_KeyFindings.pdf.

United Nations (2017b), *World Population Prospects: The 2017 Revision, DVD Edition*, Department of Economic and Social Affairs, Population Division, accessed 23 November 2017 at https://www.un.org/development/desa/publications/world-population-prospects-the-2017-revision.html.

United Nations Conference on Trade and Development (UNCTAD) (2007), *The Least Developed Countries Report, 2007*, No. UNCTAD/LDC/2007, New York, USA and Geneva, Switzerland: United Nations.

United Nations, Department of Economic and Social Affairs (2010), 'Urban and rural areas 2009', accessed March 2016 at http://www.un.org/en/development/desa/population/publications/pdf/urbanization/urbanization-wallchart2009.pdf.

United Nations, Department of Economic and Social Affairs, Population Division (2010), 'World population prospects, the 2010 revision', accessed 23 November 2017 at https://web.archive.org/web/20121028012124/http://esa.un.org/unpd/wpp/Analytical-Figures/htm/fig_8.htm.

United Nations, Department of Economic and Social Affairs, Population Division (2013), 'World Population Policies 2013', p. 205, accessed 24 November 2017 at http://www.un.org/en/development/desa/population/publications/pdf/policy/WPP2013/wpp2013.pdf.

United Nations Development Programme (UNDP) (2012), 'Going beyond GDP, UNDP proposes human development measure of sustainability', accessed March 2016 at http://www.undp.org/content/undp/en/home/presscenter/pressreleases/2012/06/20/oing-beyond-gdp-undp-proposes-human-development-measure-of-sustainability.html.

United Nations Development Programme (UNDP) (2015a), *Human Development Report 2015: Work for Human Development*, accessed August 2016 at http://report.hdr.undp.org/.

United Nations Development Programme (UNDP) (2015b), 'Human Development Index (HDI)', accessed October 2016 at http://hdr.undp.org/en/content/human-development-index-hdi.

United Nations Development Programme (UNDP) (2015c), 'Inequality-adjusted Human Development Index (HDI)', accessed October 2016 at http://hdr.undp.org/en/content/inequality-adjusted-human-development-index-ihdi.

United Nations Educational, Scientific, and Cultural Organization (UNESCO) (2016), 'International migration glossary: Poverty', accessed 3 December 2016 at http://www.unesco.org/new/en/social-and-human-sciences/themes/international-migration/glossary/poverty/.

United Nations Environment Programme (UNEP) (2015), 'The financial system we need: Aligning the financial system with sustainable development', *The UNEP Inquiry Report*, Geneva: International Environment House.

United Nations Environment Programme (UNEP) (2016a), *Global Material Flows and Resource Productivity: Assessment Report for the UNEP International Resource Panel*, accessed 3 September 2016 at http://unep.org/documents/irp/16-00169_LW_GlobalMaterialFlowsUNEReport_FINAL_160701.pdf.

United Nations Environment Programme (UNEP) (2016b), 'Green Economy', accessed 11 May 2016 at http://web.unep.org/greeneconomy/.

United Nations Environment Programme (UNEP) (2017), *The Emissions Gap Report 2017*, Nairobi: United Nations Environment Programme (UNEP).

United Nations, European Commission, International Monetary Fund, Organisation for Economic Co-operation and Development and World Bank (2009), *System of National Accounts 2008*, New York: United Nations.

United Nations, European Union, Food and Agriculture Organization of the United Nations, IMF, OECD and World Bank (2014), *The System of Environmental-Economic Accounting 2012*, New York: United Nations.

United Nations High Commissioner for Refugees (UNHCR) (2006), '2006 global trends: Refugees, asylum-seekers, returnees, internally displaced and stateless persons', accessed March 2016 at http://www.unhcr.org/ statistics/STATISTICS/4676a71d4.pdf.

United Nations High Commissioner for Refugees (UNHCR) (2015), 'UNHCR, the environment & climate change, updated version', UNHCR accessed 2 December 2017 at http://www.unhcr.org/540854f49.

United Nations High Commissioner for Refugees (UNHCR) (2016), 'Global trends: Forced displacement in 2015', accessed April 2017 at http://www.unhcr.org/576408cd7.

United Nations Secretary-General's High-Level Panel on Global Sustainability (2012), *Resilient People, Resilient Planet: A Future Worth Choosing*, New York: United Nations.

University of Sussex Science Policy Research Unit (1973), *Thinking about the Future: A Critique of the Limits to Growth*, edited by H.S.D. Cole, London: Chatto & Windus.

UN-REDD Programme (2017), 'About REDD+', accessed October 2016 at http://www.unredd.net/about/what-is-redd-plus.html.

US Bureau of Economic Analysis (2016), 'National economic accounts: Gross Domestic Product (GDP)', US Department of Commerce, accessed 2 November 2016 at https://www.bea.gov/national/index.htm#gdp.

US Census Bureau (2017), 'US and world population clock', accessed 12 October 2017 at https://www.census.gov/popclock/.

US Congress, Office of Technology Assessment (1996), *The OTA Legacy: 1972–1995*, accessed 2 September 2007 at http://www.wws.princeton. edu/~ota/.

US Congressional Budget Office (2016), 'An update to the budget and economic outlook: 2016 to 2026', accessed 19 November 2016 at https:// www.cbo.gov/sites/default/files/114th-congress-2015-2016/reports/51908- 2016outlookupdateonecol-2.pdf.

US Department of State (n.d.), 'Sustainable development', accessed December 2016 at https://www.state.gov/e/oes/sus/.

US Energy Information Administration (EIA) (2015), 'Today in energy: China and India drive recent changes in world coal trade', accessed 2 December 2016 at https://www.eia.gov/todayinenergy/detail.php?id=23852.

US Energy Information Administration (EIA) (2016a), *Capital Cost Estimates for Utility Scale Electricity Generating Plants*, Table 1, accessed 1 July 2017 at https://www.eia.gov/analysis/studies/powerplants/capital cost/pdf/capcost_assumption.pdf.

US Energy Information Administration (EIA) (2016b), *International Energy Outlook 2016, with projections to 2040*, Washington, DC: US Department of Energy, accessed 21 June 2016 at http://www.eia.gov/outlooks/ieo/ pdf/0484(2016).pdf.

US Energy Information Administration (EIA) (2017), *Addendum: Capital*

*Cost Estimates for Additional Utility Scale Electric Generating Plants*, accessed 1 November 2017 at https://www.eia.gov/analysis/studies/powe rplants/capitalcost/pdf/beret_addendum_leidos.pdf.

US Environmental Protection Agency (EPA) (2017a), *Global Greenhouse Gas Emissions Data*, accessed 30 November 2017 at http://www3.epa. gov/climatechange/ghgemissions/global.html.

US Environmental Protection Agency (EPA) (2017b), 'About smart growth', accessed 26 February 2017 at https://www.epa.gov/smartgrowth/ about-smart-growth.

US Environmental Protection Agency (EPA) (n.d.), 'Understanding global warming potentials', accessed 3 October 2017 at https://www.epa.gov/ ghgemissions/understanding-global-warming-potentials.

US Geological Survey (2006), *Minerals Information*, accessed 18 August 2007 at http://minerals.usgs.gov/minerals/pubs/stat/.

Van den Bergh, Jeroen C.J.M. (2011), 'Environment versus growth: A criticism of "degrowth" and a plea for "a-growth"', *Ecological Economics*, **70**(5), 881–90.

Van Dijk, A., H. Slaper, P.N. Den Outer, O. Morgenstern, P. Braesicke and J.A. Pyle (2013), 'Skin cancer risks avoided by the Montreal Protocol: Worldwide modeling integrating coupled climate-chemistry models with a risk model for UV', *Photochemistry and Photobiology Sciences*, **89**, 234–46.

Vargish, T. (1980), 'Why the person next to you hates limits to growth', *Technological Forecasting and Social Change*, **16**, 179–89.

Vásquez Pimentel, D.A., I.M. Aymar and M. Lawson (2018), 'Reward work, not wealth', Oxfam Briefing Paper, January, Oxfam International, accessed 23 January 2018 at https://www.oxfam.org/sites/www.oxfam.org/files/file_ attachments/bp-reward-work-not-wealth-220118-en.pdf?cid=aff_affwd_ donate_id78888&awc=5991_1516715345_0a84322c20ef396277dc8ed070 020d3e.

Veblen, T.B. (1899), *The Theory of the Leisure Class*, New York: Dover Publications.

Verspagen, B. (2006), 'University research, intellectual property rights and European innovation systems', *Journal of Economic Surveys*, **20**(4), 607–32.

Victor, P.A. (1972), *Pollution: Economy and Environment*, Toronto, ON: University of Toronto Press.

Victor, P.A. (1991), 'Economics and the challenge of environmental issues', in W. Leiss (ed.), *Politics and Ecology in Canada*, Toronto, ON: University of Toronto Press. Reprinted in H.E. Daly (ed.), *Economics, Ecology, Ethics*, San Francisco, CA: W.H. Freeman, 1980.

Victor, P.A. (2007), 'Nature as capital: Concerns and considerations', in

J. Leonard, C. Ragan and F. St-Hilaire (eds), *A Canadian Priorities Agenda*, Montreal: Institute for Research on Public Policy, pp. 171–7.

Victor, P.A. (2008), *Managing Without Growth: Slower by Design, Not Disaster*, Cheltenham, UK and Northampton, MA, USA: Edward Elgar Publishing.

Victor, P.A. (2010), 'Ecological economics and economic growth', *Annals of the New York Academy of Sciences*, **1185**(1), 237–45.

Victor, P.A. and T. Jackson (2012), 'A commentary on UNEP's green economy scenarios', *Ecological Economics*, **77**, 11–15.

Victor, P.A. and T. Jackson (2015), 'The trouble with growth', *State of the World 2015*, The Worldwatch Institute, Washington, DC: Island Press.

Vig, N.J. and H. Paschen (2000), *Parliaments and Technology: The Development of Technology Assessment in Europe*, Albany, NY: State University of New York Press.

Vitousek, P.M., P.R. Ehrlich, A.H. Ehrlich and P.A. Matson (1986), 'Human appropriation of the products of photosynthesis', *BioScience*, **36**(6), 368–73.

Von Hayek, F.A. (1956), *The Road to Serfdom*, Chicago, IL: University of Chicago Press.

Von Weizsäcker, E.U. and A. Wijkman (2018), *Come On! Capitalism, Short-termism, Population and the Destruction of the Planet*, New York: Springer.

Wackernagel, M. and W.E. Rees (1996), *Our Ecological Footprint: Reducing Human Impact on the Earth*, Gabriola Island, Canada and Philadelphia, USA: New Society Publishers.

Wang, J-J., Y-Y. Jing, C-F. Zhang and J-H. Zhao (2009), 'Review on multi-criteria decision analysis aid in sustainable energy decision-making', *Renewable and Sustainable Energy Reviews*, **13**, 2263–78.

Ward, J.D., P.C. Sutton, A.D. Werner, R. Costanza, S.H. Mohr and C.T. Simmons (2016), 'Is decoupling GDP growth from environmental impact possible?', *PLoS ONE*, **11**(10), 1–14, accessed 16 August 2017 at http://journals.plos.org/plosone/article?id=10.1371/journal.pone.0164733.

Warren, C. (2000), *Brush with Death: A Social History of Lead Poisoning*, Baltimore, MD: Johns Hopkins University Press.

Washington, R.A. (2010), 'China: Second in line: China passes another GDP milestone', *The Economist*, accessed March 2016 at http://www.economist.com/blogs/freeexchange/2010/08/china_0.

Watkins, G.C. (2006), 'Oil scarcity: What have the past three decades revealed?', *Energy Policy*, **34**, 508–14.

WCI, Inc. (2017), Western Climate Initiative, accessed 2 December 2017 at http://www.wci-inc.org.

Weart, S. (2012), 'The discovery of global warming [excerpt]', *Scientific*

*American*, 17 August, accessed at https://www.scientificamerican.com/article/discovery-of-global-warming/.

Weisz, H., F. Krausmann, C. Amann, N. Eisenmenger, K.H. Erb, K. Hubacek and M. Fischer-Kowalski (2006), 'The physical economy of the European Union: Cross-country comparison and determinants of material consumption', *Ecological Economics*, **58**(4 July), 676–98.

Wendling, Z.A., J.W. Emerson, D.C. Esty, M.A. Levy and A.M. de Sherbinin (2018), *The Environmental Performance Index*, Yale Centre for Environmental Law and Policy, accessed at https://epi.envirocenter.yale.edu/2018-epi-report/introduction.

Westheimer, J. (2010), 'Higher education or education for hire? Corporatization and the threat to democratic thinking', *Academic Matters*, accessed August 2016 at http://www.academicmatters.ca/2010/04/higher-education-or-education-for-hire-corporatization-and-the-threat-to-democratic-thinking/.

Wiedmann, T.O., H. Schandl, M. Lenzen, D. Moran, S. Suh, J. West and K. Kanemoto (2015), 'The material footprint of nations', *Proceedings of the National Academy of Sciences*, **112**(20), 6271–76.

Wiggins, S. and K. Higgins (2008), 'Pro-poor growth and development: Linking economic growth and poverty reduction', *Overseas Development Institute (ODI)* Briefing Paper no. 33, January, accessed 26 February 2017 at https://www.odi.org/sites/odi.org.uk/files/odi-assets/publications-opinion-files/825.pdf.

Wikipedia (2016), 'Nuclear power phase-out', accessed 21 June 2016 at https://en.wikipedia.org/wiki/Nuclear_power_phase-out.

Wilkinson, R.G. and K.E. Pickett (2006), 'Income inequality and population health: A review and explanation of the evidence', *Social Science & Medicine*, **62**(7), 1768–84.

Willows, R., N. Reynard, I. Meadowcroft and R. Connell (2003), *Climate Adaptation: Risk, Uncertainty and Decision-making, Part 2*, Oxford: Climate Impact Programme, pp. 41–87.

Wilson, S. (2008), *Ontario's Wealth, Canada's Future: Appreciating the Value of the Greenbelt's Eco-Services*, David Suzuki Foundation, accessed 31 July 2017 at http://www.davidsuzuki.org/publications/downloads/2008/DSF-Greenbelt-web.pdf.

Wolff, E. and I. Fung (2014), *Climate Change – Evidence and Causes: An overview from the Royal Society and the US National Academy of Sciences*, accessed 5 September 2016 at http://dels.nas.edu/resources/static-assets/exec-office-other/climate-change-full.pdf.

Woodward, D. and A. Simms (2006), *Growth Isn't Working*, London: New Economics Foundation, accessed 11 July 2007 at http://www.

neweconomics.org/gen/uploads/hrfu5w555mzd3f55m2vqwty502022006
112929.pdf.

Working Group on Mining and Human Rights in Latin America (2013), 'The impact of Canadian mining on Latin America and Canada's responsibility: Executive summary of the report submitted to the Inter-American Commission on Human Rights', accessed April 2016 at http://www. dplf.org/sites/default/files/report_canadian_mining_executive_summary. pdf.

World Bank (2007), *World Bank Demographic Projections Online*, accessed 21 August 2007 (website no longer in service) at http://devdata.world-bank.org.ezproxy.library.yorku.ca/hnpstats/dp 1.asp.

World Bank (2015), 'New country classifications', accessed 5 May 2016 at http://data.worldbank.org/news/new-country-classifications-2015.

World Bank (2016a), 'Country and lending groups', accessed June 2016 at http://data.worldbank.org/about/country-and-lending-groups#High_in come.

World Bank (2016b), *Taking on Inequality*, Washington, DC: The International Bank for Reconstruction and Development, accessed 18 November 2017 at https://openknowledge.worldbank.org/bitstream/han dle/10986/25078/9781464809583.pdf.

World Bank (2016c), 'World Development Indicators', accessed December 2016 at http://data.worldbank.org/data-catalog/world-development-in dicators.

World Bank (2016d), 'Natural capital accounting', accessed 29 September 2017 at http://www.worldbank.org/en/topic/environment/brief/environme ntal-economics-natural-capital-accounting.

World Bank (2016e), *World Bank Development Indicators*, updated 21 December 2016, accessed 15 February 2017 at http://data.worldbank. org/indicator/NY.GDP.PCAP.PP.CD.

World Bank (2017a), *Migration and Remittances: Recent Developments and Outlook*, Migration and Development Brief No. 28, October, World Bank Group, accessed 2 December 2017 at http://www.knomad. org/sites/default/files/2017-10/Migration%20and%20Development%20 Brief%2028.pdf.

World Bank (2017b), 'World Development Indicators', accessed January 2017 at http://data.worldbank.org/data-catalog/world-development-indicators.

World Bank (2017c), 'Data: Population, total', accessed March 2016 at http://data.worldbank.org/indicator/SP.POP.TOTL.

World Bank Group (2016), 'Population estimates and projections', accessed 9 November 2016 at http://data.worldbank.org/data-catalog/ population-projection-tables.

World Bank Group (2017), 'World DataBank: World Development

Indicators', accessed 27 October 2016 at http://databank.worldbank.org/data/reports.aspx?source=world-development-indicators.

World Bank Group (2018), 'World DataBank: World Development Indicators', accessed 15 June 2018 at http://databank.worldbank.org/data/reports.aspx?source=world-development-indicators.

World Commission on Environment and Development (1987), *Our Common Future*, Oxford, UK and New York, USA: Oxford University Press.

World Economic Forum (2014), 'What role does nature play in economic growth?', accessed 29 September 2017 at https://www.weforum.org/agenda/2014/08/natural-capital-accounting-sustainability-growth/.

World Economic Forum (2017a), *The Inclusive Growth and Development Report 2017*, Geneva: World Economic Forum.

World Economic Forum (2017b), *The Inclusive Economic Index*, accessed 21 December 2017 at http://reports.weforum.org/inclusive-growth-and-development-report-2017/inclusive-development-index/?doing_wp_cron=1513891370.3787980079650878906250.

World Forum on Natural Capital (2017), 'What is natural capital?', accessed 16 November 2017 at https://naturalcapitalforum.com/about/.

World Health Organization (2016), 'Obesity and overweight fact sheet', World Health Organization, accessed 13 August 2017 at http://www.who.int/mediacentre/factsheets/fs311/en/.

World Health Organization (2017), 'Obesity', accessed 16 November 2017 at http://www.who.int/topics/obesity/en/.

World Health Organization Food Safety Department (2005), *World Health Organization Food Safety Department*, World Health Organization, accessed 22 August 2007 at http://www.who.int.ezproxy.library.yorku.ca/foodsafety/publications/biotech/biotech_en.pdf.

World Nuclear Association (2016), 'Nuclear basics', accessed 21 June 2016 at http://www.world-nuclear.org/nuclear-basics.aspx.

World Resources Institute (WRI) (2014), 'Statement: WRI response to US–China climate announcement: "Make it a race to the top"', accessed 6 September 2016 at http://www.wri.org/news/2014/11/us-china-climate-announcement.

World Values Survey Association (2012), 'WVS 2010-2012 Wave, revisited master, June 2012', accessed 10 November 2016 at http://www.worldvaluessurvey.org/AJDocumentation.jsp?CndWAVE=6&COUNTRY=.

World Values Survey Association (2015), 'World Values Survey Wave 6: 2010–2014 Official Aggregate v. 20150418', accessed 8 November 2016 at http://www.worldvaluessurvey.org/WVSOnline.jsp.

World Wealth & Income Database (2017), accessed 15 August 2017 at http://wid.world/data/.

Wray, L.R. (2012), *Modern Money Theory: A Primer on Macroeconomics for Sovereign Monetary Systems*, New York: Palgrave Macmillan.

Wray, L.R. and Y. Nersisyan (2016), 'Understanding money and macroeconomic policy', *The Political Quarterly*, December, **86S1**, 47–65.

Wright, R. (2004), *A Short History of Progress*, Toronto, ON: House of Anansi Press.

Wuebbles, D.J., D.W. Fahey, K.A. Hibbard, B. DeAngelo, S. Doherty, K. Hayhoe, R. Horton et al. (2017), 'Executive summary', in D.J. Wuebbles, D.W. Fahey, K.A. Hibbard, D.J. Dokken, B.C. Stewart and T.K. Maycock (eds), *Climate Science Special Report: Fourth National Climate Assessment, Volume I*, Washington, DC: US Global Change Research Program, pp. 12–34.

WWAP (United Nations World Water Assessment Programme) (2017), *The United Nations World Water Development Report 2017. Wastewater: The Untapped Resource*, Paris: UNESCO.

WWF (2014), *Living Planet Report 2014: Species and Spaces, People and Places*, Gland: WWF International; Oakland, CA: Global Footprint Network; London, UK: Institute of Zoology; Enschede, the Netherlands: Water Footprint Network.

WWF (2015), *Living Blue Planet Report: Species, Habitats and Human Well-being*, Gland: WWF International; London, UK: Zoology Society of London.

WWF (2016), *Living Planet Report 2016: Risk and Resilience in a New Era*, Gland: WWF International.

Yap, D., N. Reid, G. de Brou, R. Bloxam, E. Piché, W. Chan, C. Cheng, M. Bitzos and S. Wong (2005), *Transboundary Air Pollution in Ontario*, Toronto, ON: Ministry of the Environment.

Zavadskas, E.K. and Z. Turskis (2011), 'Multiple Criteria Decision Making (MCDM) methods in economics: An overview', *Technological and Economic Development of Economy*, **17**(2), 397–427.

Zbinden, S. and D.R. Lee (2004), 'Paying for environmental services: An analysis of participation in Costa Rica's PSA program', *World Development*, **33**(2), 255–72.

Zekos, G. (2015), 'Re-colonization within & via economic globalization', accessed 31 December 2017 at https://ssrn.com/abstract=2573577.

Zhang, J., D.L. Mauzerall, T. Zhu, S. Liang, M. Ezzati and J.V. Remais (2010), 'Environmental health in China: Progress towards clean air and safe water', *The Lancet*, **375**, 1110–19.

Zhang, X. (2010), 'Low income measurement in Canada: What do different lines and indexes tell us?', *Income Research Paper Series, Statistics Canada*, Catalogue No. 75F0002M-No.3, accessed 5 December 2016 at http://www.statcan.gc.ca/pub/75f0002m/75f0002m2010003-eng.pdf.

# Index

acid rain 49, 99, 139, 188, 321
ALBA 90
Anthropocene era 33–6, 71
Arndt, H.W. 5, 13, 16–7, 19–21

Babe, R.E. 57, 71–2
Barnett, H.J. 103–4, 132
Base Case scenario 283–95, 299–302, 331
Baumol, W.J. 42, 61, 64, 297
Beckerman, W. 18, 102, 120
benefit–cost analysis 81–4, 92
Beveridge, W.H.B. 13, 244
biodiversity loss 33, 76, 84, 156–67, 172
biophysical limits 100, 132, 168, 181, 208, 216, 242, 269, 276, 320, 339
biosphere
    burden economies place on 26, 44, 181, 269, 274, 298
    and economic cycle 95–100
    human alterations to productivity of 34–6, 175
    use as sink 138–55, 265–6
black growth 205–6
brown capital 285, 287, 332
brown economy 1, 181–2, 287, 302
brown growth 205–7, 264–5
brown investment 274, 276, 284, 287, 331–3
Brundtland report 22–3, 306
business-as-usual 193, 274–5, 331, 340
    *see also* Base Case scenario

Cambridge capital controversy 80–81
Canada
    appetite for information about economy 4
    cap and trade programs 68
    CFCs 142
    as characterized by exploitation of natural resources 54

on climate change 24, 144, 268
economic growth
    average rates of 32–3
    and $CO_2$ intensity 204
    as insufficient for solving problems 268, 305–6
economic scenarios 282–96, 301–2
environmental indicators 266–7
environmental performance ranking 267–8
environmental policy 320–24
expenditures on goods as percentage of GDP 192
fertility rates 308
full employment
    and average hours employed 248–9
    commitment to 13
    government on 244
GDP per capita and ecological footprint 179–80
GDP percentage change, population and environmental indicators 266–7
GDP percentage from expenditure on services 191
GHG emissions 155, 189–90, 267–8, 284–5, 289, 302–3, 314, 321–2
goods as percentage of exports and imports 192–3
government
    on full employment 244
    understanding of sustainable development 23–5
    views and policies on population 308–10
green bonds 333
growth as prime policy objective 30
households
    below LIM 253–4